D1440973

ZUNI AND THE COURTS

DEVELOPMENT OF WESTERN RESOURCES

The Development of Western Resources is an interdisciplinary series focusing on the use and misuse of resources in the American West. Written for a broad readership of humanists, social scientists, and resource specialists, the books in this series emphasize both historical and contemporary perspectives as they explore the interplay between resource exploitation and economic, social, and political experiences.

John G. Clark, University of Kansas, Founding Editor
Hal K. Rothman, University of Nevada, Las Vegas, Series Editor

ZUNI AND THE COURTS

A Struggle for Sovereign
Land Rights

Edited by E. Richard Hart

WITHDRAWN

 University Press of Kansas

LIBRARY, ST. LAWRENCE UNIVERSITY
CANTON, NEW YORK 13617

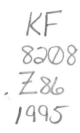

KF
8208
.Z86
1995

©1995 by the University Press of Kansas
All rights reserved

Published by the University Press of Kansas (Lawrence, Kansas 66049), which was organized by the Kansas Board of Regents and is operated and funded by Emporia State University, Fort Hays State University, Kansas State University, Pittsburg State University, the University of Kansas, and Wichita State University

Library of Congress Cataloging-in-Publication Data

Zuni and the courts : a struggle for sovereign land rights / edited by
   E. Richard Hart.
      p.   cm. — (Development of western resources)
   Includes index.
   ISBN 0-7006-0705-6
      1. Zuni Indians—Claims.   2. Zuni Indians—Land tenure.   3. Zuni
   Indians—History.   4. Indians of North America—New Mexico—Claims.
   5. Indians of North America—New Mexico—Land tenure.   6. Indians of
   North America—New Mexico—History.   I. Hart, E. Richard.
   II. Series.
   KF8208.Z86 1995
   346.7304'32'089974—dc20
   [347.306432089974]   94-44026

British Library Cataloguing in Publication Data is available.

Printed in the United States of America
Typeset by AeroType, Inc.

10 9 8 7 6 5 4 3 2 1

The paper used in this publication meets the minimum requirements of the American National Standard for Permanence of Paper for Printed Library Materials Z39.48-1984.

APR 2 9 1996

Contents

Tables and Figures

(Photographs follow pp. 26 and 102)

Preface

Governor Robert E. Lewis

When I was first elected governor of the Zuni Tribe in 1964, one of my first priorities was to see that Zuni finally got its day in court. Because our leaders had been misinformed by U.S. officials in the 1940s and 1950s, our tribe did not have a claim before the Indian Claims Commission. We were naturally incensed when that commission made a finding in the Navajo case, in which it concluded that Zuni territory belonged to the Navajos. We worked hard for many years to see that this grievous error was corrected. In 1978, because of our efforts, Congress passed an act allowing us to have our day in court. We can finally now say, in 1994, that the record has been corrected. No money can ever pay us for our losses, but at least history will now more correctly reflect the Zuni role in the history of the Southwest.

As governor of the Zuni Tribe, I am happy to introduce this book on Zuni and the federal courts. It contains a selection of very worthwhile chapters about Zuni history, archaeology, anthropology, and education. This material was prepared by scholars who have worked as expert witnesses on behalf of the Zuni Tribe in litigation for land claims and the Zuni Heaven trail easement, and this book provides a means for these scholars to share the results of their work with the Zuni people and with the outside world. The Zuni Tribe has a rich cultural heritage that we are passing on to our children and grandchildren. Knowledge about our tribal history is an important part of this heritage, and we believe this publication will help people understand how contemporary issues and concerns relate to our past problems and achievements. The Zuni Tribal Council wants all Zuni people to understand the efforts our tribal leaders have made over the past century to gain justice for our people, seek compensation for lands taken from us, develop the means to repair land damaged from erosion, and educate our young people to take their place as the future leaders of our society. The chapters in this book provide important information about our history that every Zuni should know. We think this information will also be of interest to the general public and to scholars who want to know more about Zuni, and we are glad to be able to share this book with them.

Acknowledgments

The Zuni land claims cases discussed in this book were truly driven by Zuni. All of the Zuni governors and Tribal Councils since the 1950s had pushed for litigation. The Zuni Tribal Councils that held office during the period from 1970 to 1990 were constantly faced with strategic decisions, in regard to both the legal actions and the expert testimony. Since 1990 Zuni leaders have been faced with many difficult questions in regard to the investment and expenditure of judgment funds. Governor Robert E. Lewis's tenure, and central position of authority, spanned both of these periods. Throughout, many important religious leaders have followed the cases and provided invaluable support, especially those associated with the Zuni Cultural Resources Advisory Team. Thanks also are due to the support from the Zuni Conservation Program and the Zuni Heritage and Historic Preservation Office, especially Director Roger Anyon and Cultural Preservation Coordinator Andrew Othole.

The compilation of this book and accompanying CD-ROM has been an Institute of the NorthAmerican West project. Myra Ellen Jenkins was fond of referring to the long-standing litigation as "the Zuni Wars." Indeed, the work often was an ordeal. Many of the experts who worked on the litigation are authors of chapters in this book, and many others provided effective testimony in Zuni's behalf either in court or before Congress during the course of the litigation, including Stephen G. Hall, Richard I. Ford, Patricia Limerick, James Ebert, Martin Rose, John Appel, Alberto Guttierez, Howard Sears, Robert Flavel, Barry Sadler, and Robert W. Delaney. Many other people assisted in the preparation of reports and exhibits over the course of many years, including the staff of the American West Center and the Institute of the NorthAmerican West. Avis Legler at the American West Center provided invaluable typing assistance.

T. J. Ferguson has contributed sound advice and support over the years that this volume has been in the process of being produced. The Board of Directors of the Institute of the NorthAmerican West, who have provided crucial encouragement, include Floyd A. O'Neil, Alvin M. Josephy, Jr., Vine Deloria, Jr., Patricia Limerick, and Richard White.

I want to thank several readers of the manuscript who provided excellent suggestions: Robert W. Delaney, Robert A. Williams, Jr., and Imre Sutton. I credit them for improvements in the book insofar as I have been able to respond to their advice, while at the same time I take full credit for any faults and limitations the book may have.

Introduction

E. Richard Hart

Over the past thirty years, the Zuni Tribe has been engaged in a series of major federal court cases and related legislative activities. The litigation has had a profound effect on the tribe and will continue to influence the people's future for many decades to come. The first case was a suit against the United States to establish tribal aboriginal boundaries and to seek payment for lands taken without adequate compensation. The second case was a lawsuit against the United States for damages to Zuni trust lands, damage caused by acts or omissions of the United States. The third case was a lawsuit against a private rancher by the United States, on behalf of Zuni, to establish an easement necessary for the Zunis to carry out an ancient religious pilgrimage. During the course of pursuing these cases, the tribe and its attorneys found it necessary to hire quite a number of historians, archaeologists, anthropologists, and other scientists to provide "expert testimony" before the court in both written and oral form. This book contains chapters by many of those who testified in Zuni's behalf, and all of the chapters were first written in an attempt to "demystify" the incredibly complex nature of such testimony for the benefit of the Zuni people and for non-Zunis as well. The title of the book was taken from a statement in an essay by Robert E. Lewis, who was governor of the tribe throughout much of this period and whose leadership was crucial to the tribe's success.

ZUNI 1 (DOCKET 161-79L)

Part 1 of this book is made up of chapters written by the tribe's expert witnesses on issues related to the Zuni aboriginal land claim before the United States Claims Court (Docket 161-79L). This lawsuit was similar to the claims many tribes made against the United States before the Indian Claims Commission in the 1940s and 1950s. Zuni's claim, however, was filed much later before the United States Claims Court. Over the years, Zuni leaders and the witnesses they hired to testify in their behalf on the case came to call this case "Zuni 1."

I began working for the tribe on this claim in the late 1960s. By 1978, attorney Stephen G. Boyden had managed to obtain passage of a jurisdictional act and, against all odds, had filed Docket 161-79L before the United States Claims Court. The fifteen-year legal battle that followed focused on determining whether Zuni had occupied a greater aboriginal territory at the time of U.S. sovereignty, whether acts or omissions of the United States had led to a loss of part of that land, and if so, when it had happened. Later, a second phase of the case focused on the value of the lands at the time of taking. Even though the phases of the litigation were separated by many years, certain actions taken in phase 1 had clear consequences in phase 2. For instance, when I testified to successive taking dates in phase 1, that testimony helped raise the potential value of lands at the time of taking, which was under analysis during valuation, phase 2.

Much of the written expert testimony submitted to the court in this case (and the other two cases covered in this book) is voluminous and highly technical and difficult for anyone, Zuni or non-Zuni, to read and understand. In October 1982 the Institute of the American West, with support from the New Mexico Humanities Council, sponsored a Zuni history conference for the Zunis. At this conference, witnesses for the tribe described their expert testimony to the people in lay terms. Later, these talks were published in newspaper form for other tribal members. Most of the chapters in Part 1 of this book were originally published in the *Zuni History* newspaper. The Zuni Tribe has distributed more than 20,000 printed copies of that tabloid, and the Institute of NorthAmerican West has received numerous requests to publish the articles in book form. While planning and organizing the conference, newspaper, and finally this book, I decided to orient the writing toward the general reader, including the Zuni people. The experts who testified in the various cases had to write extensive written direct testimony, rebuttal testimony, and sometimes surrebuttal testimony; they had to submit to long, exhausting depositions; and finally they had to undergo the grueling experience of court itself, with expert qualification, direct testimony, and then sometimes redirect and rebuttal. After going through all of that, the experts found that writing for a more general reader was refreshing.

Stephen Boyden, with help from Floyd O'Neil and others, identified potential witnesses for Docket 161-79L (or Zuni 1) and recommended them to the Tribal Council, which made the ultimate decision on whether to retain the expert. The attorneys and the council, to their great credit, took pains to emphasize that they did not want testimony that would flatter the Zunis or their position in court; they wanted to know what the truth was. The experts responded by producing reports that were as objective as possible. Both Governor Lewis and Boyden took pains to emphasize from the first that the primary objective was to set the historical record straight. The size of a potential judgment for the tribe was never mentioned by the attorneys, either with any of the witnesses or with the tribe.

Many issues were argued before the court in the expert reports, depositions, rebuttal reports, trial testimony, and proposed findings by each side. Complex arguments were made by both sides (Zuni and the United States) on issues related to many diverse subjects—archaeological affinity, Spanish law, anthropology, and the history of many neighboring tribes. For instance, S. Lyman Tyler and Ward Alan Minge testified extensively before the court, in both written and oral form, on the importance of Spanish recognition of Zuni aboriginal territory. Both Tyler and Minge emphasized that the Spaniards were frequently liberal in law and cruel in practice. Tyler spoke effectively about law and reality and the irony in the difference between the authorities' actual practice and the ideal under the law, an irony that may not be lost on the reader in the United States of the twentieth century. Although Spanish law was not always followed at the local or provincial level, the law did work to protect Zuni's rights. In many ways it was not until the Indian Reorganization Act of 1934 was passed that U.S. law finally mirrored Spanish law and helped protect Native American traditional rights rather than attempt to destroy them. At any rate, that Spain recognized Zuni lands helped establish Zuni's rights to those lands under the United States.

Spanish land grants were another complex issue with which the witnesses had to deal. The so-called Cruzate grants have had an important impact on the history of several of the New Mexican pueblos. Minge addressed the Zuni Cruzate grant in his study of Zuni under Spain and Mexico, which also dealt with Zuni's royal contract with Spain. He added a second study for inclusion in this volume on the subject of *reducciones*. Cruzate grants to other pueblos have been shown to be spurious, and the court found that the Zuni Cruzate grant was indeed spurious. Expert witnesses for the tribe testified that it was probably a fairly crude forgery. Today we know that it was likely drafted in the early to mid-nineteenth century. The Cruzate grants usually set aside four square leagues for each pueblo, an area measured from the center of the village. They are dated 1689, after the Pueblo Revolt but before the formal Reconquest. There has been much debate about the authenticity of the grants—whether any of the existing grants are authentic; whether there were earlier, legitimate versions of some pueblos' grants; and whether the issuance of these grants really even fit within the framework of Spanish policy of the time.

In his second chapter, Minge discusses the Provencias Internas, government units set up later, in 1776, and examines evidence relative to the Spanish policy of *reducciones*, which was carried out elsewhere in the New World under Spain. His research, observations, and arguments are important and interesting, but it is significant that in Zuni's case, the court ruled not only that the Cruzate grant was spurious but also that Spain did not utilize the policy of *reducciones* at Zuni, as the people already lived in villages. Importantly, the court ruled that Spain *recognized* Zuni aboriginal territory. There is, however, some evidence to suggest that at some point in the past Zuni did have a legitimate grant or grants from Spain or Mexico, but no copies of such legitimate grant(s) are available today.

Myra Ellen Jenkins describes how the U.S. surveyor general acquired the Cruzate grants. As Jenkins points out, under Spain the Zunis were entitled to a minimum of four square leagues, but Spain also recognized all of the lands the tribe effectively used and occupied. Under the Treaty of Guadalupe Hidalgo, the United States promised to recognize the tribal landownership that had been recognized under Spain and Mexico. In the Zuni 1 opinion, the court ruled that, had the United States surveyed Zuni aboriginal lands, as it was mandated to do, the United States would have in turn been required to recognize Zuni territory. But, as Minge suggests, tribes' claims to actual title to their aboriginal territories have generally failed in the courts. Zuni did appeal, noting that the surveyor general of New Mexico during the crucial period was himself involved in fraudulent land activities in the Zuni claim area. But eventually Zuni's claim to recognized title under the United States was also rejected. Nevertheless, Zuni's persistent efforts to work with the governments of Spain, Mexico, and the United States had measurable pragmatic results.

Surely it is true that Zuni was not completely clear on what Juan de Oñate was saying to the tribe in 1598 as he obtained the required oath to the Crown, yet the Zunis certainly were aware of the ruthless and recently displayed vicious character of the authorities, and the tribe's actions not only protected it from a slaughter similar to what Acoma endured but also put it firmly under Spanish law, as Minge points out. One must question whether there really was any "conversion" to Christianity during this visit by Oñate, but it is clear that Zuni's political actions, be they coerced or expedient, helped the tribe survive as well as it did under Spain, Mexico, and the United States.

Zuni's ability to deal with the powerful governments of these three countries through the course of four and a half centuries is indicative of the tribe's cultural strength and endurance. Much of that strength must have emanated from Zuni religion. Many of the authors in this book remark on the importance of the Zuni "lay" witnesses' contributions to the court. Appendix F lists the names of the Zunis who testified before the court in both of the land claim cases. Edmund Ladd notes that these depositions make up some of the most remarkable ethnological documents ever produced. These depositions had great impact in the cases, especially in Zuni 1.

Courts have frequently questioned the validity of tribal oral tradition as testimony. Zuni worked hard to make sure its testimony was of the highest quality. Tribal religious leaders and political leaders met and discussed what matters relating to religion could be released to the court and thus exposed to the world. Zuni generally does not want to have any religious matters opened to the public. These were difficult meetings and difficult decisions. Eventually the tribe determined who would represent the tribe in court, and these leaders (primarily prominent religious leaders) carefully responded to technical questions regarding the tribe's emergence, migration, settlement, shrines, and religious use of lands. The Zuni migration narrative referred to by T. J. Ferguson was influential in helping the court understand Zuni's claim. In fact, importantly, the court found that Zuni oral testimony had evidentiary probity, while at the same time ruling that decisions of previous courts were tertiary in nature (partly due to the language of the jurisdictional act that said the Navajo claims case findings should be ignored by the court). In my twenty-five years of interviewing Zuni religious leaders, I have found them to be uniformly dedicated to honesty in what they say.

In Part 2 of this book, Andrew Wiget analyzes all of the depositions and responds to their internal validity. He mentions the testimony of Governor Lewis, who as head of the political authority over the tribe, is expected to synthesize the views of his council and people and have "the last word." Indeed, Zuni did have the last word in this litigation. Ferguson's second chapter, dealing with Zuni anthropology, focuses on both Zuni 1 and 2 and has been arbitrarily placed in Part 2, as his work in the second claims case built on his work in the first.

ZUNI 2 (DOCKET 327-81L)

Part 2 of the book comprises chapters from witnesses and experts who worked and testified in Zuni's behalf in Docket 327-81L (which was combined with Docket 224-84L) before the United States Claims Commission. This suit involved damages to Zuni trust lands and came to be called "Zuni 2" by the Zuni leaders and their witnesses. When Zuni reached a settlement in that case, which was perhaps even more technical and complex than Zuni 1, Zuni leaders again saw a need to inform their people about the litigation. The *Zuni History* newspaper was reprinted for the tribe by the Institute of the NorthAmerican West, again with support from the New Mexico Humanities Council.

The chapters in Part 2, excepting mine on the Zuni Land Conservation Act, focus on issues that witnesses and experts faced during the litigation/legislation process. Authors explain how the resolution of the issues affected the body of thought in their own discipline. Complicated, inter-disciplinary issues confronted the court and Congress, including issues related to dendrochronology, geomorphology, history, and even lexicography. Samuel Monson's chapter is a good example. It documents the meaning of the Spanish word *arroyo* through time and was necessitated when experts for the United States falsely claimed that the historical use of the word indicated incision of a streambed.

UNITED STATES V. PLATT

Although Parts 1 and 2 of this book are related to Zuni lawsuits against the United States, the next part describes the successful efforts of the United States in Zuni's behalf. Part 3 includes two chapters: a history of the Zuni Heaven litigation and legislation and a description of the important legal decision and potential precedent that Zuni obtained in that case.

Since the passage of the American Indian Religious Freedom Act (AIRFA) of 1978 (Public Law 95-341), Native Americans have complained vehemently that, though the joint houses of Congress resolved that tribes should also enjoy freedom of religion, there are no teeth in the law, and Native Americans still do not enjoy those rights. Congress continues to consider amendments to AIRFA designed to increase tribal religious free-dom. But while the Native American Grave Protection and Repatriation Act (NAGPRA) of 1990 provides protection against the looting of graves on federal lands, the *Lyng* decision (*Lyng* v. *Northwest Indian Cemetery Protective Association*, 1988) demonstrates that tribes still do not enjoy First Amendment rights protecting their religious practices. Against this back-drop Zuni was in federal court between 1985 and 1990 attempting to protect its right to carry out a quadrennial religious pilgrimage across 110 miles of desert rangeland to *Kolhu/wala:wa* ("Zuni Heaven"). In this case, as in the two land claims cases, the Zunis were fortunate to have superb legal counsel. The United States demonstrated its power and resources defending the two land claims, as well it should, but when the United States came into this case in behalf of the Zunis, its energy was even more apparent in attorney Hank Meshorer, chief of the Indian Section for the Department of Justice. His shrewd legal strategy may be a model that will assist some tribes in pursuing religious rights.

Many disciplines are represented in this book, and even more disci-plines were represented in the actual expert testimony (see Appendix F). Readers will note some differences in style of writing by discipline. I felt it was better to preserve the style related to each discipline than to try homogenizing the chapters. I am hopeful that the book will be of interest to tribes that are seeking justice in the federal court system, and to their attorneys, who seek to preserve tribal sovereignty and rights under the judicial system. I hope that this work will demonstrate the care that was taken by Zuni in choosing its attorneys and ensuring objective testimony, with fair and honest treatment of difficult issues in the sciences and humanities, and that the reader will sense how much care went into the identification of experts and the preparation of expert testimony. Scholars and scientists from academic disciplines are sometimes criticized for being too removed from daily life, for having "ivory-tower" perspectives, and for being unable to apply their work to the lives of "normal" people. The experts who worked on these cases have demonstrated the value of their disciplines to the Zuni people. Writing expert testimony, undergoing depositions, and making court appearances are not ivory-tower experiences, but the net result has had a significant impact on the history of a people.

Postscripts provide some retrospective views of the decades of work that individuals spent on these cases. The appendices provide valuable documents related to the settlement of the litigation and the passage of legislation.

This book was put together in hopes of providing the interested reader with a broad understanding of the history of Zuni land claims, their outcome, and the significance of those decisions in a number of scholarly disciplines. The expert reports filed in these cases are voluminous. There are roughly 10,000 pages of testimony in them. In addition, another 50,000 pages of exhibits were submitted to support the conclusions in those reports. This book will make the substance of much of that material more accessible to Zuni and the general public. For those readers who would delve even further into the actual expert testimony witnesses submitted in these cases and into the depositions taken from Zuni religious leaders, the Institute of the NorthAmerican West has produced a CD-ROM, which will be available from the University Press of Kansas, that contains the full text of many thousands of pages of expert testimony and depositions submitted in behalf of the Zuni Tribe. The sum of this body of knowledge will work to meet the objective of the Zuni Tribe—to set the record straight.

PART ONE

Aboriginal Claims
(Zuni 1—Docket 161-79L)

CHAPTER 1

Zuni Archaeology and Culture History

T. J. Ferguson

Archaeologists study the distribution and patterns of artifacts and other material culture deposited in the archaeological record by past peoples. At the present time, archaeologists can only trace the cultural antecedents of the Zuni people on a broad regional basis because the data and analytical techniques necessary to trace the movement of a particular group of people from site to site in the long prehistoric era have not yet been developed. Given this, and the essentially symbolic nature of the Zuni origin accounts, it is not possible to specifically correlate archaeological culture history with the Zuni accounts of origin and migration. In general, however, the Zuni origin accounts and archaeological culture history share certain basic and major themes, including an economic shift from hunting and gathering to corn agriculture, a prevalent movement of people across the landscape, occasional violence and hostility between groups of people, and an assimilation of two cultural traditions with Zuni culture.

The earliest evidence for human use of the Zuni area dates to the Paleo-Indian period prior to 5000 B.C. A few large spear points dating from this period have been found as isolated artifacts on the mesas surrounding Zuni pueblo, but in general Paleo-Indian sites are concentrated in the more open grasslands to the east and west of Zuni in the drainages of the Rio Grande and the Little Colorado River and their tributaries. During the Paleo-Indian period, the subsistence economy was based on hunting and gathering, and the population density of the Southwest was relatively low. Small groups of people ranged extensively across the countryside, exploiting animal and plant resources as they became available through the seasons. In the Southwest, Clovis projectile points as old as ten thousand years are often found in association with the remains of the now-extinct elephantlike mammoth. In time, beautifully fluted Folsom points replaced Clovis points as a diagnostic artifact, and they are generally found in association with an extinct form of large bison. The end of the Paleo-Indian period coincided with a climatic change from the last Ice Age to the warmer conditions of today, with a corresponding decrease in grasslands

3

and increase in other biotic communities, such as forests, woodlands, and shrublands.

During the Archaic period, dating from approximately 5000 B.C. to A.D. 1, the population of the Southwest gradually increased. Hunting and gathering remained the basic way of life, although sometime after 2000 B.C. agriculture was introduced as corn, and later beans and squash, were diffused into the Southwest from highland Mexico. These domesticated plants are found in Archaic sites such as Bat Cave and Tularosa Cave in the mountains of the Mogollon Slope. Agriculture was initially adopted as a backup food production system to supplement the wild food obtained through hunting and gathering and remained of secondary economic importance throughout the Archaic period. People planted corn, beans, and squash in small amounts but did not depend on them for their livelihood.

The Archaic period ended about A.D. 1 when agriculture started to become a more important part of the subsistence system. Pithouses, a type of domestic structure excavated into the ground and roofed with wood and adobe, appeared at this time, usually accompanied by large storage pits. These architectural features indicate that people were beginning to grow enough food to store and were probably spending the winters in the vicinity of their farms, while hunting and gathering during other parts of the year. One of these early pithouse sites is located along Hardscrabble Wash, a tributary drainage of the Zuni River. As the land filled up with people through natural population increase, the mobility and resources of hunter-gatherers were constrained, and this was probably a factor in the gradual development of a sedentary agricultural way of life in the millennium after A.D. 1.

The production of pottery in the Southwest began around A.D. 200, and after that time the regional cultures that developed can be distinguished from one another on the basis of material culture. The Anasazi cultural tradition developed in the northern part of the Zuni area and is distinguished by a ceramic complex including greyware utility pottery and black-on-white decorated pottery. The Anasazi cultural tradition is also associated with circular kivas, or ceremonial chambers. The Mogollon cultural tradition developed in the southern part of the Zuni area and is associated with brownware utility pottery, redware decorated pottery, and square kivas. The Hohokam cultural traditions, which developed in the Basin and Range Province of southern Arizona, is associated with buffware pottery. All of these Southwestern cultural traditions, which developed after the advent of pottery, shared a trend toward increasing village sedentism and agriculture. The Anasazi and Mogollon cultural traditions probably each encompassed a number of separate tribes that shared a common base of material culture but probably had different customs.

The population that settled in the drainage of the Zuni River was initially part of the Anasazi cultural tradition. By A.D. 650, small villages of pithouses had begun to be located on mesa benches and other elevated landforms in the immediate vicinity of what later became Zuni pueblo. These early village settlements are similar to other Anasazi sites, such as the Flattop site in the Petrified Forest and the Cerro Colorado site in the Carrizo Creek drainage south of Zuni. By A.D. 700 to 900, Anasazi pithouse villages containing deep pithouses with associated aboveground masonry storage bins had begun to be constructed in the alluvial valley bottoms. At this time, sites in the Zuni drainage were similar to other Anasazi sites in adjacent drainages, such as White Mound Village and Allantown near the Puerco River and Kiatuthlanna near the confluence of the Zuni and Little Colorado Rivers. The pithouse villages of this time contained numerous granaries and grinding stones, indicating the increased importance of facilities and tools to store and process agricultural produce, although hunting and the collection of wild plant foods were still important in the overall subsistence system. The presence of jewelry made from shell from the Pacific Ocean and Gulf of California is evidence that these early pithouse villages were tied into a large regional trade network extending throughout the larger Southwest. In the Zuni area, these early pithouse villages are associated with a series of decorated black-on-white pottery types known as the Cibola Whitewares.

After A.D. 900 in the Anasazi area, aboveground masonry structures began to replace pithouses as the most prevalent house form. The masonry pueblos built at this time apparently developed out of the earlier aboveground masonry storage bins. Circular subterranean structures were retained, although their function changed from domestic use to ceremonial use as a kiva. The typical site plan from this period encompasses a small four- to twelve-room house fronted by a circular underground kiva with a trash mound to the south or southeast. The change from pithouse villages to aboveground masonry pueblos can be seen at sites such as K'ya:duttana and Allantown as well in the Red Mesa valley along the Puerco River and in Chiya:ma Canyon to the east of Zuni pueblo. Thousands of these small sites were occupied in the Anasazi area at this time, and in the Zuni region most of these sites are associated with Cibola Whitewares and a decorated red-slipped pottery known as White Mountain Redware. The large number of these small sites suggests that people shifted their homes around the landscape fairly frequently, perhaps in response to small changes in the amount of annual rainfall or salinization of farm fields.

From A.D. 900 to 1150, many of the small Anasazi house sites in the Zuni drainage appear to have been organized into communities oriented around a large public building encompassing forty or more rooms and associated with one or more Great Kivas, or very large ceremonial chambers. Examples of these types of community centers include the Village of the Great Kivas along the Nutria River as well as K'ya:duttana and Allantown. These community centers in turn appear to have been organized into a large regional trade and exchange system, with its center at Chaco Canyon in the San Juan basin. For reasons not entirely clear, the Chaco system began to be eclipsed after A.D. 1150, and the San Juan basin was abandoned as a location of habitation sites.

After A.D. 1150, the people living in the Zuni drainage reoriented their trade and began to interact more with other people living along the Mogollon Rim and in the mountains of the Mogollon Slope to the south of Zuni pueblo. St. Johns Polychrome, a type of White Mountain Redware manufactured in the Zuni area, was widely traded throughout the Southwest at this time. The most prevalent type of settlement consisted of small pueblos.

Between A.D. 1250 and 1300, a major change in settlement pattern occurred as people aggregated into very large and well-planned pueblos ranging in size from 250 to 1,200 rooms. These large pueblos were all oriented around internal plazas and enclosed by a high wall. They extend from Kin Tiel, through Big House Ruin in Manuelito Canyon along the Puerco River, to A'ts'ina at El Morro in the Zuni Mountains. Several of these large pueblos were located on defensible mesa tops, suggesting that warfare or raiding might have been a concern. Dismembered bodies, evidence of violent conflict, were found in archaeological excavations at a contemporaneous and related large pueblo at Mariana Mesa to the east of Zuni Salt Lake.

In the Zuni drainage alone, there were thirty-six large, plaza-oriented pueblos constructed between A.D. 1250 and 1540, extending from A'ts'ina to Hawikku. In general, the earliest of these aggregated pueblos were located in the Zuni Mountains in topographic situations that concentrated surface runoff. The presence of water control features near these pueblos indicates the people were directing water to their farm fields. This intensification of agriculture probably enabled the people to concentrate into large pueblos. The later aggregated pueblos were located downstream in areas of good soils where springs or major tributary drainages provided abundant water resources for farming. Zuni pueblo is one of these later sites and was probably founded around A.D. 1350.

Two of the types of pottery produced at the large late prehistoric pueblos in the Zuni drainage were distinctive White Mountain Redwares painted with glaze paint decoration and named Heshot Utta Polychrome and Kwa'kina Polychrome after two large pueblos along the Zuni and Pescado Rivers. The Zuni glaze-painted ceramics were traded to contemporaneous pueblos in the Mogollon area, such as Foote Canyon pueblo, and to pueblos in the Rio Grande valley. The Zuni glaze-painted pottery has a ceramic affinity with contemporaneous pottery at sites along the Mogollon Rim such as Pinedale, Four Mile, and Show Low Ruins, indicating interaction with the people who lived in that part of the upper Little Colorado River valley.

In the late prehistoric period, the population living in the upper Little Colorado River valley gradually concentrated into a fewer number of sites. At the same time, the Mogollon area to the south of Zuni was abandoned as a location for habitations, and at least some of the Mogollon people probably moved into the Little Colorado River valley. Late prehistoric sites in the upper Little Colorado area such as Table Rock pueblo, Stone Axe Ruin, Chevelon, and Homolovi show cultural affinity to both Hopi and Zuni and may have contributed population to both tribes when they were vacated. The presence of cremation and inhumation as burial practices at the Zuni sites of Hawikku and Kechiba:wa as well as the occurrence of a type of pottery known as Salado Polychrome is often cited by archaeologists as evidence of a migration of people with a Mogollon cultural tradition into Zuni from the west sometime between A.D. 1350 and 1540. This small group of immigrants was assimilated into the Anasazi population that had been long resident in the Zuni drainage, and modern Zuni culture and society emerged from the amalgam.

By the end of the prehistoric era, the population in the drainage of the Little Colorado River had consolidated at Zuni and Hopi. To the east of Zuni, between the Continental Divide and the Rio Grande valley, only Acoma pueblo was occupied. The Zuni people had concentrated their settlements into a tightly clustered group of six pueblos along the Zuni River in an optimal area of land and water resources for agriculture. This core area of Zuni settlement was surrounded by a much larger sustaining area used for hunting and collecting wild plant and animal resources. The Little Colorado River valley and mountains of the Mogollon Slope constituted important resource procurement areas used for limited activities. The Zuni pueblos at this time served as the nexus in a widespread regional trade network connecting the Colorado River area to the west with the Great Plains to the east and the Colorado Plateau to the north with the Hohokam, or Pima-Papago area, and northern Mexico to the south.

CHAPTER 2

Historic Zuni Land Use

E. Richard Hart

The Zuni people had and continue to have an understanding and knowledge of, an affinity with, and an empathy for the landscape about them. They have believed in the conservation of the landscape from the point of view of caring for a relative and not from a scientific point of view of conserving a natural resource. They have a reverence for the landscape.

The Zuni people often use a metaphor to try getting across to non-Zunis how they feel about and are attached to the landscape. They'll say, "The land is our church, our cathedral. It's like a sacred building." A mesa may be an altar in this pervasive folk metaphor or a spring, a sacred alcove. Although the entire building, the entire landscape is sacred, certain portions are especially sacred—a butte, a mesa, a mud pond, a ruin, a sacred trail. The Zunis want, above all, to have outsiders understand their depth of feeling for the landscape and their respect for the environment, the same kind of respect that they have for their friends and families. The Zunis' relationship with the environment permeates not only their religious use of land but also their utilitarian and political use. Every kind of activity that the Zunis have is associated with religious activity and religious use. The Zunis' religion is a seven-day, twenty-four-hour-a-day religion.

In a traditional sense the religious boundaries of Zuni land are a series of peaks and mountains: To the west are the San Francisco Peaks; to the east, the Sandia Mountains and Mount Taylor; to the south, the Mogollon and Tularosa Mountains; and to the north, Blue Mountain or Sierra Abajo. These form a skin around the religious lands, which are alive and connected by veins and arteries. Across this living being religious activities and all other activities take place. Inside these general boundaries are innumerable springs, ruins, cliffs, waterways, trails, mesas, buttes, all with religious significance.

Even regions can have special religious values. The Zuni people believe that after they came into the world from a spot located deep within the Grand Canyon, they searched about for many years, across what are now Arizona and New Mexico, for the "Middle Place." The spot that they eventually found is near the present pueblo and is believed to be the center of all six directions: north, south, east, west, zenith, and nadir. Each of these directions is closely associated with a color, plants, seasons, and animals as well as with religious organizations. So the entire culture and being of the Zuni people are tied inextricably to the landscape about them.

There are numerous specific shrines and sacred places within the Zuni area. Each spot along the migration trail is significant, and many stories and legends tell about the religious value associated with shrines. In the west there are the Painted Desert, Jacob's Well, and Denatsali. Each waterway is significant. Anthropologist Frank Hamilton Cushing suggested that a spring was the *most* sacred thing to the Zunis.

To the south are Zuni Salt Lake, the Zuni Plateau, and Broken Pottery Mountain. Shrines to the east include places near Agua Fria, El Morro, and Mount Taylor. To the north Chaco Canyon and the Blue Mountain have shrines. These are just a fraction of the many places that we outsiders know about, which are in turn only a fraction of the places that the Zunis treat with veneration and to which they make offerings.

The historic Zunis inherited and developed an encyclopedic knowledge of their lands. No one person could possibly tell all that there was to know about agriculture, mineral collection, plant collection, grazing, and religious use. But in the clans and religious groups, in the kivas and priesthoods, people remembered different pieces of the knowledge. It was compartmentalized throughout the tribe. In this way an incredibly vast amount of knowledge was retained about the animals that roamed over the land, the plants that grew on it, and the waterways that flowed across it.

Permanent habitation required specialized techniques to use the available resources without depleting those resources, even over a long period of time. In a good year when there was plentiful water, the irrigated agriculture and floodwater agriculture might provide a large portion of the food necessary for survival. But during a drought year, it was necessary to use all of the ancient knowledge of gathering and hunting to subsist. The Zunis maintained this knowledge year after year regardless of whether they had to use it very often.

Perhaps the most specialized techniques used by the Zunis were associated with their agricultural industries, learned over centuries by the pre-contact Zunis and their ancestors, the Anasazi and Mogollon. In an area such as this, which is arid and semiarid, every available source of water had to be used and all tillable land utilized. Much of the water in the course of a year came in the form of heavy but brief thundershowers. The rain fell on the mesas and buttes, quickly rushed down drainages into the valleys, and exited into one of the major rivers (the Little Colorado or the Rio Puerco), and was gone. There were few permanent streams or springs, so a limited amount of irrigated land was available.

Because of these climatic conditions, the Pueblo people in general, and the Zunis in particular, developed a system of floodwater irrigation. This involved the construction of check dams, diversionary dams, and mud walls in order to direct the flow of runoff water. Elaborate systems were maintained so that corn crops could grow in the silted areas behind check dams. Every drop of rainfall was used to the greatest extent possible. Floodwater fields were found wherever there was periodic runoff throughout a very large area of Zuni territory.

The Zunis grew very large crops of corn, cultivating as much as, and even more than 10,000 acres after the arrival of the Americans. It must have been an amazing sight to see a crier calling the people into the fields when a rainstorm was arriving so that the waters could be directed over the cultivated plots. Reports indicate that almost the entire Zuni valley was under cultivation in the seventeenth, eighteenth, and nineteenth centuries. People walked forty to sixty miles to cultivate every available source of water. The people had to cultivate more areas than could actually be harvested each year. In other words, because a thunderstorm would not hit every drainage every year, the Zunis had to care for fields throughout most of the drainages even though only a percentage of what they cultivated could actually be harvested in the fall. In the spring people moved out to the farming villages. But from the farming villages they went out even farther. There were Zuni people living in the 1980s who could recall their fathers and grandfathers farming as far away as the Springerville–St. Johns area.

In the process of maintaining these floodwater fields, the Zuni people effected erosion control, preventing topsoil loss from wind and water. Check dams caused a spreading of water over the surface of the land and thus prevented gullying. The planting of a row of sagebrush along the windward side of the cultivated plots prevented erosion. (When the Zunis' agricultural practices were restricted in the late nineteenth and early twentieth centuries, extensive erosion and gullying took place throughout their traditional lands.)

Corn was the Zunis' most important crop and played a central role in their spiritual, social, and ceremonial life. Wherever there were permanent springs within the Zunis' territory, the water was developed to the fullest extent. At Ojo Pescado, Ojo Caliente, and Nutria the important year-long sources of water were developed for irrigated agriculture. Reports throughout the Spanish period indicate that the Zunis had acequias, or canals, at these places. There was even one nineteenth-century report that described the Zunis' use of hollow logs in order to construct several miles of aqueducts.

After the acquisition of European seed, the Zunis sowed wheat at their ranches around these springs. Peach orchards were planted and cared for near Dowa Yalanne and elsewhere. The Zunis also cultivated "waffle gardens" (which have only recently fallen into disuse). Named for their resemblance to waffles, the gardens were planted along the Zuni River near the modern village and constructed in squares and rectangles with low mud walls. Specialty crops were grown in these plots.

The Zunis kept a two-year supply of food on hand in case of drought or insect infestation. Cord upon cord of corn were sealed in rodent-proof storage rooms in case of famine. Vegetables were dried and prepared in myriad ways for use in the cold winter months. Fruit was dried in the autumn sunshine. It was this specialized agriculture that, probably more than anything else, provided leisure time and allowed the Zunis to excel in the arts, in society, and in culture. It was the floodwater fields and the associated specialized, sophisticated technology that, more than anything else, allowed their advances.

During the 1850s, the Zunis were selling thousands of bushels, amounting to many tons of corn, to the U.S. military groups that came through the area and to the forts that were established in the area to control the Navajo. The commander of Fort Defiance in its early years indicated in his correspondence that without the corn that the Zunis were supplying, the fort could not have survived.

Hunting was also an extremely important part of the Zunis' land utilization. Among the big game animals hunted were bobcats, deer, coyotes, bear, elk, moose, antelope, mountain sheep, wild pigs, foxes, and mountain lions. The largest game was the buffalo, for which the Zunis made small-group hunting expeditions to the plains. In recent times, the Zunis have used at least seventy species of birds, including eagles, ducks, wild turkeys, hawks, jays, finches, woodpeckers, owls, crows, and blue-birds. No doubt in the past the people used nearly every species of bird and animal to be found in their areas. A small number were considered taboo or sacred and were not used.

Hunting activities were always associated with religious practices, and some hunting practices were prompted entirely by religious motives. Snares were placed for birds and small animals. There were group hunts and solitary hunters who went out after larger game. Game was treated with respect when it was killed. For instance, after a deer was killed, it was "laid in state" in the hunter's household, adorned with fine blankets and jewelry. Prayers and offerings were made at hunting shrines along the trails that led to major hunting grounds. Given the expansive territory, the wide range of altitudes and climates, and the great variety of animals hunted, it is no surprise that the Zunis maintained an extensive body of traditional hunting knowledge.

One of the most interesting kinds of hunting was the group hunts. These were carried out by large but tightly organized groups of Zunis, sometimes numbering in the hundreds. Close to the pueblos, the Zunis used boomeranglike rabbit sticks to round up and kill rabbits. In other areas of the territory, the Zunis constructed fences or drive lanes for communal hunting practices. One such fence, probably used to help capture antelopes, was reported to be seventy-five miles long. Pits were used to capture deer and were dug next to drive lanes and along existing game trails at appropriate spots.

Hunting provided the Zunis not only with a crucial supply of their meat but also with hides for clothing and other manufactured articles. Bones, sinew, fur, feathers, and every other part of the hunted animal were used and were essential to the Zunis' long-term survival. Each part of the territory provided a crop of different animals over the years, though in some years one area might not be used. In practice, the Zunis conserved the wildlife in their territory, harvesting only what was necessary to their survival and religious well-being.

Before contact with Europeans, the Zunis tended extensive flocks of turkeys. According to tradition, the Zunis "herded" these flocks over large areas of their territory, using the feathers for clothes and eating the birds themselves in times of need. How early the Zunis acquired sheep we cannot say for sure. They did have horses by 1692, which they used in full view of the Spanish, and there is evidence of the Zunis having sheep by 1721. Burros, goats, and a few cattle were also cared for, but sheep were by far the most important Zuni grazing animal. By the mid-eighteenth century, the tribe had over 15,000 sheep, and they became the important raw material source for clothing. Prior to having sheep, the Zunis had woven clothing from yucca, cotton, feathers, and other vegetal and animal materials, so they soon became expert at weaving wool into mantas and blankets. Zuni blankets had simple designs and were often black or white with simple black and brown stripes. Their weaving was known as some of the best among all of the pueblos.

Sheep also became an important supply of meat. Many thousands of lambs and sheep were slaughtered each year in anticipation of the Zunis' annual *Sha'lak'o* celebration (winter solstice and house-blessing) as well as the traditional celebration at the summer solstice. Despite the large herds of sheep, hunting continued to provide the crucial supply of meat for the people.

During the summer, several large herds of sheep were ranged as far as seventy miles from the central pueblos. Numbers of Zunis might band their herds together, and groups of Zunis would shepherd those herds communally. Tradition determined "use rights" on certain grazing areas. The finest, grassiest areas near the village were saved for the lambing period in the spring or for times when an Apache or a Navajo raid might be expected. After lambing, the Zuni herders would range their flocks far from the pueblo, avoiding the floodwater fields of corn. Several types of structures were constructed by the shepherds while they moved about with their flocks: conical and circular brush shelters or lodges for temporary shelter, cave shelters, rock houses near the lambing areas, watchtowers, fortified sheep camps, and corrals.

Sheep were the most efficient users of the available grazing lands, so only nominal numbers of cattle were maintained. Horses were used for war and for long-distance traveling, but most travel was accomplished on foot. Burros made agricultural production easier at greater distances, as crops could be brought in on the animals instead of by individual Zunis, and the burro facilitated trade of heavier goods.

By the nineteenth century, the number of Zuni sheep had grown to at least 30,000. By 1900, that number had risen to 50,000 or 60,000. The Zunis had to use good judgment in order not to overgraze the dry grasslands away from major water sources. But when the tribe was forced to pull the herds in and place them on the small reservation, much of the reservation became severely overgrazed.

Zuni mineral collection and plant collection were also very important. Many such collections still take place today. Minerals, clays, soils, samples of water, and types of rock were traditionally collected from as far away as the Pacific Ocean. Red, blue, yellow, and white clays were collected. Ochre, jasper, hematite, iron ore, and shale were used to make pigments.

There is also evidence that the Zunis mined copper ore and produced some primitive copper objects, certainly in precontact times, and there is considerable evidence that mining was carried on even until the late nineteenth century. The Zunis along with other Pueblo tribes worked the mines in the Cerrillos area. At these workings there were tunnels as deep as 200 feet and pits more than 300 feet wide. The Zunis also had diggings for copper and turquoise in the Zuni Mountains; these diggings were described in 1879 as including many "recent" and "ancient" excavations. The Zunis used native spades, digging sticks, and flint tools to excavate the copper ore. Probably in precontact times they carried the ore in a tumpline, or *zurrón*, a bag with a strap that looped around the forehead so that the individual could lift and carry the bag, sometimes for very long distances.

Plant collection included a variety of items from which the Zunis were able to fill their larders and storage bins with an amazing array of foods, medicines, ceremonial materials, basketry materials, and toiletries. Medicines for almost every type of ailment were prepared, from insect repellent to anesthetic. Pine gum gourds, cedar bark, willow root, other kinds of barks, pollen, and opiate derivatives were used by native Zuni doctors in treating illness and accidents. Burn ointments, painkillers (with different drugs for headaches, toothaches, or sore throats), and eye ointments were prepared from plants gathered throughout the region. There were depilatory preparations, narcotics, drugs for assisting women with childbirth, drugs for inducing vomiting, drugs for helping remove bullets and arrows, and preparations for healing puncture wounds.

Plants were used to construct clothes and baskets. Rabbit brush was used for baskets. Drop seed grass was woven into bunches and then attached together to make mats. In addition, there was subsistence gathering. In a drought year, if the crops failed, the Zunis were able to survive with the gathering of many other wild foods. The dozens of edible foods within the Zuni region included pine nuts, watercress, yucca, soap weed, cactus, cedar berries, and sunflowers.

Over a very long period of time, from at least A.D. 1250 to 1846, the Zuni people occupied and made exclusive use of the large area of land just described. Of course, there were times when all of the land was not being used at once or when other people were allowed to use portions of it. For instance, in the late eighteenth century many Zunis had to move in to live with their friends along the Rio Grande because of a terrible drought. The whole territory was amazed at the compassion that was aroused because the Zunis were in such need. The Zunis, who had long been friends to so many, received at that time help in return. But even then the *rancherías* of the tribe were not abandoned, and some Zunis stayed in the fields to save what crops and animals could be saved. Thus, even in the worst of times the Zunis protected their interests in their lands.

Although the Zunis controlled their lands, they often let others use them for various purposes. But if anyone else used any of the Zuni territory, it was at the leave of the Zunis — it was *permitted* by the Zunis. The Zunis were and are famous for their hospitality, so it is not surprising that other tribes were sometimes allowed to hunt, gather piñon nuts, or travel to Zuni Salt Lake. The Zunis even fed their own enemies during the *Sha'lak'o* celebration. Tribal religious leaders are quick to point out that the Zuni war gods not only protect the Zunis' lands but also help maintain order and peace for all the people in the world.

The area of traditional Zuni land use is what the Zunis required for long-term survival in a territory that even in drought could provide them sustenance for a considerable time without depleting their natural resources. They are the only people who have ever lived in this area and had an economy and a culture that could survive for a seemingly indefinite period of time without depleting the available resources.

CHAPTER 3

Zuni Oral Tradition and History

Triloki Nath Pandey

If we look at trade in a larger context, even from our twentieth-century experience, what trade really does, and did in the prehistoric or historic context, is bring together people who are isolated. It allows the uniqueness of one group to go to another. That is, it allows a kind of specialization. Through trade and commerce, people of various specializations, people of different achievements, are able to get together and exchange. Thus, trade in the historic and prehistoric context helped break down the cultural and geographic barriers that separated one group of people from another group. This is exactly what happened in the context of the Zuni people. Archaeologists tell us that the Zuni Indians had all kinds of things, things not normally found here, but things that came from various parts of the Southwest as well as areas now known as Mexico. Those things were brought by people who were trading items and very specialized knowledge about them with the Zuni people. We can get the idea from reading history books that the Zunis were isolated, as some historians have said, but that isolation has to be looked at in a cultural and historical context. The Zuni people were isolated, of course, but they were isolated in certain contexts and not in others.

There were quite a few outstanding non-Zuni individuals who became adopted Zunis. Many present-day Zunis recognize that many people were incorporated into the Zuni Tribe who were in fact either Apache (for instance, Jesus Eriacho), Navajo, Hopi, or Acoma. Over a period of time, the Zunis incorporated them into their own clans and lineages. These non-Zunis served as cultural brokers who were able to break down the cultural barriers that existed between the Zuni people and the Navajo, Apache, Acoma, and other tribal communities. From this a very interesting picture of the Zuni past emerges, one that includes other groups.

The Zuni people, who have lived here for a very long time, appreciate that physically it's very hard to live in the Southwest. It must have been even harder in the fifteenth, sixteenth, seventeenth, and eighteenth centuries. As a result, the ancestors of the Zuni people had to develop multiple strategies in order to survive. The Zuni people were not just

15

farming or collecting piñon nuts or hunting or trading. They did all these things. We have to look at all these economic and social activities in order to get a comprehensive view of the Zuni past or traditional Zuni life.

Every society has to have institutions and mechanisms to regulate the social and civic life of its people. In my work I have discussed the nature of Zuni theocracy, in particular the role of the Bow Priests and civil leaders in managing the internal law and order and the external relations of the Zuni people with groups such as the Apaches, Navajos, and other Indians and later on the Spaniards, Mexicans, and Anglo-Americans. It was in relation to these other groups that the Zunis defined their social and cultural boundaries and also ways to maintain them. In some respects, even if we look at the contemporary situation, Americans are Americans vis-à-vis Europeans, vis-à-vis Asians, vis-à-vis Australians. Whenever we define one particular unit (whatever that unit is), we define it in relation to other such units. Whenever we look at the Zuni people, how they really shaped their cultural traditions and background, we have to look at them from the other side as well—that is, from the points of view of the Athabascans, other Indian groups, whites, and others who came in contact with the Zuni Indians.

To a large extent, because of all the available scholarly specializations, we take a very narrow focus. We study either Zuni culture, Zuni history, Zuni politics, Zuni economics, or Zuni geography. But that does not mean that is the way things are in nature. Our own cultural constraints allow us to understand only a narrow segment of Zuni life. We should not ignore the other perspectives, whether it be Navajo, Apache, Hopi, Acoma, Laguna, Spanish, Mexican, or Anglo-American. It is in relation to these units that we have to understand how Zuni Indians really maintained their cultural and social boundaries and what kind of mechanisms they developed in order to safeguard their interests and values, both cultural and economic.

The fundamental idea underlying Zuni cosmology, the people's assumptions about the universe, their obligations as Zunis, and what they perceive as threats to their individual and collective lives, is that everything is predestined. What was determined by the Zuni war gods, *Ahayu:da*, in the beginning, at the time of emergence, is still the basis of Zunis' sociomoral order. In Zuni ritual poetry, in songs, in the worship of the Kachinas, in advice given by ceremonial fathers to their sons at initiations and other occasions, the same images are evoked, and the same words and phrases are repeated. Thus, the repetition of endless orderly rituals multiplied by the concentrated participation of the Zuni people combines with religious and cosmic penetration to work together to instill harmony, balance, and peace in Zuni life.

In my own society of Hindu India, a traditional society much like the Zuni, there is a great deal of emphasis on this repetition. There is a great deal of emphasis on continuity. In American culture, which developed in a very different historical context, repetition and continuity are not valued in themselves. But a study of Zuni society, a study of Indian society, or a study of Chinese society or Japanese society allows us to see what continuity really can do to cultures. Those societies that are oriented to continuing their past, or continuing their tradition, end up taking one kind of shape, one kind of orientation.

And just as words and phrases in a lost language may become of particular importance in the religious and ritual life of a people, so the ancient names of selective sacred places on the territorial limits may become sacred symbols that serve as identity or boundary markers for the people. The Zuni expert witnesses in the land claim litigation compiled a list of over 220 Zuni place-names (T. J. Ferguson played an important role in collecting this information). On the basis of this we are able to demonstrate that the Zuni people have had a much wider land base than the present reservation.

The Zuni land claim case provides an interesting opportunity to examine the role of memory in preserving certain cultural traditions and beliefs and the effect of that preservation on a people. This case raises questions about the nature of social and cultural knowledge and how it is generated by various people.

We human beings are very special. We are fragmented in many ways. We are all islands to ourselves. But we would not survive if we remained fragmented, if we remained isolated. So we must try to know each other, try to learn about each other. This social or cultural knowledge is absolutely necessary for our survival. It may not be necessary for a snake to have this kind of knowledge, it may not be necessary for a lion to have this kind of knowledge, but it is absolutely necessary for humans to have this kind of knowledge about ourselves. Without that knowledge we would not know how to survive wherever we lived. It was out of this need that various societies developed differing mechanisms to gain that kind of knowledge.

There are basically two kinds of societies: those that are oriented toward memory culture, oral tradition, and mouth-to-mouth learning, and those, which have been in existence for about 2,500 years, that are oriented toward literacy. The way the former knowledge is preserved is not just through oral tradition but also through written documents. In my own culture, the Hindu culture of India, my ancestors wrote down these things on leaves of various kinds, preserved this sacred knowledge for 2,600 years before writing became available and this information was written down.

But here I'm worried about the technology of keeping this knowledge. I'm worried about what technology does to this knowledge. In a community where history books and libraries are available, the knowledge of the past can be preserved; we don't have to do that ourselves. We can appoint a priest, a teacher, or somebody else to preserve that knowledge for us.

But the Zunis did not have access to this kind of preservation of knowledge and so had to divide themselves into various kinds of groups to do so. Medicine societies are one kind of group; the *A:shiwani,* the sacred priests, are another. There are all kinds of groups in Zuni society. One of the responsibilities that all these groups had was to have knowledge of their ecology, to have knowledge about themselves, to have knowledge about others, and to preserve that knowledge for the sake of their children and descendants. That is what really made Zuni society an extremely complex society. The Zunis stored a vast knowledge of their past in the heads of various specialists. These were the people who were the custodians of oral tradition, this oral knowledge that became the resource of those scholars whom we call anthropologists. So anthropologists were the people who started to study the leftovers, the people left out by history.

The study of orally based peoples happened in a colonial context because many of the practitioners were white and came from the centers of learning of the Western world. As a result, when they went to the non-Western countries, even to my own country, to China, and to Japan, which had a much more complex civilization than the countries the practitioners represented, they said that these people did not have history. "These people have myths. These people have folk tales. These people have oral tradition. They really do not have written documents." It was arrogance, buttressed by a feeling of technological superiority, buttressed by a mastery of written documents, that made anthropologists and others believe they could treat nonliterate peoples as inferior, with traditions not worthy of respect. But that was a long time ago.

We have now become interested not only in the nature of those disciplines but also in how those disciplines started and why they took the shape they did. That is, we have become interested in a very different kind of epistemology of knowledge, in a very different kind of cultural setup in which we have to respect each other if we are going to survive in this world together. Respect really means respecting the traditions, the values, the norms, the rules, and the regulations that govern not just our own lives but also the lives of people who may be much better than we are in certain respects.

If we really examine different kinds of society—those of India, China, Japan, western Europe, and other places—we can infer that there are basically two kinds of ordering systems for sorting out cultural complexity. One is time, sorting through chronology. In a literate culture, where history books can be written in 1920, and again in 1925, and again in 1935, and again in 1950, it is quite easy to sort out cultural and historical complexity.

The other system for sorting out cultural complexity is oral—through traditional transmission of knowledge. One way, for example, is to find out what kind of values people have about each other and nature, about their landscape. How did it happen that this way of maintaining knowledge was forgotten? It happened because in the Western world between 1200 and 1600 or 1700 there was a bifurcation between what we call ourselves and the other things that exist out there, nature. As a result, we saw nature, and other people, as something to be controlled, to be contained, to be mastered.

This is an objectification of nature. Nature is not treated as kind, as the Zuni people treat it. Nature is really not treated as a brother, a sister, a father, a grandfather—someone to be taken care of. For the Zunis, there is a reciprocity between us and nature. In Zuni tradition, we do certain things, and in return for those things nature rewards us with rain and other blessings. Neither we human beings, who are created by culture, nor nature, which is created by something else, would exist if we did not do things for nature's existence. Human beings have a very important role in keeping nature alive.

The Zuni culture, the Zuni people over a period of time, did not have Western culture's garbage-disposal type of attitude toward nature. Nature was one of them, an important part of their culture. It did not matter whether nature was land, whether it was spring, whether it was mountains, whether it was animals such as the bear or the deer. All of nature was dear to the Zunis. Unless we accord to nature's life forms the same kind of privileges as we do to our grandparents, as we do to our children, we are really not going to survive. This is what the Zunis taught us. It was the wisdom of the Zuni people to realize that they were in a partnership with nature and that they had to treat nature as a living thing, not as an object to be controlled.

Many of these things I really understood from talking with the Zuni people, including Flora Zuni, whom I have been visiting since 1964. I am interested in her life history, and Flora has always talked about her life in relation to the places that she has visited and the people she has known. That fact epitomizes one of the fundamental values of Zuni life: Emphasis is really on people, on human beings. As a result, if we want to understand the nature of the Zuni tradition, we have to consider the places that are sacred to the Zuni people, the people who are important to the Zuni people. Without bringing them into consideration, we will give a one-sided view of their past.

My effort has been to emphasize the fact that the Zuni people have retained knowledge of their past. They have developed multiple strategies to survive in the "hostile" environment of the Southwest. Unless we try to learn the Zunis' point of view, we will be unable to appreciate their past experiences inasmuch as only a fragment of those experiences has filtered through the various kinds of records compiled by scholars. I suggest that we should be conscious of the difference between oral and literate cultures and the impact of that difference on interpreting evidence from one through the tools and concepts of the other. For example, what maps, charts, and documents do in a literature society is what shrines and other sacred cultural markers do in a nonliterature society like Zuni. That's why the Zuni people have to visit these places in order to reaffirm their cultural tradition, in order to reaffirm their cultural belief. Those of us who depend on literate traditions have other rites of affirmation. But for Zuni people these are their rites of affirmation.

It is only by combining the historian's "history" with the traditional Zuni's "history" that we can be in a strong position to determine the validity of the Zuni land claim case. If we fail to do that, we are going to continue to perpetuate the inequality between the Western tradition and values and the non-Western traditions and values. Until we treat, at par, the laws and legal systems that a literate society has developed and those that a nonliterate society has developed, we are going to perpetuate inequity toward people who do not have a privileged status, who are not literate, and who do not have access to the kind of ideas and tools that literacy provides literati.

CHAPTER 4

Zuni History and Anthropology

Fred Eggan

The historical events of the past play an important part in Zuni life. Alfred L. Kroeber, the distinguished anthropologist from the University of California, spent a couple of seasons in Zuni in 1915 and 1916. He came to the conclusion almost seventy years ago that the Zunis had a different sense of history than Anglo scholars do. He claimed that he never met a Zuni who had a Western understanding of historical events and their importance.

If that may have been the case or may have been partly true some two or three generations ago, it is no longer so. The events of the past have begun to play an important role in Zuni life. When the Zunis did not file a land claims case before the Indian Land Claims Commission in the late 1940s, the Navajos claimed all the lands of the Zuni reservation as part of their aboriginal use area. Except for a small Spanish land grant of some 17,000 acres, they said all the rest of the Zuni territory was in "the exclusive use and control of the Navajos as of 1868."

The Indian Claims Commission accepted this assertion as one of its "findings of fact." The Department of Justice in later discussions said, "Well you know all of the Zuni Reservation has been carved out of Navajo aboriginal lands." Now the Department of Justice should have known better than this. It should have known that this Navajo claim was false because in 1868 the Navajos were in captivity in Bosque Redondo or Fort Summer. When they were released in midyear, they were sent to a new reservation north of Fort Defiance. They promised to stay on their reservation and not cause any more trouble with any other Indian groups. But in 1978 the Department of Justice forgot that history.

The government was supposed to have looked after the Zuni interests in these claim cases, even though the Zunis did not participate actively. So when in 1978 the Zunis got permission to file a separate claim in the United States Court of Claims, I was interested in correcting at least this one major injustice. Historians and anthropologists who testified for the Zunis and those who testified for the Department of Justice found no evidence in either history or archaeology that the Zuni River valley and the present reservation had ever been in the exclusive use and control of the

Navajos although sometimes they may have controlled a small section for a few hours.

History takes a variety of forms. All history was originally oral history, and 90–95 percent of human history has taken place in this oral phase without writing. When someone tells somebody something else or sees something else and writes it down and it comes to be a historical document, then it can be studied and interpreted. To my way of thinking, there's no fundamental distinction between history written down and history spoken. Each can be wrong or right.

Ethnohistory attempts to study the culture of any group and the historical documents that are available to provide a more complete account of what happened in the past. Historical writing about Zuni begins with Francisco Vásquez de Coronado's expedition of 1540–1542. Coronado was at Zuni and around the Southwest for two years. He came to discover the Seven Cities of Cibola, the legendary cities whose streets were paved with gold and precious stones. Coronado arrived in the summer of 1540 after traveling up through what is now Arizona and forced the submission of Hawikku and the other Zuni towns before continuing on to the Acoma and Rio Grande pueblos, where he wintered. After this he took a grand tour of the Great Plains under the leadership of an Indian nicknamed "the Turk" and came back more or less empty-handed. (There is a large volume containing the various accounts of the Coronado expedition, but most of them were written a number of years after the expeditioners got back either to Mexico or to Spain, and there are many differences between the reports.)

There were actually only six villages in the Zuni region at the time, though Coronado persisted in thinking there were seven, but the expeditioners did see the ruins of many more. Exploring parties were sent to the Hopi country, where they found seven. Coronado's group didn't look at all the villages. They probably stopped mainly at Awatovi. They heard about the Grand Canyon, and later on they sent an expedition under Pedro de Tovar to visit the Grand Canyon.

In the meantime many of the Zunis had retreated to their sacred mesa of Corn Mountain as a place of refuge from the Spanish demands for food and subservience. Juan de Oñate came to New Mexico with several hundred colonists and soldiers in 1598, almost sixty years later, settling first at San Juan pueblo and later at Santa Fe. In the 1620s, and particularly in 1629, a considerable number of Franciscan friars arrived determined to Christianize the pueblos and obliterate all traces of native religion. Their efforts led to the Pueblo Revolt of 1680, in which the priests were killed and the Spanish colonists and soldiers driven out of New Mexico for a dozen years. I think in the whole history of Spain this was the only time any of their colonies were so roughly treated.

During this period, the Zunis again returned to their sacred mountain, where each village built a set of houses, along with corrals, storage rooms, and reservoirs as a base from which to repel the Spaniards when they returned. When the Spaniards did return in 1692, under General Diego de Vargas, he pardoned the Zunis so they did not have to fight to remain in their country, and he persuaded them to descend from Corn Mountain. They came down soon after and began to build a new village at a place along the Zuni River, the site of the current village. There had been an old village on the south side of the river, but the new village of Halona, the modern village of Zuni, was the famous midpoint of the world. And here the Zunis have lived since the 1700s.

The six villages of the early historic period were now joined into one. But much more than a new set of houses was created. The Zunis reorganized their military structure, or perhaps, as Edmund Ladd has suggested, they had done that already. They also amalgamated their social groupings, ceremonies, and priesthoods into a real tribal organization (the first in the pueblo Southwest) rather then maintain a series of individual town-states, such as still exist among the Hopis, where each major village thinks of itself as independent and has very little interaction with other villages in terms of control or coordination.

This new organization was designed to allow the Zunis to meet the threat of Apache raids and Spanish reprisals. The six major priesthoods very likely represent the six major original villages, the priest of the north being the senior member and the spokesman for the sun being the spokesman for the whole group. This organization was classified symbolically in terms of the six directions. The Bow Priests were organized into a single unit, with the elder and younger brother Bow Priests as leaders, representing the war gods. The Bow Priests were charged with the protection of the population against outside aggression and against internal dissention. The kachina cult was divided among six kiva groups, even though their particular position in the village did not necessarily correspond to their direction. The matrilineal clans were organized into six major groups, or phratries. The ceremonial cycle was consolidated into a year-long series of rituals culminating in the *Sha'lak'o* performances beginning in late November or early December. The six directions, or the directional system, are a basic pueblo pattern. The Zuni organization is more complex and covers a greater variety of objects or symbolic subjects than most of the pueblos, and the pueblo system may well have had its greatest development here. As Ladd reminds up, the Zuni also added a unique seventh direction, which is right "here"; there is a shrine in the central village to represent the middle of the world.

How this consolidation was developed we do not yet know. Frank Hamilton Cushing, the young anthropologist sent out in the early 1880s to study Zuni, provided an outline of the Zuni social and ceremonial system as it had been in the recent past.[1] His "Outlines of Zuni Creation Myths" (later published in 1896 by the Smithsonian Institution) is the best model of what this system was like. But Cushing did not realize that this might have been recently developed. He knew of the periodic flight to Corn Mountain and of the structures up there, and he knew that when the Zunis came down, they were put together into one village. But he was a pioneer social anthropologist and had the whole Southwest to worry about; he didn't really think about what had happened here at Zuni. If he had, he might have consulted the old men, and they might have had oral traditions that told how this "putting together" had taken place. There may be traditions in some of the priestly societies today that refer to what happened, what the order of precedents were, and so on. When the tricentennial of the Pueblo Revolt came along in 1980, many villages searched their memories and their traditions and came up with new material that was relevant to what had happened then. So this information may still be in this oral history that Triloki Pandey talks about (in Chapter 3).

What social anthropologists can do is compare Zuni villages to Hopi villages and see what consolidation does, such as making the internal organization of Zuni, social and ceremonial, much more complicated. This complexity, this size of the structure, is one feature that distinguishes Zuni from all the other pueblos, though some of the Rio Grande ones do approach it.

Acoma gives another kind of comparison. In 1598 Acoma had the misfortune to kill about twenty Spaniards, or kill most of them; some of them jumped off the cliff and miraculously survived. But the Spaniards, having just established their first colony at San Gabriel, then part of San Juan, weren't going to let this action pass without any retaliation, particularly as the leader who had been killed was the nephew of Oñate. So in 1599 the Spaniards came in force and besieged Acoma. Acoma was divided about whether to give in or fight. And the Acomas didn't protect their places of approach very well, so the Spaniards, after a day or two of frontal assaults that got nowhere, managed to go around back and climb up with one small cannon. After three days of fighting, the Acomas gave in.

The punishment was severe. Most were taken captive, and their trial was held at Santo Domingo so everyone would know about it. The Spaniards sentenced most of the men to having one hand cut off or one foot cut off and to serving twenty years in slavery. The Acomas gradually filtered back to their mesa village, but the wall between them and the Mexicans and the Anglos has been pretty thick ever since. But what they did behind that wall, I think, was to consolidate their power structure and organization, not on the Hopi model, which is scattered among a variety of villages and individuals, but on a one-group model. One clan, the Antelope Clan, from which the cacique comes, was given more power. The cacique had the power to regulate the kachina organization and to appoint the heads of the medicine societies and so forth. This centralization enabled the Acomas to present a united front against the Spaniards whenever they might come back.

Now at Zuni there was a different situation, but again with this centralization, because when Hawikku was attacked by the Apaches in 1672 and the church and part of the community were destroyed, the Zunis from the other villages didn't seem to go to the rescue. Or if they did, by the time they got there the Apaches were down below the Mogollon Rim. By centralizing the community and its resources, the military forces, and political organization, the Zunis were able in ensuing years to repel or survive Apache and later Navajo attacks and maintain their cultural integrity down to the present day.

NOTES

1. Cushing, the first anthropologist to come to Zuni, wasn't an anthropologist when he arrived. A young man of twenty-one, he decided to stay and learn Zuni and find out what the meaning was of all the things he was seeing every day in the village, the dances, the ceremonies, the masks, and so on. He wanted to understand Zuni life as it was lived. He tried to become a Zuni, and I think so far as it was possible he succeeded. He moved into the governor's house (I recommend to our present Zuni governor that he put a good lock on his house so that no other anthropologist manages to do this), and he said, "Here I am." He stayed there. The rest of his group went off to Hopi country. He in effect threw himself on the mercies of the Zunis. They could have let him starve to death, but they didn't. They fed him. And he said, "They hardened my flesh." They made him sleep on the ground with very little covering. He survived the first winter. He said that after that living was relatively easy. He stayed four and a half years. He repaid the Zunis in a variety of ways. He was allowed to join the Society of the Bow and ultimately became at least a junior Bow Priest, the "younger brother Bow Priest." He led attacks against Apaches and Navajos who were raiding Zuni flocks of sheep and horses. He was responsible in an earlier lands claim case in the 1880s for the return to the Zuni Reservation of land that had been given to the Zunis by presidential executive order but that had inadvertently been left off the map so that the springs at Nutria and at Pescado, on which the Zunis depended for much of their irrigation and for some of the wheat and corn grown for Fort Defiance and such places, were in danger of being lost.

A group of army officers at Fort Defiance decided this would be a good place when they retired from the army to develop a cattle ranch. One of them happened to be the son-in-law of Senator John A. Logan, who was about ready to run for president. When Cushing and Sylvester Baxter, a newspaper reporter, and others blew the whistle on this outrage, Senator Logan was so angry that he threatened the Smithsonian Institution with a loss of appropriations unless it got Cushing off the Zuni Reservation. John Wesley Powell acceded to Logan's demands, but Logan lost in the next election partly as a result of the whole matter becoming public.

Cushing's writings were not completed when he died at the age of forty-three. He had the good fortune to go down to Florida and do some remarkable archaeology at Key Largo, finding carved wooden animals seen from no other site. But enjoying a meal on some type of fish, he choked on a fish bone one night and never recovered. He left a large number of essays and manuscripts. Many of them have fortunately been brought together by a young professor of English named Jessie Green. They are out in paperback under the title *The Selected Writing of Frank Hamilton Cushing,* along with the *The Zunis: Self-Portrayals* that the Zunis have done themselves.

Cushing was a controversial character. Some thought that he wrote too much about the Zunis. Others thought that he wrote too little. But the great French anthropologist Claude Lévi-Strauss praised Cushing very highly for his contributions to our understanding of Zuni society and culture. Zuni is perhaps as well known in France these days among the intellectuals as it is in this country.

Lithograph from a sketch by Richard H. Kern in 1851 showing Zuni women grinding corn. (From the Lorenzo Sitgreaves report of 1852; courtesy the Smithsonian Institution, National Anthropological Archives)

Zuni specialty crops were grown in "waffle gardens," seen here in the foreground. Cornfields can be seen in the background stretching across the valley in this 1873 photograph by Timothy O'Sullivan. (Courtesy the National Archives)

An 1873 Timothy O'Sullivan photograph showing three Zuni officers: *left to right*, the alcalde,
or municipal officer; the governor and war
chief (*Match'olth*, or Jose Maria), and the lieutenant governor. The governor carries both a
cane (symbol of secular authority) and a rifle
(as war chief).

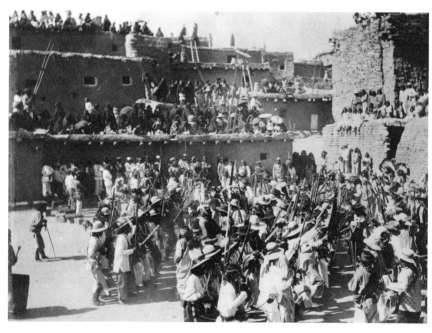

A Zuni war victory dance, ca. 1879, by John K. Hillers. (Courtesy the Smithsonian
Institution, National Anthropological Archives)

Corn drying on the rooftops of Zuni pueblo, 1879. (Photograph by John K. Hillers, courtesy the Smithsonian Institution, National Anthropological Archives)

A visitor to Zuni in ca. 1895 looks across the fields at the Zuni village of upper Nutria. (Photograph by Ben Wittick; courtesy the Southwest Museum)

"Logging in New Mexico," in the McGaffey area of the upper Zuni watershed, ca. 1910. (An H. H. Walker photograph; courtesy the Gallup Public Library)

A Zuni man works on a ditch near Toseluna Spring, "which supplies water for irrigating at Ojo Caliente." (Photograph by Matilda Coxe Stevenson, 1904; courtesy the Smithsonian Institution, National Anthropological Archives)

The failure of Blackrock Dam, December 6, 1909. "Spillway and remaining end section of dam. Looked very much like a recent upheaval." (Zuni Agency, Forestry Office, Bureau of Indian Affairs)

Women work in Zuni "waffle gardens," ca. 1912. (Photograph by Jesse L. Nusbaum; courtesy the Museum of New Mexico)

Zuni harvest wagons, 1919. (Photograph courtesy the Museum of the American Indian)

Zunis harvesting wheat near Ojo Caliente, 1919. (Courtesy the Museum of the American Indian)

"Old road degenerating into an arroyo due to improper drainage, Nutria Valley, Zuni Indian Reservation," 1930. (Record Group 75, Forestry Photographs, National Archives)

Bureau of Indian Affairs officials examine erosion in a wagon track along the Gallup Road in the Nutria valley, July 9, 1930. (Record Group 75, Forestry Photographs, National Archives)

An incision in a streambed forty feet deep and fifty-six feet wide in the Nutria area in 1939, "due to heavy use of Nutria Canyon and clear cutting of timber on adjacent private lands." (Bureau of Indian Affairs, *Forestry Annual Report,* 1939; courtesy Zuni Tribal Archives)

CHAPTER 5

Values of Zuni Oral History

Floyd A. O'Neil

I first came to Zuni working with the Doris Duke Indian Oral History Project, which was carried out at seven American institutions—the University of Utah and six others, including the University of New Mexico. S. Lyman Tyler introduced Gregory Crampton and me to the Zuni Tribal Council, and we started working on Zuni oral history but originally not on collecting—the Zunis on their own had already recorded about 925 oral testimonies, most of them stories and history from their own people.

It was there at Zuni that the University of Utah hired a translator, Alvina Quam, who along with the Zuni Tribal Council and some religious leaders selected about 400 documents for translation from Zuni into English. From those translations came the very successful book *The Zunis: Self Portrayals,* by the Zuni People. At that time I also had the pleasure of working with Wilfred Eriacho and Ralph Casebolt in the production of some other modest curricular materials for use in the Zunis' schools.

As a part of the Duke project, additional original interviews were also carried out at Zuni pueblo. A long list of people were interviewed, and about forty-seven oral interviews were carried out, including some of very great importance to the land claim cases. Some of those interviewed have since passed away, and some are still living. Between 1967 and 1973 some of those interviewed included Lorenzo Chaves; Chester Gaspar; Robert Lewis; his mother, Margaret Lewis; and Nathaniel Nasheboo, all of whose testimony proved valuable to the land claims cases. Others who provided valuable interviews included Roland Lamentino, Lucinda Nastacio, Angelina Medina, Bowman Pewa, Sam and Katy Poblano, and Alex Seowtewa. Non-Zunis who provided good factual interviews included Niles Kraft, Bernard J. Vanderwagen, other members of the Vanderwagen family, and Clara Gonzalez.

The tapes were extremely interesting and productive. In interviewing Margaret Lewis, we found that she had lived here so long that many thought she was Zuni, but she was Cherokee. I asked her what her first impression of Zuni had been when she came here in 1898. She replied, "I

27

looked from the wagon down across the valley and said, 'That's Zuni? I don't see anything but a pile of dust.' "

In that long and rich interview with Margaret Lewis, she revealed that the governor's grandmother had been born on the Trail of Tears in Cape Girardeau in Missouri in 1840, which talks a little of the antiquity of the three generations of people and the importance of each of them. When I asked Lewis to estimate how many of the Zuni people were Christian, she hesitated for a few seconds and then said, "Only me." She had lost most of the traces of being Cherokee, and I asked her if she still knew any Cherokee words, and she said, "No. God might have sent me here because I couldn't speak Cherokee and Zuni was so easy to learn." More interesting still, perhaps, was that informal session of hers when she served as the only female governor and her early efforts (after she had been there less than two decades) to negotiate for additional lands on the southern borders of the reservation.

Oral history of this type is extremely interesting and extremely rewarding if the material can be used in a land claim case. Now some of the material could be. More productive by far was another type of oral testimony, that taken in the affidavits by the lawyers and with the help of T. J. Ferguson. Collective memories are usually considered interesting, antique, and folkloric. In Indian life they are a very great deal more. This type of traditional knowledge should be maintained with great dedication.

Ever since I started coming to Zuni in 1968 in a professional relationship, I have heard a constant complaint that the oral traditions are weakening, that television often attracts the children more forcefully than the storytellers. If this is true, I hope that the role of the school might change so that the oral traditions of the people might be taught as well as the teachings of the Anglo culture. This basic change in curriculum is necessary to guard that extremely valuable folk knowledge.

The fact that there were more than 200 place names in the Zuni religious leaders' affidavits indicates the viability and importance of the present state of Zuni knowledge. As Zuni has made the transition from a nonliterate to a literate society, fewer and fewer younger people have the time the memorize all of the information that has formerly been transmitted orally. Today there are probably few people under the age of thirty-five years who could name a hundred of those names. The fact that this traditionally transmitted knowledge is indeed valuable has never been more forcefully demonstrated than it was with the land claims cases. We must hope that as much as is possible of this knowledge will be saved, whether through traditional methods of transmission, or through documentation.

Now we are told as historians that oral tradition is suspect. Historians rely on documents. However, if an oral tradition is one generation old, historians will respect it like other documents *if* someone has typed it up. So there is something flawed in the discipline of history. That same kind of bias extends to the field of law. Something said forty years ago seems to have more credibility than something said the day before yesterday. This strange kind of value in the historian's discipline and in the discipline of others is certainly questionable.

While I am addressing the value of Zuni traditional knowledge, it is worth noting the importance of the future entrenchment of this Zuni knowledge within the schools. Recent work within the Zuni school system and by the Zuni School Board is helping to integrate Zuni knowledge into the curriculum. Zuni geography, Zuni trade and traditional economics, and the Zuni political system are all subjects worthy of study within the formalized Zuni school system.

One final word about oral history. Any time people say things, anyone can find errors in them. But in Indian oral tradition I find that the long tradition of living without relying for certain types of knowledge on the written word makes the continuity of Indian oral tradition far superior to the continuity found in western European cultures.

CHAPTER 6

Zuni's Royal Contract with Spain

Ward Alan Minge

Surely a great historical event in pueblo tradition was the arrival of the Spaniards almost 450 years ago. They had high hopes and were convinced they had discovered another Indian kingdom not unlike those in Mexico for wealth, territory, population, and civilization. I am certain this image influenced Spanish concepts of the Zunis in many ways throughout the colonial period.

In the New World of 1540, Francisco Vásquez de Coronado's trip into New Mexico followed within a few years, and fresh in the memory of all, Hernán Cortés's conquest of the Aztecs in 1521, the Pizarro brothers' conquest of Peru in 1535, and the ransom of the great Aztec chieftain Atahualpa for rooms full of gold. In a few years the Spaniards had stumbled onto greater riches than the Old World had ever seen.

Holding such wealth and power were Indian emperors, kings, royal Indian families, not unlike the political structures from Europe. The Aztecs formed an empire with Montezuma ruling over many Indian kingdoms from the Taxcalans close at hand to the Zapotecs and Mixtecs a thousand miles to the south of Mexico City. The Aztecs had not been able to conquer the Tarascans, whose capital, Tzintzuntzan ("humming bird"), overlooked beautiful Lake Patzucuaro. In this country west of Mexico City, Coronado spent a couple of years before coming to New Mexico. He was a close trusted friend of Viceroy Antonio Mendoza, had been in the New World only since 1535, had married well and inherited large landholdings from this marriage, and had traveled with the influence of nobility.

With such connections Viceroy Mendoza appointed Coronado to be acting governor of Nueva Galicia, the northwestern province of New Spain or Mexico, which included numerous Indian provinces and kingdoms such as that of the Tarascans. He was largely responsible for making friends of the Indians in the region, but the Spaniards began settling Nueva Galicia rapidly because of rich gold and silver deposits. Four large Spanish settlements developed in a year or two at Guadalajara, Compostela, Purificación, and Culiacán.

In April 1539, Viceroy Mendoza appointed Coronado governor, and it was during the autumn of that year he met Father Marcos de Niza, who gave him glowing accounts of Cibola. These were not the first rumors of a rich civilization up north, and Viceroy Mendoza commissioned Coronado on January 6, 1540, to lead an exploration party, which marched on Zuni. There were between 400 and 500 Spaniards, most on horseback, some on foot, and altogether around 1,500 animals, horses, mules, and stock. Coronado stated that additionally 1,300 Indians voluntarily accompanied the expedition.

The first wholesale encounter between the Spaniards and Zunis occurred during and after the so-called Battle of Hawikku in July 1540. The report of this battle to the king of Spain and Coronado's description of Zuni constitute the first formal knowledge the outside world received:

It now remains for me to tell about the Seven Cities, the kingdom and province of which the father provincial [Fray Marcos] gave your Lordship an account. Not to be too verbose, I can assure you that he had not told you the truth in a single thing that he said, but everything is the opposite of what he related, except the name of the cities and the large stone houses. For although they are not decorated with turquoise, nor made of lime or brick, nevertheless, they are very good homes and good rooms with corridors, and some quite good rooms underground and paved, which are built for winter, and which are something like *estufas*. Most of the ladders which they have for their houses are movable and portable and are taken up and placed wherever desired. They are made of two pieces of wood, with rungs like ours.

The Seven Cities are seven little villages, all having the kind of houses I described.[1] They are all within a radius of four leagues. All together they are called the kingdom of Cibola. Each has its own name and no single one is called Cibola, but all together they are called Cibola. This one which I have called a city I name Granada (Hawikku), both because it has some similarity to it and in honor of your Lordship. In this one where I am now lodged there are perhaps 200 houses, all surrounded by a wall, and it seems to me that, together with the others which are not so surrounded, there might be in all 500 hearths.

There is another town nearby, which is one of the seven, but somewhat larger than this, and another of the same size as this, the other four are somewhat smaller. I am sending a sketch of them all, and of the route, to your Lordship. The skin on which the painting is made was found here with other skins.

The people of these towns seem to me to be fairly large, and intelligent although I do not think that they have the judgement and intelligence needed to be able to build these houses in the way in which they are built, for most of them are entirely naked except for the covering over their privy parts. They have painted blankets like the one which I am sending to you. They do not raise cotton, because the country is extremely cold, but they wear blankets, as you may see by the sample which I am sending. It is also true that some cotton thread was found in their houses. They wear the hair on their heads like the Mexicans. They are well built and comely. I think that they have a quantity of turquoises, which they had removed with the rest of their goods, except the maize, because, when I arrived, I did not find any women here nor any men under fifteen years or over sixty, except two or three old men who remained in command of all the other young men and the warriors. Two points of emerald and some little broken stones, rather poor, which approached the color of garnet, were found in a paper, besides other stone crystals which I gave to one of my servants to keep until they could be sent to your Lordship. He has lost them so they tell me.

We found fowl, but only a few, although there are some. The Indians tell me that they do not eat them in any of the seven villages, but they keep them merely for the sake of procuring the feathers. I do not believe this, because they are very good and larger than those of Mexico.

The climate of this country and the temperature of the air are almost like those of Mexico, because now it is hot and now it rains. I have not yet seen it rain, however, except once when there fell a little shower with wind, such as often falls in Spain. The snow and the cold are unusually great, according to what the natives of the country say. This may very probably be so, to judge by the nature of the country and the sort of houses they build and the skins and other things which these people have to protect themselves from the cold.

There are not fruits or fruit trees. The country is all level and is nowhere shut in by high mountains, although there are some hills and rough passages. There are not many trees fit for firewood here although they can bring enough for their needs from a clump of very small junipers four leagues distant. Very good grass was found a quarter of a league away, both for pasturage for our horses and for mowing for making hay, of which we had great need, because our horses were so weak and feeble when they arrived.

The food which they eat in this country consists of maize, of which they have great abundance, beans and game, which they must eat (although some say that they do not), because we found many skins of deer, hares, and rabbits. They make the best tortillas that I have ever seen anywhere, and this is what everybody ordinarily eats.

They have the very best arrangement and method for grinding that was ever seen. One of these Indian women here will grind as much as four of the Mexicans do. They have very good salt in crystals, which they bring from a lake a day's journey distant from here.

I have gained no information from them about the North Sea or that on the west, nor am I able to tell your Lordship which we are nearest to. I should judge that we are nearer to the western and 150 leagues is the nearest that it seems to me it can be to these. The North Sea must be much further away.

Your Lordship may thus see how extensive this country is. There are many animals, bears, tigers, lions, porcupines, and some sheep as big as horses, with very large horns, the size of which was something amazing. These are wild goats, whose heads I have also seen, and the paws of the bears and the skins of the wild boars. For game they have deer, leopards, and very large roebucks. Everyone thinks that some of them are larger than the animal with which your Lordship favored me, which belonged to Juan Melaz. They inhabit some plains eight days journey toward the North Sea. The natives here have some very well-dressed skins and they prepare and paint them where they kill the cattle, according to what they tell me.[2]

But Zuni turned out not to be Quivira, the fabulous country that Coronado traveled in search of as far east as Kansas.

The royal contract came with Don Juan de Oñate in 1598, long recognized by historians as the first successful Spanish colonizer of the far northern borders of New Spain. Oñate was more familiar and experienced with this country and the Indians than Coronado. Oñate's father had served under Cortés in conquering the Aztecs, had for a time been governor of Nueva Galicia, had fought against the beleaguered Indians there during the Mixton War, had discovered the mines at Zacatecas, and had founded the town of that name.

Don Juan de Oñate grew up during all this and married Doña Isabel de Tolosa, related by marriage to Cortés and the Aztec ruler Montezuma. He had helped his father put down several Indian rebellions in Mexico and discover mines, and with these connections Oñate had little trouble receiving a contract to settle in New Mexico as the first governor and captain general. His enemies, however, delayed his arrival into New Mexico for five years. Nevertheless, he brought with him many rights and privileges.

On April 30, 1598, Juan de Oñate, accompanied by numerous colonists, their supplies, and animals, officially took possession of the area, naming New Mexico, its kingdoms, and its provinces, "for our king our Lord." Oñate and the settlers traveled the southern route straight north following the Rio Grande. They settled first near San Juan pueblo, later moving to Santa Fe in 1608–1610 because the town was more advantageous. Oñate's relations with Zuni were scant except for one all-important visit that placed the Zuni province (or kingdom—the words were used interchangeably) officially into Spanish possessions or territorial holdings.

In addition to taking possession of New Mexico and assessing conditions for settlements, Oñate proceeded with formal Acts of Obedience and Vassalage performed by chieftains from the various pueblos, those along the Rio Grande occurring first. Zuni chieftains performed this rite later in 1598 as Governor Oñate and a select group of colonists, including some soldiers, located the salines, a source of salt near modern-day Gran Quivira, and set out to find the Pacific. No one had the slightest idea how far away the ocean might be.

The party arrived at Zuni during the first week in November 1598, and on November 9 the governor officiated over the Act of Obedience and Vassalage as performed by the Indians of Zuni. The procedure required some coaxing and negotiations, according to the governor's secretary, who drew up the official proceedings, which, signed and sealed, became the Spanish instrument of authority over the Zunis.

> Act of Obedience and Vassalage by the Indians of Zuni:
> In the name of the holy trinity . . . : Be it known and manifest to all who may see or hear of this instrument of loyalty and vassalage or who may in any way become acquainted with it that Don Juan de Oñate . . . being at the pueblo of Aguicobi in that province of Zuni, accompanied by the most reverend father, Fray Alonso Martinez, apostolic commissary of his Holiness, the friars of the order of Saint Francis, and the captains and the soldiers and there being present likewise numerous natives, including chieftains, leaders, and common people, among whom were the chiefs of the following people and pueblos:
> Negua homi and Atiz oha, who said that they were chiefs of the six pueblos named Aguicobi, Canabi, Coaquima, Holonagu, Mazaqui, and Aquima.
> All these chieftains had been summoned and assembled by the governor. Don Juan de Oñate, who had them appear in his presence and before me, Juan Velarde, secretary. With the aid of the commissary and Don Tomas, Indian interpreter, his lordship, the governor, explained to these chiefs the object of his coming.
> He told them that he had come to their lands to bring them to the knowledge of God and the king our lord, on which depended their salvation of their souls and their living securely and undis-

turbed in their nations, maintained in justice and order, secure in their homes, and protected against their enemies, and that he had not come to do them any harm. Wherefore they should know that there is only one God, creator of heaven and earth, rewarded of the good, whom He takes to heaven, and punisher of the wicked, whom He sends to hell. This God and lord of all had two servants here on earth through whom He governed. The one, concerned with spiritual matters, was the pope, the Roman pontiff, high priest and head of the church, whose representative in this country was the most reverent father commissary, whom they saw in their midst. They should venerate and respect him and all the other priests who wear the habit as ministers of God and men in His church. The other who governed the world in temporal matters, was the very Christian king, Don Philip, our lord, sole defender of the church, king of Spain and the Indies, whose representative in this country was his lordship, the governor. Consequently they should render him all respect and obedience, for it was fitting that they should give obedience and vassalage to God and the king, and in their stead to the reverend father commissary in spiritual matters and to the governor in temporal matters and in the government of their nations. Since they were free men and did not owe allegiance to any monarch or ruler, it was fitting that they should, of their own free will, submit to the authority of the king, Don Philip, our lord, great ruler and king, who would maintain them in justice and peace and defend them against their enemies and assist them in many things of their political and economic life, as would be explained to them more at length later. Thus they should consider whether they wanted to render obedience, as has been set forth.

The chieftains, when they had heard and understood this and consulted with one another about the matter, replied, with spontaneous signs of contentment and harmony, that they wished to become vassals of the most Christian king our lord, and as his vassals they desired at once to render obedience and vassalage both in their own names and for their nations.

The governor urged them to reflect and remember that to render obedience and vassalage to the king our lord meant subjection to his authority, commands, and laws, and that if the king our lord meant subjection to his authority, commands and laws, and that if they did not observe them they would be punished as transgressors of the command of their king and natural master. Therefore they should consider what they wanted to do and answer accordingly. The chiefs replied that they wished to render obedience and vassalage, as they had already stated, both for themselves and in the name of their nations. This being the case the governor said that they should rise, as a sign of obedience, for during all this time they had remained seated, and embrace the father commissary and his lordship and kiss their hands. The said chiefs rose and did as had been instructed, as a sign of obedience and vassalage.

The governor ordered me to give him written testimony of these proceedings and I did so, with my name and seal affixed. It was signed likewise by the governor and stamped with the great seal of his office, in this province of Zuni, November 8, 1598. The witnesses were Don Cristobal de Oñate, Captain Villagran, Captain Cessar, Antonio Conte de Herrera, Francisco Vido, and Cristobal de Herrera, Don Juan de Oñate.

I, Juan Velarde, secretary, was present at all the aforesaid, together with the governor, who here signed his name, as did the witnesses. In testimony of the truth, I signed. Juan Velarde, secretary.

Corrected and compared with the original, which remains in possession of the governor, who here attached his name, I had it copied by his order at San Juan Bautista, New Mexico, February 21, 1599. Witnesses to the correction were Antonio Conte de Herrera, Francisco Vido, and Francisco Villalba. In testimony of which I signed it and stamped with the seal of his lordship. In testimony of the truth. Juan Velarde, secretary.[3]

Two things in this document stand out clearly. First, the Spaniards extended the king's royal domain over the area, identified as a province, and covering western territories not at all defined or clearly understood except by the Zuni themselves. Second, Oñate pledged to protect their persons and properties.

Don Diego de Vargas reexecuted this act during the Reconquest in 1692. On Sunday November 9, ten or twelve Zunis arrived at El Morro to welcome Governor de Vargas and his group to the province of Zuni. They arrived at Corn Mountain the following day to find the Zuni main headquarters, but none could really be certain in what mood they would find the Indians.

De Vargas described the activities of the next morning:

Today, Tuesday, the eleventh of the present month of November of this year (1692), in order to climb the said rocks and enter the pueblo which the natives of the pueblos of the Zuni tribe have on its mesa-top, I, said governor and captain general, ordered the captains of the two companies to prepare five squads, with their military leaders and officers, armed, and with horses. This having been done, I, said governor and captain general, mounted my horse, with my said secretary of cavalry and the leaders to direct the troops to advance in four rows. In this order I arrived at the said rock, finding its fore part crowned with the people of the pueblo. Since the ascent was too steep and long and the footings as dangerous, it was necessary to climb up on foot, and although it took considerable effort, we were successful, and I, said governor and captain general, being on top with the soldiers, found that the said mesa was very broad and spacious. It must be about two leagues in extent. I again mounted my horse to enter the pueblo, where the natives received me with their entire population, which I could see was very large. Having dismounted my horse, I greeted all of them, saying, "Glory be," and all the said multitude came toward me and embraced me and gave me their hands, and I received them and spoke to them with great affections.[4]

Then followed the Act of Obedience and Vassalage, during which de Vargas reclaimed the "rock, its pueblo, and all this land and kingdom" for Spain and stated that the Zunis were once again vassals to the king of Spain. The day ended with the Zunis receiving absolution and baptism for both sexes and all ages, totaling 294. Governor de Vargas reported that he served as godfather for a son of the Zuni leader, while the soldiers stood as godfathers for many of the Indian children.

Understood throughout these transactions was the official recognition by the Spaniards of Indian or aboriginal boundaries. During that time, the Zunis were never required to prove what they were and what acreage was covered by their kingdom or province. The royal contract stood valid without any further qualifications throughout the colonial period and down to 1846 under the Mexicans. The official attitude toward Zuni territory appeared to have been similar to the Salinero Apache chieftain who told de Vargas that the Apaches had "always entered this land and province of Zuni on terms of peace."[5] The contract had established a large area, inhabited by the friendly Zunis, to serve as a bulwark against both unknown and common enemies.

NOTES

1. According to Frederick W. Hodge, there were only six pueblos here in Coronado's time; see Hodge, "The Six Cities of Cibola," *New Mexico Historical Review* 1 (1926): 478–88.

2. George Peter Hammond and Agapito Rey, *Narratives of the Coronado Expedition, 1540–1542*, vol. 2 in Coronado Cuarto Centennial Publications, 1540–1940 (Albuquerque: University of New Mexico Press, 1940), pp. 170–76, letter of Coronado to Mendoza, August 3, 1540.

3. George Peter Hammond and Agapito Rey, *Oñate, Colonizer of New Mexico, 1598–1628*, vol. 5 in Coronado Cuarto Centennial Publications, 1540–1940, pt. 1. (Albuquerque: University of New Mexico Press, 1953), pp. 357–59.

4. J. Manuel Espinosa, *First Expedition of Vargas into New Mexico, 1692*, vol. 10 in Coronado Cuarto Centennial Publications, 1540–1940 (Albuquerque: University of New Mexico Press, 1940), pp. 198–201.

5. Ibid., pp. 205–6.

CHAPTER 7

New Mexican *Reducciones*

Ward Alan Minge

A major issue raised by the Zuni land claim case will likely never be resolved because there are millions of acres making up Pueblo aboriginal resources in New Mexico currently owned and used by non-Indians. The issue is returning Pueblo aboriginal lands. The U.S. government conceded and acknowledged existence of widespread aboriginal holdings. The issue is strengthened by such hearings as the Zuni petition because the Indians found it difficult to accept payment in lieu of lost lands. There were many concepts skewed through these transactions and the conditions that led to the transactions. The Pueblo Indians, as past hearings made abundantly clear, still conceive of their prehistoric universe in fundamentally spiritual ways, much differently from the white man's handling of such matters, and insist that their concepts will never change. How were the Pueblos stripped of nearly all their assets, be they religious or temporal? I raised this point during the Zuni testimony, albeit somewhat obliquely, but have come to believe that there are basic considerations of law and human relationships not fully explored by the Pueblos' claim hearings. The instrument allowing this to happen was the Cruzate/league grants to the Pueblos.

For some 150 years after Francisco Vásquez de Coronado, Spain's hegemony grew through a period of geopolitical coaptation, that is, a period during which authorities assessed what they had found and were settling into while contriving to govern and control the native populations. Although politically motivated, the Spaniards accompanying Coronado's expedition reported finding "kingdoms"—the kingdom of Zuni, kingdom of Ascus, and so on—and sixty years later Don Juan de Oñate shrank the kingdoms to "provinces" in his reports. After consulting with Oñate, the king decided in 1602 "that after the Indians of those provinces have rendered obedience to me and have been persuaded by gentle means to pay some tribute, as is set forth in the ordinances for new discoveries and settlements, that is, after the Indians agree to it voluntarily, Don Juan de Oñate may levy the said tribute, provided that it does not exceed ten reals per year for each of those who are to pay it. By this decree, I authorize Don

Juan de Oñate to do this and not to act contrary to this measure in any way, for such is my will."[1] Already the areas occupied by the Pueblos had been reduced in the Spaniards' thinking from kingdoms to provinces, both terms of well-defined characteristics and specific geophysical attributes in the sixteenth and seventeenth centuries. Whether Oñate was successful in collecting the tributes was never all that clear in documents for that period.

The Act of Obedience and Vassalage was obtained by Oñate in the province of Zuni (Aguicobi pueblo) on February 21, 1599, after he had defeated and destroyed Acoma pueblo in January. The army had marched captive Acomas to Santo Domingo pueblo, where Governor Oñate sentenced Acoma males over twenty years of age to lose a foot, and most Acoma men and women he placed in servitude for twenty years, while many children were sent to be reared in Mexican convents. During these proceedings, two Hopis lost a hand each as a warning to that pueblo, and surely these two spread the news of these atrocities. As a result of Oñate's arrival at Zuni, Indian leaders who said they were chiefs of six Zuni pueblos—Aguicobi, Canabi, Coaquina, Holonagu, Mazaqui, and Aquina—assembled for the occasion.

Through an interpreter, Oñate explained the act to the assembled Indians and told them, among other things, that "he had come to their lands to bring them to the knowledge of God and the king our lord, on which depended the salvation of their souls and their living securely and undisturbed in their nations [provinces], maintained in justice and order, secure in their homes, and protected against their enemies, and that he had not come to do them any harm."[2] The chieftains were asked to submit "of their own free will" since they did not owe allegiance to any monarch or ruler. In other words, he preferred not to coerce them by force and wanted them to voluntarily discuss whether they wished to render obedience. After conferring among themselves (the report does not indicate how long), the chieftains agreed to render obedience and vassalage, whereupon Oñate explained further that they should understand that this act meant subjection to the king's authority, commands, and laws and "that if they did not observe them they would be punished as transgressors of the commands of their king and natural master."[3] The chiefs then accepted a series of symbolic rituals indicating to Governor Oñate that they agreed to all, and, doubtless fearful of the consequences if they should refuse, the Zunis became Spanish subjects.[4]

Except for ministrations by the Franciscans resident there, Spanish authorities left Zuni pretty much alone until the Pueblo Revolt of 1680. The Spanish terms for describing the pueblos as kingdoms and provinces disappeared from the formal documents altogether as governors in Santa Fe ruled the small colony through two districts, roughly corresponding to modern-day Rio Arriba and Rio Abajo. As Marc Simmons explains in

Spanish Government in New Mexico, by the eighteenth century the *jurisdic-ciones* had been gradually divided into *alcaldías,* territorial denominations known to Spanish legals and roughly corresponding to counties. The Pueblos' aboriginal dominions vanished as the governors set up rule according to existing laws.

This end was assured by the Cruzate/league grants. In 1684, during the fourth year of the revolt, at a time most of the Spanish settlers lived as refugees in El Paso, a royal decree appointed Don Domingo de Cruzate governor and captain general of New Mexico, giving him instructions for retaking the region, reestablishing towns, and authorizing the governor to issue land grants to the Pueblo Indians. The sanction held profound implications for reduction and containment of the rebellious Indians by opening their lands to returning successful settlers, leaving to recipient Pueblo villages a square league with a village in the center.

All of the preceding has become general information. How the Pueblo grants compare to reductions of Indians commonly established elsewhere in the Spanish colonies, particularly in the Provincias Internas, of which New Mexico was a part, has not, to my knowledge, been treated by historians. On two recent trips to Guadalajara to research the Real Audiencia archives, New Mexico state archivist Richard Salazar joined me in trying to locate files on New Mexico. New Mexico's have yet to be located, but working through hundreds of folios and thousands of original documents dating from the sixteenth century onward revealed clearly to us that practicing *reducciones* existed throughout the Provincias Internas except New Mexico. Spanish authorities sought to reduce the scattered settlements of a tribe by moving the families into one main village, sometimes called a *congregación.* The practice began appearing in the last half of the sixteenth century, and frequently colonies in North and South America gathered natives around military posts, mines, or monasteries for royal and religious supervision. In this manner the Spaniards could more easily conduct social, economic, and religious transactions. The *encomenderos,* owners of *encomiendas,* involving the service of these villages found the institution to their liking as well.

Historians believe the Indian hierarchy was left in control wherever possible but under Spanish supervision. The Real Audiencia records indicated that reductions in the Provincias Internas had a Spanish officer of lesser rank living either in the main pueblo or nearby. Many documents appeared to deal with problems of boundaries and water and were handled by these officers on behalf of the Indians or by the Protector of Indians, an office coming into greater influence in the eighteenth century.[5]

The significance of such settlements to the Spanish colonial government cannot be overstressed. According to one Latin American historian:

The land-holding towns with their collective property, whether of purely Indian origin or whether established after the Conquest, continued to be important. . . . It was part of Spanish colonial policy to form towns in which were gathered and settled the emancipated Indians, Indians under the King's encomienda, others held in encomienda by individuals, and nomadic Indians or those scattered in small hamlets. This movement became particularly marked in New Spain and Peru during the last half of the sixteenth century, and perhaps hundreds of such settlements were made.

The missionary-related reductions were meant for the salvation of souls but also gave the clergy control over the land and the authority to make the Indians work it.

Mechanical trades were taught; weavers, carpenters, masons, and blacksmiths were trained. Each individual had to learn some trade, but "the common trade which all had to know and be expert in was agriculture. So that tilling of the fields had to be common to all." In the "civil congregations" [reductions] the Indian village was under civil authorities (directly under its own *caciques* or *curacas*), rather than the clergy, but the general economic features of the two were similar. They formed the essence of the Spanish system of land-labor control.[6]

The Real Audiencia archives, particularly a segment labeled *Tierras y Aguas*, revealed that reductions were common to the Provincias Internas and had been in place for centuries. The *Recopilación de Leyes de los Reynos de las Indias*, volume 2, book 6, title 3, set forth all the legalities for establishing reductions. Significantly, Ley VIIII (Law 9), though brief, prohibited removing from Indians in reductions any of the lands they had formerly had.

Ley VIIII. Que á los Indios reducidos no se quiten las tierras, que ántes hubieren tenido. (D. Felipe II en Toledo á 19 de Febrero de 1560) Con mas voluntad, y prontitud se reducirán a poblaciones los Indios, si no se les quitan las tierras y grangerías, qui tuvieren en los sitios que dexaren: Mandamos que en esto no se haga novedad, y se les conserven como las hubieren tenido ántes, para que las cultiven, y traten de su aprovechamiento.

Law 9. That Indians in reductions not have lands that they formerly had taken from them. (D. Felipe II in Toledo on 19 February 1560) With utmost goodwill and timeliness, the Indian populations will be reduced, otherwise they will have taken from them the lands and farms that they formerly had in the places they will leave: We order that in this matter there should be no change and they [these lands and holdings] should be maintained for the Indians as they would have been before [the reductions], so that they may work and manage them for their own profit.[7]

The Indians were to cultivate these same lands as always and as required for their well-being. From the numerous cases appearing within the *Tierras y Aguas* papers dealing with land and water cases, the Indians in the Provincias Internas were allowed to keep their aboriginal holdings, which were protected by law and negotiated by local Spanish officials, including the protector.[8] Detailed, hand-drawn, and colored maps often accompanied the petitions, and on them were shown the major features composing the tribe's holdings. We had high hopes of finding something similar for the Pueblos of New Mexico, and we believe such a cache might yet exist. Above all, we came away from each visit certain that reductions were common knowledge to the colonials.

In New Mexico there was nothing to compare with this practice unless authorities accomplished reductions by issuing league grants. Zuni's grants, like so many of the Pueblo grants, ignored the five or more settlements occupied before the Pueblo Revolt, thereby being a strong indication of an attempt by authorities to reduce the Indian settlements to a central one. Subsequent surveys found the league grants to contain a mere 17,000 acres, more or less, thus reducing the aboriginal holdings by millions of acres in addition to contradicting Law 9. It should be concluded that the unique authorization to Governor Cruzate allowed this severe *reducción* of rebellious Pueblo Indians, certainly to achieve containment but also to free millions of acres of rich farming and grazing lands for resettlement by the Spaniards.

For the Zuni people, the full meaning and intentions of their grant surely could not have been understood until recent times. The United States surveyed the league grant in 1880, for an area of 17,581 acres. However, being constrained to use such a small area did not occur until recently as the people continued to use aboriginal lands freely during the colonial period. In actuality, Zuni had lost several million acres, and no grant appeared for the other four or five Zuni villages still occupied in 1680, the year the rebellion started.

Pueblos nearer the Rio Grande, however, felt the impact from the start. Several years after the supposed issuing of the grants in 1689 and the successful Reconquest by 1700, Santa Ana pueblo, for example, began petitioning the governors in Santa Fe for land on which to raise enough crops to feed the people because the league grant contained very little irrigable acreage. In Santa Ana's case, the U.S. survey in 1876 outlined an area of a fraction over 17,360 acres. Though the pueblo's grant lands extended over the lower Jemez River, for most of the year there was not enough water for farming after Jemez and Zia pueblos took what they needed. This hardship for Santa Ana continued until the year 1763, when the pueblo was given permission to purchase over 3,000 acres along the Rio Grande north of the Spanish town of Bernalillo.

In yet another instance, the pueblos of Sandia peoples ranged over the Sandia Mountains to the east, shared a mutual boundary with San Felipe pueblo to the north, hunted and gathered as far as the Ceja and onto the Puerco River to the west, and recognized as one of their boundaries old Highway 66 to the south. Sacred sites as well as hunting and gathering places abounded, and trails connected Sandia to neighboring pueblos, including Puaray in the Manzano Mountains. In fear of the Spaniards, the Sandia Indians relocated temporarily, from 1680 to 1748, with the Hopis in what is now Arizona, returning to receive a second grant from the Spanish governor in Santa Fe in 1748.[9] The nineteenth-century survey for Sandia in 1859 covered 24,187 acres, the grant boundaries stripped the pueblo of nearly all its aboriginal lands, and the U.S. surveyor eliminated the Sandia Mountains from the survey altogether.

A list of similar losses can be registered for each of the nineteen modern pueblos, eliminating those still occupied at the time of the Pueblo Revolt. New Mexico archives possess a multitude of grants to Spanish settlers after 1700 as those lands were legally opened to them, particularly the farming and grazing lands formerly used by the Indians. Except for more remote settlements, the Spanish authorities confined and controlled the rebellious Indians to their league boundaries and through this method practiced a form of reduction prevalent in the colonies, despite the fact that stripping the pueblos of their former lands would have been considered illegal by the Real Audiencia and the higher courts of Spain.

Trying to give some historical perspective to the Cruzate grants raises more questions because there is still so little documentation, despite renewed interests generated by the Pueblo land claims. Why hadn't the Spanish governors practiced reductions in New Mexico as was happening in other parts of the Provincias Internas? Was Governor Cruzate's authority, coming as it did in 1684, meant to be a bellicose response to conditions on this frontier during the Pueblo Revolt? And if so, did the grants themselves exempt officials in Santa Fe from laws governing regular reductions? The grants gave Spain greater power to confine the Pueblos, while placing the Spanish settlers in a much stronger position in the new century. The laws governing reductions did not apply to these outright grants, evidently, even though the Pueblos lost most of their lands. In retrospect the sanction appears to have been a deliberate and shrewd move against the Pueblos while skirting any altruistic intent by the Spanish kings in favor of the Indians and especially their concerns that the Indians be allowed to retain enough of their land and resources to sustain themselves.

NOTES

1. George P. Hammond and Agapito Rey, eds. and trans., *Oñate, Colonizer of New Mexico, 1598–1628*, Coronado Cuarto Centennial Publications, vol. 6, 1540–1940 (Albuquerque: University of New Mexico Press, 1953), pt. 2, p. 971. Cities Royal Cédula, July 4, 1602, from a copy in the Archivo General de Indias, *Indiferente General*, dossier 416; also in Charles Wilson Hackett, ed., *Historical Documents Relating to New Mexico, Nueva Vizcaya, and Approaches Thereto*, 3 vols. (Washington, D.C.: Carnegie Institution, 1923–1937), 1:402–3.

2. Hammond and Agapito, eds. and trans., *Oñate*, vol. 5, pt. 1, 357.

3. George Peter Hammond and Agapito Rey, *Onate Colonizer of New Mexico, 1598–1628*, vol. 5, Coronado Cuarto Centennial Publications, pt. 1, pp. 357–59. Translation is Agapito Rey's and an original copy was found in the Archivo General de Indias, *Patronato*, Legajo 22.

4. There exists a general belief among modern Pueblo peoples that their ancestors understood little of this ritual but obeyed Governor Oñate's requests through fear, which would certainly appear to be the case with the Zunis.

5. Real Audiencia files examined included a special large section relating to this office, and the bureaucratic structure appeared to include a branch dealing solely with *reducciones* administration as well as a section of the Real Audiencia devoted entirely to the protectors.

6. Both quotations are from Bailey W. Diffie, *Latin American Civilization, Colonial Period* (Harrisburg, Pa.: Stackpole Sons, 1947), p. 359.

7. *Recopilación de Leyes de los Reynos de las Indias* (Madrid: Por la Viuda de D. Joaquin Ibarra, Impresora de Dicho Real y Supremo Consejo, 1791; reprinted by Consejo de la Hispanidad, 1943), vol. 2, bk. 5, title 3, law 9, p. 209.

8. No Indian land and water claims have plagued the Mexican government recently.

9. The Sandia officers loaned me a copy of the Sandia Cruzate grant, dated 1689, and a copy is now on file at the New Mexico Records Center and Archives in Santa Fe.

CHAPTER 8

Zuni History During the Early U.S. Period

Myra Ellen Jenkins

Throughout the brief, problem-ridden period of Mexican sovereignty over New Mexico after 1821, Zuni pueblo was virtually ignored by the authorities in Santa Fe, whom the Zunis rarely saw except when campaigns against the Navajos were made in that area. Periodically, the pueblo was shifted from one local political jurisdiction to another, but this made little difference to the Zunis, who were probably unaware of the reassignments. As Ward Alan Minge has pointed out, an alcalde was there in 1837, but apparently only for a short time. No priest administered at Zuni during the period, although Juan Felipe Ortiz, vicar to the bishop of Durango, made one visitation in 1844 and left behind a Mauricio Arce as teacher and justice of the peace, but the latter apparently stayed for only a brief time.

FIRST CONTACT WITH THE UNITED STATES

This situation was soon to change. After Brigadier General Stephen Watts Kearny occupied New Mexico in the name of the United States, the Zunis became increasingly well known to representatives of the new government. Unfortunately, the association all too often resulted in the Zunis giving more than they received.

On August 22, 1846, four days after Kearny had run up the Stars and Stripes over the venerable Palace of the Governors in Santa Fe, he issued a formal proclamation of annexation stating that New Mexico was now a territory of the United States, of which the residents were citizens whose property, civil, and religious rights would be protected so long as they did not resist the new government. He was also instructed to protect the peaceful Pueblo Indians within its boundaries and their property from marauding parties of Utes, Navajos, and other tribes not at peace. Pueblo Indian delegations from the Tewas north of Santa Fe and from the Keres along the Rio Grande had already visited the general to pledge their allegiance and their pleasure at his presence, hoping that it would bring relief from past grievances, especially in the promised military protection against the Navajos. No pueblo had suffered more from Navajo depredation than had Zuni because of its exposed location near the area of Navajo concentrations, especially as these Navajos being pushed south from their San Juan region by the Utes. Although Zuni representatives did not come to Santa Fe to greet Kearny, that pueblo consistently welcomed and supported U.S. military and civil authorities from the first expedition into the pueblo's area during the fall of 1846.

Navajo raids along the Rio Grande caused Kearny to dispatch troops to garrison the village of Cebolleta north of the Laguna pueblo village of Paquate. Shortly thereafter, on September 25, Kearny and the main body of troops departed for the conquest of California. When raiders actually struck one Rio Grande village ahead of his forces, an angry Kearny issued a proclamation to Hispanic residents and Pueblo Indians to form war parties and recover their stock. He also sent word back to Colonel Alexander W. Doniphan, whom he had left in charge of the forces in Santa Fe, to lead an expedition into Navajo country to recover stock and captives and to secure a treaty. On October 6, Colonel Congreve Jackson, commanding at Cebolleta, on orders received from Doniphan, sent out a task force into Navajo territory led by Captain John W. Reid. The diary kept by a young private, Jacob Robinson, the only primary account of this march, contains the expedition's first mention of the Zuni people and gives a description of Zuni lands and Navajo area at the time of occupation, although his directions are difficult to follow. Taking a tortuous route northwest from Cebolleta behind Mount Taylor, the troops crossed the Chuska Mountains and for three days moved through the region of the west side of the range meeting with Navajo groups.

At the first encampment on the way back, a Zuni appeared, sent by tribal officials, to invite the soldiers "to come and see their women and children; he told us that on his side of the mountain they were very honest." Although the exact location of the camp cannot be determined, a careful reading of the entry for the following day indicates that the soldiers were in the area of Red Lake. The Zuni side of the mountain clearly referred to the Chuskas, as the camp was on the west side of the range. The Zuni also had another grievance that he hoped would be redressed: "that three of his children had been taken prisoners by the Mexicans and much stock stolen, but if he could obtain his children he would be satisfied; and that they had never yet made war against the Mexicans, and never should."[1] Leaving Red Lake, the troops rounded the southern end of the Chuskas, which was the only region of their return in which they saw Navajos, and even these were not living there but were on the move. Marching over rough terrain, then along the southern foot of Mount

Taylor, the troops came to the village of Cubero, to which the camp had been moved from Cebolleta.

While they were gone, Captain Monroe M. Parsons had on October 22 been sent in pursuit of raiders who had seized army horses and had followed them to the Chuskas, where the stock was recovered. Destitute of supplies, the detachment turned south and after an exhausting march arrived at Zuni. Private Marcellus Ball Edwards, the chronicler of the first direct contact between representatives of the new government and the actual pueblo of Zuni, had nothing but praise for the warm hospitality and generosity of its people, an experience that would continue to be related by travelers and members of later expeditions:

> As soon as our horses were unsaddled, they took them off to their fodder fields, furnished us with a house, and took us all off to different houses to eat. I went to one house where they set out a soup made of mutton and various kinds of vegetables, and a kind of bread as thin as paper. . . . They have the reputation of being the most hospitable people in the world, which I believe they merit in every respect. We were out of provision and proposed to buy from them, but they said they did not sell their provisions and more particularly to Americans. So they brought in sufficient bread and meal to last our party into camp, which is three days from here. Our saddles, bridles and every equipage whatsoever we had with us was left exposed to them, but in the morning to their great credit, not a single article was gone. Where can such a mass of honest people be found?[2]

Doniphan arrived at Cubero in early November and learned from the wily headman Sandoval that the Navajos would meet with him at Ojo del Oso, a well-known spring on the northern slope of the Zuni Mountains. Major William Gilpin, who had led a scout into Navajo country from the northeast, received word of the proposed meeting at his Canyon de Chelly camp and later commented that he had been the first to arrive at Ojo del Oso "in the territory of the Zunis," which indicated that the important watering place was recognized as within Zuni boundaries, even though the Navajos made extensive use of it. A treaty of five articles was signed on November 22.

Doniphan and the Gilpin task force returned to the Rio Grande by way of Zuni, according to Doniphan's historian, John T. Hughes, for the express purpose of securing peace between the Zunis and Navajos. The exchanges at the pueblo between the two groups were bitter, and though Hughes states that a treaty was signed between them, no copy of such a document has ever come to light. He also noted the generosity of the Zunis in furnishing the party with provisions, especially with fruit, and commented that they were known "for their intelligence and ingenuity in the manufacture of cotton and woolen fabrics."[3] The visitors were also impressed with the extensive cultivation around Zuni and with the large herds of cattle and sheep. Hughes's estimate of a 6,000 population is undoubtedly excessive, but whatever the figure, the ravages of smallpox in the following years decimated the number.

The Ojo del Oso treaty and whatever agreement was made at Zuni had little effect. Periodically, a treaty would be signed in the late fall and peace kept until after the crops were planted in the spring. Another period of raiding would take place in the summer, another military expedition would be sent, and another treaty would be signed. A bungled expedition led by Major W. H. R. Walker to Canyon de Chelly in September 1847 would have ended in complete disaster for the soldiers, who were forced to live on mule, dog, and wild parsley, had not an express arrived from Zuni. Another expedition under Colonel Edward W. B. Newby in the summer of 1848 ended in a second peace treaty with several headmen. No sooner were the troops out of the area than the Navajos met Zuni warriors near Pescado, where a battle royal raged. At the same time, a larger group from the west struck the main village but were driven off by the women and children. Attempting to turn defeat into sympathy, a Navajo delegation came to Santa Fe to complain that the Zunis had broken the treaty. The Zunis knew nothing of any treaty. Newby sent Colonel Henderson P. Boyakin with a force to Zuni. Making no investigation, Boyakin issued an order to Zuni governor Pedro Pino for his people to "cease from mistreating said Navajo Indians who made said treaty."[4] Completely innocent of any such charge, Governor Pino and war chief Antonio Chapeton nevertheless signed articles of convention providing for peace and friendship. Zuni agreed to obey the laws of the United States and was promised protection of its property and religion, a provision that, unhappily, was not to be fully honored in the subsequent years.

THE TREATY OF GUADALUPE HIDALGO

On February 2, 1848, the United States and Mexico signed the Treaty of Guadalupe Hidalgo, which transferred the Southwest to the United States. The next year gold was discovered in California, and the lure of new lands brought emigrants through Zuni on their way westward. Soon Congress was mandating massive exploration expeditions under the Corps of Topographical Engineers to map the region, plan roads and routes for transcontinental railroads, and otherwise develop the land, while the military attempted to hold hostile tribes in check. The saga of this "westward movement" would have recounted far less success had not

Zuni provided guides and supplies for the military, survey, and archaeological expeditions and replenished the stocks of emigrants.

COLONEL JOHN M. WASHINGTON

In late summer of 1849, Military Governor Colonel John M. Washington conducted another expedition and signed another treaty with two Navajo headmen, who could speak only for their bands, at Canyon de Chelly. He was accompanied by newly appointed Indian agent James S. Calhoun, who answered to the commissioner of Indian affairs in Washington. They returned by way of Zuni, where, as Calhoun wrote to his superior, the people extended them every courtesy, offering them "large quantities of fruit and bread."[5] Lieutenant James H. Simpson, who also described the feast supplied by the Zunis and a mock battle exhibition that they put on for the entertainment of the visitors, was particularly impressed by the excellence and diversity of Zuni economy. On one of his trips to copy the inscriptions at El Morro he stated, concerning the Pescado valley, "We have met today, as we did yesterday, a number of Zuni Indians carrying bags of wheat upon horses and burros to their people. These people seem to have discovered the principle of industrial accumulation, and therefore of social progress more than any Indians I have seen."[6]

As a result of experience, Calhoun was convinced that Zuni should have protection against some white travelers as well as against the Navajos. He reported that an emigrant group had commandeered stock and supplies at Zuni before the official party arrived, claiming that such action was legally authorized. Zuni had rescued from them the governor of Laguna, whom the thugs had taken in chains with them after having made similar demands on that pueblo.

No sooner had the troops left than the Navajos stepped up their attacks. On October 15 Governor Pino and other tribal representatives appeared in Santa Fe to ask Calhoun for arms and munitions to protect themselves and for permission to form an alliance of the western pueblos for mutual protection. In spite of his sympathy, Calhoun was legally unable to grant their requests, and Washington refused to do so.

As Indian agent and then as first territorial governor after New Mexico was admitted to the Union in 1850–1851, Calhoun constantly pressured his superiors in Washington to clarify the land right and title of the Pueblo Indians and to stop non-Indian trespass as well as to bring them under the wardship protection of the 1834 Indian Trade and Intercourse Act, even to signing treaties with them that would guarantee their rights. He was also in frequent confrontation with the military commanders of the Ninth Military District, who continued to be in charge of federal troops, over the failure to stop depredation or to give the pueblos the resources to protect themselves. Most of his entreaties fell on deaf ears, except that Indian commissioner Orlando Brown on April 24, 1850, gave consent to negotiate pueblo treaties. An agreement was signed by eight pueblos during the summer that obligated the United States "to adjust and settle in the most practicable manner, the boundaries of each pueblo, which shall never be diminished, but may be enlarged whenever the Government of the United States shall deem it advisable." Article 5 specifically provided that the Pueblos were to be governed by their own laws and customs.

Governor Pino and the Zuni principals again came the long way to Santa Fe and signed on August 7. In return, Pino urged Commander John Munroe to permit Zuni to attack the Navajos who had twice within the past month raided Zuni and to provide his people with arms. Munroe finally did authorize sending sixty muskets and some ammunition but ordered that these be turned over to the military on demand. While he was delaying, a detachment of soldiers accompanied Bishop of Durango Zubiria on his visitation of Zuni in October. The Navajos hit the pueblo as soon as the prelate's party had departed, actually attacking while several dragoons who had turned back to locate a missing soldier were in sight of the village. The arms arrived too late. After the raid the Navajos shifted their activities to the east, having depleted the Zuni harvest.

CAPTAIN LORENZO SITGREAVES

After inauguration as governor on March 3, 1851, Calhoun also held the title of superintendent of Indian affairs with jurisdiction over the Pueblo Indians. In July 1851 Colonel Edwin V. Sumner, the new district commander, was ordered to establish forts; conduct campaigns against the Navajos, Apaches, and Utes; and cooperate with Governor Calhoun. He forthwith led out an expedition against the Navajos. Accompanying him was a party of topographical engineers under the direction of Captain Lorenzo Sitgreaves, whose mission was to map the area from Zuni to California, following the Zuni River to its junction with the Little Colorado, to determine if it was navigable, and thence to the Colorado. In the command were cartographer Lieutenant John G. Parke and draftsman-artist Richard H. Kern, who made many sketches of Zuni life.

As the military moved out to Zuni toward the northwest, Sumner had a vivid experience with one ingenious defensive measure used by the Zunis, the construction of ten-foot-deep pits along the trails into the pueblo, with sharp stakes placed in the bottoms, on which horses would be impaled. Army surgeon Dr. P. G. S. Ten Broeck reported that several of

Sumner's mounts were lost by falling into these traps, and according to Private Josiah Rice, the colonel's own mount was one victim.

Sitgreaves described the extent of agriculture along the Zuni River: "The cornfields of the Zuni Indians extended at intervals for several miles down the stream, their crops and orchards being planted on the edge of the valley, or in the fertile gorges of the mountains."[7] Continuing down the Little Colorado, his party met a party of Coyotero Apaches on their way to trade at Zuni, one of the first mentions of the regular trade carried on between these Apaches from below the Mogollon Rim and the Zunis.

Sumner marched to Canyon de Chelly, but the campaign was a failure, with the Navajos refusing to engage in direct combat and harassing the rear guard and picket lines. The only result was the establishment of Fort Defiance, which depended largely on Zuni for its supply. Its existence brought some measure of protection from raids, especially during the command of Major Henry L. Kendrick.

LIEUTENANT A. W. WHIPPLE

Travelers and expeditions that came in 1853 also had cause to appreciate Zuni good services. Trailblazer Francois X. Aubry, returning from California in September after subsisting for a month on mule and horse flesh, was happy to reach Zuni, "where we met with a hospitable and civilized population from whom we obtained an abundance of good provisions, over which we greatly rejoiced."[8] In October, however, the dreaded white man's scourge of smallpox devastated Zuni. In spite of the plague, the survey party of Lieutenant A. W. Whipple arrived in late November, locating its camps well outside the pueblo. This expedition was a part of the War Department's project to survey the trans-Mississippi to locate the best route for a railroad to the Pacific Coast. Part of the party came by a new route that Kendrick had constructed through Wingate valley. The main body came along the new route called the Camino del Obispo, hastily constructed by Lagunas and Zunis in 1850 for the use of the bishop of Durango, which crossed the lava flow south of the Ojo del Gallo–Zuni Pass route. Passing through the Pescado valley, this group encamped at Black Rock to await the arrival of those who had gone by the northern route. German-born naturalist and expedition draftsman Baldwin Möllhausen in his journal gave excellent descriptions of the Pueblo of Zuni, its people and the extent of its agriculture and industry:

> They breed sheep, keep horses and asses, and practice agriculture on an extensive scale. The harvest was over when our Expedition passed, but in all directions, fields of wheat and maize stubble, as well

as gourds and melons bore testimony to their industry and they raise in their gardens beans, onions, and capsicums; the latter especially, immense quantities of which were hanging to dry in garlands all over the houses. Besides agriculture and cattle breeding, they, or rather their women, are skillful in the art of weaving, and like the Navajos manufacture durable blankets.[9]

Möllhausen was taken on a bear hunt some distance south of Black Rock and described seeing stubble and seasonal farm dwellings in a remote ravine along a dry streambed, an example of Zuni floodwater irrigation practice. Whipple and other members of the expedition also reported signs of widespread herding and seasonal agriculture throughout the region.

Governor Pino paid Whipple a ceremonial visit, and relations were most cordial. Realizing that the country through which he would be traveling to the west was Zuni hunting land, Whipple was anxious to secure Zuni guides. After some consideration of the request by religious leaders, the services of three guides were secured: José Hacha to lead the party to the Little Colorado, José Maria and Juan Septimo to go to the Hopi villages to obtain guides from the Little Colorado. Supplied with several hundred bushels of Zuni corn, the train moved down the Zuni River, then turned west to Jacob's Well, continued on through the Petrified Forest, and crossed the Leroux Wash on December 5, where José Hacha turned back. In the vicinity of present-day Holbrook, the other guides arrived to report that smallpox was so bad at Hopi that no guides were available; then they, too, returned to Zuni.

Navajo relations were quiet in 1854, but early in the year Zuni began to experience another problem in earnest—the problem that had so beset other pueblos since occupation: non-Indian encroachment. Hispanic stockmen in the Rio Grande valley were herding their flocks in the southern Zuni Mountains as far as Inscription Rock and even to the west of the pueblo. They were also penetrating into clearly recognized Navajo country. Major Kendrick, concerned with the resentment of both Indian people, strongly protested to Governor David Meriwether. But Governor Meriwether was no Calhoun, and in his report of the matter to the commissioner, he concurred with Kendrick's concern with respect to the Navajos but totally ignored the protests of the Zunis and disclaimed any ability to act. No action was taken to dislodge the trespassers, although Kendrick himself wrote to the offending ranchers and politely advised them to remove their stock as there would be little chance of reimbursement by the government if their animals were stolen by the Indians.

Meriwether continued to ignore the rights of the Zunis. Authorized by the Indian Office to secure a treaty with the Navajos that would delineate a reservation for them, he signed such a treaty with many headmen, together with Brigadier General John Garland, at Laguna Negra, northwest of Fort Defiance on July 17–18, 1855. The reservation line on the east and south would have run to the Continental Divide and thence to the head of Zuni River and along its north bank. The right to gather salt at Zuni Salt Lake was also reserved to the Navajos. No attention was paid to the treaty's possible effects until a year later when Kendrick visited Zuni and became aware of the threat, especially of Navajo use of the Nutria and Pescado valleys. He fired off another letter to Meriwether on August 22, 1855, pointing out that any question of Zuni title should promptly be settled by Congress. Aware of Meriwether's failure to act against the stockmen, Kendrick sent a copy to Commissioner George Manypenny. Fortunately, Congress did not confirm the treaty.

THE SURVEYOR GENERAL

Although Kendrick did not realize it, Congress had passed legislation two years before creating the Office of the Surveyor General for New Mexico to settle land titles of both Hispanic and Indian pueblos that had originated under Spain and Mexico and hence were protected by the Treaty of Guadalupe Hidalgo. Hispanic title had been by specific grant. Lands that the Pueblo Indians effectively used and occupied, however, had been protected by the extensive Spanish legal codes, and non-Indian grants were not to encroach on them. The pueblos were entitled to a minimum of four square leagues, measured a league in each direction from their mission church, and they were entitled to receive grants if additional lands were needed. The instructions to Surveyor General William Pelham read that he was "to collect data from the records and other authentic sources relative to these pueblos, so that you will enable Congress to understand the matter fully and legislate in such a manner as will do justice to all concerned."[10] But the investigation of pueblo right and title was cursory, based entirely on the false presumption that title was by written grant only. Pueblo agents were sent out to pick up any documents in the possession of the tribal authorities to tell the Indians to bring their records into Santa Fe. In the process several pueblos were found to have virtually identical documents, purportedly issued by Governor Domingo Jironza Pétriz de Cruzate in El Paso during September 1689, where the Spanish authorities were in exile during the Pueblo Revolt. These grants, or re-grants, were stated to have been made of the basis of the testimony of Bartolomé Ojeda, a Zia Indian who had been taken captive, as to the lands that had been conceded to each pueblo before the revolt. Although grants were approved and patented to several pueblos on the basis of these papers, later research proved that they were spurious, and in no case was the principle applied that the pueblos were entitled to the lands that they effectively used and occupied.

Even the perfunctory carrying out of the surveyor general's obligation was not done at Zuni. Agent Abraham G. Myers reported that he could not go to the pueblo without an escort because of the danger, and Meriwether, who told Pelham that he would check with the Zunis and Hopis as to their documents, did nothing. No attempt was made to investigate Zuni's title for some twenty years. In 1875 Zuni representatives brought a document to Santa Fe that they thought protected their lands, but it proved to be another spurious four-square-league Cruzate grant. The failure to determine what had constituted land title and right was especially critical for Zuni since no Spanish grant had ever been made anywhere near its limits, and its right to grazing, farming, hunting, and religious use areas had never been questioned by Spanish and Mexican authorities.

For the most part throughout the early U.S. period, Zuni was on good terms with the Coyotero Apaches, and trading was regularly carried on either at an agreed-on trade site on the Little Colorado or by Coyoteros coming into the pueblo. This relationship was marred in October 1856 when a band of Coyoteros, probably joined by Mogollones, seized a flock of Zuni sheep. The Zunis caught up with the raiders, killing one and recapturing the stock. Because of widespread Apache and Mogollon raiding throughout the western region, Kendrick led a patrol south of the pueblo in mid-November, accompanied by Zuni scouts and Navajo agent Henry L. Dodge, who was captured while away from the camp. A blinding snowstorm made pursuit of the captors impossible. Another band of Coyoteros and Mogollones struck Zuni on December 22, killing nine persons and driving off 1,200 head of stock. Not knowing of the raid, Kendrick dispatched a party in early February 1857 to search for Dodge's body, but no guides or supplies were furnished by Zuni. The annual feast day was at hand, and undoubtedly religious observance was combined with resentment over failure to protect the pueblo from such attacks. By September 1858, however, Coyoteros were again trading in Zuni.

LIEUTENANT EDWARD F. BEALE

Still another expedition came to Zuni in late August 1857, when Lieutenant Edward F. Beale's "Camel Corps Expedition" arrived with the mission of building a wagon route along the thirty-fifth parallel from Fort Defiance to the Colorado River. It would be interesting to know the reactions of the Zunis to the sight of twenty-five camels, which Beale was using as draft animals, lumbering down the Pescado valley. The amount of corn for which he traded was such that it took his entire crew all day and half the night to shell it. At his Jacob's Well camp two days later, in bragging on the efficiency of his camels, Beale said that each carried 750 pounds of corn. It was as well for him that he had arrived then, as the Navajos soon began their raids on Zuni cornfields and then repeated to their agent the tiresome charge that the Zunis were the aggressors when the latter retaliated. Reaching the Colorado River late in the year, Beale went on to California, then retraced his route with a small crew and minus his camels. Back at Zuni in February, he again bought corn and commented that the Navajos had just stolen 150 head of horses.

From 1858 to the mid-1860s when the Navajos were gathered up and sent to Bosque Redondo, the Zunis were in the middle of the campaigns against them, often taking the brunt of the conflict and, ironically, responsible for their own defense in spite of their assistance to the military. Guides and volunteers were willingly supplied to Colonel Dixon S. Miles during the 1858 action and were responsible for saving the army horse herd pastured near Fort Defiance from being driven off and for capturing many horses from the Navajos. The Zunis went home in disgust, however, when they were refused the right to fight under their own leadership and to use their own tactics.

Before the fighting started, a 300-wagon train of emigrants had come through Zuni on its way to California via Beale's road in August. Badly mauled by the Mohave Indians at the crossing of the Colorado River, the survivors turned back, and several straggled into Zuni to secure help for the families that were left stranded in the wagons. A relief force was immediately sent from the pueblo with food, and the starving home seekers were escorted into Zuni, where they were provisioned for their discouraging trip back east.

In December district commander Colonel Benjamin L. E. de Bonneville and Superintendent of Indian Affairs James L. Collins signed another treaty with some headmen providing for a reservation. Although the boundaries of the never-approved Meriwether 1855 agreement were modified, much Zuni land would still have been within its limits since the eastern line began at Pescado Spring and ran in a straight line to Ojo del Oso. Governor Pino was not pleased! Beale again arrived in March 1859 to buy corn for further road construction and improvement and again received both supplies and gracious welcome. In return, Pino attempted to enlist his support for grievances against the authorities by rewarding the alliance and the service of Zuni in making a separate treaty and leaving the pueblo to defend itself. Beale's arrogant answer was, "I told him I thought it served him right for meddling in things which did not concern him, and warned him for the future to avoid 'all entangling alliances.' "[11]

NAVAJO WARS

In the fall of 1860, Fort Fauntleroy, named in honor of the district commander Colonel Thomas Fauntleroy, was established at Ojo del Oso
and another campaign launched. There were no decisive engagements,
but Colonel Edward R. S. Canby's widespread infantry movements
caused the Navajos to disperse, fleeing for refuge into Zuni territory
along and north of the Puerco of the West and into the Zuni Mountains.
This time the Zunis took their own action. Troops were sent from Fort
Fauntleroy in January 1861 to pursue raiders at Agua Azul who had then
fled into a hideout deep in the mountains. The soldiers located the
camp and in it three dead Navajos: The Zunis had found the raiders first.
A preliminary treaty was signed at Fort Fauntleroy on February 18 by
a number of headmen, one article of which stated that an act of hostility against the pueblos would be considered an act of hostility against
the United States, but no attention was paid to the treaty. The continued attacks, coupled with a severe drought in the summer, had been so
severe that the Zunis, who had always provisioned others, were in a state
of near destitution. Noting their constancy, especially during the campaign, Canby appealed to the commander that they at the least be provided with seed corn and wheat, but no action on the request appears to
have been taken.

   Then came the Civil War. Most of the officers resigned their commis-
sions and joined the Confederacy, except for Canby, who became district
commander. Fort Defiance was abandoned in April 1861 and then Fauntleroy (renamed Lyon) in November, leaving the frontier undefended. In
March 1862, however, the Confederates were defeated at Glorieta, and in
September General John H. Carleton with the California column arrived
in Santa Fe and replaced Canby. Establishing Fort Sumner on the Pecos
River in an area known as Bosque Redondo as reservation for the Mescalero Apaches and the Navajos, he launched a systematic campaign of
subjugation. The Mescaleros were rounded up by the following spring,
and the famous Kit Carson was ordered to Navajo country in early summer. Fort Wingate had been constructed near Ojo del Gallo and was
garrisoned with four companies under Lieutenant Colonel J. Francisco
Chaves. Old Fort Defiance was reactivated as Fort Canby. For the next five
months, Carson's swift strike forces kept the Navajos on the move as they
again scattered into outlying Zuni lands and Hopi areas to elude the
troops. This tactic combined with the "scorched earth" policy of crop
destruction and the capture of the Navajos' great Canyon de Chelly fortress in January 1864 virtually ended the campaign, although harried and
hungry bands continued to be rounded up or to surrender for the next two
years, while others remained in hiding.

The Zunis took action of their own and furnished supplies and guides for Carson, who had frequent high praise for their services. Interestingly enough, in the midst of the campaign Bishop John B. Lamy and Father J. M. Coudert, with an escort from Fort Wingate, arrived in Zuni in late September 1863. The prelate witnessed a scalp dance, baptized some 100 children, and performed other pastoral rites before continuing to California.

But the Zunis were a compassionate people, and with the danger of constant attack over in 1864, they took no action against small Navajo bands nearby and even permitted some to come into the pueblo for food. The Coyoteros were also in to trade in spite of the opposition of the military.

The situation changed in 1865, however, and again Zuni sent out war parties against those who had taken refuge inside its boundaries or renewed their raiding. In fact, Barboncito, one of the leading headmen holed up in the Sierra Escudilla, sent word by refugees who were turning themselves in at Wingate that he would surrender but wanted to go directly to Bosque Redondo and not come into the fort for fear of the Zunis.

Bosque Redondo Reservation was no solution. On June 1, 1868, after three days of negotiation and pleas by the headmen that they be allowed to return to a reservation established in their homeland, the Treaty of Bosque Redondo was signed. Peace commissioners General William T. Sherman and Samuel F. Tappan, for the United States, and twenty-nine headmen, with Barboncito as chief spokesman, agreed that the new reservation's south boundary would be an east-west line passing through the Cañon Bonito site of old Fort Defiance. Thus, the area did not conflict with Zuni lands, and the Navajos relinquished their rights to occupy land outside the reservation. Barboncito also promised Sherman that his people would stay together during the long trek back to the fort at Ojo del Oso, now renamed Wingate as the installation of that name at Ojo del Gallo was abandoned. From there they were dispersed within the new reservation, and Fort Defiance was rehabilitated to serve as the agency headquarters.

Some confrontation again occurred between the Zunis and Navajos who left the reservation to renew their raiding habits or who never actually went within its limits. On November 5, 1869, Governor Pedro Pino, accompanied by sixty-five Zunis, was knocking on the door of Superintendent William Clinton in Santa Fe demanding protection again from depredation. In April of the following year, Pino stopped at Ojo del Oso on his return from leading a pursuit of thieves into Navajo country, where he received a written commendation from post commander Captain James R. Brown.

Periodically, other incidents occurred into the 1870s, but by and large the danger from constant attack was over by 1870. Regular trade with the

Coyoteros at the Little Colorado rendezvous and at the pueblo was continuing. Zuni lands were still largely intact. With the rapid expansion of the Southwest following the Civil War and the subjugation of hostile tribes, new threats of encroachment arose for Zuni. Thus far, non-Indians, welcomed and supplied by the Zunis, had moved through their lands. Soon, however, they would enter in large numbers and remain, undeterred and even encouraged by the policies of U.S. authorities.

NOTES

1. Jacob S. Robinson, *A Journal of the Santa Fe Expedition under Colonel Doniphan*, ed. Carl L. Cannon (Princeton: Princeton University Press, 1932), p. 53.

2. Ralph P. Bieber, *Marching with the Army of the West, 1846–1848*, vol. 4 of Southwest Historical Series (Glendale, Calif.: Arthur H. Clark Company, 1936), pp. 204–5.

3. William Elsey Connelly, *Doniphan's Expedition and the Conquest of New Mexico and California* (Topeka, Kans.: Printed by the author, 1907), pp. 311–12.

4. Boyakin Order no. 41, July 1, 1848, Hodge-Cushing Collection, Southwest Museum, Los Angeles.

5. Annie Heloise Abel, *The Official Correspondence of James S. Calhoun* (Washington, Government Printing Office, 1915), p. 30.

6. Ibid., p. 125.

7. Captain Lorenzo Sitgreaves, "Report of an Expedition down the Zuni River," 33rd Congress, 1st sess., Senate Executive Document No. 59, 1854, pp. 5–6.

8. Ralph P. Bieber and Averam B. Bender, eds., *Exploring Southwestern Trails* (Glendale, Calif.: Arthur G. Clark Company, 1938), pp. 372–73.

9. Baldwin Möllhausen, *Diary of a Journey from the Mississippi to the Coasts of the Pacific with a United States Government Expedition*, 2 vols. (London: Longman, Brown, Green, Longmans, & Roberts, 1858), 2:97–98.

10. Senate Executive Document No. 1, 33rd Congress, 2d sess., 1854, p. 93.

11. *Wagon Road—Fort Smith to Colorado River*, 36th Congress, 1st sess., 1860, House Executive Document No. 42, p. 40.

CHAPTER 9

The Zuni Indians Under the Laws of Spain, Mexico, and the United States

S. Lyman Tyler

Although Zuni territory was within the exterior boundaries of what the Spanish rulers considered their domain, and although the United States recognized the forty-second parallel to be the northern boundary of Spanish territory in the west at the time of the Adams-Onis, or Transcontinental, Treaty of 1819–1821, Zuni leaders had actually continued to govern themselves, as provided for under Spanish laws and continued under Mexico, and there had been no permanent occupation of Zuni territory by the Spaniards or Mexicans at the time representatives of the United States arrived in New Mexico during the Mexican War in 1846. There was no sustained effort by European Americans to challenge the property rights of the Zuni Indians until after U.S. institutions replaced Mexican institutions in the area.

On June 3, 1846, the secretary of war issued the following instructions to Colonel Stephen W. Kearny: "Should you conquer and take possession of New Mexico or California, or considerable places in either, you will establish civil governments therein . . . abolishing all arbitrary restrictions that may exist, so far as it may be done with safety. In performing this duty, it would be wise and prudent to continue in their employment all such of the existing officers as are known to be friendly to the United States and who will take the oath of allegiance to them."[1]

When the military forces of the United States occupied New Mexico in 1846, their commanding officer, now General Stephen W. Kearny, instructed Colonel Alexander W. Doniphan, with the assistance of Willard P. Hall, to prepare a code of laws for the governance of the people of New Mexico. This was printed in Spanish and English. The Spanish translation was done by Captain David Waldo. This bilingual document was published in October 1846 as *Laws of the Territory of New Mexico*. We find under "Administration," section 1, "The laws heretofore in force concerning descents, distributions, will and testament, as contained in the treatise on these subjects written by Pedro Murillo De Lorde, shall remain in force so far as they are in conformity with the Constitution of the United States and the State laws in force for the time being."[2] Under "Laws," section 1, we find: "All laws heretofore in force in this territory, which are not repugnant to, or inconsistent with the Constitution of the United States and the laws thereof, or the statute laws in force for the time being, shall be the rule of action and decision in this Territory."[3] Thus, the laws of Mexico, and of Spain as they had come down through the Mexican period, became the laws of the territory of New Mexico (which included Arizona until 1863) until those laws were replaced by the laws enacted by or for New Mexico as a part of the United States.

Under Spain, and continuing under Mexico, recognition was given to the local-level governmental structures of the Indians by the respect shown to the caciques, or Indian leaders.[4] In the established Indian towns, Indian officials chosen at regular elections had the authority to carry on local government. Spaniards, Negroes, mestizos, and other outsiders (with the exception of missionaries) were instructed by law not to live in Indian towns. Traders were not to remain there for more than three days.[5]

From the earliest contacts, the rulers in Spain had tried to control the actions of Spaniards toward the Indians. These two groups were frequently adversaries, and the kings regularly issued decrees to protect the interests of the Indians. Some of the institutions developed under the direction of the king and the Council of the Indies to carry the Spanish system to the Indians were the mission, the presidio, and settlements established by selected Spanish leaders and their followers. The role of the mission, protected by the presidio, is explained by C. H. Haring:

> The mission in Spanish America was not only a religious, proselytizing institution. It was also one of the most conspicuous pioneering devices of the Spanish government, a military and political agency designed to push back and defend the frontiers, pacify the natives, and open the country to European occupation.
>
> The mission therefore was an agent of the State as well as of the Church, a vital part of Spain's pioneering system. And in many cases it was largely supported by the State, receiving an annual stipend of several hundred pesos. The more obvious the political and material ends to be served, the more liberal was the royal subsidy. If necessary, military protection was also supplied, a *presidio* or garrison of half a dozen armed soldiers.[6]

The use of the mission, of the presidio, and of settlements in securing the title to territory in the Americas in order to follow through after discovery and after the papal donation was part of a well-developed plan.

It was necessary to occupy territory in order to maintain title against other European nations. Occupation involved the development of relationships between Spanish subjects and the Indians.

Although the people of Zuni had encountered Spanish representatives in 1539—the black man Esteban and the Indians who accompanied him—the first Spaniards entered their territory under the leadership of Don Francisco Vásquez de Coronado in 1540. The Zunis did not sit passively at Hawikku awaiting the arrival of the Spaniards but had scouting parties out observing their progress. As described by Herbert E. Bolton:

> At Rio Bermejo, four natives of Cibola appeared before Cardenas, making signs of peace, saying through the interpreters that they had been sent to welcome the Spaniards, and that on the morrow all the visitors would be supplied with food—the most joyous news imaginable to the famished soldiers!
>
> Giving two of the emissaries a cross, Cardenas instructed them to return to Cibola and tell their people to remain quietly in their houses, because Coronado was coming in the name of the Emperor to defend and aid them. The two other Cibolans were held as hostages until the general should arrive. . . . It was this episode on the Little Colorado that Casteneda had in mind when he wrote years afterward: "Here it was," at Rio Bermejo, "that they saw the first Indians in that land."[7]

After the encounter at Hawikku, there were years of peace between the people of Zuni and the Spaniards.

By the time the Spaniards carried their discoveries, pacification, and settlement methods northward into what is now the United States, some changes had occurred in the rules governing movements into areas occupied by the more highly organized Indian societies of central Mexico and the Andean area. The contract between Juan de Oñate and the Crown for the settlement and pacification of New Mexico was made under the "Ordinances of His Majesty for the New Discoveries, Conquests and Pacification"[8] compiled by Philip II in July 1573. This compilation specified precise patterns to be followed as new discoveries were made and new territories occupied by the Spaniards:

> No person of any status or condition will undertake new discoveries under his authority either by sea or by land, or will establish new settlement or exploration in those parts already discovered or to be discovered, unless permission and provision from Us or from those empowered by Us shall be issued, under the penalty of losing his life and all of his possessions which will be assigned to our Treasury. We

also order our Viceroys, Audiencias, Governors, and other Royal Officials of the Indies not to issue permission for new discoveries without first consulting Us and having our authorization for doing so; however, we allow them to issue permission to establish the necessary settlements in that part of the land already discovered, provided that they observe the order put forth by the laws of this book in which the form to establish these settlements is specified, and that they send Us a report about the settlement of the population.

Under no circumstances or for any reason whatever there could be will the discoverers, either by land or by sea, get involved in warfare, or conquest, or help any Indians to fight against other groups, or be involved in arguments or fights with the natives or take anything away from them against their will, but they will trade with them and exchange things with them when they wish to do so. . . .

If there are priests and missionaries who wish to pass to the Indies with the purpose of serving Our Lord and who would go to discover new lands to preach the Holy Gospel there, they will be preferred to any other persons to carry out these discoveries; they will be given permission for doing so, giving them and supplying them with the necessary supplies to carry out this holy and good purpose at Our expense.

The discoverers will observe the ordinances of this book, especially those issued in favor of the Indians. . . .

After the Region, Province, Portion or Land has been chosen by experienced discoverers, the places for the establishment of capitals and principal towns will be chosen without causing any harm to the Indians, since these towns will be situated in uninhabited places or in other parts provided with the consent of the Indians.

If the natives want to defend the location against the settlers, they will be given to understand that the settlers wish to live there and not cause them any harm or take their properties away from them. They will let them know they want to be friends with them and teach them how to improve their lives, to learn about God and about His Law, by which they can achieve salvation. The settlers will give them to understand this through the religious, clergymen and persons assigned this duty by the Governor, and through interpreters. They will endeavor by all possible favorable methods to establish the settlement with their good will and consent. If the natives still cannot be persuaded to receive them by said methods, the settlers will make their settlement there without taking anything which belongs to the Indians, and without harming them any more than necessary, in order to establish the settlement and protect the settlers. . . .

After the establishment of peace with them and an alliance with their nations, they will strive to associate closely with them. The preachers, with the greatest possible dignity and with much benevolence, will begin to convince them that they should want to know about those matters related to the Holy Catholic Faith. They will begin to teach them with great prudence and discretion, according to the method of Book One under the Title of the Holy Catholic Faith, making use of the most gentle means available, that their wish for learning will grow. In order to do this, they will not begin by rebuking them for their vices or their pagan gods, or by taking their wives or their idols away from them so that they become offended or turn into enemies of the Christian doctrine. Rather, the natives must first be taught and, after they have been instructed, they will become convinced to abandon those things which are contrary to our Holy Catholic Faith and to the evangelical doctrine of their own free will. . . .

Those Indians who have been brought to Our obedience and apportioned out will be persuaded that in recognition of the Lordship and Universal Jurisdiction that We have over the Indies, they must present us with tributes in moderate amounts of the fruits of the land, in accordance with what has been ordered in the section which deals with this matter. It is Our wish that they be exacted by the Spaniards to whom they have been allotted in order to comply with the duties for which they are obligated, reserving for Us from those tributes of the principal towns and seaports the necessary amounts to pay the salaries of those persons in charge of governing and defending the land and the administration of Our Treasury. If it would be better to grant the natives exemption from paying tribute for some period of time in order to bring peace more easily, this will be agreed to as well as other privileges and exemptions. Whatever shall be promised to them will be observed.[9]

The foregoing ordinances were incorporated into book 4 (on "Discoveries, Pacifications, and Settlements") of the *Recopilación,* and in this form they continued to be part of the basic laws of the Indies during the remainder of the colonial period. The ordinances were referred to frequently after the establishment of the Mexican nation until Spanish laws concerning land, water, and so forth could be replaced by Mexican laws.[10]

Some of the laws of book 4, title 12, on behalf of particular interests of the Indians merit attention. In connection to assigning land to settlers, Law 5 stated, "They shall leave the lands, cultivated properties and pastures of the Indians, for the Indians, in such a way that the Indians may not lack what they need, and that they may have all the relief and repose possible for the support of their homes and families."[11] In regard to Indians' frequent complaints about the livestock of Spaniards getting into Indian fields, Law 12 said, "Because farms of cattle, mares, hogs and other large and small livestock cause great damage to the cornfields of the Indians, and especially when they wander apart and without being watched, We command: that no such farms shall be given in parts or places where damage may result; and as this may not be possible to avoid, such farms shall be far from the Indian towns and their planted fields."[12]

During the eighteenth century, the Pueblo Indians also had numerous sheep, goats, and horses and were in need of grazing as well as agricultural land. With the added mobility brought by the horses, the Pueblos could more freely and frequently make use of resources acquired by hunting and gathering. Oakah L. Jones reports "that the pueblos of Laguna, Acoma, and Zuni (all western pueblos) each possessed more horses than any Spanish settlement, and that Laguna alone had almost as many as all of the Spanish settlements together."[13] His references are to statistics from the mid-eighteenth century.

Under Spanish law, Pueblo lands effectively used by the Indians were supposed to be protected. According to Law 18,

> We order that the sale, benefit and *composición* of lands be managed with such care that more than all the lands that belong to the Indians shall be left to them, to the individuals as well as the communities, and also the waters and irrigations. The lands in which they have created ditches, or any other benefit by which through their personal industry they may have fertilized them, shall be reserved for them above all; and in no case may they be sold or given away.[14]

And Law 19 maintained that the Spaniards who had not possessed lands for ten years were not entitled to *composición*, although they could allege possession. Also, "The Indian communities shall be given preference over other individual persons, and they shall be afforded every convenience."[15] Felix Cohen acknowledges that the Indians were widely oppressed by the Spaniards but suggested that "the oppression was in defiance of, rather than pursuant to, the laws of Spain."[16] Recognition of the unsavory actions of individual Spaniards in the face of protective laws should not startle us, Cohen writes, "once we recognize that although the behavior of our own citizens and officials towards the Indians has frequently been marked by acts of cruelty and treachery, it is by our own courts and laws that these acts of cruelty and treachery have been denounced, the perpetrators of these acts punished, and the victims of these acts, or their descendants, recompensed in the only kind of measure that human compensation for such acts can follow. So it was with Spain."[17]

The kings of Spain used the laws of the Indies to protect individual Indians and Indian communities from the Spaniards, just as laws of the United States have been used to protect the Indians from the Anglos. Local Indian communities continued to be self-governing entities, with their own Indian leaders, under Spain. Royal officers, local administrators, and representatives of the church were to see that the laws on behalf of the Indians were obeyed. If they didn't, the king stated in the laws, it would be on their conscience and not on his. Also, the protectors of the Indians and other legal officers of the Crown, sometimes prodded by Indian leaders, could bring those who took unlawful advantage of the Indians into court, where their rights would be defended.

With allowances for unrest and upheaval both at the center of government in Mexico and in outlying localities, it was the intention of the Mexican government to continue much of the body of laws inherited from Spain, which included a vast accumulation relating to the rights of Indians, until replaced by specific Mexican laws. Ordinances on land and water were thus taken from the laws of the Indies and included in a work by Mariano Galvan Rivera in several editions beginning in 1842. Translations were made from this work by Thomas E. Massey for the guidance of James S. Calhoun in 1852 while he was territorial governor of New Mexico. Thus, the body of laws that pertained to Indians in Spanish America was handed down from the Spanish government to the Mexican government and into the period under the United States, where they would influence decisions concerning the rights of Indians and other inhabitants of Arizona, New Mexico, and other parts of the United States.[18]

It was the policy of both Spain and the United States, which they would uphold in law, if not always in practice, that aboriginal occupancy gave title to the Indians that would be recognized against third parties. However, it took the time that elapsed between the decision in *United States* v. *Anthony Joseph* (1877) and in *United States* v. *Felipe Sandoval* (1913) for the Supreme Court of the United States to discover the similarities among Spanish, Mexican, and U.S. policies as they referred to the Pueblo Indians. The experience of the Pueblo Indian cases in the courts during that thirty-six-year interim period is worthy of a close look.

Although agents had been assigned to the Pueblo Indians since the 1850s, in order to weaken one of the grounds of the *United States* v. *Lucero* decision (1869), an agent for "the Pueblo Agency" was called for in the Appropriation Act of May 29, 1872, to make the relationships with the Pueblos seem more similar to those with other Indians.[19] By such action, U.S. representatives renewed their efforts to protect the Pueblo lands from trespass. The territorial court found the statute inapplicable to the Pueblos. This time, an appeal was taken to the Supreme Court, which in *United States* v. *Anthony Joseph* affirmed the position of the territorial court and set a precedent that would be followed until it was overruled by the *Sandoval* decision in 1913.

Although I agree with the findings of the Court in some particulars, I must disagree with the idea that because the Pueblo Indians have certain qualities, they are therefore not entitled to similar protection under the United States to that which they received under Spain and Mexico. As I review the actions of the territorial legislature of New Mexico and consider the findings of the territorial courts, and even the Supreme Court, as they examined these actions in the light of U.S. laws pertaining to Indians generally, two points demand consideration. First, the legislators, lawyers, and judges were uninformed in some cases and misinformed in others about the nature, lifeways, and law-ways of the Pueblo Indians and of the Indians of the United States in general. Second, what impressed the Anglos involved at the time was the extent to which the Pueblo Indians were *unlike* the Indians of the United States generally and how much they were *like* the ideal Hispanos and Americans—good Catholics, good farmers, good citizens, not troublemakers. There was no discussion of the ideal *Pueblo Indian*.

In a 1940 paper by William A. Brophy, then special attorney for the Pueblo Indians, we find information concerning the period under discussion:

The Mexican policy was misinterpreted by the courts of the United States. Shortly after the acquisition of New Mexico by the United States, litigation was instituted in the New Mexico courts which resulted in the decision that the Declaration of Iguala took away from the Pueblo Indians the protections which the Spanish Government had given them and especially that these Pueblo Indians were not entitled to the benefits of Federal guardianship. The United States courts reasoned that the Plan of Iguala made the Pueblo Indians citizens of Mexico and removed all restrictions upon the alienation of their lands. Since they had been citizens of Mexico, they were citizens of the United States, because under the treaty of Guadalupe Hidalgo Mexicans who remained in the ceded territory for a year without having declared their intention to retain Mexican citizenship became citizens of the United States. It therefore followed, said these courts, that the Pueblo Indians were citizens of the United States and consequently their lands were taxable by the Territory of New Mexico. They could sell their lands without any governmental approval, and the statutes of the United States which prohibited settlement upon Indian lands by non-Indians and forbade the sale of intoxicating liquors to Indians did not apply to the Pueblo Indians, but applied only to the nomadic Indians of the territory. . . .

Ten years of strife and dispute over land ownership and the status of the Pueblo Indian followed the Sandoval decision, in 1913. Congress, through the Senate Committee on Indian Affairs, investigated the matter with the aim of devising some plan which would settle the problem. Numerous plans were suggested, but in 1924 Congress passed the Pueblo Lands Board Act, which permitted settlement of the existing land dispute. Our Commissioner of Indian Affairs, Honorable John Collier, led the forces which defeated discriminatory legislation aimed at settling the problem by giving the land to the non-Indians, in devising a plan for settling this land dispute and in carrying the dispute to a conclusion which was reasonably satisfactory to the Indians. . . .

The Commissioner of Indian Affairs was fully aware of the threats which still existed against Pueblo Indian lands, and the lands of other Indians. He was intimately acquainted with the Pueblo Life and government. He had been companion to many Pueblo men during the long struggle to preserve their lands between 1913 and 1930, and had successfully concluded that dispute. He was familiar with the history of these Pueblos and the protections granted them under Spain. Consequently, it is not surprising to find that upon John Collier's assuming the office of Commissioner of Indian Affairs, he caused to be prepared and introduced into the Congress of the United States the Indian Reorganization Act. The passage of this Act by the Congress and its approval by the President of the United States on June 18, 1934, brought the policy of the United States into accord with the policy of Spain as it existed under Philip IV. No transfer of restricted Indian lands can be made by the Indians or approved by the Government. The general allotment act was repealed, and the policy of giving 80 or 160 acres to individual Indians out of tribal lands no longer is in vogue or possible under existing statutes. The act recognizes the common ownership of Indian reservation lands by tribes as units, and enables tribes to continue to hold their lands, to exist as a people, and to carry on tribal government.[20]

Actually the language in regard to citizenship in the Treaty of Guadalupe Hidalgo (1848), Article 8 was stated in the future tense: "Those who *shall* prefer to remain in the said territories, may either retain the title and rights of Mexican citizens, or *acquire* those of the citizens of the United States." And those who had not so declared their intention "*shall* be considered to have elected to become citizens of the United States."[21] Article 9 explained that Mexicans remaining in the ceded territories *could* become citizens and "*shall* be incorporated into the Union of the United States, and be admitted *at the proper time* (to be judged by the Congress of the United States) to the enjoyment of all the rights of citizens of the United States" and *"in the mean time"* could enjoy their "liberty and property" and be secure "in the free exercise of their religion without restriction."[22] Thus, it seems apparent that it would have taken action by Congress to "at the proper time" confer "all the rights of citizens" on the Pueblo Indians of New Mexico. They had to wait for these rights until they came as a blanket grant to all Indians of the United States who were not yet citizens as a result of the Indian Citizenship Act of 1924.

In regard to the property rights of the Zuni Indians after their territory was included within the exterior boundaries of the United States, we must look to the Indian Trade and Intercourse Act of June 30, 1834,[23] which was the basic law governing relations with Indians at the time U.S. military forces took over the government of New Mexico. This act expressed the power the Constitution had bestowed on Congress to deal with Indian tribes on behalf of the United States. It defined Indian country and prescribed methods of making contacts with Indians. It empowered the commissioner of Indian affairs to appoint traders and to regulate trade goods to be sold to Indians. It provided that interests in Indian lands could be acquired only by treaty or other agreement formalized under the direction of duly constituted authorities of the United States. Penalties were also provided for trespassers on Indian properties.

In the case of *United States, as Guardian of the Hualapai Indians of Arizona* v. *Santa Fe Railroad Co.* (1941), the Supreme Court held, "This Court has continuously recognized that aboriginal possession creates a possessory right legally enforceable against everyone except the United States."[24] As a result of the Treaty of Guadalupe Hidalgo, the aboriginal possessions of the Zuni Indians were brought within the exterior boundaries of the United States. These possessions included the land occupied and used by the Zuni Indians that had come down through the Spanish and Mexican periods undisturbed. These Indians now looked to the United States for protection of their property rights.

An oft-quoted expression of the rights of aboriginal Indian governments is found in the case of *Worcester* v. *Georgia* (1832): "The Indian nations had always been considered as distinct, independent, political communities, . . . and the settled doctrine of the law of nations is, that a weaker power does not surrender its independence—its right to self-government—by associating with a stronger, and taking its protection."[25] Indeed, the Indians did not surrender their property rights. These were taken from the Indians because the new "stronger" power, the United States, which had taken over the territory that included the possessions of the Zuni Indians, failed to fully protect Zuni property rights as guaranteed by the Treaty of Guadalupe Hidalgo and the Indian Trade and Intercourse Act. However, the Indian Claims Commission Act (1946)[26] permitted

Indian tribes to bring claims against the United States for actions on the part of its representatives that resulted in the confiscation of lands, loss of property, and other unfair and dishonorable dealings. Special legislation by Congress permitted Zuni pueblo, a federally recognized Indian community, to seek justice under the laws of the United States for losses suffered during the century following 1846.

NOTES

1. *California and New Mexico*, H. R. Exec. Doc. no. 17, 31st Cong., 1st sess. 238 (1850).
2. *Laws of the Territory of New Mexico* (Santa Fe: October 7, 1846), "Admin.," sec. 1, p. 19.
3. Ibid., "Laws," sec. 1, p. 83.
4. *Recopilación de Leyes de los Reinos de las Indias* (Madrid: 1943), vol. 3, pp. 245–49 ("Concerning the Caciques," bk. 6, title 7). Originally published as nine books in four volumes in Madrid, 1681. Republished almost without change in 1756, 1774, 1791 (3 vols.), and 1841. The books are divided into titles and the titles into laws.
5. Ibid., "Concerning *Reducciones* and Towns of the Indians," pp. 207–25.
6. C. H. Haring, *Spanish Empire in America* (New York: 1947), pp. 202–3; Herbert E. Bolton, "The Mission as a Frontier Institution in the Spanish American Colonies," in *Wider Horizons of American History*, ed. Bolton (Notre Dame, Ind., 1939), pp. 107–48.
7. H. E. Bolton, *Coronado, Knight of Pueblos and Plains* (Albuquerque: University of New Mexico Press, 1949), p. 114.
8. S. Lyman Tyler, ed. and comp., *Spanish Laws Concerning Discoveries, Pacifications, and Settlements Among the Indians*, Occasional Paper no. 17 (Salt Lake City: American West Center, University of Utah, 1980).
9. Ibid., pp. 1–42.
10. Ibid., pp. 61–315.
11. Ibid., p. 158.
12. Ibid., pp. 161–62.
13. Oakah L. Jones, *Pueblo Warriors and Spanish Conquest* (Norman: University of Oklahoma Press, 1966), pp. 123–24.
14. Tyler, *Spanish Laws*, pp. 166–67.
15. Ibid.
16. Felix Cohen, "The Spanish Origin of Indian Rights in the Law of the United States," in Lucy Kramer Cohen, ed., *The Legal Conscience: Selected Papers of Felix S. Cohen* (New Haven, Conn.: Archon Books, 1960), p. 243.
17. Ibid., p. 239.
18. Mariano Galvan Rivera, *Ordenanzas de tierras y aguas o sea formulario geometricojudicial* (Paris, 1868; original ed., Mexico, 1842).
19. 18 Stat. 165 (1872). The *United States* v. *Lucero* ruling was that Pueblo natives were not "Indians."
20. William A. Brophy, "Spanish and Mexican Influences upon Indian Administration in the United States" (Paper prepared for the First Inter-American Conference on American Life, Pátzcuaro, Michoacán, Mexico, 1940), pp. 1–8.

21. Hunter Miller, ed., *Treaties and Other International Acts of the United States of America* (Washington, D.C.: GPO, 1937), vol. 5, pp. 217–18, Article 8; emphasis added.

22. Ibid., Article 9, pp. 219, 241–42; emphasis added.

23. 4 Stat. 729 (1834).

24. 314 U.S. 342 (1941).

25. 6 Peters 515 at pp. 559–60 (1832).

26. 60 Stat. 1049 (1946).

CHAPTER 10

Zuni Relations with the United States and the Zuni Land Claim

E. Richard Hart

The earliest reports of Zuni from the chronicles of Europeans describe a tribe that conducted itself as a sovereign nation in relations with other tribes, treaties, wars, dominion over territory and over the affairs within the territory, both among Zunis and non-Zuni visitors. There are many stories about Indians being awed by the first white men who came into the Indians' territory. That was not the case with the Zunis. The tribe was not awed by superior military technology, and the people were not converted to European materialism (nor have they been today). Information available today suggests that at the time of contact with Europeans the tribe had a type of theocratic government, with a competent and confident political leadership. From the narratives of the Coronado expedition we learn that when Francisco Vásquez de Coronado reached the Zuni villages, the Zunis still had the bones of Esteban and were advising other tribes that the Europeans were mortal and should be killed. Furthermore, said the Zunis, if the other tribes were afraid to do it themselves, the Zunis would do it for them.

The development of an advanced trade network and system of trails or precontact roads and the resulting contact with many different cultures from vastly distant places helped Zuni develop such an effective organization for dealing with foreigners. Trade was a way of life for the tribe for centuries before the arrival of the Europeans. Hawikku had become a center of trade in the Southwest, from which contacts were made with tribes in what is now Mexico, with the Pacific Coast, and with the buffalo plains. To keep trade routes open was a high priority. Zuni war chiefs would act against any party that was restricting or endangering Zuni trails, just as they would respond to encroachments on their territory. The Zunis not only allowed numerous and diverse groups to travel within their territory in order to carry out trading operations, they also encouraged such trade and travel. Many groups traveled the Zuni roads to reach the center of trade at Hawikku and later Halona:wa, and many groups of Zunis and individual Zunis traveled out across those roads in order to trade with other tribes, although prior to 1846 Zuni trading parties were more likely to be communal affairs.

The Zunis' commerce in trade was important to their early relationship with the U.S. government. During the early years of the Mexican period, the Zunis encountered their first visitors from the United States, trappers who came out across the trails to Zuni in order to outfit themselves at the "last outpost of civilization" before going out into what were to them unknown lands. One report even suggests that in 1834 the Zunis allowed a Mexican trader, Pedro Sanchez, to establish a trading post along the southern Zuni trail to the Apaches, perhaps to facilitate the developing trade with American trappers. The Zunis welcomed these American trappers and encouraged their activities.

The promise of improved commerce was one reason the Zunis welcomed the U.S. government into New Mexico. The tribe also looked forward to U.S. rule in the territory because of the promise of self-rule and freedom of religion, which were guaranteed not only by U.S. leaders but also by constitutional law. That law recognized that since "time immemorial," Zuni had had an inherent right to self-government. Zuni exercised that right in terms of both inner, self-government and its relationship to outside entities prior to the time of contact with non-Indians. Prior to the arrival of the Spanish in the Southwest, Zuni had true external and internal sovereignty. Spain and Mexico exercised external sovereignty over the Zunis' aboriginal homeland and in so doing restricted, though not eliminated, their external rights to sovereignty. However, Spain defended Zuni's right to its own territory and made no significant impact on Zuni's relationships with other tribes. At the end of Spanish and Mexican rule in 1846 and at the beginning of U.S. rule, the Zunis had full control over their aboriginal homelands. Their traditional lands remained intact, and their ability to control them had not been affected by the government of either Spain or Mexico (see Figure 10.1).

Zuni looked forward to the relationship with the U.S. government. The people had fought religious oppression under Spain and Mexico, and under Mexico the economy had become very poor. The tribe went out and met the first U.S. officials, expressing their willingness to work for an enduring order in that part of the country. In essence they created an alliance between themselves and the United States. The Zuni political leaders, on behalf of the Zuni religious leaders and in the name of all the Zuni people, signed a series of treaties with the United States and agreed that they would not go to war against the Navajos, Apaches, or anyone else without the express permission of the authorities in Santa Fe. There was never a battle between the tribe and the United States. In return, the Zunis

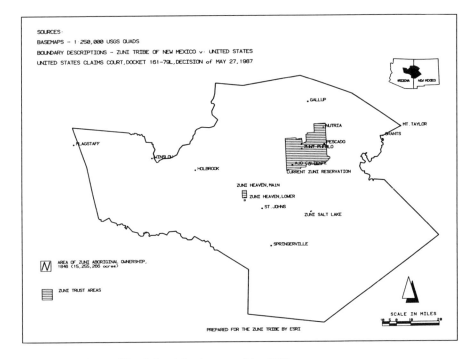

Figure 10.1. Area of Zuni aboriginal ownership, 1846.

were promised—guaranteed—the rights of self-government and freedom of religion. They were assured that they would receive those rights, but those assurances have still not been fulfilled.

The Zunis fed the U.S. troops that came into their territory, first in small groups, and then, when forts were established at Cebolleta and Fort Defiance (which, by the way, was on the boundary between Zuni and Navajo country), the tribe supplied great amounts of corn to the military government. The Zunis' support for those forts made it possible for the United States to maintain a foothold near Navajo territory in the 1850s. The tribe also acted as a military ally of the U.S. government. It sent out hundreds of well-organized men who fought side by side with U.S. troops against the Navajos and Apaches. On occasion the Zunis saved U.S. troops from ambush.

After the final subjugation of the Navajos and Apaches and the Navajos' return from Bosque Redondo in 1868, the United States found it convenient to turn its back on all of the agreements it had made with the Zunis. Bit by bit the U.S. government began to encroach on Zuni territory and to encourage others to do the same. In sometimes direct, sometimes subtle and very powerful ways, the government maneuvered to allow non-

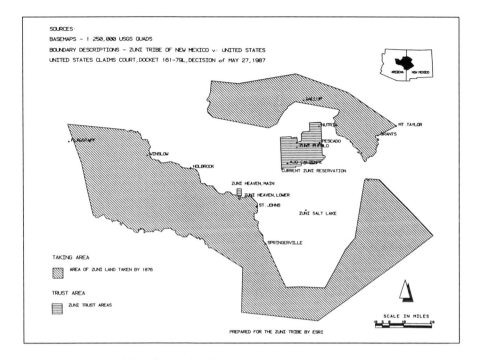

Figure 10.2. Area of Zuni land taken by 1876.

Zunis access and title to what had been Zuni tribal lands. Congress allowed homesteading on Zuni lands. It allowed the railroad to take checkerboard sections along a right-of-way through Zuni territory, which in turn led to eventual settlement. The United States encouraged, in fact forced, other tribes to settle on Zuni land (see Figure 10.2).

In 1877, by a presidential executive order, the Zuni Reservation was established as a part of a major effort to pressure the tribe into a tinier and tinier piece of land. An agent was sent to administer Zuni affairs, and soon troops began to enforce the wishes of the agent, the superintendent of Indian affairs in New Mexico, or the commissioner of Indian affairs in Washington, D.C. The U.S. government made every effort to take away the people's right to self-sufficiency and their land base. Perhaps the most reprehensible attack was the government's attempt to destroy much of the Zunis' culture—to suppress dancing and religious observances, to prevent traditional industries and social events, and to force the people to become like white men and women (see Figures 10.3 and 10.4).

At first the Zunis did not know where the boundaries of their reservation were, nor did the agent or anyone else for that matter. It was many years before an adequate survey was accomplished. But the tribe was

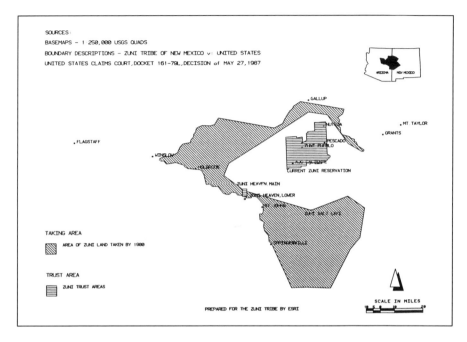

Figure 10.3. Area of Zuni land taken by 1900.

eventually forced back into the reservation. By the late 1930s, the tribe had
lost most of its traditional territory. As the Zuni political leaders became
aware of the actual size of their reservation, they protested to Congress
and to U.S. officials, asking for its enlargement. Within five years from the
time of the establishment of the reserve, they were demanding that the
boundaries at least include Zuni Salt Lake. Thirty-five years later, some
Zunis were saying and believing that Zuni Salt Lake was within their
reservation. Zuni leaders were also protesting the land that had been
taken from them. Between 1877 and 1982, Zuni leaders protested, sought
redress, and attempted to find the justice that had been promised them
under their agreements with the U.S. government.

Even with the establishment of the reservation, the Zunis continued
to use large amounts of land outside it. (And they continue to use lands
outside the reservation today.) They collected minerals and plants. They
hunted and grazed their animals. Grazing is one of the best evidences we
have in the early years of the twentieth century of Zuni land use outside
the reservation. Between 1877 and 1900, as economic forces pressed in on
the Zunis, their herds increased. By the turn of the century, the Zunis had
60,000 head of sheep. And they herded these sheep well outside their

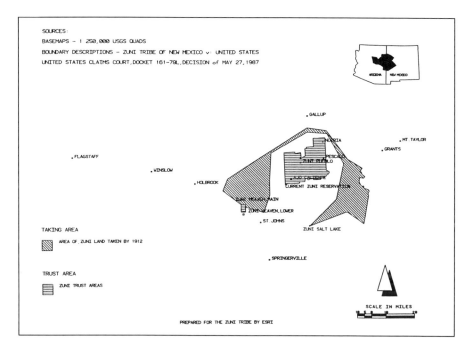

Figure 10.4. Area of Zuni land taken by 1912.

reserve, using in the early twentieth century at least 1.5 million acres outside the reservation (see Figure 10.5).

They continued to hold onto traditional lands outside their reservation for many years. They fought—maybe not always in violent ways because the Zuni people have historically been able to avoid violence—against the encroachment of non-Indians on their land. Pressures by the U.S. government culminated in 1935 when a fence was built around the reservation that prevented herders from going outside (see Figure 10.6).

In 1939 there was one final broken promise—let us hope, anyway, "final"—in regard to tribal lands. Commissioner of Indian Affairs John Collier rescinded an agreement that he had made. He had personally come to the Zunis and negotiated a boundary between them and the Navajos, who were rapidly pressing south, out of their established reservation. But the Zunis lost another series of townships when Collier allowed the Navajos to go beyond the negotiated boundary into a section of land above what is now known as the North Purchase Area (see Figure 10.7).

Throughout the period from 1877 to the present, Zuni leaders used every means at their disposal to prevent the loss of their lands and to call attention to the injustice taking place. Early Zuni leaders, such as Pedro

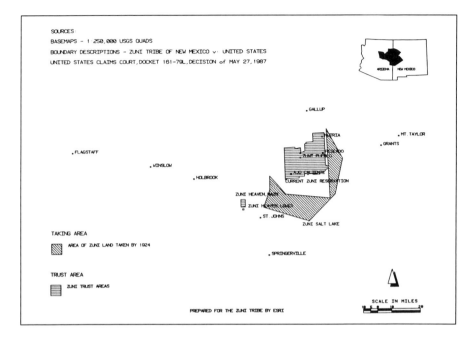

Figure 10.5. Area of Zuni land taken by 1924.

Pino (Lai-iu-ah-tsai-lu) and his son Patricio Pino (Ba:lawahdiwa), battled long and hard in diplomatic ways to achieve justice for the tribe. In the 1880s and 1890s, Zuni leaders protested against encroachment on their traditional hunting, grazing, and agricultural lands. With the Americans came disease, famine, poverty, war, and gangs of desperados, not to mention military and government pressures against the Zunis' traditional religion and culture. By 1906 the tribe had been prohibited from gathering salt at the salt lake, and the population had nose-dived to less than a fifth of what it had once been. In 1909 Zuni governor Quanantonio and his councilmen again petitioned the government to have the reservation expanded to include more of their traditional domain. Three years later William J. Lewis (father of later governor Robert E. Lewis) was made governor of Zuni. He immediately petitioned the commissioner of Indian affairs about the size of the reservation and took his wife, Margaret Lewis (who acted as interpreter), and Lieutenant Governor Dick Tsanaha on a trip to Washington, D.C., to air his and the tribe's grievances.

Zuni political leaders continued to petition Congress in the 1920s, asking for the return of lands that had been taken from the tribe. In the 1930s the Zunis pressed to have lands added to the reservation and to have religious areas protected. Henry Gaspar was one Zuni governor during

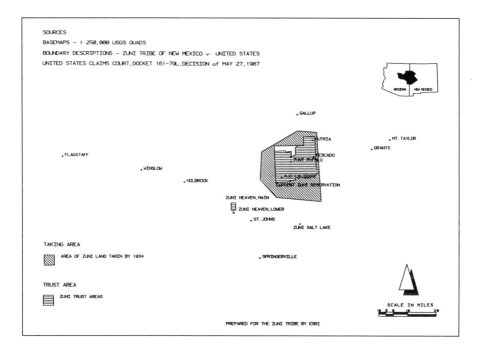

Figure 10.6. Area of Zuni land taken by 1934.

the period to make requests for restitution of Zuni land. He took U.S. officials to visit sacred areas that he testified had been held by the Zunis for centuries. Governor Gaspar's attempts to find justice continued into the 1940s when he not only petitioned for the return of lands but also managed to get dozens of letters from Zuni cattlemen, who testified that they formerly had used much land that now had been taken from them. Governor Gaspar also testified about the tribe's need for additional lands.

Under U.S. laws, a person, or an Indian tribe, cannot sue the government without first receiving permission for the suit from the government itself. It wasn't until 1855 that the United States Court of Claims was established, making some of such suits possible. But in 1864 Indians were exempted from using the Court of Claims, which meant that they could not seek redress in the U.S. judicial system for the many injustices they had suffered. So for many years tribes had no recourse whatsoever in seeking justice for the lands that had been unconscionably and unlawfully taken from them.

In 1928 the Meriam Report was issued, a turning point in Indian affairs. It was one of the steps that eventually led to the passage of the Indian Reorganization Act, which in a way attacked the traditional

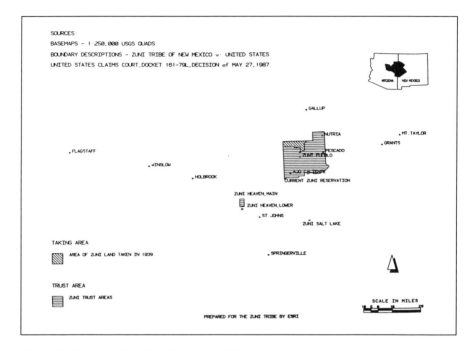

Figure 10.7. Area of Zuni land taken in 1939.

government of the Pueblos but also was meant to clear a way for Pueblo religious freedom. The Meriam Report, in addressing all of the great problems then facing tribes, noted that tribes did not have any way to seek redress for many of the wrongs done to them.

In the ensuing years a strange mixture of those supporting "termination" of tribes and those favoring tribes' justice in the courts led to the passage of an act allowing tribes to sue for damages for lands taken unjustly. In 1946, after the close of World War II and during the administration of Commissioner William Brophy, the Indian Claims Commission Act was passed, giving Indian tribes a specific judicial avenue through which they could sue for damages for lands taken without compensation. The original statute of limitations for filing a claim under the act ran from August 13, 1946, through August 13, 1951.

The Bureau of Indian Affairs (BIA) was asked to go out to Indian tribes and explain their right to sue the government. In 1947 Governor Gaspar was replaced by Leopoldo Eriacho, who continued Gaspar's efforts to enlarge the reservation and to protest the loss of Zuni land. Indeed, by this point, making some kind of a land claim against the U.S. government had become a nonpartisan political effort. By June 1947 the Indian Claims

Commission (ICC), through the BIA, had begun its explanation to tribes of what the Indian Claims Commission Act meant. A letter was forwarded to Governor Eriacho explaining the act, but for some reason the Zuni leaders at that time did not have the implications of the act explained to them. It is clear that Governor Eriacho was working toward filing some kind of claim, however, both from his petition to the commissioner in 1948 and from the papers he filed with the tribes' land claim papers in Santa Fe in 1951. As the statute of limitations came closer, the BIA made an attempt to obtain an official response from the Zuni regarding the ICC, though the Zunis still did not understand what was involved.

On April 11, 1951, in the midst of a Zuni political factional dispute and just before BIA officials believed the statute of limitations on the claims act was about to run out, a letter was obtained from the Zuni Tribal Council declaring that the tribe had no claim against the government. It is now clear that the governor and the council were improperly advised about what they were signing. Those leaders later explained that they had thought the statement had something to do with "allotment," and of course they had not wanted the tribe to allot. They had believed they were fighting to *protect* their own lands.

Zuni leaders continued undaunted against odds that now appeared to be insurmountable to press for a land claim against the government, though they had lost their chance for a hearing under the ICC. Governor Fred Bowannie and Governor Calvin Eustace both worked toward establishing some kind of claim, but in the period from 1953 to 1960 the Eisenhower administration would not even approve a contract so the tribe could hire an attorney. In the early 1960s, however, a contract was finally approved between the tribe and attorney Raymond Simpson, who called and tape-recorded an important meeting of tribal leaders in 1961, under the administration of Governor Bowannie and Lieutenant Governor Eustace. Important information on the Zuni claim was recorded and documented at that meeting.

In 1965 Governor Robert E. Lewis took office at Zuni, nearly a hundred years since the establishment of the Zuni Reservation and fifty-six years since his father, William J. Lewis, had petitioned the government about the Zunis' loss of traditional land. Governor Lewis eventually contracted work through Floyd O'Neil at the American West Center in Salt Lake City to examine possibilities for a land claim suit, work that led to a 1974 report on the matter, which I authored and which was submitted to the tribe, its attorneys, and Congress. Governor Lewis and his council also approved a claims counsel contract with the firm of Boyden, Kennedy and Romney. Contracts such as this required Interior Department approval and were subject to congressionally mandated regulations. For instance, although attorneys normally receive anywhere from 33 percent to 50 percent of any judgment received, the fee agreed upon in this case was 20 percent.

On February 27, 1975, Stephen Boyden's work culminated in an early success when Senators Joseph Montoya (D-N.Mex.), Pete Domenici (R-N.Mex.), and James Abourezk (D-S.Dak.) submitted a bill to the Senate that would confer jurisdiction for a Zuni claim to the United States Court of Claims *and* authorize what amounted to a return of some important religious lands, the lands around Zuni Salt Lake. Most certainly, the tribe's near-century of lobbying had a significant effect on the attorney's success. During the same year, a new Zuni administration was elected, led by Governor Edison Laselute, who continued the work on the Zuni land claim. It was under Governor Laselute's tenure that Public Law 95-280 was passed by the Ninety-fifth Congress and reads as follows:

92 STAT. 244
Public Law 95-280, May 15, 1978
95th Congress

An Act

To direct the Secretary of the Interior to purchase and hold certain lands in trust for the Zuni Indian Tribe of New Mexico, and to confer jurisdiction on the Court of Claims with respect to land claims of such tribe.

Be it enacted by the Senate and House of Representatives of the United States of America in Congress assembled, That (a) the Secretary of the Interior (hereinafter in this Act referred to as the "Secretary") shall acquire, through purchase or exchange, the lands described in subsection (b).

(b) The lands to be acquired under subsection (a) are lands in the State of New Mexico upon which the Zuni Salt Lake is located and which are more particularly described as follows: Lots 3 and 4, east half southwest quarter, west half southeast quarter, section 30, township 3 north, range 18 west, lots 1 and 2, east half northwest quarter, west half northeast quarter, section 31, township 3 north, range 18 west, southeast quarter southeast quarter, section 25, and east half northeast quarter, section 36, township 3 north, range 19 west, all of the New Mexico principal meridian, New Mexico, containing approximately 618.41 acres, more or less.

(c) Title to the lands to be acquired under subsection (a) shall be taken and held in trust in the name of the United States for the benefit of the Zuni Indian Tribe of New Mexico (hereinafter in this Act referred to as the "tribe"), and such lands shall be exempt from State and local taxation.

Sec. 2 (a) Notwithstanding sections 2401 and 2501 of title 28, United States Code, and section 12 of the Act of August 13, 1946 (60 Stat. 1052; 25 U.S.C. 70k), jurisdiction is hereby conferred upon the United States Court of Claims to hear, determine, and render judgment on any claims of the Zuni Indian Tribe of New Mexico against the United States with respect to any lands or interests therein in the State of New Mexico or the State of Arizona held by aboriginal title or otherwise which were acquired from the tribe without payment of adequate compensation by the United States; *Provided*, That jurisdiction is conferred only with respect to claims accruing on or before August 13, 1946, and all such claims must be filed within three years after approval of this Act. Such jurisdiction is conferred notwithstanding any failure of the tribe to exhaust any available administrative remedies.

(b)(1) Any award made to any Indian tribe other than the Zuni Indian Tribe of New Mexico before, on, or after the date of the enactment of this Act, under any judgment of the Indian Claims Commission or any other authority, with respect to any lands that are the subject of a claim submitted by the tribe under subsection (a) shall not be considered as a defense, estoppel, or setoff to such a claim, and shall not otherwise affect the entitlement to, or amount of, any relief with respect to such claim.

(2) Any award made to the tribe pursuant to subsection (a) shall not be considered as a defense, estoppel, or setoff to the claims pending before the Indian Claims Commission on the date of the enactment of this Act in docket 196 (filed August 3, 1951) and docket 229 (filed August 8, 1951), and shall not otherwise affect the entitlement to, or amount of, any relief with respect to such claims.

Approved May 15, 1978

The passage of the act was choreographed by the Boyden firm, with valuable help from Representative Wayne Owens (D-Utah), who, on behalf of the Zunis and the law firm, lobbied for the bill's passage on the floor of Congress.

Public Law 95-280 had two parts to it. The first part provided that the U.S. government, through the Department of the Interior, purchase the land surrounding Zuni Salt Lake and return that area and the lake to its rightful owners, the Zuni Tribe. The second part provided an avenue for the tribe to sue for *compensation* for lands taken without any payment. The Tribal Council under Governor Lewis, who had now been reelected, consulted with religious leaders and former political leaders of the pueblo and weighed the pros and cons of filing such a suit, knowing that it would be highly unlikely that another suit would ever be allowed in the U.S. courts if they did not file under this jurisdictional act. The council was aware that the adjudication of such a suit would finally and permanently quiet title to Zuni aboriginal territory, but it would also provide compensation for the large amount of land taken in past years. The council decided to file the suit but to withdraw certain religious lands from it that the tribe believed should remain in legal title to the tribe. The land around the sacred *Kolhu/wala:wa*, or "Zuni Heaven," was not included in the suit for that reason. The tribe also believed that legal access and easements along religious pilgrimage routes should be provided to the tribe so that its age-old religious practices could continue unimpeded.

Thus, on April 27, 1979, the Zuni Tribe of Indians filed suit against the U.S. government in the U.S. Court of Claims to seek compensation for tribal lands taken without payment between 1846 and 1946 (Docket 161-79L). The tribe hired seven expert witnesses to provide testimony in the ensuing trial: E. Richard Hart, Ward Allen Minge, Myra Ellen Jenkins, Fred Eggan, Triloki N. Pandey, T. J. Ferguson, and S. Lyman Tyler. John O. Baxter was added later. Floyd A. O'Neil and Kathryn MacKay at the American West Center in Salt Lake City coordinated the submission of thousands of exhibits and other materials before the court and also produced, with the help of Catherine J. Patillo, a set of large, impressive maps illustrating Zuni land use.

The trial was held in the Utah Supreme Court chambers in Salt Lake City in March 1982. In addition to the expert witnesses for the plaintiff and Justice Department, a number of Zuni political leaders and religious leaders testified. Tom Awelagte, Oscar Nastacio, and Fred Bowannie provided depositions to the court but were unable to testify in person in the trial. Those who testified included Chester Mahooty, Frank Vacit, Alonzo Hustito, Ralph Quam, Theodore Edaakie, Mecalita Wytsalucy, Sefferino Eriacho, Chester H. Gaspar, Alvin L. Nastacio, and Governor Lewis. Also present at the trial, representing the tribe but not testifying, were Cynthia Kaskalla and Alex Boone.

The precedents set in the Indian Claims Commission and in the other Indian cases throughout the past 100 years create a tight set of definitions within which the court *must* work. In order to prove title to traditional lands, the court uses a definition of "long and continuous, exclusive use"; other complexities are involved as well. In almost all cases such as this one, the court cannot return title to lands to the tribe. It pays compensation for the lands at the value of the lands at the time they were taken. In many cases this has meant that tribes have received eighty, fifty, or even twenty-five cents an acre for lands that today may be worth billions of dollars.

There is obvious inequity in this. But no judgment of dollars can ever repay the Zunis for the loss of much of their ancient, sacred homeland.

Money simply cannot repair the cultural damage or bring back the lost lives or assuage the tribal grief at lost shrines. However, what happens in court does represent the U.S. government's effort to redress the wrongs that Congress has recognized were inflicted on the tribe. Zuni has had a history of dealing honestly, openly, and fairly with the U.S. government, and the tribe entered these legal proceedings in that spirit. Zuni religious leaders spent long hours determining what knowledge could be revealed to the outside world regarding Zuni sacred sites.

Before providing testimony to the court, these leaders made what amounted to an amazing recitation of evidence of land use in the Zuni traditional territory—only an indication of the wealth of knowledge available in the oral tradition but a great gift to the outside world in itself.

The tribe was well aware that the court could take several years to reach a decision in this case and that the outcome was a completely unknown factor, but the initiation of the suit gave an indication of the tenacity and persistence of the Zuni political leaders, who, along with their predecessors, had striven to have their day in court and had learned and used the complex American judicial and political system to seek justice for past inequities. The suit was a triumph in itself for the Zunis' political leadership and the Zunis' ability to live within the strictures of their own religion while successfully dealing with an alien and often hostile U.S. system.

Since the passage of the Indian Reorganization Act in 1934, the Zunis have had a tremendous challenge in building a tribal government that is democratic under the laws of the United States yet embraces the traditions, ethics, and rights of tribal self-government as well. In recent years the Zunis' government has been a leader among tribes in pointing a direction for assuming self-determination and achieving a proper relationship with the BIA.

In this particular day and age, when new and sophisticated pressures are being mounted for termination, perhaps the Zunis have a certain edge over many other Indian tribes. They have not only a reputation, both contemporary and historical, for industry and hospitality but also the experience of nearly four and a half centuries in dealing relatively successfully with Spain, Mexico, and the United States. In relations with the U.S. federal government in the last twenty years, the Zunis have at times displayed national leadership. Today the Zunis must continue to exercise their *sovereignty*, their *rights*, and their *traditions*, for there are still those who would take them away.

CHAPTER 11

The Zuni Land Claim Victory

E. Richard Hart

The preceding chapters briefly summarize the expert testimony submitted to the United States Court of Claims during the trial on Docket 161-79L. This trial was to determine (1) whether the United States had taken lands that had been held exclusively by the Zuni Tribe and (2) if so, when they had been taken. Many complex issues were raised at the trial, and there was much conflicting testimony offered by witnesses for the United States. Zuni waited five years for Judge Judith Ann Yannello to ponder the evidence and reach a decision. Finally, on May 27, 1987, she filed her decisions with the United States Court of Claims. The text of her decisions, which is more than 100 pages long, represented a great victory for Zuni. Judge Yannello accepted the testimony of the Zunis and their experts and rejected the arguments set forth by the United States. She found (1) that the Zunis had held "aboriginal title" to a large portion of what has become the states of Arizona and New Mexico and that as a result of acts or omissions of the United States, Zuni was deprived of 14,835,892 acres; and (2) that these lands were taken by gradual encroachment between 1876 and 1939. The maps that describe the taking of Zuni lands are almost exactly the same as those published in *A Zuni Atlas*, written by T. J. Ferguson and myself, and includes maps drawn from the evidence developed for the case showing the various pieces of land and the dates they were taken from Zuni.

Following the decision by the Court of Claims on the amount of land taken from Zuni and the time of the taking, the case entered into the valuation phase. But before the valuation phase could move forward, Zuni filed a motion relative to recognized title. The court ruled that Zuni had what amounted to recognized title to its aboriginal territory. As a result, Zuni filed a motion asking the court to issue a finding on U.S. recognition of Zuni title. This would have allowed Zuni to receive "just compensation" (values at today's rates) or actual title to lands. When the court ruled that the United States did not recognize Zuni's aboriginal title (on the technicality that Zuni land had never been surveyed), Zuni decided it was left with no recourse but to seek payment for the lands at their value at the time of taking.

Between 1987 and 1990, appraisers for both the Department of Justice and the Zuni Tribe worked to determine the value of the land at the time it was taken. As I indicated in my earlier chapter on the Zuni land claim, many tribes have been forced to settle their claims for amounts that represent very small per acre values. Zuni hired two appraisers, R. Howard Sears and Robert H. Flavel. Zuni also hired other experts to help with the valuation phase work, including me and T. J. Ferguson. As a result of historical testimony, Zuni claimed that it was due a minimum of at least $1.25 an acre for any lands taken. The appraisers for the United States and for the tribe differed dramatically in what they thought the claim was worth.

In late 1990 Stephen Boyden, representing the tribe, entered into negotiations with the Department of Justice in an effort to settle the case at a value the tribe believed was just. He and the tribe hoped to receive the total amount that their appraisers had suggested the claim was worth. The negotiations were difficult, but the Department of Justice dealt fairly with the tribe, and on November 30, 1990, the two parties agreed to a settlement of $25 million, or about $1.69/acre. Boyden and tribal officials were delighted with this settlement because it was the total amount that their appraisers had concluded the claim was worth. Should the case have gone to court, it might have been years before the tribe received its judgment, and the judgment could have been smaller. By settling out of court, the tribe will receive several years' additional interest on the settlement amount.

The settlement was next approved by the attorney general of the United States and the secretary of the Interior. After that, the money was put in a temporary trust under the supervision of the Albuquerque area office of the Bureau of Indian Affairs. The tribe then was asked to agree on a plan for the use of the funds. On May 26, 1992, that plan was presented to the people of Zuni.

After paying attorneys fees and outstanding bills for expert services, the remainder of the judgment fund, approximately $19 million, was placed in the special trust account pending the tribe's decision on a plan for the use of the funds. The Tribal Council submitted a plan, which was subsequently approved by the Department of the Interior and which called for the funds to be invested and managed by the secretary of the Interior. The plan restricted expenditures to authorized purchases for the benefit of the tribe as a whole and forbade the use of any funds for per capita payments. Funds were approved to repay a loan the tribe had previously obtained from the Jicarilla Indian Tribe and from a bank in order to prosecute the claims, and $1.7 million were approved to aid in paying for the construction of a new elementary school at Zuni. Funds for a purchase of land near *Kolhu/wala:wa* were also approved. The council's decisions on the use of these funds for these purposes should have a positive bearing on the future of Zuni children, grandchildren, and children born in the next century.

PART TWO

Damages to Zuni Trust Lands
(Zuni 2 — Dockets 327-81L and 224-84L)

CHAPTER 12

The Zuni Land Conservation Act of 1990

E. Richard Hart

On October 31, 1990, President George Bush signed into law the Zuni Conservation Act of 1990 (Public Law 101-486). The passage of this act represented a negotiated settlement of Zuni tribal claims against the United States for damages to Zuni trust lands for which the United States was responsible. On May 12, 1981, the tribe filed its second claim against the United States under the authority granted by a congressional act of May 15, 1978 (Public Law 95-280). During the 1980s, among Zuni tribal leaders and the experts working for the tribe, this claim came to be known as Zuni 2 and represented Docket 327-81L in the Court of Claims as well as Docket 224-84L, which was filed May 3, 1984, and expanded the period covering the claimed damages to the Zuni Reservation.

In early 1983 Stephen Boyden contracted with me to provide a preliminary report on damages to Zuni trust lands. My report was presented to his firm in March of that year. The report outlined potential types of damages to Zuni trust lands that might have been caused by the United States. It also suggested disciplines that could be used to test the various hypotheses posed by experts to explain causation. After reviewing the report, Boyden immediately began arrangements with the tribe to hire a team of experts to testify.

In 1984, while the experts worked on their written testimony, Boyden conducted depositions with twenty Zunis, who provided information about damages that had occurred in their lifetimes or about which they had learned from their parents and grandparents. Those Zunis who provided depositions were Belle Bowannie, Fred Bowannie, Clarence Calavaza, Sefferino Eriacho, Calvin Eustace, Frank Ghaccu, Mazone Harker, Tom Idiaque, Dempsy Kanteena, Robert E. Lewis, Chester Mahooty, Sidney Neumayah, Lowell Panteah, Pacque Ondulacy, Sol Ondulacy, Ella Pinto, Kathlutah Telsee, Joe Tsabetsaye, Frank Vacit, and Bob Walewa.

In 1985 expert reports were submitted by Jeffrey S. Dean (dendrochronology); T. J. Ferguson (ethnohistory and archaeology); Richard I. Ford (ethnobotany); Alberto Gutierrez and John Appel of Geoscience

Consultants, Ltd. (geomorphology and hydrology); Stephen A. Hall (geo-morphology); E. Richard Hart (history); and Martin Rose (dendroclimatol-ogy). In 1987, nearly two years later, the United States finally responded with rebuttal testimony from seven witnesses. Between 1987 and 1990, the Zuni expert witnesses also submitted rebuttal testimony, and five addi-tional experts filed reports in behalf of Zuni. These new experts were John O. Baxter (history), James I. Ebert (photogrammetry), Patricia Limerick (history), Samuel C. Monson (etymology and lexicography), and Andrew Wiget (folklore and oral history).

THE DAMAGES

The Zuni Tribe and their experts were able to document serious damages that had occurred to the Zuni Reservation as a result of actions or omis-sions of the United States. These damages included the following.

Erosion

In 1846, when the United States first expressed sovereignty over the 15.2-million-acre Zuni aboriginal territory, the Zuni Tribe was the wealth-iest and most secure political force in that region of the Southwest. The core of the tribe's traditional lands was the watershed of the Zuni River, with headwaters in the heavily wooded Zuni Mountains and the mouth emptying into the Little Colorado River in what is now Arizona. U.S. officials quickly noticed the wealth of timber in the Zuni Mountains, the beautiful mountain pastures with three- to four-foot-high grass, and the thousands on thousands of acres of agricultural lands cultivated by the Zuni Indians. During the next thirty-five years, many travelers marveled at the quality of the Zuni landscape—its timber, its water, its grass, and its cultivated lands.

The Zuni Tribe immediately allied with the United States in the mid-nineteenth century. The tribe never fought a single battle against U.S. troops and in fact has fought alongside such troops in the nation's conflicts ever since. Gradually, under U.S. rule, the Zunis' traditional territory was reduced to less than 3 percent of its original size, and the small portion of the territory that remained in trust status became seriously damaged by erosion.

In the mid-nineteenth century, the Zunis were cultivating between 10,000 and 12,000 acres of crops, enough to harvest sufficient corn to help support U.S. military posts in the region, including one, Fort Wingate, that was established just a few miles to the northeast of the Zuni farming village of Nutria. The Zunis' thousands of sheep grazed over grasslands within a 2-million-acre area. Their salt from Zuni Salt Lake had been famous for centuries and provided another important unit of trade.

Between 1846 and 1876, as the United States used every means to encourage non-Indian settlement of the West, the Zunis lost control of some 9 million acres of territory. Fort Wingate officers established ranching operations and a sawmill in the Zuni Mountains. Nevertheless, the Zunis retained most of their grazing land and almost all of their upper watershed. The next fifty years, however, would prove disastrous to the Zuni Tribe, which had long enjoyed its preeminent position in the region.

Having determined that the construction of a southern transcontinental railway would be beneficial to the nation, Congress had made a vast land grant to the Atlantic and Pacific Railroad in order to underwrite the expense of that monumental endeavor. As the railroad approached Zuni territory, many government actions signaled the changes that were coming. A territorial line was surveyed between New Mexico and Arizona, huge contracts for timber were let by the railroad company, and the federal government set aside a small tract of land it said would suffice for the Zuni Reservation. In 1881 the tracks cut a swath through what had been Zuni territory, and lumbermen with contracts for tens of millions of board feet of lumber cut roads into the Zuni watershed.

The railroad not only opened up immense tracts of southwestern lands for non-Indian settlement; it also created enormous opportunities for business ventures and land speculation. With the railroad now available for shipping lumber, the value of the native stand of pine timber in the Zuni Mountains was quickly realized. In 1886 officers at Fort Wingate incorporated and purchased 40,000 acres of the choicest lands of the Zuni Mountains from the railroad. The commander of the fort, who also became the president of the Cibola Land and Cattle Company, arranged a beef contract between his company and the fort and soon had 12,000 cattle ranging on the Zunis' watershed. In 1892 another concern purchased 300,000 acres of timbered lands in the Zuni Mountains, including most of the rest of the Zuni watershed. Giant sawmills began to process millions on millions of board feet of lumber. During the same decade, over 200,000 sheep were herded into the Zuni Mountains. At the same time, the Zunis' own grazing area was being restricted, and their flocks were being pushed back in toward the heart of their territory. As a result of the damage to the upper Zuni watershed caused by the overgrazing of stock and the cutting of timber, in about 1885 streams began to cut channels into the mountain valley floors above the Zuni Reservation.

By the early 1890s Congress had been alerted to the fact that serious damage was taking place on the public lands in the West. In 1891 an act of Congress gave the president authority to set aside national forests. In 1897 a special report to Congress from the National Academy of Sciences described in detail the erosion that was occurring in western forests as a result of overgrazing and improper logging practices. In 1898 Gifford Pinchot became head of the Division of Forestry in the Department of Agriculture. Both the Forestry Division and Division R in the General Land Office carried out investigations in the West to determine which forest lands should be set aside in order to preserve important watersheds and provide a future supply of timber for the nation. A forest reserve was suggested for the Zuni Mountain area, and in 1899 and again in 1900 special agents of Division R visited the Zuni Mountains, examined the watershed and the timber, took affidavits from concerned individuals in the area, and then reported back to the General Land Office. When New Mexico territorial officials learned of the possible move to establish a national forest in the Zuni Mountains, they quickly took advantage of an 1898 act of Congress that gave the territory the right to choose lands in the public domain and selected a vast tract of 153,000 acres, covering much of the best remaining timber lands. The timber on this land would be sold during the next fifteen years to provide income to benefit various territorial interests.

The special agents for the General Land Office reported that as a result of the overgrazing of cattle and then sheep in the Zuni Mountains, deforestation was occurring, the vegetative cover had been removed from much of the mountain range, and incisions in the watershed that had begun in the 1880s now were becoming widespread and severe. The government agent for the Zuni Indians warned the General Land Office that if the mountains were not protected, more serious damage could occur to the Zuni watershed, and the Zunis' thousands of acres of agricultural land would be in jeopardy. Unfortunately, the federal government did not act at this time to preserve the Zuni Mountain timber and watershed.

During the first decade of the twentieth century, logging and overgrazing intensified in the Zuni watershed and, combined with two major dam failures, had catastrophic results. During that decade, the Zunis lost control of another half million acres, much of it constituting their traditional grazing land. As a result, their flocks were pushed back in on an area inadequate to provide sufficient grass. Non-Indian flocks of sheep were already decimating the upper Zuni watershed. At the same time, logging interests built railroads into the Zuni watershed, and intensive commercial logging operations focused on the portion of the Zuni Mountains just above Nutria. By 1911 many millions of board feet of lumber were being cut from tens of thousands of acres within the watershed. Section after section was cut over by loggers whose practices did not include elimination of "slash" and who cut virtually 100 percent of the marketable timber, leaving no chance for reseeding of the forest, let alone reforestation.

During the same period, the two major dam failures compounded the problems and increased the erosion in the Zuni watershed. In 1905, downstream from some of the major timber operations, the Ramah Reservoir failed. Inside of twenty-four hours, 20,000 acre feet of water gushed through the Zuni River channel, overnight cutting an incision ten feet deep in the Zuni riverbed seventeen miles away from the failed dam.

Although the Zunis had long been farmers and had been productively cultivating thousands of acres of land for centuries, the U.S. government believed that the traditional agricultural practices of the Zunis were uncivilized. In addition, prominent U.S. political and military officials wanted to take over Nutria for their own purposes. For these reasons, the United States set out to allot very small parcels (Zuni's superintendent suggested ten acres) of land to adult, male Zunis and then open the remainder of the reservation to non-Indian use under the Dawes Allotment Act. In order to carry this plan out, in 1904 the government began constructing a large dam at a gap in the basalt cliffs along the Zuni River near the tribe's main village. When the dam was finally finished and filled for the first time in 1909, it failed. The "engineers" in charge of the dam had not taken into account a stratum of sand a few feet under the spillway, which allowed water to seep out of the reservoir when it was filled. On September 6, 1909, the spillway and a portion of the dam collapsed. The contents of the reservoir poured out, washing over, under, and through Blackrock Dam. At the height of the calamity, between 7:00 and 11:00 P.M., 72 million cubic feet of water left the reservoir in a rampaging torrent, leaving the dam a shambles and the river channel and surrounding countryside looking like a war zone.

By 1912, when the General Land Office did a survey of much of the Zuni Reservation, incisions in the watershed were widespread, at least twenty or thirty feet deep. By that time, even with the dam rebuilt and perhaps a thousand acres available under the new government ditches, the total of Zuni cultivated lands had declined from 10,000 to 12,000 acres in the nineteenth century to about 8,000 in 1912. By that time about 50 percent of the prime timberland in the Nutria drainage had been cut over.

Between 1912 and 1940, all but 5,000 acres of the remaining merchantable timber in the Zuni Mountains was cut over. Although logging methods improved later in the twentieth century, the Forest Service in 1940 complained that the Zuni Mountain area had been left denuded and cut through with gullies. During the period 1929–1937, seven additional dams were constructed by the government on the Zuni Reservation. Each of them failed at least once. The Zunis also lost another million acres of traditional territory during the same period. The effects of the timber operations, overgrazing, and failed dams on the Zuni watershed included increased erosion through the 1930s, heavy siltation in the government dams, lowered water tables in the alluvial aquifers, destruction of wildlife, and decreased carrying capacity on the grazing lands. In the 1930s and 1940s, the United States Soil Conservation Service, the National Forest Service, and the Bureau of Indian Affairs all acknowledged the damages and the causes of those damages. To Zuni, the most important damage the tribe had suffered was the loss of agricultural land. By 1934 only 5,200 acres were under cultivation; by 1968 the number of acres under cultivation had dropped to 2,185. Today only 1,370 acres are being cultivated. At least 11,000 acres of prime irrigable lands have been lost to Zuni agricultural use as a result of the damaged watershed and other government acts on the Zuni Reservation.

Water

One of the first settlements of non-Indians within the Zuni traditional territory was made in the 1870s by a colony of Mormons who established the farming town of Ramah just to the east of the Zuni farming village of Pescado. In 1898 they began construction on a dam to impound the waters of the Pescado tributary of the Zuni River in what at that time was an immense reservoir. After raising the height of the dam between 1901 and 1903, the reservoir came to have a capacity of 13,500 acre feet. It was not until 1920 that the Mormon cattle company sought a formal water right from the New Mexico State Engineer's office.

Zuni had been using the water in the Pescado drainage for the irrigation of cultivated fields for centuries. The Indian Department was well aware of this fact and protested against the pending application for a water right, noting that the Zunis had a prior right to all of the water in the Zuni River basin drainage. The government irrigation supervisor on the Zuni Reservation notified all parties, including the State Engineer's Office, that the Zuni claimed all of water flowing from the Zuni River and its tributaries, including flood flows, whether inside or outside the reservation boundaries and cited the authority of the United States to back his claim, which had been approved by the commissioner of Indian affairs. However, the government did not follow up this protest, and a water right was issued by the state to the Ramah Irrigation Company in 1923. The water in the Pescado drainage continues to be diverted from Zuni use into the Ramah Reservoir, which impounds it for non-Zuni agricultural use.

Reservation Timber

Between 1910 and 1946, the government operated a sawmill on the Zuni Reservation. Although agency officials failed to keep adequate records, or at times any records at all, it is clear that over the years millions of board feet of lumber were cut from timbered lands on the reservation without payment to the tribe. Most of this timber was cut in the Nutria area, but when that area was damaged by improper logging practices, the agency sawmill was moved first to Pia Mesa and then to a location amid the thick timber in the Miller section of the reservation. Analysis of aerial photography taken in 1935 (at roughly the time the agency sawmill was moved as a result of damage in the watershed) indicates that at least 2,560 acres were cut over in that area alone.

Salt

Since Francisco Vásquez de Coronado visited the Zuni villages in 1540, the white, pure salt of Zuni Salt Lake has had a fabled reputation. Its commercial value was recognized centuries ago, and salt from the lake was an important trade item for the tribe until the early twentieth century, when the government allowed non-Zunis to enter into commercial operations at the lake. In the early 1970s, the tribe used hard-gained tribal funds to lease its own lake and protect it and the salt that annually rises out of the unique saline springs that feed the lake. In 1978 Congress recognized Zuni's aboriginal title to those lands. Recently, a deed was provided to the tribe for the section of land on which the lake is located.

Coal

Between 1908 and 1946, tens of thousands of tons of coal were mined on the Zuni Reservation by the U.S. government, but without payment to the tribe. In 1908 the first mine was authorized, but it was abandoned when veins of coal played out in 1914. A second mine was opened. A third mine also operated for a period of time. The documentary record suggests that during the period from 1907 to 1937 between 50,000 and 70,000 tons of coal were mined on the reservation without any payment to the Zunis. Today the improperly managed coal tailings from these mines continue to damage a portion of the Nutria watershed.

Trespass

From the time of the establishment of the Zuni Reservation in 1877 until 1946, consistent, widespread, and notorious trespass took place on areas of the reservation. At one point the government even allowed non-Zunis to make homesteads on Zuni trust land. Many thousands of acres of Zuni grazing land were either temporarily overgrazed, damaged, or restricted from Zuni use as a result of this trespass. White ranchers not only illegally grazed their stock on the reservation but were also allowed to use the reservation as a drive lane for moving stock, with the full knowledge of government officials. As late as the 1940s, government officials admitted that they had not reported all of the trespass that was going on for fear they would have been criticized for not stopping that trespass.

Damage to Archaeological Sites

Between 1916 and 1946, Bureau of Indian Affairs road-building operations damaged nearly 2,000 archaeological sites on the Zuni Reservation. Graves were unearthed, ancient villages plowed with bulldozers, and the cultural heritage of the Zuni people despoiled by construction practices that were illegal under the laws of the United States.

Appropriation of Zuni Land for Non-Zuni Use

During the past century, the U.S. government has not only allowed but at times has also encouraged the appropriation of Zuni trust land for non-Zuni use. Land has been given to traders, missionaries, churches, and myriad government facilities without payment to the tribe. Land has been appropriated without payment to make roads, reservoirs, and rights-of-way.

THE SETTLEMENT

By the late 1980s, it had become apparent to the tribe that if the court dockets were to continue at their current pace, it might be another ten years or more before the case went to trial and a judgment was rendered. In the meantime, erosion continued and the tribe struggled with an inadequate funding base and high unemployment. The case was extremely complex, and the cost of pursuing it through the courts was mounting. Tribal leaders decided to attempt to settle the case in Congress. To do so, Zuni had to receive a legislated package that satisfied their claims in court. In exchange for this legislation, the Zunis would agree to dismiss their complaint in the court. The tribe was assisted by officials in the Bureau of Indian Affairs at Zuni and the Albuquerque area office, including former superintendent John Gray, Superintendent H. B. Simpson, and area director Sid Mills.

After long and careful deliberation with experts and attorneys, Zuni decided it was willing to settle these two outstanding dockets (Zuni 2) for a total of $20 million. After the deduction of attorneys' fees, the costs of the work of the expert witnesses over the years, and some additional costs associated with obtaining title to all necessary lands at *Kolhu/wala:wa*, the remaining funds would be placed in a permanent trust fund, the interest from which would be used by Zuni to maintain a sustainable development plan for Zuni human, cultural, and natural resources. The decision by Zuni to use these funds for permanent sustainable development purposes has been widely applauded by national and international leaders.

The effort to obtain passage of a Zuni claims settlement act was led by tribal attorney Stephen G. Boyden. Governor Lewis and his entire Tribal Council worked tirelessly between 1988 and 1990 in the effort to lobby Congress for passage of the bill. By 1988 Representative Bill Richardson (D-N.Mex.) had been persuaded that the Zunis' cause was just, and he introduced the Zuni Claims Settlement Act in the House. A hearing was held before the House Interior and Insular Affairs Committee, at which Boyden, Hart, and Lewis testified in person, while all other experts for the tribe submitted written testimony. In addition, two leading figures in the national and international conservation community testified in Zuni's behalf: Peter Jacobs, representing the International Union for the Conservation of Nature (IUCN) and Don Lesh, representing the Global Tomorrow Coalition. Barry Sadler, who worked both with the Institute of the NorthAmerican West and IUCN, also submitted written testimony.

In 1988 Zuni's efforts to get the bill introduced in the Senate were unsuccessful, and Congress failed to take any action. Perhaps this was a good thing because by 1990 the tribe, after reviewing new information from its experts, had decided that it should receive $25 million to settle the case. Boyden, Lewis, and the Tribal Council continued to persist in their efforts to push the bill, and by 1990 they had convinced Senator Pete Domenici (R-N.Mex.) to introduce and back the bill before the powerful Senate Select Committee on Indian Affairs. A hearing was held before that committee on May 7, 1990. Again the Zunis' experts all submitted written testimony. Lewis, Boyden, and Hart testified in person. Also testifying in support of the tribe's bill were two additional experts, Robert W. Delaney and Floyd A. O'Neil, both historians. Both Senator Domenici and Representative Richardson made strong statements before the committee, which was chaired by Senator Daniel Inouye (D-Hawaii). Although the Department of Justice opposed the bill, with the support of Senators Domenici and Inouye the bill quickly passed the Senate.

In the House, the bill was again introduced by Representative Richardson, and a hearing was scheduled before the House Interior and Insular Affairs Committee on July 12, 1990. Again Lewis, Hart, and Boyden testified in support of the bill. This time, however, the Department of Justice showed much stronger opposition to the proposed legislation and promised to try persuading President Bush to veto the bill should it be passed. Zuni did not waiver in the face of this opposition. Richardson determined to have the bill passed on the Suspension Calendar (those bills for which the rules are suspended because they are not controversial). In the following months, there were difficult negotiations between the Department of Justice and Zuni, with the offices of both Domenici and Richardson assisting the tribe. Ferguson and Hart prepared a detailed, issue-by-issue response to the allegations raised by Department of Justice experts. In the meantime, a University of New Mexico geologist led a rather acrimonious attack against the Zunis, their experts, and the legislation. Many independent scholars wrote to defend the Zunis' position. After reviewing all of the evidence, on September 1 the House Interior Committee issued House Report 101-727 in which the majority of the committee strongly supported the bill and rejected the arguments that had been raised by the Department of Justice. As the congressional session came closer and closer to ending, Richardson was finally able to bring the bill to the floor of the House. During the prior week, Boyden and Lewis were engaged in intense negotiations with the Department of Justice. During the weekend before the bill came to the floor, the Department of Justice finally agreed to back the legislation if several changes in the bill's language were made. The United States formally disclaimed any liability for the damages to Zuni lands. But none of the changes affected the content of the bill as it had been originally drafted by the tribe or the total that the tribe was to receive—$25 million. The settlement was satisfactory to Zuni. On October 10, Richardson substituted the new language, and the bill was passed on the Suspension Calendar. On October 15, President Bush signed the Zuni Land Conservation Act of 1990 into law.

The bill called for an appropriation of $25 million and set out the details of the Zunis' goal for a permanent sustainable development plan. After payment of expenses, a total of at least $17 million was placed in a permanent trust fund. At the time of the appropriation, the tribe asked the United States Court of Claims to dismiss Dockets 327-81L and 224-84L. The control of the interest from the trust fund would be subject solely to the authority of the Zuni Tribe through the authority of the duly elected Zuni Tribal Council. The tribe had two years after the appropriation to finalize its sustainable development plan. The annual interest from the fund was then to be used to implement the sustainable development plan.

THE ZUNI SUSTAINABLE DEVELOPMENT PLAN

Zuni traditional religion, philosophy, and actual land use methods all emphasized utilizing only those natural resources that were actually needed. In Zuni society, industriousness, hospitality, and moderation are highly admired values, so it is no surprise that those same terms have been used so frequently by others over the past centuries to describe the

Zuni Tribe. Again and again visitors have described the Zunis as hard-working, religious, and hospitable. My experience with the tribe over a period of some twenty years also leads me to the same characterization of Zuni culture.

About a century and a half ago, when U.S. troops first marched into Zuni territory, they found a prosperous trading and agricultural people who had over 10,000 acres of corn in cultivation and harvested enough crops to supply their new allies in Fort Defiance with all the food necessary for the troops and their horses. The Zunis' success was due not only to their industry, sharp trading, and well-organized political and military capabilities but also to a complex system for dealing with their environment. Potential erosion was controlled with the same techniques by which crops were cultivated. The Zunis' agricultural technology was tested over centuries and, combined with their encyclopedic knowledge of the landscape, enabled them to make the best use of the excellent soil in their valleys. Most of the water that they had available during their relatively short growing season came in the form of floodwater runoff.

Where there were permanent supplies of water, the Zunis had farming villages with systems of small diversion dams and reservoirs and canals to feed the crops. Specialty crops, like coriander, beans, onions, and cotton, were cared for meticulously in waffle gardens along the Zuni River, where the alluvial aquifer provided wellwater a few feet from the surface of the ground, even in dry years. After the Spanish arrived in the sixteenth century, the Zunis also cultivated peach orchards on benches along the edges of their mesas. But these farms and gardens were not sufficient to provide for all the Zunis' needs. In addition, the Zunis cultivated vast tracts of land along the streambeds (or arroyos) that drained the Zuni Mountains and the mesas and plateaus surrounding their villages.

Check dams constructed in the arroyos not only served to spread water out into fields to irrigate corn but also provided nutrients to the crops in the form of the silt found in solution in the floodwater. The check dams also protected the arroyos from erosion. Silt backed up behind the thousands of dams throughout the tributary system prevented incision in the streambed or filled incipient erosion with silt. Zuni farmers also guarded against wind erosion by planting rows of perennial species where they could serve as windbreaks. Many thousands of acres of land were cultivated using this floodwater technology. Historical records indicate that the Zunis maintained a two-year supply of corn in case of drought and that they usually harvested enough corn to trade an ample supply to their neighbors. But during the period from 1885 to 1935, overgrazing, timber operations, and the improper building and maintenance of dams caused enormous damage to the Zuni watershed. Virtually all of the arroyos in the Zuni watershed were cut by deep channels. Thousands of acres of prime agricultural land were lost to Zuni use as a result of this episode of erosion.

Following a number of years of discussions with the Zuni Tribe, on May 10, 1988, by a Zuni tribal resolution the Institute of the NorthAmerican West was asked to provide technical assistance in helping the Zuni Tribe establish a sustainable development plan for its renewable natural resources. By the time the Zuni Conservation Act was passed in 1990, it was clear that internally Zuni had all the resources necessary to draft and complete the sustainable development plan. Tribal member James Enote was chosen to lead the new Zuni Conservation Program, with a professional staff of Zunis and non-Zunis under him.

With an eroded agricultural base, diminished herds of sheep, and drastically reduced overall land base, all occurring at the same time as a rapidly increasing population, the tribe knew that planning for the future was crucial. The tribe desired to establish a permanent fund, the interest from which would be used to rehabilitate the eroded Zuni landscape and work to sustain Zuni cultural, human, and natural resources. Both traditional Zuni technology and contemporary state-of-the-art scientific methodology were drawn on in creating the model for Zuni sustainable development over a two-year period as described in Public Law 101-486. Under this plan a number of positions were established for Zuni professionals, who will direct and administer activities on the reservation and throughout the watershed. A seasonal Zuni labor force will work each season building check dams, planting in eroded areas, and providing information from monitoring stations. Proper management of archaeological resources will be integrated into the plan and tribal code. A digitized geographic information system will provide instant monitoring data on stream flow, sediment yield, and arroyo incision depth throughout the watershed. Under the Zuni resource development plan, the tribe will establish sustainable yields for timber and cropland within its watershed. Water will be developed from runoff channels as well as from the Zunis' aquifers in order to bring agriculture back to the reservation. Land acquisition may also be possible with some of the funds. The tribe desires a labor-intensive program, one that will not only result in the long-term rehabilitation of the landscape but also provide educational and employment opportunities for many Zuni people.

Interest in the development of this plan has been widespread. Passage of the Zuni Conservation Act allowed Zuni to begin rehabilitating the landscape, creating a tribal sustainable development plan, and providing a model that demonstrates the value of erosion control and the principles of sustainable development in an arid landscape.

Check dam used to control erosion on the Zuni Reservation in the 1960s. (Bureau of Indian Affairs, Forestry Department, Zuni Tribal Archives)

Zunis offering prayers at the Grand Canyon during fieldwork to verify the location of Zuni land-use sites during the Zuni 1 research. *Left to right,* Jack Peynetsa, Ben Kallestewa, Allen Kallestewa, Victor Niihi, Chester Mahooty, and Edmund J. Ladd. (Photograph by T. J. Ferguson)

Head Priest Mecalita Wytsalucy at a Docket 161-79L pretrial meeting in Salt Lake City, March 27, 1982. (Photograph by E. Richard Hart)

Interpreter Edmund J. Ladd and Stephen G. Boyden at a Docket 161-79L pretrial meeting in Salt Lake City, March 27, 1982. (Photograph by E. Richard Hart)

Governor Robert E. Lewis at a Docket 161-79L pretrial meeting in Salt Lake City, March 27, 1982. (Photograph by E. Richard Hart)

Witnesses for the Zuni Tribe at the March 1982 trial on Docket 161-79L, Salt Lake City. *Front row, left to right,* Lieutenant Governor Theodore Edaakie, Frank Vacit, Chester Mahooty, Alonzo Hustito, Alvin Nastacio, Edmund J. Ladd (interpreter). *Second row, left to right,* Triloki Nath Pandey, Alex Boone, Cynthia Kaskalla, Ralph Quam, S. Lyman Tyler, Ward Alan Minge. *Third row, left to right,* Chester Gaspar, Mecalita Wytsalucy, Sefferino Eriacho, Myra Ellen Jenkins, John Baxter. *Fourth row, left to right,* Floyd A. O'Neil, Governor Robert E. Lewis, and T. J. Ferguson. (Photograph by E. Richard Hart)

Senator Barry Goldwater with Councilwoman Rita Enote Lorenzo at the 1984 Zuni celebration honoring Senator Goldwater for his role in securing title to *Kolhu/wala:wa* for the Zuni Tribe. (Photograph by E. Richard Hart)

Governor of Zuni Chauncey Simplicio honors Senator Barry Goldwater for his assistance in gaining title to *Kolhu/wala:wa*, at a tribal celebration, October 17, 1984. (Photograph by E. Richard Hart)

Governor Robert E. Lewis and Councilman Barton Martza examine erosion in Bosson Wash on the Zuni Reservation, February 1990. (Photograph by E. Richard Hart)

Hank Meshorer addresses the tribal celebration of the court's decision in the Zuni Tribe's favor in *United States* v. *Platt*, September 5, 1990. (Photograph by T. J. Ferguson)

Left to right, Curtis Lanyate, Philip Vicente, John Niiha, Hank Meshorer, Floyd A. O'Neil, Solen Lalio, Mecalita Wytsalucy, and Miss Zuni at the tribal celebration of the court's decision in *United States* v. *Platt*, September 5, 1990. (Photograph courtesy of E. Richard Hart)

Left to right, E. Richard Hart, Stephen G. Boyden, and Governor Robert E. Lewis, in Washington, D.C., October 2, 1990, for a hearing on the proposed Zuni Land Conservation Act. (Photograph by E. Richard Hart)

T. J. Ferguson and Sefferino Eriacho at the tribal celebration of the passage of the Zuni Land Conservation Act and the settlement of Docket 161-79L, December 4, 1990. (Photograph by E. Richard Hart)

Chester Mahooty and Stephen G. Boyden at the tribal celebration of the passage of the Zuni Land Conservation Act and the settlement of Docket 161-79L, December 4, 1990. (Photograph by T. J. Ferguson)

Councilman William Tsikewa, Lieutenant Governor Pesancio Lasalute, Senator Pete Domenici, Governor Robert E. Lewis, Councilman Virgil Wyaco, and Councilman Barton Martza at the tribal celebration of the passage of the Zuni Land Conservation Act and the settlement of Docket 161-79L, December 4, 1990. (Photograph by E. Richard Hart)

CHAPTER 13

An Anthropological Perspective on Zuni Land Use

T. J. Ferguson

Anthropological evidence has been used to investigate two fundamental issues raised in the Zuni land claims litigation: (1) the extent and organization of Zuni land use and (2) the relationship between human land use and environmental degradation. The anthropological perspective developed in this chapter is based on archaeological and ethnohistorical data.[1] Other valuable anthropological perspectives on Zuni land use were developed by scholars using ethnological, ethnobotanical, and dendrochronological data, and their research complements the conclusions summarized in this chapter.[2]

THE EXTENT AND ORGANIZATION OF ZUNI LAND USE

The extent of Zuni land use in 1846 was a fundamental issue in the Zuni 1 litigation for lands taken without payment. Two types of anthropological evidence were helpful in determining the extent and organization of nineteenth-century land use: archaeological data and ethnohistorical information derived from Zuni oral history.

Archaeological Data

The area claimed by the Zunis as their sovereign territory in 1846, and confirmed as such by the United States Claims Court,[3] is depicted in Figure 13.1. The prehistoric archaeology of this area was reviewed in detail in my testimony "Zuni Settlement and Land Use: An Archaeological Perspective." Archaeological evidence does not support a conclusion that all people who lived in this area in prehistoric times were members of the Zuni Tribe, and the Zuni Tribe did not make such a claim. However, based on similarities between the archaeology of the Zuni Indian Reservation and the styles of prehistoric pottery,[4] the settlement patterns, and the

103

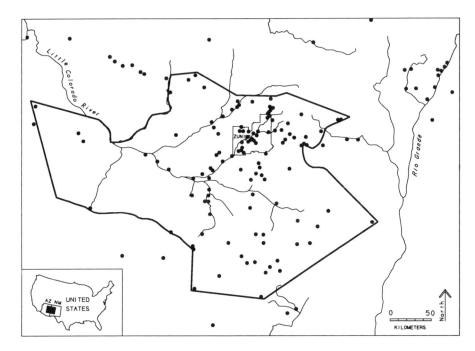

Figure 13.1. The boundary of Zuni lands taken without payment superimposed on the distribution of Zuni land-use sites documented in depositions of Zuni elders. The boundaries of the Zuni Indian Reservation are shown in the northeastern quadrant of the claim area.

architectural forms found throughout the claim area, a conclusion was made that the Zunis have a cultural affinity to the prehistoric people who lived in the Zuni claim area. The prehistoric occupants of the Zuni claim area were culturally ancestral to the modern Zuni people.

During the course of prehistory in the Zuni claim area, there was a trend toward the occupation of a fewer number of larger sites through time. This trend culminated in the founding and occupation of the set of six or seven large villages encountered by Esteban and Francisco Vásquez de Coronado in the first Spanish *entrada* of 1539–1540.[5] These villages were all founded circa 1350–1400 and were thus already ancient settlements at the beginning of the historic era. The use of the outlying parts of the Zuni claim area for habitation sites was gradually relinquished in favor of consolidation of settlement in the Zuni River valley. As this process occurred, some people emigrated to the Zuni villages and were incorporated into the Zuni Tribe; other people emigrated elsewhere. The Zuni immigrants must have brought with them a detailed knowledge of the resources of the areas they had formerly inhabited, and in my opinion they also brought with them the proprietary rights to use those resources.

The archaeological concept of "abandonment" is negatively correlated with the use of an area for habitation sites—that is, when an area is no longer used for habitation sites, many archaeologists call it "abandoned." In a legal sense, however, the term *abandonment* means the "complete and final giving up of property or rights with no intention of reclaiming them and to no particular person."[6] Since there is some archaeological evidence that the Zunis continued to use the claim area after habitation sites in the area were relinquished, I concluded that the Zuni claim area was never abandoned, even though there was a major reorganization of the way in which land was used. Occupation of habitation sites was consolidated in a small area containing the best agricultural lands and water resources in the claim area. The surrounding land was not abandoned but used as a sustaining area for the hunting and gathering of the wild resources that were essential for survival during the occasional droughts in the Southwest that resulted in agricultural failure. The presence of late prehistoric and early historic Zuni ceramics at mountaintop shrines in the claim area is archaeological evidence of the continuing use of the claim area.[7]

A backup subsistence strategy, as was provided by the use of the Zuni claim area, is essential for a self-sustaining economy in the arid Southwest. A similar sequence of settlement patterns and land use as occurred in the Zuni area is evident in the neighboring Hopi and Acoma areas. These Pueblo tribes share an affinity with Zuni to some portions of Zuni claim area in relation to its prehistoric occupation. By the beginning of the historic era, however, all three tribes were occupying small core areas with habitation sites, surrounded by very large resource areas that I think were intentionally kept free of habitation in order to conserve and manage the natural resources they contained. It is my opinion that the earlier prehistoric pattern of many small settlements scattered widely over the landscape became untenable as the population of the region gradually increased. With that increase, new settlements were founded in the hunting and gathering areas of existing communities, and this degraded the natural resources essential for survival. The late prehistoric shift to relatively small core areas of settlement surrounded by large sustaining areas was an adaptive shift in land use that enabled the long-term occupation of the large permanent settlements occupied at the beginning of the historic era.

The Zunis' use of the claim area following the consolidation of settlement in the Zuni River valley produced an archaeological record that, with a few exceptions, has been largely ignored by archaeologists. The exceptions are the studies that document late prehistoric and early historic Zuni ceramics on mountaintop shrines. The hunting, gathering, and religious use of the claim area produced small campsites and undiagnostic artifact scatters that are ubiquitous but not well studied. These sites are not very "glamorous" in comparison to the substantial pueblos with large assemblages of painted pottery that have been the focus of most archaeological research in the region. As a result of the Zuni land claim, the archaeological investigation and dating of small campsites and artifact scatters have emerged as a high-priority research activity that needs to be addressed in order to fully document the late prehistoric and early historic use of the region.

Ethnohistorical Information

Valuable new ethnohistorical information on the extent and organization of Zuni land use was produced during the Zuni 1 litigation in the form of twelve depositions of Zuni civil and religious leaders.[8] A deposition is testimony under oath in the form of written statement by a witness for use in court. The twelve depositions were taken during February 1980 at Zuni pueblo. Attorneys for both the pueblo and the Department of Justice questioned the deponents about Zuni land use in direct and cross-examinations, with the testimony documented by a court reporter. Edmund J. Ladd served as an interpreter, compiling a list of 194 place-names mentioned in the depositions. Triloki Nath Pandey and I were also present during the depositions, contributing questions asked through the Zunis' attorney and observing the proceedings. The depositions, totaling 571 pages of testimony, were submitted as court exhibits in the evidentiary trial held in March 1982 in Salt Lake City.

The twelve Zuni deponents ranged in age from thirty-seven to ninety-three, with an average age of seventy. The Zuni religious organizations represented by the deponents included all six of the kivas, six out of fifteen clans, five out of twelve medicine societies, and several priesthoods, including the *Kyaklo*, the *Koyemshi* (Mudheads), and the *A:shiwani* (Rain Priests). In addition, five past or current tribal councilmen were among the deponents, as were a former governor and the current lieutenant governor.

Supplementary fieldwork was conducted to verify the locations of a sample of land use sites documented in the depositions. Between February and June 1980, I accompanied ten Zuni men on four field trips covering approximately 2,700 miles. Thirty-five of the 194 sites referenced in the depositions were located and photographed (often from a distance to respect the sacred nature of shrines). Twenty additional land use sites were recorded during this fieldwork, and another 18 sites were documented in interviews with Zuni stockmen, bringing the total number of documented Zuni land use sites to 232. The distribution of Zuni land use sites is depicted in Figure 13.1.[9]

There are several limitations to the data collected in the Zuni 1 depositions. First, the information represents the knowledge of only a relatively few men in a population of about 9,000 people. Not all of the Zuni clans, medicine societies, and priesthoods were represented by the deponents and other consultants, and additional sites would undoubtedly have been elicited if members of other religious organizations had testified. Second, no depositions were taken from women, and those aspects of Zuni land use and resource procurement most closely associated with women are therefore underrepresented. Third, knowledge about many land use sites associated with hunting and gathering was lost as the subsistence economy of the Zuni became integrated with the American market system in the twentieth century. Information about land use sites associated with subsistence activities is therefore underrepresented.

The sites of Zuni land use documented during Zuni 1 research are depicted in Figure 13.1, with the exception of religious sites on the Zuni Indian Reservation, which are too numerous to plot at the scale of the map. Although these sites do not represent a total inventory of Zuni land use, they do provide extremely valuable information about the overall patterns of Zuni land use. Most of the sites illustrated in Figure 13.1 were areas where several types of land use occurred. A particular site, for instance, may have been used for hunting, plant collection, and religious activities. Religion pervades the Zuni culture, and most traditional subsistence activities had religious elements to them. There are a few shrines and sacred areas, however, whose only use was religious.

The information derived from the depositions of Zuni elders is depicted in Figure 13.2 as a general model showing the extent and organization of Zuni use in the mid-nineteenth century. This model illustrates a system with concentric zones of different types of land use radiating out from a core area of settlement. The configuration of these zones is determined by topography and the general course of streams and rivers. All of the activities in the outer zones were also practiced in the zones contained within their exterior boundaries, meaning that hunting also took place in the grazing area, grazing also took place in the farming area, and so forth. The lines demarcating the zones of land use in Figure 13.2 were drawn by analyzing the sites identified in the depositions by different types of land use and encircling the sites with a similar use. These boundaries are conservative estimates of the extent of Zuni land use. Using documentary data, E. Richard Hart has drawn boundaries of land use with slightly different configurations, but the overall pattern is very similar.[10]

The core area of settlement is located along the upper Zuni River and its tributary drainages, the Rios Pescado and Nutria. It is within this area, roughly corresponding to the present Zuni Indian Reservation, that the Zunis have established their major settlements since the prehistoric era.

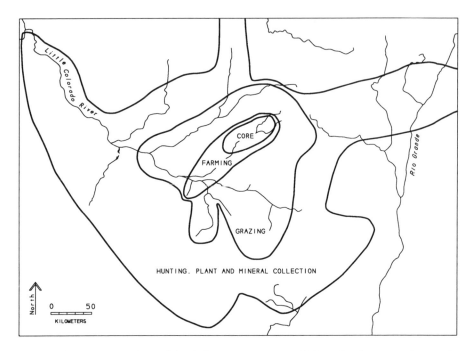

Figure 13.2. A general model of the organization of Zuni land use in the mid-nineteenth century.

Throughout the historic period, the settlement patterns in the core have entailed occupation of multiple villages situated in the prime areas of agricultural land and water resources. There has been a shift, however, from the occupation of multiple permanent pueblos to the occupation of a single permanent pueblo used in conjunction with the seasonal occupation of multiple farming villages.

When the Europeans arrived at Zuni in 1539 and 1540, the Zuni Indians occupied six or seven villages along a twenty-mile stretch of the upper drainage of the Zuni River and its tributaries. After the Pueblo Revolt of 1680, the Zunis coalesced into a single permanently occupied village at Zuni pueblo, which was one of the villages occupied during the first Spanish *entrada*. Accompanying this consolidation into a single pueblo was the establishment of a number of seasonally occupied farming and ranching settlements scattered throughout the core area of settlement.

In the eighteenth century, there were five major seasonal settlements as well as more numerous and smaller sites associated with the Zuni livestock industry.[11] The major villages were located on the hilltops or the sandy benches of mesas, and several of them were associated with large peach orchards. In the nineteenth century, occupation of the first set of seasonally occupied farming villages was relinquished in favor of the development of a second set of farming villages located in areas where ditch-irrigated agriculture was possible. This settlement shift accompanied an intensification of Zuni agriculture in response to a new market for agricultural products created by the entry of the U.S. Army into the Southwest in 1846.[12]

The agriculture conducted at the settlements in the core area supported the sedentary lifestyle of the Zunis and enabled them to reside in a large community where a rich cultural life could be maintained. As discussed, however, in the arid Southwest agriculture is a precarious occupation, and the vicissitudes of precipitation require that a population has an alternative subsistence strategy to rely on during times of crop failure caused by drought. The large sustaining area surrounding the core area of settlement provided the Zunis with essential resources to use when needed as well a supply of various necessities and luxuries during better times.

Surrounding the core area of settlement and extending to the southwest was a larger area used for the Zunis' extensive agriculture. Seven specific farming sites and three general agricultural areas were referenced in the depositions, constituting 3 percent of the total number of land use sites. Ditch-irrigated agriculture was practiced at Ojo Caliente, Nutria, and Pescado, but runoff-irrigated farming using sheetwash, and the overflow from stream channels was conducted over a more extensive area. The most distant farming site documented in the depositions is *Shoto:k'a:wan'ahonn'a*, or "Red Shell Stream," located sixty miles from Zuni pueblo along Concho Creek in Arizona. Some farming was conducted as a secondary economic activity in conjunction with other land use activities. Stockmen herding sheep on distant ranges in the summer, for instance, would plant gardens in areas with sufficient soil and moisture along the banks of the Zuni River and adjacent drainages in the Little Colorado River. These gardens would provide melons and other produce that could be consumed at the end of the growing season before livestock was driven back to the core area for the winter.

The Zunis' grazing area formed a large zone encompassing the Puerco River to the north of Zuni, the upper Little Colorado River to the west of Zuni, and the Carrizo Creek to the south of Zuni as well as the drainage of the Zuni River. The twelve Zuni deponents and six stockmen interviewed identified twenty-five grazing areas, representing 11 percent of the total number of land use sites.

The Zunis developed a livestock industry in the seventeenth and eighteenth centuries following the introduction of sheep, goats, cattle, and horses by the Spaniards. Grazing livestock provided a means for the Zunis to harvest the grass on pastures far from the core area of settlement, converting the vegetal biomass into animal products (protein, hides, and wool), which could then be transported on the hoof back to Zuni pueblo for use and consumption.

Before the Zuni Reservation was fenced in 1934, the Zunis had a flexible grazing pattern over a widespread land base. A number of families often herded livestock together, mostly sheep and goats, sometimes using as many as ten herders. The choice grazing areas near Zuni pueblo were reserved for lambing season in the spring, when there was the greatest need to protect the herds and have access to a large labor pool at Zuni pueblo. Following lambing, herders would take their livestock onto the grasslands surrounding the core area of settlement, as far as fifty to seventy miles from Zuni pueblo. While on the range, herders supported themselves with simple, easily movable camps of canvas tents and occasionally with camp structures similar to forked-stick hogans made from juniper wood.

After harvest in October, the herds were brought into the core area to graze in and near the farming areas. Crops were occasionally grown in fields for that purpose. After the crops were harvested, the numerous corrals at the seasonal farming villages were used to pen livestock, and the farming villages became the winter outposts of the livestock industry. The Zunis coordinated and scheduled their agricultural and livestock activities to maximize use of the core area of settlement and to facilitate the use of the surrounding sustaining area.

Surrounding the grazing area was a very large zone used for hunting and for collection of plants and minerals. This zone extended to the Grand Canyon on the west and to the Rio Grande and beyond to the east. A hunting corridor to the north extended to Abajo Mountains in southern Utah. Prime hunting areas included all of the forested mountains surrounding Zuni as well as the grasslands along the Little Colorado River and in the plains of San Agustin. Forty-seven hunting sites were documented, constituting 21 percent of the Zuni land use sites.

Hunting was an activity the Zunis practiced both individually and collectively, depending on the type of game animal being sought. Zuni hunting parties often stayed in hunting areas for a month or more, sundrying meat into jerky to preserve and transport it. Rabbit drives conducted in the Zuni River valley were one form of Zuni communal hunt. Another form was the impoundment of deer and antelope in game drives to the west and south of Zuni. Many of the Zuni deponents stressed that hunting was also a ritual activity, with religious responsibilities, songs, prayers, and places of offering that had to be attended to as part of ensuring a good hunt.

Twenty-nine sites used for the collection of minerals were documented in the depositions, constituting 13 percent of the total number of land use sites. Minerals collected at these sites included azurite, malachite, hematite, jet, obsidian, salt, galena, serpentine, petrified wood, clay, mud, silt, sand, and turquoise. The area in which minerals were collected extended from the Grand Canyon in the west to the Jemez and Sandia Mountains in the east. Fifty-eight percent of the sites of mineral collection were also religious sites, and many of the minerals collected by the Zunis were used in religious ceremonies and rituals. One of the most important mineral resources in the Zuni sustaining area was Zuni Salt Lake, located in a volcanic cone forty miles to the south of Zuni pueblo. The salt produced at this lake provided an important economic and nutritional resource, and the lake itself had great religious significance to the Zuni Indians.

Forty-two plant collection sites were referred to in the depositions, representing 19 percent of the total number of sites. Plant collection generally occurred in the same area as mineral collection, but at a greater number of sites. Like mineral collection, plant collection was closely associated with religious activity, and 64 percent of the plant collection sites were also religious sites.

The testimony in the depositions about plant collection was largely focused on the plant collecting still conducted for religious and medicinal purposes. Although virtually all Zunis still collect piñon nuts when they are in season, plant collection is not a major subsistence activity at the present time. Only the older deponents discussed the subsistence collection of plants such as piñon nuts, oak seeds, juniper seeds, wide-leaf yucca fruits, and cactus fruits. These were considered starvation foods to be relied on when crops failed. The use of plant collection areas, in conjunction with hunting and grazing, provided critical backup subsistence systems to support the Zuni population during times of agricultural failure.

Most of the sites outside of the Zuni claim area illustrated in Figure 13.1 were primarily used for religious purposes, with secondary uses for collection of resources used ceremonially. The religious use of the landscape constituted one of the most important components of the Zuni land use system. A total of 139 religious sites were documented in the depositions, representing 71 percent of the land use sites. Sixty-two of the religious sites were located outside of the Zuni Indian Reservation. These religious sites included shrines, offering areas, sacred springs, mountain peaks, ancestral sites mentioned by name in the Zuni origin and migration narrative, and other place-names referenced in prayers, songs, and religious history.

The Zunis used these religious sites as spiritual resources in religious activities conducted to promote fertility, productivity, and well-being in their land. In the context of the land use system, the use of religious sites also functioned to create opportunities for the Zunis to monitor the environment, keeping them informed about the economic resources available in the sustaining area. Formal religious pilgrimages to *Kolhu/wala:wa* (near the confluence of the Zuni and Little Colorado Rivers) and Zuni Salt Lake and periodic visitation of many other shrine areas took the Zunis into all parts of their sustaining area on a regular basis.

Most of the religious sites are still used by the Zunis to collect resources for religious use and to leave prayers and offerings. The use of religious sites is currently the most prevalent land use activity conducted off of the Zuni Indian Reservation. The Zuni Tribal Council withdrew the lands around *Kolhu/wala:wa* from their claim for lands taken without payment since they considered that the Zuni Tribe's continuing use of this important area meant it had not been taken from them. The Zuni Tribe successfully lobbied the U.S. Congress for legislation, passed in 1984, authorizing the addition of this area to the Zuni Indian Reservation.[13] Other types of land use in the Zuni sustaining area were marked by sites that included trail markers, campsites, battle sites, boundary markers, and place-names. Thirty-seven sites falling into this category were recorded, representing 17 percent of the total sites.

The ethnohistorical data about Zuni land use documented in the twelve depositions have utility for the Zuni Tribe beyond their use in the Zuni 1 land claims. With the passage of the Native American Graves Protection and Repatriation Act in 1990, and with the inclusion of traditional cultural properties as a type of historic site managed through the National Historic Preservation Act, the Zuni Tribe is routinely asked to identity the area within which it has a claim of cultural affinity. The area and sites depicted in Figure 13.1 provide an initial source of the information needed for consultation with federal and state agencies in this regard. Of course, given that these sites do not constitute a complete inventory, additional research is often needed to fully document concerns about specific locations. When specific locations used by religious groups not represented by the Zuni 1 deponents are threatened, the Zuni Tribe must consult with religious leaders from these groups to identify their concerns in management of the sites.

HUMAN LAND USE AND ENVIRONMENTAL DEGRADATION

The Zuni 2 litigation involved claims of damages to the Zuni Indian Reservation caused by the acts and omissions of the United States in its role of trustee. One of the major issues in this litigation concerned the relationship between human land use and environmental degradation.

Erosion was one of the principle damages claimed by the Zuni Tribe, and the experts for the Department of Justice asserted that erosion was a natural, cyclical process not related to human land use. This assertion therefore had to be examined using data from all of the research disciplines applied by Zuni experts, including anthropology. In addition to contributing information pertinent to this issue, anthropological data were useful in documenting damage to archaeological sites caused by road construction on the Zuni Indian Reservation.

The Relationship of Human Land Use and Erosion

The timing and causation of erosion are complex issues whose explication requires the analysis and theoretical synthesis of data from a number of disciplines, including hydrogeology, geomorphology, dendroclimatology, dendrochronology, and environmental history.[14] Such a synthesis is beyond the scope of this chapter, which concentrates only on the conclusions reached using anthropological data. Actual presentation of all of the anthropological data is too voluminous for a brief chapter, and readers interested in these data are referred to the written testimony submitted to the United States Claims Court and other publications based on these data.[15] In this chapter several conclusions contrasting traditional Zuni land use and the land use practices sponsored by U.S. government agencies are briefly discussed to identify the role human land use plays in environmental conservation and degradation.

Fifty-two Zuni tribal members and two non-Zuni residents of Zuni pueblo were interviewed during anthropological research for the Zuni 2 litigation.[16] Richard I. Ford; his assistant, Dana Lepofsky; and I worked as a team conducting and transcribing interviews during the summer of 1984. All of our information was pooled and shared for use in our individually prepared testimony. The information contributed by Zuni tribal members was extremely valuable and formed the basis for many of the conclusions reached by expert witnesses. Without the active participation of Zuni tribal members in the research, much less information about Zuni land use would have been documented by the anthropologists.

Traditional Zuni land use entailed a socioeconomic system in which the means of subsistence production were available to all tribal members. Although access to the relatively scarce ditch-irrigated farmland was not evenly distributed among tribal members, the usufruct rights to any land not already in production could be claimed by any tribal member through the act of developing the land for agriculture using techniques of floodwater irrigation. In addition, the livestock industry was based on an open range with no individual ownership rights to particular areas. This meant that any Zuni could participate in the livestock industry.

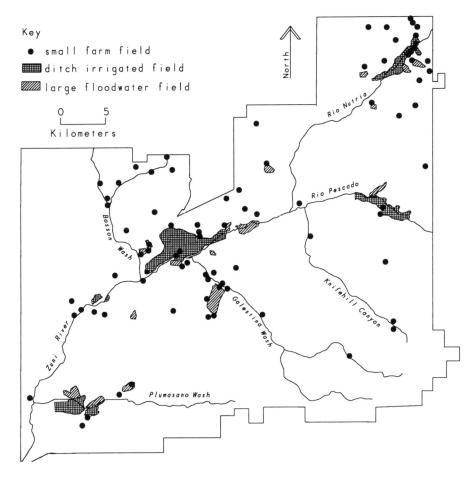

Figure 13.3. Distribution of Zuni agricultural sites documented during Zuni 2 research.

The agricultural system was based on small zones of ditch-irrigated farming near Zuni pueblo and the farming villages, each surrounded by a much more extensive area in which floodwater farming was practiced. Figure 13.3 illustrates the distribution of agricultural areas on the Zuni Indian Reservation as documented in Zuni 2 interviews with tribal members. The major areas of traditional ditch-irrigated agriculture were located along the Rio Nutria, the Rio Pescado, and the Plumasano Wash. The large area of ditch-irrigated land in the center of the reservation was the Zuni Irrigation Unit developed by the Bureau of Indian Affairs (BIA).

The fields mapped in Figure 13.3 are not an inventory of all farmland on the Zuni Indian Reservation, and the figure serves only to depict the extensive area managed by traditional Zuni agricultural techniques. These techniques entailed the construction of many small check dams and other rock structures designed to control surface runoff by slowing water down and spreading it out using a low-cost, labor-intensive technology. Earthen enclosures of various sizes were used to conserve available water. These techniques were appropriate for the semiarid environment of the Zuni Indian Reservation and were instrumental in controlling the surface flow of water across the reservation to retard soil erosion. Similar types of water control features as used in agriculture were constructed by Zuni sheep-herders to repair incipient soil erosion on the open range.

The United States implemented a new system of land use on the Zuni Indian Reservation that restricted access to land for farming and grazing, forced some farmers to stop cultivating floodwater-irrigated fields, and in general reduced the total acreage maintained by traditional Zuni water control techniques. The BIA constructed Blackrock Dam and Zuni Irriga-tion Unit in the first decade of the twentieth century as part of an effort to allot Zuni lands to individual Zuni farmers. About half of the Zuni farmers were induced to give up their farmland in the outlying farming districts and concentrate their agricultural activities in the newly constructed irri-gation unit fed by the Blackrock Dam. This devastated the labor pools at the farming villages and forced the remaining farmers to adopt mecha-nized agricultural techniques since the communal work parties that tradi-tional agriculture was based on were no longer viable. The Blackrock Reservoir rapidly lost most of its capacity because of siltation, and there was never enough irrigation water to farm all the land the United States developed at Zuni pueblo. Because of the exigencies of the Zuni land tenure system and policy decisions by the BIA, the farmers who had given up their farmland in the outlying districts could not return there. The development of Blackrock Dam thus played a major role in the decline in Zuni agriculture in the twentieth century. There was a drastic reduction in the number of acres farmed on the Zuni Indian Reservation.

In the 1930s, as agriculture became increasingly less viable economi-cally, the BIA implemented policies that favored development of the live-stock industry over farming. As the Zunis' access to grazing land off the reservation was reduced by the lands taken by the United States without payment, there was increased pressure on the grazing lands on the reser-vation. Although the Zunis voluntarily reduced the number of their live-stock as these lands were taken, the problem of soil erosion related to overgrazing finally became so acute that the BIA implemented further stock reduction in conjunction with regulation of grazing land. The Zuni Reservation was divided into assigned grazing units, and the number of stock an individual could own was determined by a permit system. A limitation in the number of available permits resulted in many Zunis being unable to participate in the livestock industry. As with farming, many Zunis were excluded from access to the means of subsistence production.

The policies implemented by the BIA also favored stockmen over farmers in terms of the regulation land use. Under the traditional Zuni land use system, for instance, stockmen were responsible for any damage livestock caused to crops growing in unfenced floodwater fields. Under the BIA policies implemented in the 1930s, farmers were required to fence their fields in order to have a claim. The cost of fencing was prohibitive to many farmers, who gave up farming of floodwater fields as a result. In addition, the BIA policies precluded the development of new floodwater fields in areas assigned for grazing. These policies had the cumulative effect of reducing the amount of acreage farmed and the amount of surface runoff controlled by traditional water management techniques. In conjunction with other changes in land use occurring at the same time (e.g., logging in the Zuni Mountains), the decrease in the area managed by traditional water control contributed to erosion on the reservation.

The water control system implemented by the United States entailed capital-intensive, large-scale water impoundments requiring a technology funded and administered by the BIA. The reservoirs built by the United States were all damaged by siltation, decreasing their capacity for flood control and irrigation. Many of the dams also suffered structural failure resulting in the incision of stream channels, the covering of farmland with silt, and other damage to reservation land. The mechanized agriculture based on impounded water promoted by the BIA required large flat fields, which reduced water conservation in ditch-irrigated fields and necessitated expensive equipment and fossil fuels that Zuni farmers could not afford without a subsidy from wage labor. Such farming also reduced the soil moisture on sandy soils used for floodwater farming.

The United States physically altered the landscape and fluvial system on the Zuni Indian Reservation by (1) constructing large-scale dams, reservoirs, and other waterworks; (2) channelizing Bosson Wash, Plumasano Wash, the Zuni River, and other watercourses; and (3) building a road network. The construction of many roads on the Zuni Indian Reservation aggravated erosion by redirecting sheetwash into narrow channels. This made many traditional land use practices involving the spreading of surface runoff impossible. Some erosion control practices implemented by the BIA and Soil Conservation Service in the 1930s were similar to traditional Zuni land use techniques, with the exception that they were one-time treatments, not continual practices. The effects of these techniques, although initially helpful, were negligible over the long run.

In summary, the actions of the United States resulted in erosion and other land damage on the Zuni Indian Reservation. These actions included (1) changing the social and technological organization of Zuni land use; (2) reallocating resources on the reservation to restrict access to productive resources; (3) physically altering the landscape and fluvial system of the reservation; (4) constructing large dams that failed; (5) taking Zuni land off of the reservation, resulting in overgrazing of the reservation; and (6) failing to institute a permanent erosion control program to replace the traditional water control system rendered inoperable by BIA agricultural and livestock programs.

Damage to Archaeological Sites from Road Construction

In addition to identifying land damage in the Zuni 2 litigation, the Zuni Tribe had to evaluate that damage in financial terms. Information about the damage to archaeological sites caused by road construction was one of the quantifiable damages the Zuni Tribe pursued through anthropological research. Archaeological sites on the Zuni Indian Reservation are a physical embodiment of the Zuni cultural heritage. They constitute a fragile and irreplaceable cultural resource considered important by the Zuni Tribe. Many archaeological sites on the reservation are eligible for inclusion on the National Register of Historic Places.

Construction of a road through an archaeological site destroys irreplaceable artifacts and their associated archaeological deposits. Critical information about the stratigraphic context of archaeological sites is lost forever when sites are bulldozed. Where road construction does not entirely destroy an archaeological site, the remaining deposits are often subjected to increased erosion that continues to damage the site. At many sites, cultural materials and human burials are eroding from unpaved road surfaces or from steep cutbanks where a road has been cut to grade through a hill. Some drainage ditches and road culverts focus water into channels that become incised, causing further erosion of cultural deposits. Routine road maintenance also contributes to continuing damage.

Damage to archaeological sites by the road construction activities of the United States was first reported in 1916.[17] Since then, road construction has continued to damage archaeological sites. Few roads on the Zuni Indian Reservation have been adequately surveyed for cultural resources, so the exact number of archaeological sites damaged by road construction is not known. The work of the Zuni Archaeology Program, however, demonstrates that the problem is widespread. Damaged archaeological sites have been documented along thirteen roads and two state highways on the reservation.[18] Only 20 miles of roads have had damage to archaeological sites adequately mitigated by scientific study, leaving a total of 380 miles of road rights-of-way with unmitigated damage to archaeological sites.[19]

An estimate of the total number of sites damaged by road construction was generated using the average site density per mile of linear survey on the Zuni Indian Reservation. Seventeen archaeological surveys encompassing 163 miles of linear survey of roads, pipelines, transmission lines, and other projects yield an average site density of 0.95 sites per mile of right-of-way. Actual site density varied from 0.1 to 4.8 sites per mile.

When I multiplied the length of the roads on the reservation with no mitigation of damage to archaeological sites by the average number of sites per mile, I estimated that 361 archaeological sites have been damaged by road construction.

In addition to archaeological sites, there are other cultural materials in road rights-of-way that have been subjected to damage. These cultural resources include isolated artifacts and extremely low density artifact scatters. The appropriate measure for these resources is not the number of sites per mile but the total acreage impacted by road construction. Multiplying the total length of roads by an average right-of-way of 150 feet yields 7,277 acres, or 11.36 square miles of damaged landscape.

Road construction has substantially damaged the archaeological sites and regional distribution artifacts on the Zuni Indian Reservation. To quantify this damage in financial terms, Roger Anyon, the director of the Zuni Archaeology Program, provided figures about the cost of scientific data recovery on a number of recent projects the Zuni Tribe had undertaken to mitigate damage to archaeological sites along road rights-of-way. These figures were used to calculate, in 1990 dollars, a very conservative estimate of $5 million of damage to archaeological sites.

An anthropological perspective on Zuni land use was useful in both the Zuni 1 and Zuni 2 litigation. The data contributed by anthropological research helped document the extent and organization of the Zunis' land use in their aboriginal territory. Examination of the traditional organization of land use on the Zuni Reservation and how this was changed by the policies of the United States helped articulate the causal linkage between human land use and land damages, including erosion and destruction of archaeological sites.

NOTES

1. T. J. Ferguson, "Zuni Settlement and Land Use: An Archaeological Perspective" (Expert testimony submitted to the United States Claims Court as evidence in the case *Zuni Indian Tribe* v. *United States*, Docket 161-79L, 1980); T. J. Ferguson, "Rebuttal Report" (Expert testimony submitted to the United States Claims Court as evidence in the case *Zuni Indian Tribe* v. *United States*, Docket 161-79L, 1981); T. J. Ferguson, "Patterns of Land Use and Environmental Change on the Zuni Indian Reservation, 1846–1985: Ethnohistorical and Archaeological Evidence" (Expert testimony submitted to the United States Claims Court as evidence in the case *Zuni Indian Tribe* v. *United States*, Dockets 327-81L and 224-84L [Ct. Cl., filed May 12, 1981], 1985); T. J. Ferguson, "Rebuttal Report: Land Use and Land Damage on the Zuni Indian Reservation, 1846–1988" (Expert testimony submitted to the United States Claims Court as evidence in the case *Zuni Indian Tribe* v. *United States*, Dockets 327-81L and 224-84L [Ct. Cl., filed May 12, 1981], 1988).

2. For an ethnological perspective, see Fred Eggan, "Aboriginal Land Use of the Zuni Indian Tribe" (Expert testimony submitted to the United States Claims Court as evidence in the case *Zuni Indian Tribe* v. *United States*, Docket 161-79L, 1980), and Triloki Nath Pandey, "Some Reflections on Aboriginal Land Use of the Zuni Indian Tribe" (Expert testimony submitted to the United States Claims Court as evidence in the case *Zuni Indian Tribe* v. *United States*, Docket 161-79L, 1980). For an ethnobotanical perspective, see Richard I. Ford, "Zuni Land Use and Damage to Trust Land" (Expert testimony submitted to the United States Claims Court as evidence in the case *Zuni Indian Tribe* v. *United States*, Dockets 327-81L and 224-84L [Ct. Cl., filed May 12, 1981], 1985). For dendrochronological data, see Jeffrey Dean, "Dendrochronological Dating of Floodplain Erosion on Zuni Indian Lands, Northwestern New Mexico" (Expert testimony submitted to the United States Claims Court as evidence in the case *Zuni Indian Tribe* v. *United States*, Dockets 327-81L and 224-84L [Ct. Cl., filed May 12, 1981], 1985).

3. *Zuni Indian Tribe* v. *United States*, 161-79L (Ct. Cl., May 27, 1987), Indian Claims; extent of aboriginal land and title.

4. During the Zuni 1 evidentiary trial in Salt Lake City, examples of the major pottery types found on the Zuni Indian Reservation were introduced as illustrative evidence. The distribution of these ceramic types throughout the claim area was reviewed as a basis for this conclusion. The collection of ceramics used in the Zuni 1 trial was provided by Roger Anyon of the Zuni Archaeology Program.

5. Keith Kintigh, *Zuni Settlement, Subsistence, and Society in Late Zuni Prehistory*, Anthropological Papers of the University of Arizona, 44 (Tucson: University of Arizona Press, 1985), pp. 77–82.

6. Daniel Oran, *Oran's Dictionary of the Law* (St. Paul, Minn.: West Publishing, 1983), p. 3.

7. Charles H. Greenwood and C. W. White, "Mogollon Ritual: A Spatial Configuration of a Non-Village Patter," *Archaeology* 23 (1970): 298–301; Elizabeth Morris, "High Altitude Sites in the Mogollon Rim Area of Arizona and New Mexico" (Paper presented at the Jornado Mogollon Conference, Las Cruces, New Mexico, 1980).

8. These depositions were given by Tom Awelagte, Fred Bowannie, Theodore Edaakie, Sefferino Eriacho, Chester Hart Gaspar, Alonzo Hustito, Chester Mahooty, Alvin Lynn Nastacio, Oscar Nastacio, Ralph Quam, Frank Vacit, and Mecalita Wytsalucy.

9. The names and uses of each of the sites depicted on Figure 13.1 are published in T. J. Ferguson and E. Richard Hart, *A Zuni Atlas* (Norman: University of Oklahoma Press, 1985), pp. 36–57, 125–39.

10. Ibid., pp. 36–57.

11. Frank Hamilton Cushing, "Outlines of Zuni Creation Myths," in *Thirteenth Annual Report of the Bureau of American Ethnology, 1891–1892* (Washington, D.C.: GPO, 1896), p. 332; Ward Alan Minge, "Zuni in Spanish and Mexican History" (Expert testimony submitted to the United States Claims Court as evidence in the case *Zuni Indian Tribe* v. *United States*, Docket 161-79L [Ct. Cl., filed April 27, 1979] 1980), pp. 51–56; Leslie Spier, *An Outline for a Chronology of Zuni Ruins*, Anthropological Papers vol. 18, pt. 3 (New York: American Museum of Natural History, 1917), pp. 230–33.

12. Barbara J. Mills, Barbara E. Holmes, and T. J. Ferguson, "Performance Report for an Architectural and Historical Study of the Zuni Farming Villages" (Manuscript, Zuni pueblo, Zuni Archaeology Program, 1982).

13. Public Law 98-408, To Convey Certain Lands to the Zuni Indian Tribe for Religious Purposes.

14. On hydrogeology, see Geoscience Consultants, "Changes in Geomorphology, Hydrology, and Land Use on the Zuni Indian Reservation, McKinley and Cibola Counties, New Mexico, 1846–1985" (Expert testimony submitted to the United States Claims Court as evidence in the case *Zuni Indian Tribe* v. *United States*, Dockets 327-81L and 224-84L [Ct. Cl., filed May 12, 1981], 1988). On geomorphology, see Stephen A. Hall, "Erosion on Zuni Indian Reservation Lands" (Expert testimony submitted to the United States Claims Court as evidence in the case *Zuni Indian Tribe* v. *United States*, Dockets 327-81L and 224-84L [Ct. Cl., filed May 12, 1981], 1985). On dendroclimatology, see Martin Rose, "Present and Past Climate of the Zuni Region" (Expert testimony submitted to the United States Claims Court as evidence in the case *Zuni Indian Tribe* v. *United States*, Dockets 327-81L and 224-84L [Ct. Cl., filed May 12, 1981], 1985). On dendrochronology, see Dean, *Dendrochronological Dating.* On environmental history, see Richard E. Hart, "The Zuni Mountains: Chronology of an Environmental Disaster" (Expert testimony submitted to the United States Claims Court as evidence in the case *Zuni Indian Tribe* v. *United States*, Dockets 327-81L and 224-84L [Ct. Cl., filed May 12, 1981], 1988); T. J. Ferguson and E. Richard Hart, "Rebuttal Report: Interpretation of Historical and Contemporary Photographs" (Expert testimony submitted to the United States Claims Court as evidence in the case *Zuni Indian Tribe* v. *United States*, Dockets 327-81L and 224-84L [Ct. Cl., filed May 12, 1981], 1988).

15. T. J. Ferguson, "The Impact of Federal Policy on Zuni Land Use," in *Seasons of the Kachina: Proceedings of the California State University, Hayward, Conferences on the Western Pueblos, 1987–1988*, ed. Lowell John Bean, Anthropological Papers no. 34, (Menlo Park, Calif.: Ballena Press, 1989), pp. 85–131.

16. The Zuni interviewees were Tom Awelagte, Nitsa Bescalente, Neoma Bobelu, Belle Bowannie, Fred Bowannie, Clarence Calavaza, Lettie Cawyoka, Amy Chuyate, Leroy Dewa, Sefferino Eriacho, Wekeema Eriacho, Calvin Eustace, Tom Walker Idiaque, Chester Gaspar, Frank Ghaccu, Silas Gjahate, Mazone Harker, Litsa Kaaymassee, Dempsy Kanteena, Scotty Kaskalla, Frank Lalacita, Meda Waikanema, Edison Laselute, Lidaneta Lasiloo, Pesancio Lasiloo, Jimmy Lonjose, Rita Enote Lorenzo, Chester Mahooty, David Mateya, Nathaniel Nasheboo, Leo Nastacio, Sidney Neumayah, Pacque Ondelacy, Sol Ondelacy, Russell Owaleon, Remijo Panteah, May Peina, Adam Penketewa, Dennis Peynetsa, Patterson Peynetsa, Ella Pinto, Gabriel Pinto, Mary Poblano, Ethel Poncho, Dallas Quam, Chauncey Simplicio, Kathlutah Telsee, Joe Tsabetsaye, Sadie Tsipia, Frank Vacit, Bob Walela, and Calvin Weeke. The non-Zuni interviewees were Daisy Nampeyo Hooee and Elaine Thomas.

17. Spier, *An Outline*, p. 234.

18. Frances Hayashida, "Preliminary Assessment of Damage to Archaeological Sites Caused by Road Construction and Maintenance, Zuni, New Mexico" (Manuscript, Zuni pueblo, Zuni Archaeology Program, 1987), pp. 1–22 and accompanying maps.

19. Measurements were made using the English system rather than the metric system since this is congruent with the standards used in road construction on the Zuni Indian Reservation.

CHAPTER 14

Problems of Land Use Within a Portion of the Zuni Land Claim Area

John O. Baxter

For centuries preceding the arrival of U.S. forces in 1846, the pueblo of Zuni successfully maintained dominion over the tribe's traditional land base. Lying within well-known boundaries, Zuni's homeland comprised more than fifteen million acres spreading over western New Mexico and eastern Arizona. While fending off intrusions by both European invaders and neighboring tribes, the Zuni people sustained themselves on their lands by farming, hunting, grazing, and gathering a variety of indigenous products adapted to their lifestyle. All these activities were conducted in an ecologically sound manner without excessive exploitation of any resources. After the signing of the Treaty of Guadalupe Hidalgo in 1848, by which the United States annexed most of the Southwest, the tribe's situation deteriorated rapidly. Within the next one hundred years, the Zunis lost all but a tiny portion of their original territory as government officials responsible for protecting Indian rights looked the other way. Before 1900 Anglo-American entrepreneurs had obtained access to millions of acres of Zuni land for livestock ranching, lumbering, and mining. Establishment of these industries not only prevented the Zuni people from using their customary resources but also brought devastation to the land itself. Deleterious practices such as overgrazing and clear-cutting brought widespread erosion and environmental deterioration still in evidence today.

Hoping to right a great wrong, Zuni leaders pleaded with authorities in Washington to provide compensation for the tribe's lost lands. Decades of effort were finally rewarded with passage of a law on May 15, 1978, that allowed Zuni to present its case before the United States Court of Claims. Subsequently, in a separate action the tribe also sought restitution for the environmental spoilation that had occurred while the pueblo's lands were controlled by other interests. To support that claim, Zuni's legal advisers assembled a team of experts from various disciplines in the sciences and humanities to document the environmental degradation that had been caused by many years of misuse. One of the reports submitted concerned a specific tract of about 55,000 acres in New Mexico located northeast of the pueblo village in the Zuni Mountains. The report presented a detailed history of the tract from about 1870 to 1940, a period in which stock growers and lumbermen invaded the Zuni Mountains to obliterate grass and timber that had grown there for centuries. Together with reports based on physical evidence prepared by experts in the sciences, it served to document the ecological decline throughout a much larger area in the same era (see Figure 14.1).

Situated west of the Continental Divide in McKinley and Cibola (formerly Valencia) Counties, the tract considered in this study included most of the land in four contiguous townships (Townships 12 and 13 North, Ranges 15 and 16 West). Government surveyors platted the townships in 1881 and 1882, but removal from the public domain began earlier. On February 18, 1870, an executive order gave the U.S. Army 64,000 acres on the north side of the study tract near Bear Springs to establish Fort Wingate Military Reserve. In 1881, a second order extended the south boundary two and a quarter miles, adding another 8,640 acres of higher, timbered county to provide building material for the fort.

A much larger expropriation resulted from a congressional act passed in 1866 to encourage construction of the Atlantic and Pacific Railroad, originally intended to follow the thirty-fifth parallel from St. Louis to California. The legislation provided for a land grant to the railway company of all the odd-numbered sections in a strip reaching fifty miles on each side of the right-of-way. No tracks were laid until 1881, but authorities later decided that the grant became effective on March 12, 1872, the date on which the secretary of the interior received a map of the proposed route to California. Running straight across the Zuni homeland, the grant comprised more than three million acres in New Mexico, including all the odd-numbered sections in the study area.

After 1884 some homesteading took place in the adjoining even-numbered sections, but most of them remained public lands until the territory of New Mexico selected them for withdrawal under the terms of the Fergusson Act of 1898. Sponsored by the territory's nonvoting delegate to Congress, Harvey B. Fergusson, the act gave title to certain lands and the resources thereon for the support of public schools and other educational and custodial institutions. The act was intended to alleviate financial problems caused by New Mexico's long wait for statehood.

At first, Atlantic and Pacific executives found the land grant to be something of a white elephant. The region's remote location, aridity, and distance from markets discouraged large investors; railroad policymakers opposed sales of small parcels to settlers. Within the study area, however,

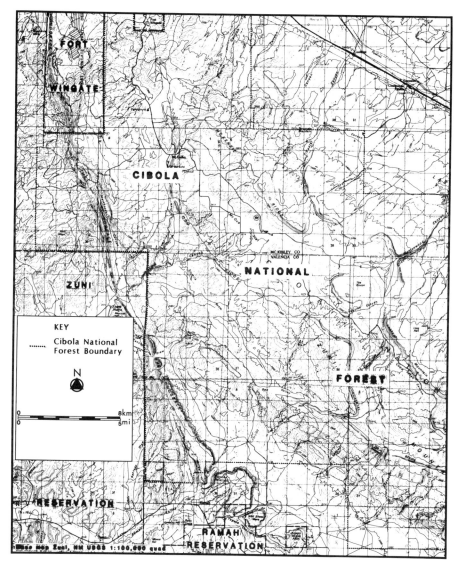

Figure 14.1. Zuni watershed study area.

there were a few exceptions. In 1886 the railroad sold 41,592 acres from the odd-numbered sections to the Cebolla Cattle Company of Fort Wingate for fifty cents per acre. Beginning at the south boundary of the Wingate Reserve, the Cebolla lands formed a rectangle about twenty-one miles long and six or seven miles wide, which included the west half of the study area. Because the purchase gave control of the adjoining even-numbered sections as well, the company secured use of about 100,000 acres for a little more than $20,000 (see Figure 14.2).

Incorporated on January 26, 1886, the Cebolla Cattle Company was organized by officers from Fort Wingate to profit from the ranching boom then sweeping the West. Having capitalized the firm at $250,000 (25,000 shares at $10 each), the original investors adopted the "Box S" as their brand for cattle and horses. Little is known of the company's affairs prior to 1884, when Colonel Eugene A. Carr came to Wingate as commanding officer of the Sixth Cavalry. Known for his vigorous campaigning against hostile Indians, Carr soon became an important shareholder in the Cebolla ranching operation. During the same year, Carr's son, Clark M. Carr, a recent graduate of Phillips Exeter Academy, joined his father in New Mexico and threw himself into the livestock venture with great enthusiasm. By January 1, 1889, father and son were serving as the cattle company's president and secretary/general manager, respectively. During the following year, 1,500 mother cows and 500 steers grazed on the Cebolla range.

When the company purchased its ranch lands from the railroad, the shareholders had to decide what to do about a small but tenacious colony of Mormons that had squatted on the Atlantic and Pacific grant in the 1870s. By 1882, the settlers had established a community known as Ramah (a name taken from the Book of Mormon), less than twenty miles east of Zuni pueblo. At first, the Carrs ordered their uninvited tenants to vacate, but hard cash eventually softened their attitude. Thanks to a large subsidy from church elders in Salt Lake City, the Mormons resolved the matter by buying a section of land at the very high price of $10 per acre, for a total of $6,400.

Despite this windfall, cattle company affairs did not go smoothly during the 1890s, a time when crippling drought combined with low cattle prices to eliminate profits for stockmen. In a gloomy report released early in 1893, general manager Clark Carr complained that lack of grass and water caused cattle to scatter, making them easy prey for rustlers. In the previous year, Box S cowboys had branded only 383 calves. As a result, expenses had exceeded receipts, and corporate debt had risen alarmingly. The only glimmer of hope came from the possibility of a quick sale of the company's timberlands.

Financial difficulties caused the shareholders to split into factions, with each group intent on protecting its particular interests. All agreed,

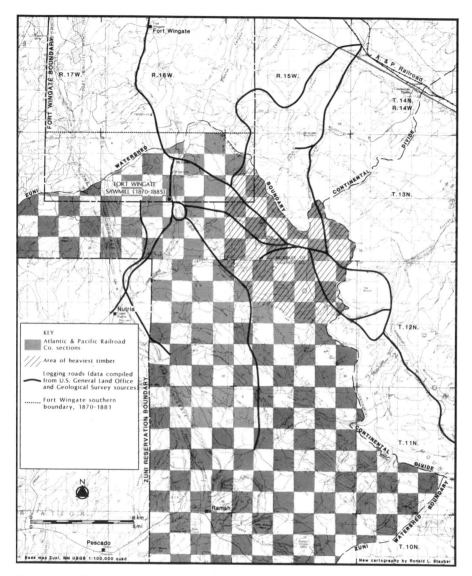

KEY

▓ Atlantic & Pacific Railroad Co. sections

/// Area of heaviest timber

━━ Logging roads (data compiled from U.S. General Land Office and Geological Survey sources)

········ Fort Wingate southern boundary, 1870-1881

Base map Zuni, NM USGS 1:100,000 quad

New cartography by Ronald L. Stauber

Figure 14.2. Timber cut in the Zuni watershed, 1870–1885.

however, that liquidation of assets offered the only chance to prevent disaster. In the spring of 1894, Clark Carr and his father, then a brigadier general, contracted with their former adversaries, the settlers at Ramah, to round up all Box S cattle on the range for eighty-five cents per head. Once gathered, the Carrs took over the stock at $5 per head as payment for old debts owed to them by the company. A few months later, they sold 370 cows to the Mormons for $11.50 each, throwing in the calves at $2, apparently turning a substantial profit. The sale also included the Box S brand, thus ending the company's livestock enterprise.

During the next five years, General Carr became the principal creditor of the company through cash advances for expenses and purchases of notes owed to other lenders. On January 30, 1899, the general brought suit against the company for about $7,000. A court-appointed appraiser valued the lands at thirty-three and a third cents per acre, a total of $14,237.39, less $3,328.47 in overdue taxes and interest, giving the property a net worth of $10,908.92. On April 24 General Carr purchased the company's lands for $7,287.56 at a sheriff's auction conducted on the steps of the Valencia County courthouse in Los Lunas, New Mexico. Having secured clear title to the original railroad purchase, the Carrs began a vigorous campaign to find a purchaser and realize a profit from their investment. In 1901 Clark Carr returned home after service in Cuba during the Spanish-American War to join his father in a major effort to promote the sale.

As an attraction for potential buyers, the younger Carr wrote a detailed description of the property that emphasized the valuable timber resources. Estimating the stumpage at approximately 125 to 150 million board feet, Carr characterized the trees as large and thrifty, very similar to the white pine found in Michigan and Wisconsin. He also indicated that the territory of New Mexico owned the intermediate even-numbered sections and would soon sell the timber on them as authorized by the Fergusson Act. Carr helpfully offered to handle negotiations with territorial officials for the stumpage, which he judged would yield another 125 million board feet. The owners offered to sell their deeded sections at $5 per acre or the timber standing on them at $1.25 per thousand board feet, estimating that each acre would yield 7,000 to 10,000 feet of sawed lumber. Having prepared the necessary promotional material, the Carrs organized a small lumber company of their own to provide some cash flow and return on investment until a buyer materialized for their 40,000 acres.

Even before the demise of the cattle company, entrepreneurs had begun exploitation of the vast timber reserves of the Zuni Mountains. During construction of the Atlantic and Pacific Railroad in 1880 and 1881, lumbermen supplied huge numbers of crossties and bridge timbers to extend the line across New Mexico and Arizona. The contractors included John W. Young, a flamboyant son of Mormon leader Brigham Young, who agreed to provide 500,000 ties, enough for two hundred miles of track. Surveyors working in the area reported locations in the mountains where great quantities of ties and lumber had been removed. As railroad crews pushed west, timber cutting subsided rapidly, but large-scale logging resumed in 1890 when Austin and William Mitchell, brothers from Cadillac, Michigan, bought more than 300,000 acres of railroad land at $2 per acre. Also made up of odd-numbered sections, the huge tract lay east of the Box S ranch on both sides of the Continental Divide and included the east half of the study area. Experienced lumbermen, the two brothers envisioned an enormous enterprise with headquarters at a siding on the railroad's mainline known as Mitchell (now Thoreau), where they built a new sawmill. To carry logs from the woods to the mill, they laid out six miles of narrow gauge track. Lumber production began in late June 1892, but suddenly, after less than three months of operation, the Mitchells closed the mill and returned to Michigan. Although the Mitchells offered no explanation for their departure, the shutdown can be safely attributed to the severe business depression that gripped the nation during much of the 1890s. Because of low demand, a decade passed before logging resumed in the Zuni range.

Confidence revived, and change began in 1901, when the American Lumber Company, recently incorporated in New Jersey, purchased almost all of the Mitchell lands in New Mexico. The price, $1.1 million, must have allowed the sellers to recoup their investment and realize some additional profit. American Lumber soon became one of New Mexico's most important industries with the construction of a large sawmill complex just north of Albuquerque on a 110-acre site with easy rail access. To carry timber out of the mountains, the company built a standard gauge line south from Thoreau that allowed flatcars of logs to be switched onto the main line without reloading. The first train arrived in Albuquerque on October 25, 1903, and the mill began operations the next day (see Figure 14.3).

During 1904 and 1905, the Albuquerque plant turned out approximately 35 million board feet each year. To ensure efficient logging operations and avoid boundary squabbles, lumber company officials purchased the stumpage on the territory's even-numbered sections interspersed among their own. In 1904 American Lumber secured the timber on 34,000 acres of territorial land at $2.50 per acre. The agreement stipulated that no trees would be cut with a diameter smaller than twelve inches and that accumulated slash would be disposed of according to government regulation. A year later Clark Carr obtained a similar contract to buy the timber on 12,640 acres of territorial land adjoining his property.

Within months after negotiating a contract with the territory, the Carrs finally sold most of their timber property at an extremely lucrative

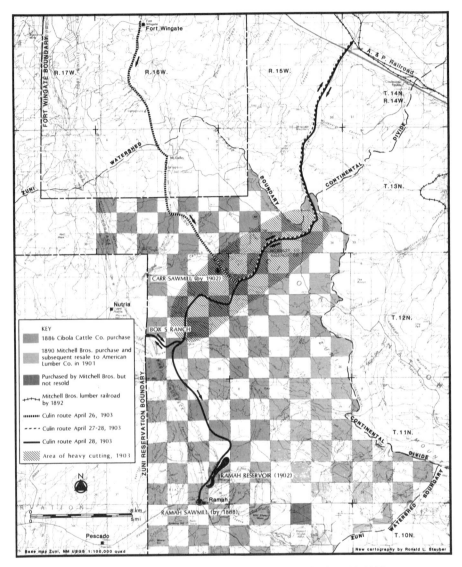

Figure 14.3. Lumber company activity in the Zuni watershed, 1886–1903.

price. In the spring of 1906, Clark Carr, acting for his father, reached an agreement with John R. Gordon, John Garvin, and William McFarlane of Marquette and Ontonagon, Michigan, to sell 18,400 acres at $6.20 per acre. The Michigan men also assumed a balance of $27,644 due to the territory for its timber and agreed to pay the Carrs about $5,500 for their interest therein. Finally, the buyers contracted the timber on the unsold Carr lands at $1 per thousand. Altogether, the total return of more than $120,000 must have been very gratifying for the Carr family.

At about the same time that McFarlane and his associates took over the Carr lands, New Mexico's logging industry became embroiled in a major political scandal. In 1907 disposal of territorial public lands and natural resources rocked the administration of Governor Herbert J. Hagerman, eventually forcing his resignation. On the basis of the timber contracts just mentioned and others like them, special investigators from Washington brought suit against the American Lumber Company, Clark Carr, and other operators in district court. The accused were charged with violating a provision of the Fergusson Act that limited the amount of land acquired by a single individual or corporation for exploitation to 160 acres. Although the issue generated intense publicity, in the end no one was prosecuted. However, the court did issue an injunction restraining the loggers from cutting timber on the territorial sections. Before the contracts expired in 1909, they were renewed with the injunction still in force. After New Mexico finally attained statehood in 1912, the state replaced the federal government in the timber litigation, but the new attorney general declined to further prosecute the cases. On March 12, 1913, Judge William H. Pope dissolved the injunction, but the matter did not end there. More lawsuits followed.

Despite troubling legal difficulties, the timber cutters gradually extended their railroad network over twenty-three townships stretching northwest from the west side of Acoma pueblo's land grant to the southeast corner of the Fort Wingate Military Reservation. By May 1, 1907, American Lumber had cut more than 141 million board feet from 27,000 acres, averaging slightly more than 5,000 feet per acre. Lands cleared by that date included almost 10,000 acres within the study area. To avoid payment of property taxes, the company began selling off its deforested lands as early as 1906. On October 17, Silvestre Mirabal, a Hispanic sheep rancher from San Rafael east of the Zuni range, paid $4,225 for 4,080 acres. Scattered over a vast area, Mirabal's purchase consisted of many small parcels that seem to have been chosen to control springs and waterholes. In later years Mirabal bought much more cutover land, slowly accumulating enormous holdings to pasture his flocks.

On January 2, 1907, the Atchison, Topeka, and Santa Fe Railway, which had taken over the Atlantic and Pacific, entered into a three-way contract for 1 million crossties to improve its roadbed. Under the contract's terms, American Lumber provided the timber and delivered the ties to Thoreau over its branch line. The third party, Amasa B. McGaffey, agreed to cut and pile the ties at trackside loading points in the woods. A native of Vermont, McGaffey moved from Albuquerque to Thoreau in 1903, where he entered the mercantile business and became interested in logging. Specializing in ties, his forestry enterprises prospered, and the New Englander soon became a leader in New Mexico's timber industry. In 1911 he submitted the high bid for merchantable timber on a tract of thirty sections in the southern part of the Fort Wingate Reserve just north of the former Carr lands. Officials of the Zuni National Forest, who managed the sale, estimated the yield at 42 million board feet. With the contract confirmed, the energetic Yankee set up a sawmill with a capacity of 50,000 board feet per day about ten miles south of the Santa Fe's main line. Adjacent to the mill, he established a company town, appropriately named McGaffey, that boasted a store, post office, and school. Logging began in November 1912 (see Figure 14.4).

After two years of cutting south of Fort Wingate, McGaffey bargained for additional timber to supply his mill. In 1914 he obtained the stumpage on the former Carr lands purchased eight years earlier by Gordon, Garvin, and McFarlane. Recently, the Midwesterners had run afoul of New Mexico's commissioner of public lands, Robert P. Ervien, over terms of the contract for timber on the intermediate sections, which had expired. To protect their interests, McFarlane and his partners hurriedly negotiated a new ten-year agreement that raised the price for timber from $2.50 to $3 per acre. During the discussions, they further promised to buy the state sections outright for an additional $3 per acre. On December 28, Commissioner Ervien issued a patent that gave each investor an undivided fraction of the whole tract.

While McGaffey's employees laid new rail lines south from the mill, woodsmen began felling timber on the McFarlane tract, as the Carr lands became known. To improve transport of logs and lumber, McGaffey purchased a new locomotive and other equipment. The town grew and prospered. However, a major setback occurred in March 1917 when the mill caught fire and burned to the ground. McGaffey rebuilt immediately, installing new machinery with greater capacity, but after that time his interest focused increasingly on other timber properties in Arizona. His career ended abruptly on September 3, 1929, when he died in a commercial airline disaster. En route to Los Angeles, McGaffey's plane became lost in clouds west of Albuquerque and crashed into Mount Taylor, the highest peak of the San Mateo range. Everyone on board was killed. Soon after his death, logging stopped on his Zuni Mountain properties. During 1930 the McGaffey mill was closed and dismantled, ending an important timber enterprise.

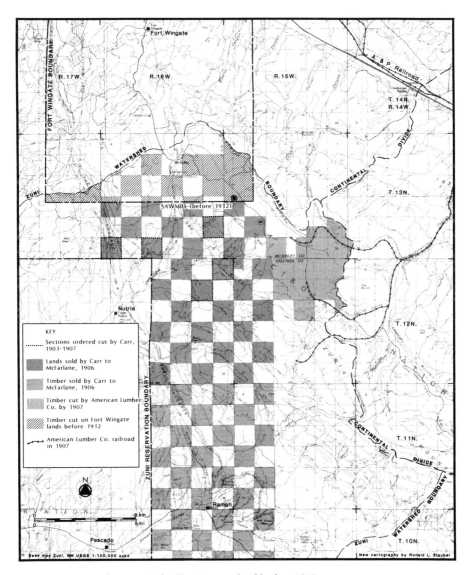

KEY

Sections ordered cut by Carr, 1903-1907

Lands sold by Carr to McFarlane, 1906

Timber sold by Carr to McFarlane, 1906

Timber cut by American Lumber Co. by 1907

Timber cut on Fort Wingate lands before 1912

American Lumber Co. railroad in 1907

N

Figure 14.4. Timber cut in the Zuni watershed before 1912.

At the end of 1913, several months before McFarlane and his partners concluded their land purchase from state officials, the American Lumber Company found itself in serious financial difficulty. After terminating all operations in September, the corporation defaulted on interest payments due January 1 to service a series of mortgage bonds and soon went into receivership. Plant and equipment remained idle for three years, but the situation changed late in 1916 when American Lumber's receivers sold all of its assets to Otis and Company, investment bankers from Cleveland, for $445,000. Within two months, the Ohio firm had assigned the property, including the mill at Albuquerque, the branch railroad, and 300,000 acres of timberland, to a new corporation known as the McKinley Land and Lumber Company. Incorporated in New Mexico, the latter organization was controlled by George E. Breece, a West Virginia lumberman with timber interests all over the nation. New ownership seemed to promise renewed activity, but World War I intervened, and the big sawmill remained closed until September 1919. Logging in the mountains had resumed several weeks earlier.

While lumberjacks and millhands waited for a call back to work, management of the new company took stock of the recent acquisition. Assurance of an adequate timber supply loomed as a pressing concern since many sections on the original railroad purchase had already been cut over. After Judge Pope had lifted the injunction that prevented logging on the even-numbered sections, Commissioner Ervien, on June 19, 1913, had extended the American timber contracts for ten years, but with some important changes. Like the McFarlane group, company negotiators agreed to a raise in fees for timber still uncut to $3 per acre and an additional fifty cents per acre for those lands previously logged. When McKinley Land and Lumber acquired the property, it assumed those contracts and further compensated the state by making a large purchase of the same lands in fee simple. On August 6, 1918, the company bought almost 100,000 acres in the Zuni Mountains for $3 each, indicating optimism for the future. As was customary, the state received payment as the timber was removed. The purchase included almost all the lands in the study area not previously acquired by American Lumber, the McFarlane partners, or scattered homesteaders.

For several years McKinley Land and Lumber Company harvested timber under agreements with the state, but controversy erupted again shortly before expiration of the 1913 extension. In March 1922 State Land Commissioner Nelson A. Field suddenly refused to accept the company's regular payment for timber cut, declaring that the extension of the 1904 contracts had violated state law in two ways. First, no new bids had been called for, and second, timber taken had been paid for by the acre rather than by stumpage, which would have given a greater return.

Despite his strong words, the commissioner failed to initiate litigation, leaving McKinley management believing that the extension remained valid. No further action took place until after the election of 1922, which brought a whole new slate of state officers to Santa Fe.

On May 28, 1923, a few days before expiration of the 1913 extension, George Breece and E. W. Dobson, president and general counsel, respectively, of the lumber company, tendered two checks to Field's successor, Justiano Baca. The first, in the amount of $6,667.20, paid for logs recently cut, and the second, in the amount of $53,653.94, represented compensation for all timber still standing on lands covered by the original 1904 contracts and subsequent extensions thereof. Unsure of the legal issues, Baca sought advice from the new attorney general, Milton J. Helmick. According to the *Albuquerque Morning Journal*, $100,000–$150,000 hung in the balance. After three months of research, Helmick issued an opinion on September 1 urging Baca to accept the payments. Writing at some length, the attorney general found that the agreement reached in 1913 had been an extension, not a new contract, and therefore was not in violation of state law. Furthermore, purchase of the land in 1918 gave the company a right to the remaining timber as long as it complied with the earlier contracts for disposition of the stumpage.

Helmick's opinion effectively settled the issue. Two years later, on October 1, 1925, New Mexico's land commissioner conveyed the state's interest in all timber still standing on lands covered by the 1904 contracts. Although the company secured the stumpage on 16,589 acres in this transaction, only 320 acres remained in the area on which this chapter is focused. All the other state lands had already been logged.

While McKinley's executives acquired uncut timberland with one hand, they continued to sell off deforested tracts with the other. By doing so, they realized considerable savings in property taxes. Always looking for sheep range, Silvestre Mirabal remained the company's most active buyer. On January 6, 1920, the rancher from San Rafael paid "$100 and other valuable considerations" for 88,000 acres located in odd-numbered sections from the old railroad grant. Several months later he bought another 10,000 acres, mostly former state lands. On May 2, 1932, Mirabal further enlarged his grazing empire by assuming responsibility for the balance due to the state for 20,500 acres purchased by McKinley Lumber under the contracts of August 6, 1918 (see Figure 14.5).

During the years when the big lumber companies removed timber from the Zuni Mountains, their employees adopted few conservation practices. Without exception, the corporations sought to maximize profits and showed little consideration for progressive ideas such as sustained yield cutting or retention of a residual stand for reseeding. One observer recalled that lumberjacks left only two seed trees per acre when cutting

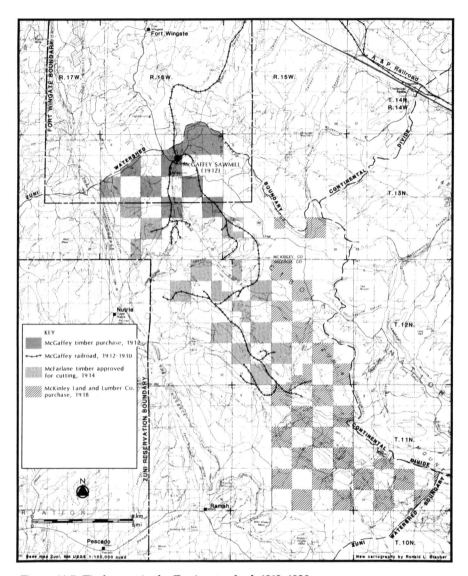

Figure 14.5. Timber cut in the Zuni watershed, 1912–1930.

private lands, although more remained on those sections managed by the Forest Service. In a report prepared in 1940, when logging had almost ended in the region, Forest Service personnel painted a grim picture of how the Zuni range had been affected by several decades of unrestrained timber extraction. One ranger described the situation thusly:

> The logging methods used in this almost continuous operation have been very destructive. The timber is first cut for sawlogs, utilizing only clear, sound logs, other merchantable logs are left as waste. This is followed by small portable tie mills which cut every tree that will make one eight foot tie, wasting everything else. Then the mine timber operators cut everything suitable for props and stulls. These successive operations result in clear cutting everything except cull trees and small poles, with no provision made for seed trees or brush disposal. The picture presented is one of desolation and waste. . . . Both [operations] are excellent examples of exploitation of natural resources.[1]

The same writer estimated that to reestablish timber production fifty years in the future, 100,000 acres would have to be replanted with ponderosa pine seedlings.

Frequently, overgrazing coincided with clear-cutting as large flocks owned by Mirabal, George Breece, and other livestock owners followed in the wake of the loggers. By 1940 soil erosion had become acute over large areas in the Zunis and "hypercritical" on a number of particular tracts, according to Forest Service reports. For example, Cottonwood Canyon, just east of the study area, had deteriorated from a trout stream lined with willows to a deeply incised arroyo with banks ten to twenty feet high and subject to devastating flash floods. Such erosion represented the culmination of sixty years of neglect and misuse. During that period, exhaustive exploitation left a badly damaged environment within the area covered by this study and over much of the Zuni Mountains. Ironically, the exploiters sometimes found themselves at the mercy of forces beyond their control and experienced severe losses or bankruptcy caused by swings in the business cycle. Nevertheless, the ecological excesses continued as new profiteers appeared in place of the old. Throughout the process, the Zuni people were denied a voice as their ancestral lands deteriorated.

After their resources had disappeared, however, the tribe did receive a measure of retribution. Once the team of experts had completed the necessary research and prepared reports to support Zuni's claim for compensation, the Pueblo's attorneys brought the case before Congress. Various House and Senate committees held hearings to consider the mass of evidence provided. In 1990 success rewarded the long effort.

Congress passed the Zuni Land Conservation Act, which was subsequently signed by President George Bush. The bill included a $25-million appropriation to be placed in a permanent trust fund for the benefit of the Zuni people. Interest generated by the fund will be used to establish a permanent sustainable resource development plan to reclaim and improve the Pueblo's land base.

NOTES

1. Edwin A. Tucker, "Preliminary Report, Acquisition Purchase, Zuni Mountain Area," Albuquerque, March 20, 1940, pp. 7–8, Record Group 75, Interdepartmental Rio Grande Board, Project Subject Files, 1937–1942, National Archives, Denver Branch, Denver, Colorado.

CHAPTER 15

Recapturing the Landscape: Use of U.S. Government Surveys in Zuni Land Claims Research

Ronald L. Stauber

In 1854 the net of the public land survey was cast in the New Mexico territory to capture the landscape from its original inhabitants. In 1984 the Zuni Tribe began using information from these government surveys as evidence in the United States Claims Court to document claims against the government.

The American military began occupying the Southwest in 1846 and intensified its occupation after the signing of the Treaty of Guadalupe Hidalgo in 1848. Actions by Congress in 1854 and 1862 instructed the surveyor general of New Mexico to survey the New Mexico territory.[1] The surveys provided a legal framework for granting lands and stimulating new settlement. Railroad land grants were also being made to foster economic activity.[2] By law, the taking of land required that the region first be surveyed to divide it into a rectangular township and range network. This network provided the necessary legal boundaries from which homestead lands could be further subdivided. As a result, the surveys became a "paper trail" leading back to the past.

Examination of these surveys began after the initiation of the Zunis' claim of the U.S. government's negligent or intentional damages to Zuni trust lands (Zuni 2).[3] Many crucial research questions were posed by the tribe's attorneys to their expert witnesses. These questions included, What were the resources and condition of the aboriginal Zuni lands, and how were the Zunis using them? Were there damages to or removal of resources from the Zunis' land? What were the nature and extent of the losses or damages? When did the damages take place? Who and/or what was responsible for the damages? Expert witnesses in ethnohistory, archaeology, history, geomorphology, and hydrology recognized the usefulness of the primary data contained in historical cartographic documents in answering these questions. Of these documents, the United States General Land Office (GLO) cadastral surveys of the late nineteenth and early twentieth centuries offered the most help in answering some of these questions.

THE U.S. GENERAL LAND OFFICE SURVEY

GLO surveyors were charged with the task of both classifying and quantifying the landscape. Their surveys provide a wealth of historical and spatial information about the landscape and its use. Each township survey is a large-scale historical geography providing specific information about a thirty-six-square-mile area at a single point in time. Taken together, the notes and plat maps in the GLO archive form the historical equivalent of a modern geographical information system.

The GLO surveyors' field notes consisted of accurate measurements of the locations of cultural and natural features. Many of the feature types recorded in the Zuni area can be found in the following list:

Natural Features	Cultural Features
Rivers	Farming villages
Streams	Homesteads
Springs	Structures
Drainages	Roads
Timber	Trails
Coal outcroppings	Fences
Soils	Farm fields and crops
Landforms	Irrigation ditches
Grassland	Archaeological sites
Ponds and lakes	Livestock and corrals
	Stock ponds
	Dams
	Sawmills

In addition to identifying features and their geographical locations, surveyors also measured drainage channel depth, stream width and depth, large spring flow, and timber trunk diameter. A "General Description" at the end of each survey broadly characterized the township according to the perceived value of the land for agriculture, grazing, mining, and timber. Specific information about the people living in the township was often provided. GLO survey plats (survey maps) were drafted from the data supplied in the field notes. In addition to field notes, the surveyor also made a field sketch-map, which helped resolve ambiguities of language in the notes. The sketch-map, made on site, allowed the plat cartographer to connect the dots, as it were, through unsurveyed areas.

Research problems with the GLO surveys vary depending on the survey, surveyor, or, at times, even the surveyor general.[4] Some surveys had improper omissions, or inconsistent recording, of features in the field notes. Hastily or inadequately written general descriptions or incomplete or poorly drafted plats were also a problem. Important methodological and theoretical limitations noted by one expert witness are that the coverages of the GLO surveys were linear samples rather than complete areal inventories of the landscape and that the primary concern of the GLO survey was to establish legal boundaries; observation, though important, remained secondary.[5]

Two GLO Survey Examples

Most of the GLO surveys in the Zuni Reservation area were conducted between 1880 and 1912. Examples of the range of data compiled during the research are seen in two 1911 surveys. The first (Figure 15.1) shows the area around Zuni pueblo (Township 10 North, Range 19 West), and the second (Figure 15.2) shows the Zuni farming village of Ojo Caliente (Township 8 North, Range 20 West).[6] Each plat provides a good picture of the extent of land use and settlement in its township.

Over 3,000 acres of agricultural land are illustrated around Zuni pueblo in Township 10 North, Range 19 West (Figure 15.1).[7] Most of this farmland was irrigated by ditches, but some was irrigated with runoff. Numerous small Zuni-constructed irrigation ditches branch out from Zuni Canal to the north, following natural land contours. In Sections 35 and 36, two peach orchards are shown on the slopes of Dowa Yalanne, a large mesa and the site of a Zuni refuge village during the Pueblo Revolt.

Eleven roads and a telephone line radiate out from Zuni pueblo, marking the major transportation routes. Four corrals and a barn give evidence of livestock activities. The ruins of the Zuni refuge village of *Wimaya:wa*, occupied during the Spanish colonial period, is shown in Sections 10 and 11. Sacred Springs, near Blackrock Dam, was described as the source of water supplying the school and government buildings at Blackrock.

Zuni pueblo itself was often mentioned in the survey. A trading post called Sabin's store was located where a Thriftway convenience store now stands. The Zuni Day School was mapped on the northern edge of the village. A catastrophic loss of Zuni people during a measles epidemic was laconically recorded in the "General Description" by the surveyor, who noted that over 150 bodies were buried in the mission "burial ground" in the spring of 1911.

The Zuni farming village of Ojo Caliente in Township 8 North, Range 20 West (Figure 15.2) is bisected by Plumasano Wash, which drains a large

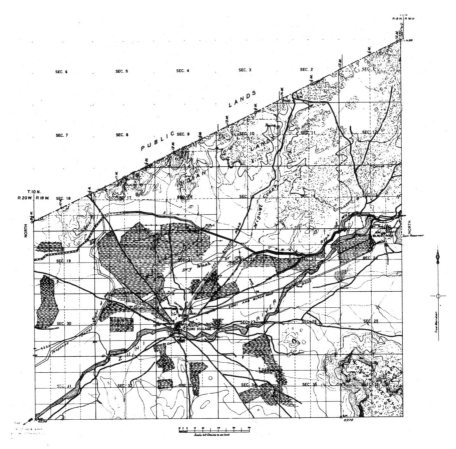

Figure 15.1. United States General Land Office Survey plat: Township No. 10 North, Range No. 19 West of the Principal Meridian, New Mexico, Zuni Indian Reservation (1911).

portion of the reservation into the Zuni River to the west. In 1911 the area of agricultural lands depicted in this township was over 1,400 acres. A little less than half of the area was under cultivation at the time of the survey, while the rest was fenced but fallow. A large portion of Plumasano Wash was surrounded by brush or wire fences to keep stock away from crops. Fences also enclosed areas around drainages feeding Plumasano Wash from the north and south. Except for one enclosure with deep channel incision, these last fenced areas had cultivated portions that were presumably irrigated by runoff. Fields near the Ojo Caliente Spring were watered by a ditch network. The irrigation ditches averaged about 3.5 feet in width.

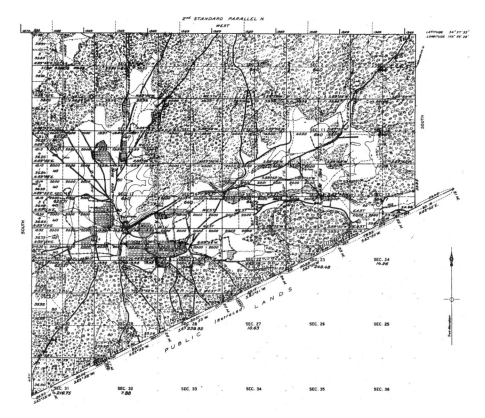

Figure 15.2. United States General Land Office Survey plat: Township No. 8 North, Range No. 20 West of the Principal Meridian, New Mexico, Zuni Indian Reservation (1911).

There was no channel incision recorded for areas under cultivation in the upland drainages. Some of these drainages had channel deepening elsewhere, often in proximity to a nearby road. Although the surveyors traversed Plumasano Wash fourteen times, this major drainage had only two incised channel depths recorded for it in this township. The first was at the end of a long bend. The other was near an intersection with another drainage and a road at the edge of a cultivated area. Other drainages in the township, however, had recorded depths away from cultivated areas of three to twenty feet.

GLO surveyors measured the flow from Ojo Caliente Spring, called Rainbow Spring on the Ojo Caliente Reservoir, NM USGS 7.5′ quad, and found it to be discharging "fine water" at a rate of 500 gallons of water per minute. Sacred Spring, shown in Section 20 on the USGS quad, was not noticed on this survey, although the ground in the area was observed to be "swampy."

The surveyors recorded more than a dozen structures and three corrals at Ojo Caliente. Two of the structures, both in Section 20, are still visible on the modern USGS quad. Nineteen roads converged on Ojo Caliente, four of which were claimed by the surveyors to lead to Zuni Salt Lake. The ruins of the pre-seventeenth-century Zuni villages of Hawikku and Kechiba:wa were mentioned but not named.

Identifying and Quantifying Damage to Zuni Lands

The GLO surveys were valuable to the Zuni land damages case. They contained information not only about who was using the Zuni landscape and what resources were present but also about how *much* of those resources was being used and what condition they were in at the time of the survey. Zuni's expert witnesses compared this information with other historical and current data to calculate the changes that had taken place in the landscape.

Research Methods

The bulk of the Zuni 2 GLO research consisted of compilations from the survey field notes.[8] Approximately 2,000 pages of GLO survey field note and map documents were examined to record pertinent information about the historical conditions of Zuni trust lands. The compilations were based on the following criteria, which were determined to be relevant to the research interests of the Zuni Tribe's expert witnesses:

    Environmental Criteria
       Landform characteristics
       Soil type and quality
       Vegetation species and condition
       Timber species, quality, and quantities
       Minerals present and quantities
       Watercourse, lake, and spring characteristics
       Drainage characteristics
       Meteorological conditions, if any
    Cultural Criteria
       Soil and water control features
       Agriculture and agricultural features
       Grazing and grazing features
       Architecture
       Transportation and communication networks

Mining, lumbering, and industrial operations
Any ethnographic or historic information relating to nineteenth-
century attitudes or activities

These preestablished criteria helped ensure that the researching procedure would be as straightforward and noninterpretive as possible. Interpretation and use of the data were left up to each expert.

The geographic scope of the work was limited to the examination of
forty-two GLO township surveys of public and Indian lands, either partially or completely within present-day Zuni Reservation boundaries.[9]
Portions of surveys of the second standard parallel north line (GLO) and of
the western boundary of New Mexico were also examined where their
lines co-occurred with Zuni lands.[10] The GLO surveys under study began
chronologically with the New Mexican boundary survey of 1875, ranged
through public land surveys of 1881–1893, and ended with Indian land
surveys of 1911–1912.[11]

The original survey notes were perused line by line for pertinent data.
These data then were assembled into a manageable and accessible tabular
format for use by the Zuni Tribe's expert witnesses in preparing their
testimony. Because of time constraints imposed by the case, the research
notes were taken manually and eventually entered into a digital database.
Agricultural land areas were calculated using a polar planimeter device.
Observations about the surveys themselves were made that might aid in
the user's interpretation and understanding of the information the surveys contained. Field notes, trends, or key words (e.g., arroyo) in a given
survey were flagged if they were thought to be of particular significance
within the claims case criteria. The scope of the GLO research, though
circumscribed spatially by the boundaries of the Zuni Reservation and
temporally by the survey dates, was designed to be very broad and
inclusive in its subject matter. The mandate governing the compilation
and recording of survey notes was to preserve all data or information
falling within the case criteria.

Use of GLO Data for Analysis

The GLO surveys helped demonstrate loss of agricultural and grazing
lands at Zuni through misdirected government policies and actions involving dam construction, logging, grazing, mining, and road building.
The results of these government activities forced detrimental changes in
Zuni farming and grazing practices and the eventual loss of the Zunis'
previously successful subsistence economy.

Spatial patterns of Zuni land use and agricultural practices recorded
in the GLO surveys of 1881–1912 were similar to those dating to the

beginning of the American period in 1846.[12] Agricultural field polygons, peach orchards, buildings, and corrals for the entire reservation were compiled from the GLO plats into a single scaled map.[13] This map formed a data baseline from which ethnohistorians, geomorphologists, and others could take measurements and draw comparisons with later sources.

Researchers using photogrammetry compared GLO records of agricultural lands and drainage channel depths with other measurable sources.[14] United States Soil Conservation Service and other aerial photos from 1934, 1957, and 1978 as well as contemporary (1985) field measurements at the same location were used to track damages to farm fields and erosional changes in drainages. Interviews with Zuni informants, archaeological fieldwork, and historical record research provided information that could also be compared and contrasted with the GLO data.[15]

The question of causation was, on the Zuni side, tied to both the succession of events and the rate at which they occurred. The GLO surveys provided a fixed quantity, anchored to a fixed point in time, that was important to the case. The U.S. government's own surveys provided both qualitative and quantitative answers to the legal questions of what resources the Zunis originally had, what condition those resources were in at the time of the survey, who was responsible for maintaining those conditions (i.e., the Zunis), and to what extent damages were occurring through time. The crucial question of who was responsible for damages might eventually become an easier one for the Claims Court to answer.

Gathering evidence of erosion-causing changes to lands in the Zuni watershed off reservation rose to primary importance when government lawyers began to focus their own experts' testimony against Zuni's assertions. Zuni claimed that the episodes of erosion on Zuni trust lands were geologically recent and the result of a synergistic combination of several factors. One of the most critical of these factors was the impact of a long series of swift and intense, silt-laden runoff events originating on the west slope of the Zuni Mountains in the Zuni River watershed. The reasons for this runoff, Zuni asserted, were the government-sanctioned timber clear-cutting and livestock overgrazing on the western slope of the mountains from the late 1870s through the 1920s. Zuni's evidence consisted of extensive documentation of timber sales, grazing leases, and historic photos of logging operations.[16] Photogrammetric analysis of early aerial photos clearly showing checkerboard patterns of timber clear-cutting was also submitted to the court.[17]

The U.S. government's witnesses admitted that logging and grazing operations did occur. They argued, however, that these operations did not begin in the Zuni River watershed before 1912 and were not extensive enough to cause erosion at Zuni. They tried to demonstrate that much of the area Zuni maintained as having been heavily logged was, in fact, "natural" grassland. Grassland soils, by definition, could never have supported commercially valuable timber.[18] At the center of the watershed area the government's experts chose for their rebuttal was Section 32 of Township 13 North, Range 15 West. The paper trail left by the GLO surveys vividly contradicted these government denials, both in the survey plat (Figure 15.3) and in the following "General Description":

> The Land in the South tier of Secs. and S.W.Cor. of this Twp. at the fork of Zuni Ridge [McKenzie Ridge] is good and covered with good Pine Timber, and plenty of Grass. Red Rock Spring is in the S.E.Cor. of the [Ft. Wingate] Military Reservation and contains a good supply of water. From Mountain Ridge bearing S.E. from N.W.Cor. of Ft. the country slopes rapidly to N.&-N.E., is Rough, Broken and Rocky. Covered with Pine, Pinon and Cedar. A Deep Rocky Cañon runs N. through the sec. tier of Secs. from E.bdy. and contains abundance of water, in Secs. 2 and 11. A Road has been opened through this Cañon at considerable labor and expense by the A. and P.R.R. Co. to obtain the Pine Timber in the country S. of Ridge, which is valuable for Lumber.[19]

All of Section 32 and most of the surrounding sections were depicted in 1881 as covered with "heavy timber." The plat visually confirms what was stated in the first and final sentences of the "General Description."

Scientific, legal, and historical research has usually required some form of measurable graphic presentation of data. Charts, graphs, photos, and maps are necessary to illustrate a large quantity or complexity of data at one time. Even a table, though primarily textual in content, is also a graphical array of data that conceivably might require many pages of prose to otherwise elucidate. As a research tool, the GLO survey is both graphical (plat) and textual (field notes), each validating the other by separate means. Ideally, the GLO plat format provides for the observer a translation into "immediate" spatial perception what the survey notes contain in consecutive format: Free association leading to spontaneous pattern recognition can be stimulated by the interaction of both formats. The researcher may choose to apply either a ruler to the plat or a calculator to the notes or do both.

Speculation aside, as a purely historical document, the GLO survey has the same validity—and carries the same caveats—as any other official document. As a legal document, it has the distinct advantage of being illustrative as well as expository. In the United States Claims Court or in Congress, where only a preponderance of evidence must wring a just

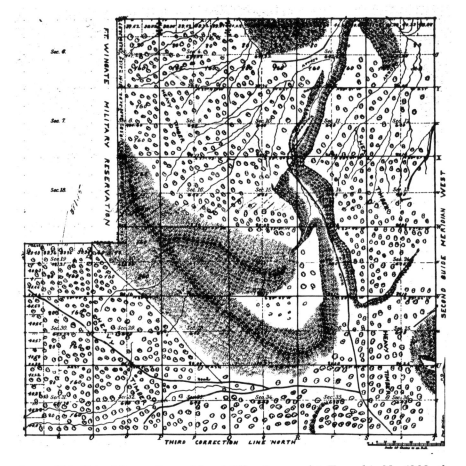

Figure 15.3. United States General Land Office Survey plat: Township No. 13 North, Range No. 15 West of the New Mexico Principal Meridian (1881).

decision, graphic displays of evidence such as the GLO surveys often carry the greatest weight.

The Zuni 2 case was, in effect, settled through congressional action and never argued to conclusion in the United States Claims Court.[20] Even so, Zuni successfully presented its evidence to Congress. The quantitative and qualitative information the GLO surveys furnished in settling the Zuni land claim was perhaps unequaled as a baseline for calculating specific damages to Zuni lands and the circumstances of their occurrence. This same set of data is now providing a model from which to measure the success of the land rehabilitation program the Zuni people began implementing in 1992.

NOTES

1. C. Albert White, *A History of the Rectangular Survey System* (Washington, D.C.: U.S. Department of the Interior, Bureau of Land Management, 1983), pp. 118, 132.

2. Ibid.

3. *Zuni Indian Tribe* v. *United States,* Dockets 327-81L (Ct. Cl., filed May 12, 1981) and 224-84L (Ct. Cl., filed May 3, 1984).

4. During the 1870s and 1880s in New Mexico and Arizona, several surveyors general were either removed from office or forced to resign for their roles in massive land fraud schemes. These fraudulent activities were in regard to both Spanish and Mexican land grants as well as the filing of false homestead claims and surveys. See Floyd A. O'Neil and E. Richard Hart, "Fraudulent Land Activities by United States Officials Affecting Title to Zuni Lands: Conclusions" (Expert testimony submitted to the Select Committee on Indian Affairs, U.S. Senate, 101st Cong., 2nd sess., May 7, 1990), pp. 2–3, items 10–24. White, *A History,* p. 216, lists the surveyors general for each state or territory and how they left office.

5. T. J. Ferguson. "Patterns of Land Use and Environmental Change on the Zuni Indian Reservation, 1846–1985: Ethnohistorical and Archaeological Evidence" (Expert testimony submitted to the United States Claims Court as evidence in the case *Zuni Indian Tribe* v. *United States,* Docket 327-81L [Ct. Cl., filed May 12, 1981]), p. 39.

6. R. A. Farmer, "Field Notes of the Survey of the Section Lines and Subdivisional 1/16 and Center Lines of Fractional Township 10 North Range 19 West, Zuni Indian Reservation," July 24, 1911 (or 1912?), and accompanying plat, Bureau of Land Management Archives, Santa Fe, New Mexico. All dates on the plat give 1911 as the survey year; all survey dates on typewritten office copy of field notes say 1912, but the number "2" is written in by hand and appears to overwrite something else. Farmer was surveying at Zuni both years. R. A. Farmer, "Field Notes of the Survey of the Section Lines and Subdivisional 1/16 and Center Lines of Fractional Township 8 North Range 20 West, Zuni Indian Reservation," September 12, 1911 (or 1912?), and accompanying plat, Bureau of Land Management Archives, Santa Fe, New Mexico.

7. Areas given in these two examples are revised and are not the original areas calculated with the planimeter. They have been taken from E. Richard Hart, "Rebuttal Report: Damage to Zuni Trust Lands" (Expert testimony submitted to the United States Claims Court as evidence in the case *Zuni Indian Tribe* v. *United States,* Dockets 327-81L [Ct. Cl., filed May 12, 1981] and 224-84L [Ct. Cl., filed May 3, 1984]), p. 60.

8. Most of the information in this section can be found in Ronald L. Stauber, "Method of Researching United States Government Surveys for Zuni Trust Land Damages Claim" (Testimony submitted to the United States Claims Court in the case *Zuni Indian Tribe* v. *United States,* Docket 327-81L [Ct. Cl., filed May 12, 1981]).

9. U.S. General Land Office Survey Notes and Plats, Bureau of Land Management, Santa Fe, New Mexico.

10. Chandler Robbins, "Field Notes of the Survey and Establishment of the Western Boundary of New Mexico," 1875, New Mexico State Records Center and Archives, Santa Fe, New Mexico.

11. Most of the earliest GLO surveys at Zuni were of public lands, which were originally intended by the United States to be part of the Zuni Reservation. They were left out of the boundaries because of a surveyor "error" that conveniently

excluded from the reservation the most valuable agricultural and grazing areas (Nutria and Pescado farming villages) available to the Zunis by the 1880s.

12. Ferguson, "Patterns" pp. 38–39.

13. Ibid., Map 1.

14. Geoscience Consultants, "Changes in Geomorphology, Hydrology, and Land Use on the Zuni Indian Reservation, McKinley and Cibola Counties, New Mexico, 1846–1985" (Expert testimony submitted to the United States Claims Court as evidence in the case *Zuni Indian Tribe* v. *United States*, Docket 327-81L [Ct. Cl., filed May 12, 1981]).

15. Ferguson, "Patterns."

16. E. Richard Hart, "The Zuni Mountains: Chronology of an Environmental Disaster" (Expert testimony commissioned by the Institute of the NorthAmerican West, in behalf of the Zuni Indian Tribe, for submission to the United States Claims Court in the case *Zuni Indian Tribe* v. *United States*, Dockets 327-81L and 224-84L).

17. James I. Ebert, "Historic Photographs: Photointerpretation and Photogrammetry Using Terrestrial and Aerial Photographs in and Around the Zuni Indian Reservation to Define the Nature and History of Watercourse Erosion and Forest Cutting" (Expert testimony submitted to the United States Claims Court as evidence in the case *Zuni Indian Tribe* v. *United States*, Dockets 327-81L [Ct. Cl., filed May 12, 1988] and 224-84L [Ct. Cl., filed May 3, 1984]), pp. 114–49.

18. Robert Balling, Laurence Lattman, Loren Potter, Yale Weinstein, and Stephen Wells, "Response of Department of Justice Experts to Statements Made in Justification of Legislative Settlement of Zuni Claims" (Washington, D.C.: United States Department of Justice, Environment and Natural Resources Division, 1990), pp. 33–39. This is the summary of the response commissioned by the Department of Justice to be included in testimony before the Senate Select Committee on Indian Affairs against passage of S. 2230, a bill, subsequently enacted into law in a modified version, to settle all Zuni claims of damages against the U.S. government. Sur-rebuttal Report (Defense Exhibit 19,000): "Interdisciplinary Report—Logging Issues, Zuni River/Zuni Mountain Watershed, New Mexico" (Washington D.C.: United States Department of Justice, Environment and Natural Resources Division, 1990).

19. Ricard L. Powel, "Field Notes of the Survey of the Subdivisional Lines of T. 13 N., R. 15 W.," May 29, 1881, and accompanying plat, Bureau of Land Management Archives, Santa Fe, New Mexico, pp. 81–82.

20. Zuni Land Conservation Act, 1990 (Public Law 101-486).

CHAPTER 16

Dendrochronological Dating of Alluvial Deposition and Erosion in the Zuni Area

Jeffrey S. Dean

Natural science research undertaken in connection with the Zuni land damage case had two basic objectives: (1) to document the nature, magnitude, and timing of physical damage to lands traditionally occupied by the Zunis; and (2) to assess the contribution of human activity to the recent deterioration of the environment. Dendrochronology illuminates both topics. The most direct dendrochronological approach to environmental analysis is the reconstruction of climatic variables such as annual precipitation. In addition to their intrinsic value, such retrodictions (1) provide a long-term, quantitative baseline against which the magnitude and direction of recent climatic variations can be assessed and (2) delineate possible climatic causes of other environmental changes. Reconstructions of Palmer Drought Severity Indices and summer precipitation are available in the supplementary documentation to this volume.[1] Rather than duplicate these efforts, I apply tree-ring research to another aspect of recent environmental change in the Zuni area.

When used in conjunction with geological data, dendrochronology is capable of accurately dating depositional and erosional events in the histories of alluvial floodplains.[2] In addition to contributing to an understanding of past environmental variability, the alluvial chronologies are vital to evaluating the impact of human activities on floodplain conditions. For example, specific alluvial changes can be attributed to human actions that preceded the changes but not to acts that followed them. Dendrochronological dating of erosion episodes is used to construct a chronology of alluvial events and to evaluate the possibility that these events could have been caused by the unwitting or intentional acts of human agents.

Research connected with the Zuni land damage case has identified activities of the U.S. government and private concerns that could have caused or accelerated the floodplain erosion of the last century. First,

149

extensive, unregulated logging in the Zuni Mountains depleted the natural ground cover in the headwaters of the Zuni River, which increased surface runoff, enhanced stream flow, and increased the frequency and magnitude of erosive floods.[3] Second, the forced replacement of traditional Zuni land use practices, which were well adapted to local conditions, with environmentally inappropriate Anglo farming, grazing, and water control methods exposed the Zuni River valley to erosion.[4] Third, federal dam construction on the Zuni River and its tributaries altered runoff patterns and caused damaging floods and serious erosion.[5] Particularly disastrous was the failure of Blackrock Dam in 1909, which released a flood that, if it did not actually cause downstream channel incision, certainly accelerated the erosion.

My approach to the problem of causality uses dendrochronological evidence to test the hypothesis that arroyo cutting followed large-scale Anglo logging, soil conservation, and water control activities of the late nineteenth and early twentieth centuries. Rejection of this hypothesis would establish that erosion predated, and therefore cannot be attributed to, the specified acts. Failure to reject the hypothesis would strengthen the possibility that these actions were responsible for the environmental deterioration.

Logically, it would be preferable to test the alternative hypothesis that arroyo cutting preceded 1900. Rejection of this proposition would unequivocally place erosion within the time frame of Anglo responsibility. For example, twentieth-century dates for trees rooted below the present valley surface or for buried structures would show that alluviation intervened between 1900 and the incision of the stream channel and that the extant arroyo could not have formed before 1900. Unfortunately, neither situation was discovered at Zuni, and the somewhat less satisfying hypothesis that arroyo cutting postdated 1900 must be tested.

DENDROCHRONOLOGY

Dendrochronology is "the method of employing tree-rings as a measurement of time . . . and the process of inferring past environmental conditions that existed when the rings were being formed."[6] Only the first aspect of dendrochronology (dating) is employed here. Tree-ring dates and age estimates for trees and sagebrush growing on valley margins and dissected floodplains help place temporal limits on recent erosion and deposition episodes that occurred along the Zuni River and its tributaries. The second aspect (dendroclimatology) is employed by Martin Rose and Gordon Jacoby to reconstruct past climatic variability in the Zuni area.[7]

Although dendrochronology commonly is referred to as tree-ring dating, the method is applicable to any plant that produces anatomically distinct rings at the rate of one ring per year and whose radial growth is controlled by the same environmental factors that regulate tree growth. Sagebrush (*Artemisia*) meets these criteria,[8] and, unless specifically qualified, statements about trees in the following discussion apply also to sagebrush.

Although the age of a tree can be determined by counting the annual rings visible in the cross-section of the trunk, absolute dating of tree rings is achieved through crossdating.[9] In this chapter, crossdating involves the matching of identical patterns of ring-width variation among ring series from different trees. Averaging many different crossdated ring series produces composite, or master, ring chronologies that record annual variation in ring widths with each value dated to the year in which it was produced.[10] A wood sample of unknown age is absolutely dated by finding the unique point where its ring-width pattern crossdates that of a master chronology. Once a match has been achieved, every ring in the sample is assigned to the year in which it was grown, and under ideal circumstances the exact years of tree germination and death are determined.

GEOLOGICAL TREE-RING DATING

Although tree-ring dating is most commonly linked with archaeology, it is applied here to geological events associated with alluvial deposition and erosion. The first tree-ring placement of alluvium was accomplished by James Lewis Giddings, who in 1937 crossdated spruce trunks rooted in silt deposits near Fairbanks, Alaska.[11] Early attempts at alluvial tree-ring dating in the Southwest by Lionel Brady on the Rio de Flag and Ernst Antevs in Tsegi Canyon failed because of the poor quality of the wood samples.[12] In the 1940s, John Hack applied tree-ring dates from buried archaeological features to the enclosing sediments.[13] Following these pioneering efforts, Southwestern alluvial dendrochronology languished until 1972, when dead and living trees buried in and growing on the floodplain of a tributary of Dinnebito Wash were absolutely dated. Tree-ring dates from this and other "buried forests" provide an alluvial chronology for the last 600 years on the southern Colorado Plateau.[14]

The geological processes of floodplain aggradation and erosion combine with the biological processes of tree germination, establishment, and growth to create situations in which tree-ring dates accurately date events in the histories of floodplains. Southwestern drainages are characterized by periods of sediment accumulation (alluviation or aggradation) alternating with intervals of erosion and arroyo cutting (degradation).[15]

Aggradation is generally accompanied by rising alluvial water tables and degradation by falling groundwater levels.[16] These processes have produced a widely distributed set of floodplain features, including deep alluvial deposits, buried erosion channels and soil horizons, erosional and depositional terraces, and integrated systems of deep arroyos.

The relationships between floodplain features and tree-ring dates result from the germination and growth of trees on stable floodplain surfaces, that is, surfaces that are neither eroding nor aggrading. Seeds are not likely to germinate or seedlings to survive on surfaces that are being scoured by floods, buried by alluviation, or stripped by erosion. Furthermore, trees do not survive when the root zone is saturated by high alluvial groundwater levels. Trees invade valley floors after the surfaces have stabilized and after the water table has dropped far enough to ensure aeration of the root zone.

Because trees normally invade valley floors soon after these surfaces have stabilized, living trees provide minimal ages for the topographic features on which they are growing. Stabilization of a particular surface — terrace, arroyo bank, or floodplain — cannot have occurred later than the age of the oldest tree rooted on that surface. For example, the presence of fifty-year-old trees on an alluvial surface establishes that the arroyo enclosing the surface existed prior to 1940 and also that the surface had stabilized by that date.

Germination is the datable event in a tree's life that is most directly related to erosional and depositional events. This relationship derives from the tree's association with a particular topographic or stratigraphic surface. Germination marks the establishment of a tree on the surface in question, and the germination date provides an accurate estimate of when the surface became stable enough to support permanent tree cover. Thus, the tree-ring dates of primary interest here are those relevant to tree germination.

Two dates, which represent the time span of the rings present on the sample, are routinely supplied for each dated specimen. The first date applies to the innermost ring on the sample, which can be either the initial (pith) ring or a later ring when the inner part of the sample is missing. Because the base of a tree is older than the top, the nearer a sample is to the roots, the closer the pith date is to the germination date. When the pith ring cannot be absolutely dated because of anomalous ring growth, its date is approximated by counting the rings between the pith ring and the first dated ring.

A pith date establishes an upper time limit for the germination of a tree; that is, the tree must have germinated in or before the year of the pith ring. This ring, however, can only rarely be surely identified as the very first ring produced by the tree; therefore, the pith date is a highly accurate estimator of germination date. The accuracy of this estimate is enhanced by sampling the tree as close to the roots as possible. When this is done, germination is unlikely to have occurred more than one or two years prior to the pith date. When the inner growth rings cannot be crossdated, germination precedes the estimated pith date by zero to an unknown number of years.

The second date supplied for each sample is that of the outermost ring. When the sample includes the exterior surface of the trunk, this date specifies the last year in which the tree was alive. Since nearly all the trees and shrubs examined for the Zuni case were alive when sampled, most of the outermost rings date to the year, 1984, in which the sampling was done. Clearly, this date is irrelevant to dating past geological events. Therefore, except for the dating of a buried archaeological feature, outermost ring dates are not considered further.

Living-tree samples that fail to date against a master chronology are useful for geological dating, even though absolute calendar dates cannot be assigned to them. A sample's failure to match a master chronology can be due to any one of three factors. "Complacent" samples lack the ring-width variability necessary to establish a link with a master sequence. "Erratic" samples exhibit extreme ring-width variability that cannot be crossmatched with a master sequence. Finally, some samples have too few rings to specify a single, unique match with a master chronology. Undated living-tree samples are still useful because the date of the outermost ring—that is, the year of collection—is known. Subtracting the number of counted rings from the collection year yields an approximate "date" for the innermost ring. Although not dendrochronologically valid, an estimated pith date derived in this fashion from a fairly young (less than 100 years) tree is a good indicator of the germination date. Germination could not have occurred after the estimated pith date or more than a few years before that date.

Sometimes it is necessary to correct for removal of a sample's pith area by decay, weathering, or breaking. In such cases, a pith date is estimated by adding the number of rings judged to have been in the missing portion of the sample to the number of rings counted in the existing part. Estimated pith dates are at best rough approximations of the true germination dates.

TREE-RING DATING OF FLOODPLAIN EROSION
IN THE ZUNI AREA

Dendrochronology's contribution to understanding the recent alluvial history of the Zuni area lies in the dating of successive geological events

events that produced the floodplain configuration that now character-izes the area. Tree-ring dates and age estimates from living trees grow-ing on various land surfaces associated with these floodplains pertain to the stabilization of the surfaces, subsidence of alluvial groundwa-ter levels, and sequential episodes of channel incision. The relevance of the dates and age estimates to these events lies in the associations between the sampled trees and the topographic features and in the high accuracy, precision, and resolution of tree-ring dates and age estimates.

The tree-ring samples were collected in conjunction with Stephen A. Hall's geological research in the Zuni area.[17] The tree-ring dates are tied to his analysis and can be understood only by reference to the stratigraphic cross-sections presented in his expert testimony. Rather than duplicate these illustrations here, they are referenced collectively.[18] The reader should consult the figure or figures pertinent to each study locality.

Site Selection and Sample Collection

Sample collection was designed to optimize the relevance of the tree-ring dates and ages to the chronological placement of various features of the study localities. Geological considerations predominated in Hall's selec-tion of sampling loci. Choice of location was governed by the extent of the exposure, degree of erosion, clarity of stratigraphic relationships, rele-vance of the section to the general alluvial history of the area, and presence of trees or sagebrush associated with relevant features of the floodplain. Hall thoroughly documented topographic and stratigraphic relationships and the associations between the terrain features and the sampled plants. Every attempt was made to sample the oldest trees and shrubs to achieve the maximum age possible for the surfaces.

Collection of samples was performed in two stages. First, Hall and I visited several localities on Galestina, Bosson, and Cheama Washes that Hall had identified as potentially informative on the erosional history of the area. Using principles of tree selection developed during previous geological studies on the Colorado Plateau, we sampled several living trees at the Galestina Wash 2 locality and conferred on future sampling at the Cheama and Bosson Wash localities. In addition, we collected charcoal specimens from roasting pits exposed in the arroyo banks of Bosson and Cheama Washes. During the second stage, Hall did the collecting using tree selection criteria developed during the first stage.

Field procedures involved the removal of study samples from tar-get trees and shrubs and the careful documentation of their geolog-ical relationships. Samples were taken as close as possible to the bases of the plants to ensure that the pith dates provided the best possible estimates of germination dates. Ponderosa pine trees were cored. Other trees and sagebrush were sampled by removing cross-sections from the bases of the stems.

Sample Analysis

Thirty-five geological samples and eight archaeological samples from roasting pits buried in floodplain alluvium were analyzed at the Laboratory of Tree-Ring Research at the University of Arizona in Tucson. A thirty-sixth geological sample (field number [FN] 29) was lost in transit. Standard dendrochronological techniques were employed in the analysis of this material.[19] Samples were skeleton plotted, and the plots were dated against the Cibola master tree-ring chronology.[20] Many samples could not be dated because of short, complacent, or erratic ring sequences. In such cases, ring counts were made to determine minimum ages for the plants. On completion of the analysis, the samples were added to the laboratory's permanent collections.

Results of the analysis of the geological and archaeological tree-ring samples are presented in Tables 16.1 and 16.2. The "Provenience" column of these tables lists the sampling localities, whose exact locations are given in Hall's chapter. "Spec. Number" is the tree-ring laboratory's catalog designation. "Species" abbreviations are "JUN" for juniper (*Juniperus*), "PNN" for piñon (*Pinus edulis*), "PP" for ponderosa pine (*Pinus ponderosa*), "Populus" for cottonwood (*Populus*), and "Sage" for sagebrush (*Artemisia*). "Form" specifies the nature of the sample: wood, charcoal, section, core, or fragments. An "X" in the "Cutting Date" column indicates that the terminal growth ring could be assigned an absolute date through crossdating. The "Dating" column lists the "Inside" and "Outside" dates that apply, respectively, to the innermost and outermost rings of those samples that were absolutely dated. The symbols accompanying these dates are explained in Table 16.3. "Not dated" in this column means that crossdating with a master chronology could not be achieved. The "Remarks" column contains data such as field number, nature of the ring series, number of rings if not dated, presence or absence of pith ring and bark, estimate of the number of rings in missing parts of the sample, and estimated germination date.

Evaluation of the Geological Tree-Ring Dates

Following Hall's organization of the data by drainage and site, I present the dendrochronological implications of the dates and tree ages relative to the terrain features with which they are associated. Field numbers are given along with the catalog numbers to facilitate comparison with Hall's

Table 16.1. Geological Tree-Ring Samples from the Zuni Indian Reservation, Northwestern New Mexico

Provenience	Spec Number	Species	Form	Cutting Date	Dating Inside	Dating Outside	Remarks
Bosson Wash, Locality 1	ZUN-841	JUN	Wood Sec	na		Not dated	FN 31. Erratic; false rings. Approximately 84 rings. Bark and pith. Germinated approximately 84 years before sampling: ca. 1900.
Bosson Wash, Locality 2 Terrace 1	ZUN-846	JUN	Wood Sec	x	1916 ± p−1984cB		FN 36. False rings. Dated from 1984 to 1940; ring count from 1940 to pith. Germinated before 1916.
Bosson Wash, Locality 3 Terrace 1	ZUN-827	Sage	Wood Sec	na		Not dated	FN 14. 6 rings. Bark and pith. Germinated at least 6 years before sampling: 1978.
Terrace 1/2	ZUN-830	JUN	Wood Sec	na		Not dated	FN 10. Erratic. 49 rings. Bark and pith. Germinated at least 49 years before sampling: 1935.
Terrace 2	ZUN-824	Sage	Wood Sec	na		Not dated	FN 11. 13 rings. Bark present. Estimated 1 or 2 additional rings to pith. Germinated at least 15 years before sampling: 1969.
	ZUN-825	Sage	Wood Sec	na		Not dated	FN 12. 12 rings. Pith and bark. Germinated at least 12 years before sampling: 1972.
	ZUN-826	Sage	Wood Sec	na		Not dated	FN 13. 13 rings. Bark and pith. Germinated at least 13 years before sampling: 1971.
Terrace 3	ZUN-828	Sage	Wood Sec	na		Not dated	FN 15. 9-11 rings. Bark and pith. Germinated at least 9–11 years before sampling: 1973–1975.

Provenience	Spec Number	Species	Form	Cutting Date	Dating Inside	Outside	Remarks
Bosson Wash, Locality 4 Terrace 2/3	ZUN-831	JUN	Wood Sec	x	1944p–1984cB		FN 16. Germinated no later than 1944.
Terrace 3	ZUN-829	Sage	Wood Sec	na	Not dated		FN 17. 10 rings. Bark and pith. Germinated at least 10 years before sampling: 1974.
Bosson Wash, Locality 5 Terrace 1	ZUN-842	JUN	Wood Sec	na	Not dated		FN 32. Erratic. 25 rings. Bark; pith area rotted away. Germinated more than 25 years before sampling: before 1959.
Terrace 2	ZUN-843	JUN	Wood Sec	na	Not dated		FN 33. Erratic; false rings. Approximately 48 rings. Bark and pith. Germinated approximately 48 years before sampling: ca. 1936.
Bosson Wash, Locality 6 Valley Slope	ZUN-844	JUN	Wood Sec	x	1638 ± p–1984rB		FN 34. False rings. Dated from 1984 to 1700; ring count from 1700 in to pith. Germinated before 1638.
	ZUN-845	JUN	Wood Sec	x	1788p–1984cB		FN 35. Germinated no later than 1788.
Nutria River Locality Terrace 1	ZUN-814	Populus	Wood Sec	na	Not dated		FN 30. Complacent. 39 rings. Bark and pith. Germinated at least 39 years before sampling: 1945.
Galestina Wash, Locality 1 Terrace 1	ZUN-832	JUN	Wood Sec	na	Not dated		FN 18. Erratic. 46 rings. Bark and pith. Germinated at least 46 years before sampling: 1938.
	ZUN-833	JUN	Wood Sec	na	Not dated		FN 19. Erratic. 52 rings. Bark and pith. Tree germinated at least 52 years before sampling: 1932.

continued

Table 16.1 (continued).

Provenience	Spec Number	Species	Form	Cutting Date	Dating		Remarks
					Inside	Outside	
Galestina Wash, Locality 2 Terrace 1	ZUN-804	PP	Wood Core	na	Not dated		FN 7. Complacent. 43 rings. Bark. Estimated 1 or 2 additional rings to pith. Germinated at least 45 years before sampling: 1939.
	ZUN-805	PP	Wood Core	na	Not dated		FN 8. Complacent. 43 rings. Bark. Estimated 1 or 2 additional rings to pith. Germinated at least 45 years before sampling: 1939.
	ZUN-835	JUN	Wood Sec	na	Not dated		FN 22. Complacent. 55 rings. Bark and pith. Germinated at least 55 years before sampling: 1929.
	ZUN-836	JUN	Wood Sec	×	1925p	1984cB	FN 23. Germinated no later than 1925.
	ZUN-837	JUN	Wood Sec	×	1932p	1984cB	FN 24. Germinated no later than 1932.
Terrace 2	ZUN-807	PP	Wood Core	na	Not dated		FN 5. Complacent. 55 rings. Bark. Estimated 1 or 2 additional rings to pith. Germinated at least 57 years before sampling: 1927.
	ZUN-810	PP	Wood Core	na	Not dated		FN 6. Complacent. 55 rings. Bark and pith. Break in sample may throw ring count off by 1 or 2 years. Germinated at least 57 years before sampling: 1927.
	ZUN-815	JUN	Wood Sec	na	Not dated		FN 21. Erratic. 57 rings. Bark and pith. Germinated at least 57 years before sampling: 1927.
	ZUN-838	JUN	Wood Sec	×	1928p	1984cB	FN 25. Germinated no later than 1928.

Provenience	Spec Number	Species	Form	Cutting Date	Dating Inside	Outside	Remarks
	ZUN-813	JUN	Wood Sec	na	Not dated		FN 26. Complacent. 49 rings. Bark and pith. Germinated at least 49 years before sampling: 1935.
	ZUN-839	JUN	Wood Sec	x	1925p	1984cB	FN 27. Germinated no later than 1925.
	ZUN-840	PNN	Wood Sec	x	1923p	1984cB	FN 28. Germinated no later than 1923.
Terrace 2/3	ZUN-808	PP	Wood Core	na	Not dated		FN 4. Complacent. 57 rings. Bark. Estimated 1 or 2 additional rings to pith. Germinated at least 59 years before sampling: 1925.
Terrace 3	ZUN-806	PP	Wood Core	na	Not dated		FN 9. Complacent. 31 rings. Bark and pith. Germinated at least 31 years before sampling: 1953.
	ZUN-834	JUN	Wood Sec	na	Not dated		FN 20. Erratic. At least 65 rings. Bark and pith. Germinated at least 65 years before sampling: 1919.
	ZUN-811	JUN	Wood Sec	na	Not dated		FN 3. Erratic. 55 rings. Bark and pith. Germinated at least 55 years before sampling: 1929.
	ZUN-812	JUN	Wood Sec	na	Not dated		FN 2. Erratic. 52 rings. Bark and pith. Germinated at least 52 years before sampling: 1932.
Tributary Channel	ZUN-809	PP	Wood Core	na	Not dated		FN 1. Complacent. 33 rings. Bark. Estimated 1 or 2 additional rings to pith. Germinated at least 35 years before sampling: 1949.

Table 16.2. Tree-Ring Samples from Buried Roasting Pit, Cheama Wash, Zuni Indian Reservation, Northwestern New Mexico

Provenience	Spec Number	Species	Form	Cutting Date	Dating		Remarks
					Inside	Outside	
	ZUN-820	PNN	Charcoal Fragment	No	1428–1550 + vv		No FN.
	ZUN-819	PNN	Charcoal Fragment	No	1383–1551 + vv		No FN.
	ZUN-817	PNN	Charcoal Fragment	No	1405–1562 + vv		No FN.
	ZUN-818	PNN	Charcoal Fragment	No	1456 ± p–1589 + + vv		No FN. Ring count from pith to 1466; ring count from 1580 to outside ring.
	ZUN-821	PNN	Charcoal Fragment	No	1533–1695 + + vv		No FN. Ring count from 1665 to outside ring.
	ZUN-816	PNN	Charcoal Fragment	No	1512 ± p–1719 + vv		No FN. Ring count from pith to 1530.

Table 16.3. Tree-Ring Research Symbols

Symbols used with the "Inside" date

p   The innermost ring on the sample is the pith ring.
± p   The innermost ring on the sample is the pith ring, but an exact date
         cannot be assigned to it because of the difficult nature of the ring series
         near the center of the sample.
∅   No symbol indicates that the innermost ring is not the pith ring.

Symbols used with the "Outside" date

B   Bark is present indicating that the outermost ring is the last ring pro-
         duced by the tree before dying or being sampled.
c   The outermost ring is continuous around the complete circumference of
         a full cross-section.
r   The outermost ring is continuous around the outer surface of a sample
         that represents less than a full cross-section.
v   Indicates a subjective judgment on the part of the dendrochronologist
         that the outermost ring is close to the actual terminal ring produced by
         the tree.
vv   Indicates that there is no evidence as to how far the outermost ring is
         from the actual terminal ring.
+   Indicates that the nature of the dating is such that one or more rings may
         be locally absent near the end of the ring series and that their presence
         or absence cannot be verified because the sample does not possess
         enough additional rings to provide an adequate check.
+ +   A ring count was necessary because the ring series of the sample
         cannot be matched with that of a master chronology beyond a certain
         point.

stratigraphic illustrations. Terraces are numbered from lowest (latest) to
highest (earliest) at each locality; therefore, number identities do not
denote contemporaneity.

Bosson Wash Locality 1. Sample ZUN 841 (FN 31) is rooted on a terrain
feature distinct from the floodplain and the arroyo. Therefore, its estimated germination date indicates only that juniper trees were present in
this locality by around A.D. 1900 at the latest. Such trees could have served
as seed sources for the colonization of the floodplain once it had stabilized
after the onset of arroyo cutting.

Bosson Wash Locality 2. Sample ZUN 846 (FN 36) was crossdated from
the bark back to 1940, inside which a count added fourteen rings to
produce an estimated date of 1916. It is unlikely that this tree germinated
much before 1916, and the first terrace on which it is growing must have
stabilized by that year. Erosion that produced the deep channel below this
tree probably began before 1916, but no dendrochronological estimate of
when it reached its present depth is possible.

Bosson Wash Locality 3. This locus produced six samples from juniper trees and sagebrush growing on four topographic surfaces. The estimated germination date of ZUN 830 (FN 10) indicates that the arroyo face between the first and second terraces, on which this juniper tree is rooted, predates 1935. In fact, erosion down to the level of the first terrace probably also predates 1935 because the arroyo bank above it is unlikely to have stabilized until active downcutting had ceased.

Superficially, the estimated germination dates of five sagebrush associated with the three terraces seem too recent to contribute much to the dating of geological events. In fact, these ages may reflect a recent sagebrush invasion of valley floors, perhaps as a result of grazing. Sagebrush, however, does not normally grow where the water table is close to the surface. Therefore, the estimated germination age of ZUN 827 (FN 14) may indicate that the groundwater level dropped away from the first terrace only a few years before 1978 and that the present inner channel was incised not long before 1978 as well. If so, this is the latest tree-ring dated downcutting episode in the Zuni area.

Bosson Wash Locality 4. The pith date of ZUN 831 (FN 16) indicates that the second and third terraces and the arroyo faces above them had stabilized by 1944 or slightly earlier. Stabilization of these surfaces was probably associated with the channeling that formed the first terrace; therefore, the arroyo between the second and first terraces probably preceded 1944 as well. The estimated sagebrush germination age of 1974 (ZUN 829 [FN 17]) contributes nothing to dating the arroyo cutting at this locality.

Bosson Wash Locality 5. Estimated germination ages based on ring counts are consistent with the morphology of the channel cross-section at this locus. The second terrace stabilized prior to 1936 (ZUN 843 [FN 33]), probably as a result of the incision of the channel separating the second and first terrace levels. The size and curvature of the rings near the inside of ZUN 842 (FN 32), which lacks the pith area, suggest that this tree germinated no more than ten years before 1959. Thus, the first terrace had stabilized by around 1950, an event that probably accompanied the cutting of the channel that currently forms the arroyo bottom.

The dendrochronological picture is particularly clear at this locality. The first and second arroyo cutting episodes preceded 1936, the former by an unknown number of years, the latter by no more than a few years. Between about 1936 and 1950, the arroyo floor lay at the level of the first terrace. After about 1950, the channel cut to its present maximum depth at this locus.

Bosson Wash Locality 6. Two trees, ZUN 844 (FN 34) and 845 (FN 35), produced pith dates significantly earlier than any of the other Zuni study trees. Both these trees grew on the slopes above the present valley floor and are irrelevant to the dating of floodplain events. They do, however, establish the presence since 1640 of juniper trees that could have supplied seeds for the colonization of the floodplains. The absence of junipers from the floodplains after that date must therefore be attributed to floodplain conditions rather than to a lack of seed sources.

Nutria River Locality. Since cottonwood trees rarely fail to produce one ring per year, the count of thirty-four rings undoubtedly yields an accurate pith date for ZUN 814 (FN 30). This tree germinated a few years before 1945, probably on the active floodplain of the Nutria River, which then flowed at the level of the present first terrace. Downcutting to this level obviously preceded that date, and incision of the present channel followed 1945. Alternatively, this cottonwood may have germinated on the first terrace after the arroyo had achieved its present configuration, in which case all features predated 1945. In either case, major incision of the Nutria River at this locality occurred before 1945.

Galestina Wash Locality 1. Estimated germination dates of two junipers, ZUN 832 (FN 18) and 833 (FN 19), establish 1932 as the latest possible date for the erosion that produced the first terrace at this locus. The trees probably did not germinate until after the water table dropped when the present arroyo floor was formed. Thus, it is likely that both instances of channel incision preceded 1932.

Galestina Wash Locality 2. Estimated germination dates and topographic relationships of fourteen trees growing along a short reach of Galestina Wash reveal the present channel configuration to have been produced by a rapid series of erosion events. An estimated date for a juniper tree (ZUN 834 [FN 20]) growing inside the ruin of a Zuni field house on the third terrace is relevant to two events, one historical, one geological. First, for the tree to have germinated inside the ruin, the house must have been vacated and partially dismantled or fallen into disrepair by 1919. Second, because structures are rarely built on active floodplains, stabilization of this level of the valley floor must have preceded 1919. Since stabilization is commonly associated with channel incision, initial arroyo cutting also probably occurred before 1919. The field house may have been abandoned in response to field destruction by the incision of the present arroyo.

The erosion associated with the pre-1919 stabilization of the third terrace removed a tremendous amount of alluvium in a short time to produce the broad, deep arroyo now present in this locality. That this erosion was complete by 1923 is shown by an estimated germination date from a piñon tree (ZUN 840 [FN 28]) rooted on the second terrace some seven meters below the surface of the third terrace. This estimated germination date is based on a dendrochronological pith date, which means that germination did not precede 1923 by more than a couple of years. Estimated germination dates of six juniper trees (ZUN 807,

810, 813, 815, 838, and 839 [FN 5, 6, 26, 21, 25, and 27]) growing on the second terrace and of a ponderosa pine tree (ZUN 808 [FN 4]) rooted on the arroyo face separating the third and second terraces range from 1925 to 1935 and support the dating of the second terrace by ZUN 840 (FN 28). Given that the tree species involved do not colonize flood-plains until the water table has drained away from the surface, the erosion that produced the arroyo floor represented by the first terrace probably also dates to the early 1920s. This inference is confirmed by an estimated germination date of 1925, which is based on an actual pith date for ZUN 836 (FN 23), a juniper tree rooted on the floor of the old arroyo channel (Terrace 1). The three junipers (ZUN 835–837 [FN 22–24]) growing on this feature could neither have germinated nor survived there while it was an active streambed; therefore, they must have germinated after the stream migrated horizontally several meters eastward, cut off the original channel, and left it susceptible to arboreal colonization. This old channel never experienced significant stream flow after its surface stabilized around 1923.

Yet another episode of downcutting produced the present arroyo floor. Estimated germination dates of two ponderosa pine trees (ZUN 804 and 805 [FN 7 and 8]) growing on the first terrace adjacent to the most recent channel indicate that this surface stabilized a few years before 1939. This stabilization was probably associated with the cutting of the present channel, which can also be dated to around 1939.

Dendrochronological data provide a tight chronology of the major erosional events that produced the extant cross-section of the Galestina Wash arroyo at this location. During the nineteenth century, a floodplain that probably extended all the way across the valley and a fairly high alluvial water table supported fields tilled in the traditional Zuni fashion. Sometime before 1919, rapid erosion dissected the floodplain, and by 1923 an arroyo more than 100 meters wide and around seven meters deep had been incised into the sediments of the valley floor. Removal of the sediments combined with depression of alluvial groundwater levels would have destroyed the agricultural potential of the valley floor while at the same time rendering it suitable for colonization by juniper trees. Downcutting paused briefly at the second terrace level but resumed by 1923. By 1925 downcutting had produced a smaller channel within the main arroyo. Also by 1925, the stream had moved laterally far enough to cut off a portion of the original inner channel and create an environment there for the germination and survival of junipers. No later than 1939, further incision lowered the streambed to its present level and left the former arroyo floor as a first terrace. Since that time, downcutting and groundwater subsidence sufficient to prepare new surfaces for arboreal invasion have not occurred at this locality.

Cheama Wash Locality. Tree-ring dates from charcoal in a roasting pit buried to a depth of 30 to 100 centimeters in the alluvium of Cheama Wash establish a lower temporal limit for the intrusion of this feature into the floodplain. Dating an archaeological feature such as this pit depends on the dates of the outer, rather than inner, rings of the samples. This is so because the death, rather than the germination, of a tree is most closely associated with the human activity that produced the feature. A piece of wood cannot be used for fuel before the tree has died. Therefore, the last utilization of the Cheama Wash roasting pit postdated 1719. Given that this noncutting date may not represent the last year of the tree's life and that dead wood is commonly utilized for fuel, the pit could have been used some years after 1719, perhaps as late as 1750–1800.[21] Minimally, however, the ground surface from which the roasting pit was dug must predate 1719, and the postpit sediments deposited on that surface must postdate 1719. Thus, nearly one meter of alluviation occurred in the late eighteenth and/ or early nineteenth century.

Summary of Dating

In the aggregate, estimated germination dates of trees associated with various floodplain surfaces in the Zuni area fail to exhibit the patterning that should result from synchronous episodes of channel incision and surface stabilization. There is little dendrochronological evidence that terrain surfaces within the modern arroyos were produced by a regular sequence of erosional events common to all drainages or even to different loci within single drainages. Instead, the dates suggest that, once initiated, arroyo cutting progressed in a somewhat discontinuous manner within and between drainages to produce the different topographic expressions represented by the channel cross-sections at the study loci. Although different expressions between localities is the norm, orderly progression of erosional events is evident within localities.

At the two study loci with suitable data, Bosson Wash 5 and Galestina Wash 2 (Table 16.4), earliest germination dates progress from early to late, with increasing distance of growth site beneath the level of the valley floor, exactly as would be expected if these arroyos had been produced by successive episodes of downcutting. Eleven possible instances of downcutting (erosion) and fifteen possible instances of surface stabilization (terraces and arroyo floor) can be dendrochronologically dated (Table 16.4). Seven of the former and eight of the latter predated 1944–1945. The three earliest of these events predated 1920, whereas the majority fell between 1910 and 1940.

The chronology of erosional events helps date the onset of the latest episode of arroyo cutting. Clearly, this downcutting must have preceded

Table 16.4. Tree-Ring Chronology of Terrace Stabilization and Channel Incision Events, Zuni Indian Reservation, Northwestern New Mexico

Locality	Third Terrace	Erosion	Second Terrace	Erosion	First Terrace	Erosion	Arroyo Floor
Galestina 2	1919	1919–1923	1923	1923–1925	1925	1939	1939
Bosson 4		1944	1944				
Bosson 5			1936	1936	1950	1950	1950
Bosson 3				1935	1935–1978	1978?	1978?
Bosson 2					1916	1916	
Galestina 1					1932	1932	1932
Nutria					1945	1945	1945?

the germination date of the oldest tree growing within the arroyo. Therefore, the oldest estimated germination date at a particular locality provides an upper temporal limit for the formation of the arroyo and of the floodplain into which the channel is incised. Based on this criterion, the latest possible dates for arroyo cutting at seven dendrochronologically dated localities range from 1916 to 1945 (Table 16.4). The dating establishes the widespread occurrence of deep arroyos in the Zuni area by 1936. Within this general temporal frame, only two localities produced dates contextually relevant to dating the actual inception of arroyo cutting. Initial downcutting predated 1916 at Bosson Wash 2 and occurred before 1919 at Galestina Wash 2.

Having shown that fully developed arroyos existed at several localities by the first decade of the twentieth century, dendrochronology does not place a maximum age limit on the inception of downcutting—that is, a date after which arroyo cutting must have begun. Nevertheless, some tree-ring data do bear on this issue. The presence of juniper trees adjacent to the floodplains by 1640 (ZUN 844 [FN 34]) means that seeds would have been available for colonizing the floodplains whenever these surfaces became suitable for germination and seedling survival. The evident lack of such colonization prior to the twentieth century suggests that from at least as early as 1640 to around 1900, the floodplains were unstable as a result of erosion or deposition. The post-1720 accumulation of alluvium on top of the Cheama Wash roasting pit indicates that aggradation, rather than erosion, prevented juniper invasion of the floodplains well into the nineteenth century. Only the Galestina Wash 2 locality yielded tree-ring data relevant to the earliest possible date for the onset of downcutting. If ZUN 834 (FN 20) represents as rapid an invasion of the highest (third) Galestina Wash 2 terrace as occurred on the first terrace, floodplain stabilization, water table subsidence, and arroyo development probably occurred not long before 1919.

RATE OF ARBOREAL INVASION OF STABLE
SURFACES

The tree-ring dating of alluvial events in the Zuni area is based on the
critical assumption that in localities suitable for the plant species involved,
trees rapidly invade floodplains rendered suitable for seed germination
and seedling survival by the surface stabilization and groundwater subsidence that accompany channel incision. If, however, colonization was
slow, germination dates would yield only a nebulous upper limit for the
time of surface stabilization, which could have occurred many years before
invasion by the trees.

Jacoby maintains that germination on alluvial surfaces requires favorable (wetter than normal) climatic conditions as well as advantageous
hydrological and depositional circumstances.[22] He further argues that
if factors other than surface stability cause trees and shrubs to colonize floodplains, the immediacy of the connection between stabilization
and germination is destroyed. Given these considerations, he concludes
that alluvial surfaces may be much older than the vegetation growing
on them and that plant germination dates cannot be directly applied to
these features.

The idea that floodplain colonization is due to unusually favorable
climatic conditions, rather than to the stability of the ground surface,
is contradicted by two lines of evidence. First, if woody plant colonization of floodplains reflects favorable climatic conditions, most of the
trees and shrubs now growing there should have germinated during two
unusually wet intervals indicated by both instrumented climatic records
and dendroclimatic reconstructions: 1905–1920 and 1935–1945.[23] Of the
thirty-three alluvial trees and shrubs previously analyzed, twenty-three
actually germinated during unfavorable (dry) intervals. Eight of the ten
trees that germinated during favorable climatic intervals did so during the
less favorable (1935–1945) of the two. Second, the common lack of a climate
signal in floodplain trees indicates that climate is not vital to their
establishment.

Evidence from Zuni and elsewhere contradicts the idea that stable
surfaces are much older than the oldest plants growing on them. If trees
and shrubs do not rapidly invade stabilized surfaces, there should be
no correspondence between the germination dates of the oldest plants
rooted on the surfaces and the time sequence of the surfaces. Under
such conditions, dating disparities should be common, and younger surfaces should often support plants older than the oldest plants growing on
earlier surfaces. No such reversals have been noted in all the tree-ring
dated stratigraphic sections on the Colorado Plateau or in the Zuni area
(Table 16.4).[24]

Considerable positive evidence for the assumption that arboreal plants quickly colonize newly stabilized alluvial surfaces exists. The difference of only two years in estimated germination dates for trees growing on the second and first terraces at the Galestina Wash 2 locality could result only from the immediate colonization of newly stabilized floodplain surfaces. At Klethla Valley Buried Forest 2, two juniper trees that germinated around 1900 are rooted in a channel that formed after 1880, which means that these trees must have become established on the arroyo floor almost immediately after it stabilized.[25] At Klethla Valley Buried Forest 3, juniper trees growing on an arroyo face that stabilized in the 1930s germinated in the early 1940s.[26] These considerations establish the validity of the key assumption that trees and shrubs commonly invade alluvial surfaces almost immediately after stabilization that is due to erosion and declining groundwater levels. Therefore, the geochronological inferences based on the germination dates of trees and shrubs rooted on topographic features are accurate.

COMPARISONS

Tree-ring data from eight study loci on four drainages in the Zuni area provide the basis for the chronology of erosional events that produced the present configurations of these arroyos. This tree-ring-based chronology will undoubtedly be refined by future geological and historical research in the area. At this point, however, the dendrochronological erosion chronology must be formulated independently so that it can be compared to the results of the other studies.

Tree-ring dates from a buried roasting pit on Cheama Wash indicate that alluviation occurred after 1719. This coupled with the failure of junipers to colonize the valley floors suggests that aggradation continued well into the nineteenth century. As far as can be determined dendrochronologically, the current episode of arroyo cutting at Zuni began not long before 1910. Certainly, deep channels existed by the 1910s and 1920s. Once channel incision began, downcutting continued at irregular intervals, with the majority of datable secondary erosion episodes occurring in the 1930s and 1940s. The latest securely dated channel incision probably occurred in the 1950s. Since that time, minor erosional and depositional events have failed to produce surfaces suitable for juniper colonization. Combining the tree-ring dates with a more sophisticated appreciation of the geological data, Hall independently arrived at an erosional chronology essentially identical to that presented here.[27]

The tree-ring-based chronology of erosional events is congruent with Hall's findings that "the major period of arroyo incision at Zuni occurred during the 1910s with continual scouring through the 1930s and to a lesser extent after about 1940 through to the present (1984)," with Geoscience Consultants' statement that "analysis of the aerial photographs has shown that most arroyo cutting on the Zuni Reservation occurred between about 1900 and 1934," and with historical references to severe gullying in the 1920s and 1930s.[28] Furthermore, examination of Jacoby's geological tree-ring loci disclosed no conflicts between his dates and those just outlined.[29] The congruence of five independent investigations into the timing of erosional events in the Zuni area enhances confidence in each set of results and in the general chronology of progressive channel incision that emerges from them.

The research also revealed that the alluvial chronology of the Zuni area is similar to that developed for the Colorado Plateau in general.[30] Ninth-century archaeological sites buried under more than one meter of alluvium near the Galestina Wash 2 locality testify to a stabilization of the valley floor contemporaneous with the primary hydrologic-aggradation decline between 750 and 925 identified elsewhere on the plateau. The eighteenth-century surface stabilization represented by the Cheama Wash roasting pit is probably a local expression of the secondary hydrologic-aggradation decline centered on 1700. The major episode of arroyo cutting that is placed before 1900 in the Zuni area is a local aspect of the large-scale erosion that occurred throughout the Southwest after 1880. These correspondences indicate that fluvial processes in the Zuni area were integrated into the broader geohydrological systematics that controlled alluvial processes in the Southwest.

Even though the Zuni area was subject to the same floodplain events that characterized the region as a whole, dating the onset of the current arroyo cutting to shortly before 1900 supports the contention that Anglo activities of the late nineteenth and early twentieth centuries contributed materially to the timing and magnitude of erosional damage to the Zuni valley. If these operations did not actually cause the erosion, they undoubtedly severely impacted an alluvial system poised on the brink of instability. Thus, Anglo acts that reduced the natural plant cover, increased surface runoff, and proscribed traditional Zuni land use may have initiated the downcutting and certainly exacerbated a precarious natural situation. Intensive logging in the Zuni River watershed, the construction of dams and other water control devices on the streams, and interference with traditional Zuni land use practices through the imposition of "modern" land and water management techniques altered surface runoff patterns, with disastrous consequences for a highly susceptible alluvial system. The flood caused by the failure of the Blackrock Dam in 1909 may have been the "trigger" that upset the delicately balanced alluvial system and initiated the arroyo cutting that disastrously altered the Zuni environment.

NOTES

1. Martin R. Rose, "The Present and Past Climate of the Zuni Region" (Plaintiff's Exhibit 5000; expert testimony submitted to the United States Claims Court as evidence in the case *Zuni Indian Tribe* v. *United States*, Docket 327-81L, 1985), Gordon C. Jacoby, "Dendrochronological Investigation of the Zuni Indian Reservation" (Defendant's Exhibit 14,000; expert testimony submitted to the United States Claims Court as evidence in the case *Zuni Indian Tribe* v. *United States*, Docket 327-81L, 1987).

2. Jeffrey S. Dean, "Dendrochronology and Paleoenvironmental Reconstruction on the Colorado Plateaus," in *The Anasazi in a Changing Environment*, ed. George J. Gumerman (Cambridge: Cambridge University Press, 1988), pp. 119–67; Eric T. Karlstrom and Thor N.V. Karlstrom, "Late Quaternary Alluvial Stratigraphy and Soils of the Black Mesa – Little Colorado River Areas, Northern Arizona," in *Geology of Central and Northern Arizona: Geological Society of America Rocky Mountain Section Guidebook*, ed. James D. Nations, C. M. Conway, and Gordon A. Swann (Flagstaff, Ariz.: Geological Society of America, 1986), pp. 71–92; Thor N.V. Karlstrom, "Alluvial Chronology and Hydrologic Change of Black Mesa and Nearby Regions," In *The Anasazi in a Changing Environment*, ed. George J. Gumerman (Cambridge: Cambridge University Press, 1988), pp. 45–91.

3. E. Richard Hart, "Damage to Zuni Trust Lands" (Plaintiff's Exhibit 1000; expert testimony submitted to the United States Claims Court as evidence in the case *Zuni Indian Tribe* v. *United States*, Docket 327-81L, 1985); E. Richard Hart, "The Zuni Mountains: Chronology of an Environmental Disaster" (Plaintiff's Exhibit 13,000; expert testimony submitted to the United States Claims Court, Dockets 327-81L and 224-84L, 1988). Also see Chapter 12.

4. T. J. Ferguson, "Patterns of Land Use and Environmental Change on the Zuni Indian Reservation, 1846–1985: Ethnohistorical and Archaeological Evidence" (Plaintiff's Exhibit 6000; expert testimony submitted to the United States Claims Court as evidence in the case *Zuni Indian Tribe* v. *United States*, Docket 327-81L, 1985); Richard I. Ford, "Zuni Land Use and Damage to Trust Land" (Plaintiff's Exhibit 7000; expert testimony submitted to the United States Claims Court as evidence in the case *Zuni Indian Tribe* v. *United States*, Docket 327-81L, 1985). See also Chapter 13.

5. Hart, "Damage to Zuni Trust Lands"; Geoscience Consultants, "Changes in Geomorphology, Hydrology, and Land Use on the Zuni Indian Reservation, McKinley and Cibola Counties, New Mexico, 1846–1946" (Plaintiff's Exhibit 2000; expert testimony submitted to the United States Claims Court as evidence in the case *Zuni Indian Tribe* v. *United States*, Docket 327-81L, 1985).

6. Bryant Bannister, "Dendrochronology," in *Science in Archaeology: A Comprehensive Survey of Progress and Research*, ed. Don Brothwell and Eric Higgs, rev. ed. (London: Thames and Hudson, 1969), p. 191.

7. Rose, "The Present and Past Climate"; Jacoby, "Dendrochronological Investigation."

8. Charles W. Ferguson, "Growth Rings in Woody Shrubs as Potential Aids in Archaeological Interpretation," *The Kiva* 25 (1959): 24–30; C. W. Ferguson, "Annual Rings in Big Sagebrush: *Artemesia tridentata*," Papers of the Laboratory of Tree-Ring Research, no. 1 (Tucson: University of Arizona Press, 1964).

9. Bannister, "Dendrochronology"; Jeffrey S. Dean, "Tree-Ring Dating in Archaeology," University of Utah Anthropological Papers, no. 99 (Salt Lake City: University of Utah Press, 1978), pp. 129–63.

10. Dean, "Tree-Ring Dating," pp. 136–37.

11. James L. Giddings, "Buried Wood from Fairbanks, Alaska," *Tree-Ring Bulletin* 4 (4) (1938): 3–5.

12. Lionel F. Brady, "The Arroyo of the Rio de Flag: A Study of an Erosion Cycle," *Museum Notes* 9 (1936): 33–37; Paul B. Sears, "Pollen Analysis as an Aid in Dating Cultural Deposits in the United States," in *Early Man: As Depicted by Leading Authorities at the International Symposium, the Academy of Natural Sciences, Philadelphia, March 1937,* ed. George Grant MacCurdy (London: J. B. Lippincott, 1937), pp. 61–66; Paul B. Sears, "Palynology and the Climatic Record of the Southwest," *Annals of the New York Academy of Sciences* 95 (1961): 632–41.

13. John T. Hack, "The Changing Physical Environment of the Hopi Indians of Arizona," in *Papers of the Peabody Museum of American Archaeology and Ethnology* (Cambridge, Mass.: Harvard University, 1942), vol. 35, no. 1.

14. Jeffrey S. Dean, Robert C. Euler, George J. Gumerman, Fred Plog, Richard H. Hevly, and Thor N. V. Karlstrom, "Human Behavior, Demography, and Paleoenvironment on the Colorado Plateaus," *American Antiquity* 50 (1985): 540, Fig. 1a; Robert C. Euler, George J. Gumerman, Thor N. V. Karlstrom, Jeffrey S. Dean, and Richard H. Hevly, "The Colorado Plateaus: Cultural Dynamics and Paleoenvironment," *Science* 205 (1979): 1096–97, Fig. 4; Karlstrom, "Alluvial Chronology," pp. 45–91.

15. Euler et al., "The Colorado Plateaus," pp. 1096–97.

16. Dean et al., "Human Behavior," p. 540; Eric T. Karlstrom, "Soils and Geomorphology of Northern Black Mesa," in *Excavations on Black Mesa, 1981: A Descriptive Report,* ed. F. E. Smiley, Deborah L. Nichols, and Peter P. Andrews, Center for Archaeological Investigations Research Paper, no. 36 (Carbondale: Southern Illinois University, 1983), p. 329.

17. Stephen A. Hall, "Erosion of Zuni Indian Reservation Lands" (Plaintiff's Exhibit 3000; expert testimony submitted to the United States Claims Court as evidence in the case *Zuni Indian Tribe* v. *United States,* Docket 327-81L, 1985).

18. Hall, "Erosion," Figs. 1–8, maps.

19. Marvin A. Stokes and Terah L. Smiley, *An Introduction to Tree-Ring Dating* (Chicago: University of Chicago Press, 1968), pp. 37–53.

20. Dean, "Tree-Ring Dating," pp. 144–46; Jeffrey S. Dean and William J. Robinson, *Expanded Tree-Ring Chronologies for the Southwestern United States* (Tucson: Laboratory of Tree-Ring Research, University of Arizona, 1978), pp. 33–34.

21. Dean, "Tree-Ring Dating," pp. 147–48.

22. Jacoby, "Dendrochronological Investigation," pp. 3–4.

23. Robert C. Balling, "Analysis of Zuni Indian Reservation Precipitation Patterns During the Period of Instrumental Record" (Defendant's Exhibit 15,000; expert testimony submitted to the United States Claims Court as evidence in the case *Zuni Indian Tribe* v. *United States,* Docket 327-81L, 1987), p. 64; Rose, "The Present and Past Climate," Figs. 7.2, 7.4; Jacoby, "Dendrochronological Investigation," Fig. 3.1.

24. Karlstrom, "Alluvial Chronology," pp. 70–91.

25. Ibid., p. 83, Fig. 3.11.

26. Ibid.

27. Hall, this volume; Hall, "Erosion," pp. 20–24.

28. Hall, "Erosion," p. 34; Geoscience Consultants, "Changes in Geomorphology," p. 26; Hart, "Damage."

29. Jacoby, "Dendrochronological Investigation"; Jeffrey S. Dean, "Rebuttal Report: Dendrochronological Dating of Floodplain Erosion on Zuni Indian Lands"

(Plaintiff's Exhibit 4000 [rebuttal]; expert testimony submitted to the U.S. Claims Court as evidence in the case *Zuni Indian Tribe* v. *United States,* Dockets 327-81L and 224-84L, 1989), pp. 10–13; Stephen A. Hall. "Rebuttal Report: Erosion of Zuni Indian Reservation Lands" (Plaintiff's Exhibit 3000 [rebuttal]; expert testimony submitted to the U.S. Claims Court as evidence in the case *Zuni Indian Tribe* v. *United States,* Dockets 327-81L and 224-84L, 1988).

    30. Dean et al., "Human Behavior," Fig. 1.

CHAPTER 17

Recovering the Remembered Past: Folklore and Oral History in the Zuni Trust Lands Damages Case

Andrew Wiget

Indian claims, such as those advanced by the pueblo of Zuni, have necessitated the evidentiary use of oral tradition in modern litigation. However, with few exceptions, oral tradition has been viewed only as a useful complement to documentary or archaeological evidence, both of which were deemed to be inherently more objective (Wiget 1982). Although our understanding of both archaeology and historiography has changed dramatically in the forty or so years since Indian claims cases began to be filed, this bias, as Thomas Wessell's testimony for the defendant indicates, still persists in some quarters. Oral tradition was accepted only insofar as it confirmed (or more accurately, was confirmed by) the documentary or archaeological record (Day 1972; DeLaguna 1958; Prendergast and Meighan 1959). The problem of how to substantiate claims that depend on testimonies from oral tradition is an especially serious one for traditional peoples for whom large spans of their history and large areas of their domain lack written documentation and whose conceptions of history do not always conform to Western notions (Eggan 1967).

The question is not whether data exist—testimonies of credible deponents abound—but whether the data are trustworthy enough to have evidentiary value. This concern can be reformulated as a question of method: Can one establish the reliability and validity of oral traditional testimonies, apart from any external forms of corroboration, so that one can discriminate different kinds of data in the same testimony according to their evidentiary value? In the Zuni cases, the urgent need was for a method to identify and evaluate the internal structure of an oral tradition composed of dozens of testimonies in order to develop the shared sense of the remembered past as a larger context for evaluating testimony concerning discrete data within that tradition.

The sheer quantity of the oral testimony in the Zuni case was enormous. I reviewed twenty depositions totaling nearly 1,300 pages of

testimony taken at Zuni during September 1984 in conjunction with
Dockets 327-81L and 224-84L. Some of the deponents spoke English
well; others required the assistance of an interpreter at least occasionally. The youngest was 57 at the time of deposition; the oldest, 101.
Between these extremes, the ages of the deponents ranged from 67 to
89. All could confidently remember the time of their youth, around
1910–1920. Deponents included Zuni farmers and stockmen, former tribal
councilors and governors, and the tribal governor at the time of the deposition, Robert E. Lewis. In addition, for comparison purposes, I reviewed
thirteen depositions, totaling around 550 pages, from the Aboriginal
title case, Docket 161-79L. These were useful in establishing the reliability of memory of some of those individuals who were deposed in
both cases.

Some limitations necessarily qualified my judgments. First, because
the practical constraints of this review precluded review of data gathered
by other expert witnesses, especially in the area of long-term or regional
variations in climate and erosion, I could not directly test the validity
of these testimonies with corroborating testimony of other forms. Moreover, I was deliberately isolated from the data developed and conclusions drawn by scientific experts in order to assure that my interpretations
of the oral tradition were not influenced by potentially corroborative
or contradictory information, a strategy that later proved very useful
in revealing the integrity of the tradition. Therefore, any judgments
about validity must be understood as inferences based on formal and
thematic elements in the testimonies themselves and subject to corroboration. Second, much of the usefulness of oral testimony depends
on a determination of the speaker's emphasis, derived from changes in
volume and inflection, which are impossible to get from a transcript.
Third, I played no role in structuring the lines of inquiry developed for
taking the depositions.

THE SHAPE OF THE PAST

The past, precisely because it is past, is irrecoverable. The sum of *lived-
through experiences* is inaccessible even to the subject who is the focus
of those experiences. Only incomplete records of the past are available,
the sum of which will always fall short of the sum of the lived-through
experiences. The incompleteness of the record is the result of several
factors. First, the construction of a historical record, either in memory
or on paper, is motivated by a need to share certain kinds of information
with an identifiable audience. That need to share with a particular
audience necessitates a *partial* record, compelling the inclusion of some

kinds of information and the exclusion of others. The recall of these records is also specifically motivated, and that motivation structures the past-as-remembered. Finally, the past-as-remembered only "makes sense" when it is thematized, which occurs when a temporal sequence is supplied with a motivational or causal framework. By virtue of being thus emplotted into some kind of narrative, otherwise discrete remembered elements of experience are provided a context within which they can be related to each other. These observations are as true for the documentary record as they are for the memory record and are equally applicable to written as to oral narratives. Once cannot assume, therefore, that oral records are necessarily of lesser value than written records. The majority view of most historians is best summed up by Alice Hoffman (1984: 72): "One might say that oral history is simply one among several primary sources. It is no worse than written documents. Archives are replete with self-serving documents, with edited and doctored diaries and memoranda written 'for the record.' In fact, when undertaken in the most professional way, oral histories may be superior to many written records in that there is a knowledgeable interviewer present accurately seeking to promote the best record attainable." The usefulness of any historical record, then, depends on understanding the ways in which the motives of its maker and the circumstances of its construction have shaped the record.

Three tasks must be accomplished in order to effectively address these issues. First, the depositions must be evaluated in terms of the degree of veracity exhibited by the deponents, which reflects on the motives and circumstances behind the record as recalled. Second, the form of the testimonies must be evaluated in terms of their validity, reliability, and consistency in order to establish the shape of past-as-remembered at Zuni, which reflects on the record as stored. Third, a particular tradition, called here the Zuni "golden age," must be extensively analyzed, which reflects on the motives and circumstances surrounding the record as constructed.

VERACITY OF THE ZUNI DEPONENTS

Evaluation of oral testimony taken in depositions must begin with the assumption that in whatever circumstances, the purpose for which the deposition is taken shapes the testimony by forcing on the deponent a concern for "relevance," which is further focused by the interrogatory nature of the examination process. A deponent is never absolutely free to order his recollections as he wishes but concedes much of this to external direction. Consequently, it is significant that so many of the testimonies feature explicit statements or dialogic strategies that indicate that the deponents have formed some "settled sense" of the past, the shape of which they are not willing to alter. Despite the pressures exerted by the questioner, this settled sense of the past often motivates the deponent's reluctance to volunteer some kinds of information:

> Q: Were there roads constructed on the reservation prior to 1946 that caused similar problems?
> A: Well, I guess in some areas it does, but where I am up there, that's about the only road that was put out by water that I know of. But I think in some parts of the reservation, of course, I don't go all over the reservation to know. That wasn't my job anyway. (Eriacho 29)

Concern that counsel understand the limits of the deponent's knowledge is especially acute in the testimony of Dempsey Kanteena (1984), who insists he can testify only to what he saw while on the reservation from 1931 to 1947. Sometimes this concern for the nature of the truth to which one is testifying takes more subtle forms, as in this portion of Sol Ondelacy's testimony, where the shift from eyewitness reportage to speculation is signaled by the introduction of the verb *imagine*.

> Q: Was there anything that you've seen recently, have you been up there in the last few months?
> A: Oh, I've been up there I don't know how many times, but then I've seen that was there and noticed it a while ago, since back in around about '40, I think that was about the last time I went up there and picked up—harvest the corn from my aunt's, where they had the field. It's been that way ever since, but I imagine its been slowly cutting it down every year or every raining season, when there's a lot of rain that comes on the top of the mesa, Galestina Mesa, I imagine there would be a lot of water coming through that wash.

The recollected past also has nebulous areas at its margins, which a reflective witness will hesitate to enter:

> Q: We were just trying to locate where it was you were grazing sheep. You said it was way up in the canyon—
> A: Yes sir, over clear down to the Navajo Reservation. I was—I grazed all over.
> Q: Sure; now, when—when did you—or where did you see this big arroyo that you were talking about?
> A: Well, when I was herding sheep, that was around 1937, '39, I remember that a little bit then. (Harker 23–24)

The settled sense of the past may be contradicted by the implications of counsel's questions, as when Sol Ondelacy (122–30) disputes the Justice Department defense attorney's leading questions about the locations of the original watercourse and the subsequent Bureau of Indian Affairs channel in Bosson Wash near the highway.

THE FORM OF THE TRADITION

Although it appears from the depositions that Zuni deponents are unlikely to alter or fabricate a past in response to the perceived demands of the questioning attorney, nevertheless a question remains concerning the integrity and value of the remembered record offered as evidence in deposition. The question focuses on the familiar criteria of validity, reliability, and consistency.

Validity

According to Alice Hoffman (1984: 70), director of the Oral History Program at Pennsylvania State University, validity refers to "the degree of conformity between reports of the event and the event itself as recorded in other primary source material such as documents, photographs, diaries and letters." Insofar as validity is a measure of external corroboration, it was not measurable within the constraints set out for this review. I was purposely prohibited from reviewing other forms of evidentiary material in order to safeguard the integrity of my interpretations of oral traditions in the depositions. There are enough corroborative points in the depositions, however, that validity could easily be measured. These would include specific dates, such as that given for the big snow of the early 1930s or of the first grasshopper infestation at Nutria as well as dates for the terms of tribal officials or of construction projects. By trying to corroborate these with physical evidence from climatology, hydrology, and geomorphology, for instance, one ought to be able to test some generalizations as well as specific dates. These generalizations would include assertions about a period of decreasing rainfall after the big snow or about the size of arroyos in a person's youth. In regard to the latter, however, a phenomenon must acquire a certain significance, through size, frequency, rarity, or other factors, before it becomes memorable. Memorableness, in other words, is relative, and a certain "threshold of awareness" must be achieved before something is deemed remarkable enough to be remembered. The testimonies bear witness to phenomena after they have achieved that threshold. Thus, arroyo cutting may have, indeed probably did, begin a little earlier than testified to. Similarly, rainfall may have decreased considerably during the 1930s, not in an absolute sense but relative to the informant's memory of the 1920s.

Reliability

Reliability is defined by Hoffman (1984: 70) as "the consistency with which an individual will tell the same story about the same events on the different occasions." Reliability is a function of replicability. Because few deponents were asked to address the same issue again in cross-examination, I examined reliability by comparing testimonies from those few individuals who had been deposed in both the present Zuni trust lands damages case and the aboriginal title case, Docket 161-79L. The purpose here was to check the degree of reliability when reporting the same information on two occasions five years apart. This is an important consideration because oral historians generally concede that forms of testimony that are structured by a number of culture-specific rules are generally more reliable (not necessarily more valid) than forms less structured by cultural requirements, such as elicited testimony.

Of the four individuals who testified in both cases, only the depositions of Frank Vacit elicit no correlatable material. In both cases, Sefferino Eriacho refers to the fall roundups formerly held in the Fence Lake area, even invoking for the benefit of counsel the same frame of reference: the roundup as portrayed in Western movies, complete with chuckwagon. In the earlier deposition Eriacho recalls that his parents had about 800 head of cattle (16), a figure that rises to 900 in the second deposition (9–10). Fred Bowannie, however, testifies earlier that his father had about 50 head of livestock, but in the second deposition that number drops to 35. Chester Mahooty testifies in the aboriginal title case that there were "no problems" with livestock damaging farm crops. It is unclear whether "no problems" means that such situations never happened or that, having happened, they were always happily resolved. He does attribute this harmonious relationship between farmer and stockman, however, to the fact that in the old days people lived according to prayers (38). In the trust lands deposition, he indicates that such problems did happen but that they were resolved in the customary way: by having the stockman provide an animal as compensation for the damaged crops (37–38). The discrepancy between these two responses, it seems to me, is only apparent. I am inclined to read the first testimony in the second of the two ways suggested. The appearance of discrepancy is attributable to the context of elicitation, which stresses the sacredness of custom and tradition in the Zuni title case and traditional Zuni conservation practices in the second case. These few instances are the only examples of correlatable material and are not sufficient to establish any kind of pattern. However, the degree of change is relatively small, and there are no signs of exaggeration, both of which are somewhat remarkable when the information being recalled is nearly eighty years old.

Consistency

Consistency may be defined as the degree to which the form or content of one testimony conforms with other testimonies. It differs from reliability by being a measure of conformity between, rather than within, traditions. The testimonies show that consistency varies in relation to the different forms that the elicited testimony takes. Testimony for which absolute dating is sought for a singular event is quite variable. The big snow is variously dated at 1932 by Robert Lewis (26), 1935 or 1933 by Lowell Panteah (19), or 1929 or 1930 by Joe Tsebataye (14), who a few minutes later recalls it as happening in 1931 or 1932 (20). The first grasshopper infestation at Nutria is remembered by Tom Idiaque as having happened in 1930 (20, 17) and by Fred Bowannie as having occurred in 1938 (39). The drought is remembered fairly consistently as having happened in 1921 (Ondelacy 145–47). Equally consistent is the recollection that the Emergency Conservation Works (ECW) began work in 1934. Accounting for the inconsistency is not difficult, however, in the case of the big snow; at a distance of half a century that inconsistency is not as great as it first seemed. More interesting is the consistency for the drought and the ECW dates. The latter may be mentally associated with increased government activity that followed the Indian Reorganization Act (IRA) of 1934.

By far the preference of deponents throughout is for relative, rather than absolute, dating and for customary, rather than absolute, measurements. Relative chronology is focused around a few singular events: the construction of Blackrock Dam, World War I, the measles epidemic, return from school, the big snow, the fencing of the reservation, World War II. Of particular interest, and requiring further research, is the reliance on the customary measurement called "a Zuni step." When Lowell Panteah talks about measuring the line for the north purchase boundary, he refers to the "step" as a lineal measurement (20). However, both Sidney Neumayah (8) and Sol Ondelacy, in discussing the surface of Blackrock Dam, use the "step" as an areal measurement.

Recurrent events, for which absolute dating is not essential, are remembered quite clearly. This is especially true for a number of Zuni customs that are reported the same way by every deponent, though they are remembered from a distance of thirty to fifty years. Several deponents testify that in the period before interior fencing on the reservation, if livestock strayed into a farm area and damaged crops, the livestock owner was liable and typically compensated the farmer with one or more head from his herd (Eustace 55; Mahooty 37–38). The method of plugging gullies by setting rows of cedar branches and brush weighted with rock in a trench across a watercourse is described in identical terms by Bob Walewa (12–14) and Mahooty (8–9). The use of native irrigation techniques, including small diversion dams (Harker 12) and wooden shunts (Idiaque 16), is frequently mentioned. Ubiquitous, too, are the mentions of "dry-farming" techniques, including the use of the "wooden leg," or digging stick. What is significant is that these techniques and processes are consistently described in nearly identical ways, suggesting not merely that these are familiar experiences but that ways of speaking about them have become almost stereotyped. This is especially evident in the descriptions of gully plugging.

THE ZUNI GOLDEN AGE TRADITION

Several of the testimonies represent the Zuni environment of the deponent's youth as considerably better than the environment is at present. Oral historians know that, especially when speaking of broad patterns of behavior, informants frequently, though not universally, recollect the past as a much better time than the present, a "golden age of youth." Such a view of the past frequently conflicts with data from other sources. When such an evaluation contrasts with "empirical" data, what does it represent? To put the worst face on the matter, Are such testimonies "delusions" or even "fabrications"? (For contrasting evaluations of another range economy, see Schneider 1987.) More precisely, the problem is, apart from external evidence, what clues might one gather to determine whether the several testimonies that represent the past in almost glowing terms are emotionally enhanced recollections or factual representations?

Tradition and Structural Coherence

Five of the Zuni testimonies—Eustace, Ghaccu, Harker, Lewis, and Telsee—directly attest to the golden age, two of them rather simply. Kathlutah Telsee merely observes that in former times the land (Nutria) was good (7) and later observes that today there is a lack of rain (29) and the dam is silted up (29). Frank Ghaccu similarly observes that now there is neither much rain nor much Gramma grass (21), both of which were, by implication, plentiful in former times. The rain, Ghaccu asserts, stopped during the 1930s (22).

Two other depositions are much more complex. Mazone Harker observes that formerly there was plenty of grass and water (11) and that everything was much greener (18). The Blackrock Dam produced record growths of alfalfa (19) until it silted up (18), and maintenance of the main ditch fell off because since it had come to depend on equipment instead of horses, it had become time consuming and expensive. Robert E. Lewis provides the most extensive recollection of this golden age. At that time it was green everywhere, even where there was no irrigation (28), and everywhere there was good grazing (35). This fruitful time during the 1920s coincided with the time when the Blackrock Dam was not silt filled and the ditch was clean (25). The big snow of 1932, Lewis claims, marked a long-term change in the climate, characterized by very irregular precipitation (26). This claim is unique to Lewis's testimony. Now the range is overgrown with noxious weeds (35).

Intermediate between all these is Calvin Eustace's testimony. He asserts that in his youth there were plenty of good feed grasses (69), which have now been replaced by noxious weeds (69). The Blackrock Dam has silted up, he avers, because of overgrazing in the Nutria area (70).

There are several recurrent motifs in these testimonies, sometimes expressed in the positive ("There was better grass then"), sometimes in the negative ("The grass is not good now"), which can be divided into before and after thematic units:

Before
1. Generalized verdure without irrigation (not to be confused with grazing or farming fertility)
2. Plenty of rain
3. Good grazing
4. Effective irrigation (communal ditch maintenance and lack of siltation)

After
1. Less rain or irregular precipitation
2. Less quality range grasses
3. Appearance of noxious weeds
4. Ineffective irrigation (silted dam and/or no ditch maintenance)

The most widely shared motifs are the change in precipitation and in rain conditions, which appear in almost every testimony (Harker and Eustace lack the precipitation difference). These most common elements are the least helpful in trying to understand how these testimonies are related to one another. To determine which of the parties had shared their sense of the past at some point prior to the deposition, I looked at the infrequent motifs as diagnostic.

- Lewis and Eustace share the noxious weeds motif.
- Lewis, Telsee, and Harker share the silted dam motif.

- Lewis and Harker share the generalized verdure motif.
- Lewis alone specifies the snow of 1932 as a trigger for climate change, but if one eliminates the causative claim and retains only the temporal claim, his testimony agrees with Ghaccu's, who avers that precipitation became scarcer in the 1930s.

From this array, I concluded that it is more likely that Lewis's testimony synthesizes motifs provided by others than that it is that he disseminated those motifs to the other deponents. I reached this conclusion for two reasons. First, Lewis's responses to counsel's questions are longer than those of the other deponents. Throughout his testimony, he demonstrates an aptitude for building extended narratives, showing a real competence in creating causal and temporal transitions to link discrete events. This is not a skill that appears in most of the depositions. Using the big snow as a sign of climactic change is a marvelous device (and one familiar to folklorists), which he contextualizes in such a way as to make it entirely plausible. The question is not whether such a big snow ever happened or even whether it "triggered" climactic change; rather, it is how Lewis has made it serve as a "sign" to link together in his story two periods that are quite distinct in his mind.

Second, Lewis's golden age narrative is by far the most complex of all such narratives, both in the number of motifs and the varieties of ways in which they cohere. Testimonies, especially those elicited in response to a very narrowly circumscribed line of questioning, hardly ever have the thematic coherence or formal and performative features of stories per se. This supports the conclusion that the more unstructured testimonies are the original ones and that a narrative, even a purportedly historical one, as well formed as Lewis's is a secondary synthesis. Such a conclusion is supported by the fact that the necessary conditions existed in Lewis's case to produce such a synthesis. As governor, Lewis occupies a position of responsibility in which he gathers information from the deponents about the changing condition of the Pueblo's lands and is compelled to fashion a coherent narrative through having to repeat the testimony many times in the course of preparing for the case and having to integrate idiosyncratic testimony not corroborated by others.

What does this mean for evaluating Lewis's testimony? It means that the least reliable aspects of his testimony—"reliable" here being an index of replicability without change—are the causal and temporal junctions he creates to bind episodes together. It means, moreover, that his crafted golden age testimony is less reliable *taken as whole* than the more fragmented testimonies of the others. In its parts, however, especially insofar as they are incorporated from the testimonies of others, it is at least as accurate as the others.

Individualized Thematic Coherence, Multiple Causation, and Single-Factor Generalization

I have been discussing how Lewis creates a structural coherence in his narrative by integrating discrete materials into a single causal and chronological frame. Another, related issue in these testimonies is the development of thematic coherence. Individuals create and interpret narratives under the pressure of what Norman Holland calls "individual identity themes." These themes structure narratives by imposing an interpretive framework on a set of events that is consistent with the teller's fundamental values or central experiences.

These personal identity themes are clearly at work in a number of the depositions. Telsee, for instance, continually refers throughout his deposition to situations or incidents that enable him to demonstrate that he is a man of many useful skills, such as clearing land or breaking horses. For Clarence Calavaza, the key moment in his life was the stock reduction that cost him many of his beloved horses. Harker's deposition displays two themes that are not consistent with each other (identity themes need not be). One is his continual reaffirmation of the work ethic; the other is the cunning of the white man, who will outwit an Indian no matter how hard he works. This personal thematizing is sometimes reinforced by the deponent's occupational focus. Calvin Eustace, for example, responds not as a Zuni but as a Zuni stockman, whose expertise in that area is valued. This tends to elicit testimony that foregrounds that dimension of his experience while diminishing others.

These identity themes structure the deponent's response by providing an interpretive framework for recalled information. This is most clearly seen in those testimonies in which the deponent represents the present condition as deriving from some single factor in the past. Clearly, history is more complex than any single-factor analysis suggests, but the deponents, having built much of their own identities on key events or values, need to substantiate their present lot by reference to some single factor. For Calavaza, the loss of draft horses led to a dependence on machinery, which in the end proved too expensive and too time consuming and so drove many Zunis out of farming. For Eustace, fencing led to overgrazing, overgrazing to erosion, and erosion to the ensiltation of the dams. For Lewis, much was attributable to a great change in climate following a big snow. The deponents are not necessarily incorrect in their identification of causative factors; they only overvalue them in the exclusivity they attribute to each.

The Underlying Value Theme: Options Foreclosed

The depositions speak to a perception that the quality of life at Zuni has diminished considerably in this century. Formerly, Zunis derived their subsistence from many sources in an economy that effectively balanced both exploitation and conservation of the environment. Intervention by the federal government upset that balanced economy. Fencing precluded free movement of stock, which led to overgrazing and erosion, all of which made herding more difficult. Silted dams, limited rainfall, changed watercourses, erosion and ruined floodplain fields, and a shift to Anglo farm machinery have limited the extent and effectiveness of farming. In short, technology dependence, management policies, and government support have effectively limited the number and quality of subsistence resources. This is clearly experienced as a "loss of options," though identification of the causes is less clear. It is to this generalized sense of loss, rather than to its exact dimensions or specific causes, that the depositions as a group most cogently testify.

Wessel's remarks and my response to them suggest a context of issues that might frame arguments over oral testimony. I earlier argued that the value of oral tradition is a function of reliability and validity and that these frequently correlate with the degree of formal structure a culture requires for different kinds of oral tradition. It may be argued, in response, that because these depositions have no indigenous Zuni counterpart, they are essentially anecdotal and thus have a low probability of validity or reliability.

As a rejoinder to this anticipated counterargument, I recommended that in using the present testimonies, one should undertake three tasks. First, differentially evaluate the several aspects of the testimony on the bases of reliability and validity to preclude a comprehensive evaluation of all the testimony as being of little value. Aspects can be rated as

a. *Excellent* for long-term, recurrent behaviors and for evaluation of events from Zuni cultural perspective
b. *Very good* for historical periodicization (i.e., chunking the remembered past into accurate chronological units)
c. *Fair* for analysis of causation because of personal thematizing, occupational focus, and public role (Lewis: governor; Eustace: range code)

d. *Fair* for absolute dating of idiosyncratic events
e. No *poors* because of the deponents' veracity

Second, emphasize the depositions' high degree of consistency, along with general reliability and validity. Third, vouch for the veracity of the deponents and their refusal to speak beyond their knowledge.

Isolating me from the data and conclusions developed by other members of the expert witness team provided independent corroboration concerning not only important data within the oral tradition but also the methodology I used to support my interpretation. After I presented my report to the defense expert witness team in Salt Lake City on May 26, 1988, John Appel of Geoscience Consultants, another expert witness, showed me a graph of annual precipitation on the Zuni reservation that can reasonably be interpreted to indicate a decline in average annual precipitation on the reservation during the 1930s, which especially contrasted with the 1920s. Moreover, E. Richard Hart, who headed the expert witness team, confirmed my conclusion that Robert Lewis, in accordance with his responsibilities as governor, had augmented his own personal knowledge by synthesizing testimonies gathered from others. In my final report ("1990"), I was able to establish that Zuni oral tradition accurately preserved a broad but detailed picture of the degradation of Zuni lands for which the federal government had trust responsibilities.

Cases such as the Zuni trust lands damages case are fertile ground for promoting the dialogue between oral historians, who are accustomed to work with topically focused personal reminiscences, and folklorists, who more frequently work with well-formed narratives. The need for such a dialogue persists even today, when the professional methodologies of both disciplines have advanced significantly toward convergence. Usually the oral historian comes to the problem from a background of prior research in the documentary history surrounding the issue and with a specific focus on content and questions of validity. The folklorist may lack prior knowledge of the specific disputed issue but brings to the table a familiarity with the shape of a community's oral traditions as a whole; with a special knowledge of forms, genres, and styles; and with a concern for matters of reliability. The validity of oral testimony is often established by corroboration with other forms of evidence, but in many aspects of Indian claims cases such other evidence is often missing or itself subject to dispute. In such instances, the only guarantor of the validity of oral testimonies is the reliability or internal integrity of the tradition. And it is here that the folklorist can make an important contribution in differentiating several dimensions of the oral tradition's representation of the past and determining the degree of confidence that can be invested in them.

REFERENCES

Primary Sources

1. Depositions from Zuni Aboriginal Title Case, Docket 161-79L
   Bowannie, Fred.
   Eriacho, Sefferino.
   Mahooty, Chester.
   Vacit, Frank.

2. Depositions from Zuni Trust Lands Damages Case, Dockets 224-84L and
   327-81L
   Bowannie, Fred. 21 September 1984. 81 pp.
   Calavaza, Clarence. 21 September 1984. 64 pp.
   Eriacho, Sefferino. 17 September 1984. 72 pp.
   Eustace, Calvin. 24 September 1984. 129 pp.
   Ghaccu, Frank. 25 September 1984. 25 pp.
   Harker, Mazone. 21 September 1984. 74 pp.
   Idiaque, Tom. 17 September 1984. 23 pp.
   Kanteena, Dempsey. Interview by T. J. Ferguson, Zuni Pueblo, New Mexico, 14
      August 1984.
   Lewis, Robert Edward. 22 September 1984. 192 pp.
   Mahooty, Chester. 25 September 1984. 82 pp.
   Neumayah, Sidney. 18 September 1984. 44 pp.
   Ondelacy, Sol. 19 September 1984. 175 pp.
   Panteah, Lowell. 24 September 1984. 45 pp.
   Telsee, Kathlutah. 18 September 1984. 41 pp.
   Tsabetsaye, Joe. 24 September 1984. 28 pp.
   Walewa, Bob. 18 September 1984. 19 pp.

3. Expert Witness Statements
   Wessel, Thomas R. "Federal Government Activity on the Zuni Reservation."
      Expert witness statement for the defendant. Prepared for the U.S. Depart-
      ment of Justice, Washington, D.C., pp. v–vi.
   Wiget, Andrew. 1990. "Summary and Analysis of Testimony by Zuni Elders."
      Zuni Land Claims and 1937 Housing Act. Hearing before the Senate Select Com-
      mittee on Indian Affairs. S. Hrg 101–878. May 1990. Washington, D.C.: GPO,
      1990, pp. 223–31.

Secondary Sources

Day, Gordon M. 1972. "Oral History as Complement." *Ethnohistory* 19: 99–107.
DeLaguna, Frederick. 1958. "Geological Confirmation of Native Traditions, Yaku-
   tat, Alaska." *American Antiquity* 23: 434.
Eggan, Fred. 1967. "From History to Myth: A Hopi Example." *Studies in South-
   western Ethnolinguistics,* ed. Dell Hymes and William E. Bittle. The Hague:
   Mouton, pp. 33–53.
Hoffman, Alice. 1984. "Reliability and Validity in Oral History." In *Oral History: An
   Interdisciplinary Anthology,* ed. David K. Dunaway and Willa K. Baum. Nashville,
   Tenn: American Association for State and Local History, pp. 67–73.

Prendergast, David M., and Clement W. Meighan. 1959. "Folk Tradition as Historical Fact: A Paiute Example." *Journal of American Folklore* 72: 128–33.

Wiget, Andrew. 1982. "Truth and the Hopi: An Historiographic Study of Documented Oral Tradition Concerning the Coming of the Spanish." *Ethnohistory* 29: 181–99.

CHAPTER 18

Changing Meanings of Arroyo

Samuel C. Monson

The Zuni Tribe filed suit against the U.S. government, alleging that government policies had led to the degradation of the farmland on the Zuni Indian Reservation. The government contended as part of its defense that early reports of arroyos on tribal farmlands proved that such degradation had not occurred. That contention was based on interpreting the recent geological meaning: "an incised channel; a channel of an ephemeral or intermittent stream, usually with vertical banks of consolidated material 2 feet or more high"[1] as the basic meaning of arroyo. In rebuttal, the plaintiff presented as evidence the history of the word as exemplified by suggested etymologies and meanings in both Spanish and English as they changed over the course of four centuries—meanings determined both by dictionary definitions and examples of actual usage.

Dictionary etymologies suggest forms and meanings in earlier languages. Dictionary definitions indicate that a meaning has become widespread. Citations—that is, occurrences of the word *arroyo* in accounts of exploration and settlement in the southwestern area of the United States—determine what the word meant to those who used it. Since arroyo entered the English language from Spanish, which was the language used by early explorers of the Southwest, writings in both Spanish and English were relevant. Translations from Spanish into English allowed comparison of meanings in the two languages.

Determining changes in meanings of arroyo as accurately as possible ruled out any citation, etymology, or definition not dated. Sources consulted—a total of 124—comprised 4 from the 1500s, 4 from the 1600s, 16 from the 1700s, 40 from the 1800s, and 60 from the 1900s. Of these, 70 were dictionaries of lexicons in Spanish, English, Spanish-English, and English-Spanish; 36 were journals and accounts of early exploration; and the rest were scientific treatises, mainly geological.

Some people consult a dictionary to determine the meaning of a word, then base their usage of the word on the dictionary definition or definitions. Usually, however, people use words with meanings deduced from the contexts in which the words have occurred in their listening and reading. Lexicographers base their definitions on meanings revealed by contexts that suggest limitations on the meaning of a word. Other contexts, of no use in defining, reveal little except that a word exists.

ETYMOLOGIES

The source of a word taken into a different language is more difficult to determine than is its meaning once it is there. The origin of a word used first in writing is usually easier to trace than that of one borrowed into the spoken language. A spoken word is often used for many years before lexicographers, who base most of their dictionary work on written sources, notice that its usage is widespread enough for them to record. During the period of oral transmission, the word may have dropped, altered, or added sounds to the extent that its actual origin is difficult to recognize. It may also have gained new meanings or lost its original one. Dictionary etymologies then become guesses, and several different origins may be suggested in different dictionaries. Lexicographers plagiarize freely from the work of their predecessors, with the result that several different dictionaries will repeat an etymology that may have been based on shrewd guesswork rather than certainty. None of the etymologies studied here from sources dated before 1961 suggest any meaning for the antecedents of arroyo other than "running water" or "stream." Identification of arroyo with late *arrugia*, with its idea of something dug out, was added very late, although the Roman author Pliny had used *arrugia* in A.D. 79.

DEFINITIONS

Since dictionaries derive their meanings of words from usage, they seldom record new meanings until such meanings have become fairly common. New definitions (as distinguished from meanings) may appear in other publications before being recorded in dictionaries or lexicons.

There was a slow accretion of geographical meaning to arroyo recorded almost entirely in Spanish sources. Nongeographical definitions have been omitted:

1587   a stream or small river
1623   a little river, a running brook of water [in a Spanish-English dictionary published in London]
1817   small volume of water which flows all the time; and the bed where it flows
1826   small volume of water which runs almost always; and the bed where it flows

1854   In the streets the place where the water runs, when it rains and at other times.
1860   When to the side of *un valle grande* [a large valley] exist others of less importance, they are called *valle pequeño* [small valley], *vallecito* [little valley], *barrance* [ravine], *cañada* [dale], *arroyo*

Although arroyo was used sometimes by people writing in English about the Southwest during the nineteenth century, they usually considered the word Spanish, not English. *The Oxford English Dictionary*, published in England, was the first English dictionary (other than English-Spanish dictionaries) to enter the term but indicated that arroyo was a Spanish word. Its definition added "gully," a concept in no previous dictionaries.

1888   a rivulet or stream; hence, the bed of a stream, a gully (in United States)
1889   enters as an English word in an American dictionary, *Century Dictionary and Cyclopedia*
1889   a watercourse; a rivulet [southwestern United States]; also *arrollo*
1895   more extensive entry in *A Standard Dictionary of the English Language*, published in New York
1895   a small stream, or its dry bed; in geology, a deep dry gully

More complete technical meanings appeared in geological and geographical journals:

1902   An arroyo is a steep sided, narrow gulch cut in a previously filled gravel and adobe valley in the arid west.
1929   The ephemeral streams of the region have channels which are dry except for a few days a year. These channels are known as arroyos or washes. "Wash" or "dry wash" is the common local term. In the logs the term "arroyo" is used when there is a single definite channel with a sandy or gravelly bed and banks 2 to 10 feet high. "Wash" is used where the banks are low and there are numerous channels.

These additions to the meaning of the word were later noted in American dictionaries:

1944   This is a Spanish word meaning *rivulet*. It is used almost exclusively in the Southwest, where a small stream is capable of cutting a deep channel for itself in the soft earth, and the name has come to mean a narrow gorge having precipitous walls of dirt.

1951   a brook or creek, also a channel, gully, dry wash, stream bed, or valley.

It is interesting to note that, although the meaning "the bed of a stream" (which suggests the intermittent nature of small streams in the U.S. Southwest) was recorded in a dictionary as early as 1817, it was not until 1888 that "gully," which suggests erosion, was first used in defining arroyo.

CITATIONS WITH DEFINING CONTEXTS

A search through the journals of explorers, accounts of travelers, and articles by scientists uncovered many occurrences of arroyo, but relatively few in which the context would help in ascertaining its meaning. Here is a selection of citations of arroyo with defining contexts that extended the meanings of arroyo beyond what was suggested by earlier citations. The earliest suggestion of a change in meaning is given, as well as several subsequent citations that support the change. Repetition of a date indicates a different source:

1594   Proceeding on our way on the eighth, we went five leagues through the forest, by a good trail, stopping by a stream of water which we called El Arroyo de los Alamillos.

1630   The Arroyo de Abó was situated, was the only perennial stream in the region.

1706   The little stream above, very miry and marshy, I ordered called El Arroyo de las Ansias, because of the many troubles I had in cutting through it.

1776   This pueblo has no river, but an arroyo which flows only in a very rainy season or when the snows melt.

The same stream which lower down they call Arroyo del Canjilon, or Arroyo Seco [Dry Arroyo].

In this place there was no permanent water, although we found a little in an arroyo near the broken ground to the east-southeast.

On the bank of another arroyo, which is called Rio de las Nutrias, because, although it is of permanent and running water, apparently during all or most of the year it stands in pools where they say beavers breed.

We halted for siesta at an arroyo which the guides thought had water, though we found it entirely dry.

We entered the bed of an arroyo, and having traveled along it a league to the east we came unexpectedly to a large pond of good water.

Through a low valley in which runs as much water as two good-sized furrows would hold, although it does not continue throughout the valley, for in places it completely disappears, yet in some places it runs and in others it can be seen in pools like stagnant rainwater. . . . Following the bed of an arroyo where the water disappears and comes out again on the north bank, we traveled northwest a league and a half and camped in the bed of the arroyo.

We again passed close to the arroyo. Here the beaver have made with logs such ponds that at first they look like a fairly good-sized river.

He said . . . that this was an arroyo, not a river, but that it might have water now.

We swung to the northwest, taking as a road the bed of an arroyo. . . . We continued along the arroyo which led us imperceptibly into a closed canyon, high on both sides, with no passable terrain other than the bed of the arroyo.

We halted . . . near a creek of good water which we called Arroyo de San Andrés. . . . It appears to flow continuously and therefore is rather a small river or creek than an arroyo.

We arrived at an arroyo which appeared to have much water, but we found only some pools in which it was difficult for the animals to drink. . . . All along the arroyo there was a sort of white, dry and narrow bank which from a distance looked like stretched canvas, for which reason we named it Arroyo del Tejedor.

On the bank of the arroyo . . . where there was a large supply of water and good pasturage.

Descended to a dry arroyo and a very deep canyon.

Going half a league closer to the arroyo or canyon to which formerly we had been unable to descend.

1782 The mission of Nuestra Señora de Guadalupe of Zuñi Indians . . . rests on a flat plain with a spring for the supply of the Pueblo. At a league distant from it runs an arroyo.

1842 Crossing a number of dry and timbered arroyos, we travelled until late through open oak groves, and encamped among a collection of streams.

The dry bed of a large sand-creek, four or five hundred yards wide, known as the Kuyawa. The banks of this arroyo are very steep and high, disclosing, now and then, spreads of beautiful bottom lands with occasional groves of cottonwood. At this season of the year its waters are lost in the quicksand and gravel.

1850   The frightful desolation of the country, and the deep gullies of arroyos with which it is seamed. In the beds of these they would often lose the trail, occasioning them many hours' search to recover it.

Dry, gravelly arroyos, in and out of which we went with a plunge and a scramble, marked the courses of the winter streams.

The trail was crossed by deep, dry arroyos, which in the rainy season make the country almost impassable.

Our crossing of the arroyos would have startled even an Allegheny stage-driver. When one of these huge gullies yawned before us, there was no check of our speed. We dashed sheer off the brink at an angle of fifty degrees; there was a giddy sensation of falling for an instant, and in the next our heavy vehicle regained the level, carried half-way up the opposite steep by the momentum of our descent.

A week of wet weather turns the dusty plain into a deep mire, the hollows into pools, and the stony arroyos into roaring streams.

1851   Immediately on their arrival, they prepared their nests; one of these, built in the gravel bank of an *arroyo seco* or dry creek, I examined.

1852   The face of the country to-day has been generally level—a few arroyos (dry beds of streams) intersecting it at intervals.

Our route to-day . . . was generally in a northwesterly direction, and, besides being . . . rough and uneven on account of sand hills and arroyos, did not furnish us a drop of water throughout its whole extent.

1854   On the third of July the first rain fell. . . . The arroyo, which passes through the village, and which furnishes barely water enough for our party and the animals, became so much swollen as to render it difficult to cross; and by the time it had received the numerous mountain torrents which fall into it within a mile from our camp, it became impassable for wagons, or even mules. The dry gullies became rapid streams, five or six feet deep, and sometimes fifty feet or more across.

An arroyo, or place where there was slight depression in the desert, marked by some mezquit bushes, whose freshness showed that water sometimes reached their roots.

Near the arroyo, where water sometimes finds its way, a few mazquit bushes have attained the height of ten feet.

1854   Three miles from San Antonio, we crossed the bed of the arroyo Alazan, now reduced to a dry mass of gravel.

1859   The points named are where deep wells have been dug. "New River," though usually set down, is a dry arroyo.

1864   Roaring torrents have become dry arroyos.

1872   For the first twenty minutes the road was hard and smooth and level; after that gentle, shallow undulations began, and at last, at brief intervals, were sharp narrow arroyos (ditches eight or nine feet wide).

1878   For the distance of upwards of a hundred miles south of the Zuni village there is an arroya [sic] embracing a series of small valleys, watered by mountain streams and a system of natural springs which, could the device of man cause to share their lot with the otherwise fertile soil of the so called deserts of the western part of the State, would cause that emblematic desert rose to assume all its brilliancy.

1878   It was decided to go westward up the arroyo we were on. . . . The two days we followed the arroyo, grass was abundant, and water enough found in the limestone "pockets," which appear occasionally along these canons.

1884   The *arroyos* or depressions in the *mesas* contain fine groves of mesquit.

1884   Crossing the city of Monterey from west to east is a little valley, the *arroyo* of Santa Lucia, into which, midway in its passage, comes through another arroyo of a few hundred yards in length the water from the *ojo de agua*.

1888   The Smoky heads in the prairie of eastern Colorado, and while a mere sandy arroyo enters Kansas just south of the parallel mentioned, and cuts its valley deeper as it descends the slope of the State.

1893   Its site is a wee bead of a valley, strung upon a deep and ragged arroyo.

These citations indicate earlier changes in the meaning of arroyo than those indicated in dictionaries: 1776 rather than 1826 for "intermittent stream," 1776 rather than 1817 for "the bed of a stream." In fact, as early as 1776 Father Escalante suggested that it was wrong to call a stream that flowed year round an *arroya*. Some of the citations indicate that some arroyos (the streams or even intermittent streams) might occur in mountains and form canyons. That was not a necessary condition for recognizing an arroyo in 1854, when arroyo was characterized as a "slight depression in the desert," or in 1884, when arroyos were "depressions in the mesas." Nor was it in 1895, although John Wesley Powell's description of the Grand Canyon suggests how impressive an effect a "dry arroyo" might have: "The mesas are carved out of platforms of horizontal or nearly horizontal rocks by perennial or intermittent streams, and as the climate is exceedingly arid most of the streams flow only during seasons of rain, and for the greater apart of the year they are dry arroyos. Many of the longer channels are dry for long periods. Some of them are opened only by floods that come ten to twenty years apart."[2]

In the United States today arroyo seems to be losing its original meaning of "small stream," while retaining the meaning of "dry stream bed." Increasingly, the word suggests erosion as well, of the sort described by Kirk Bryan in 1925:

> Nearly all streams in southwestern United States flow between vertical banks of alluvium that vary in height from ten to as much as one hundred feet. Although subject to great floods, these streams no longer overflow their banks, nor build up their adjacent flood-plains. Floods merely deepen and widen the channels (arroyos) which continually grow headward into the undissected valley floors of headwater valleys and tributaries. . . .
>
> It is evident to all observers that the formation of the channel trenches is recent as early settlers in the region can remember the time when many of these valley flood plains were intact and the floods spread widely. At that time, meadows, belts of cottonwood or willow trees, and even swamps characterized the floors of valleys that now support only scattered sage, greasewood or mesquite. . . .
>
> Duce has described the formation of *arroyos* (channel trenches) in southern Colorado. The pioneer settlers found the bottom land low and rounded, with no suggestion of an arroyo in the center. He gives various types of evidence that the arroyos are recently formed and sets the time as since the early government surveys of 1860 and 1870 and since the settlement of the country—that is, since 1860–65 in southeastern Colorado and since 1870–80 in southwestern Colorado.[3]

A careful study of the changing meanings of arroyo helped contribute to the decision of the U.S. government to settle the Zuni claims out of court rather than contesting them in a trial.

NOTES

1. *Glossary of Geology and Related Sciences*, 2d ed. (Washington, D.C.: American Geological Institute, 1962), p. 15.

2. John Wesley Powell, *The Exploration of the Colorado River and Its Canyons* (New York: Dover Publications, 1961), p. 46.

3. Science 62 (1925): 338–44.

PART THREE

The Barefoot Trail
(United States v. *Platt)*

CHAPTER 19

Protection of *Kolhu/wala:wa* ("Zuni Heaven"): Litigation and Legislation

E. Richard Hart

For more than a century, Zuni political and religious leaders have attempted to protect their ownership and use rights to *Kolhu/wala:wa*, or "Zuni Heaven," as it is commonly known to non-Zunis. According to the Zuni religion, *Kolhu/wala:wa* is the place where all Zunis go after death and where the supernatural *Kokko* reside under a sacred lake fed by the waters from a precious spring. *Kolhu/wala:wa* is located near where the Zuni River flows between two mountains and then into the Little Colorado. On one of the mountains is an opening into the underworld, where Zuni religious leaders can enter subterranean chambers in order to attempt to communicate with their ancestors and the *Kokko*. Near the end of the other mountain is the location where the *Koyemshi*, or "Mudheads," were created. Many of the *Kokko* were themselves created in the lake under which they now reside and where departed Zunis go to dance with them. *Kolhu/wala:wa* is both conceptually and geographically central to the Zuni religion. The ancient Zuni origin and migration narratives all tell of *Kolhu/wala:wa* and explain its place in the story of the Zunis' search for the Middle Place.

Every four years, between forty and sixty Zunis set out on a strenuous religious pilgrimage that takes four days and covers more than 110 miles. During this solemn, ceremonial trek, the Zunis who make the pilgrimage represent all of the tribal members as they make offerings, say prayers, gather sacred paint pigments, and eventually reach *Kolhu/wala:wa*, where their religious activities and prayers are aimed at bringing peace, order, and prosperity not only to the Zunis but also to the entire world. Prayers to the supernatural beings and to the Zunis' ancestors are focused on bringing rain to the Zuni region to enable the crops of the Zunis to grow and nurture the fields of their neighbors as well. Sometimes in periods of drought, special pilgrimages have been made in "off years" in order to pray for rain.

The historical records of non-Zunis provide proof that Zunis have been making this quadrennial pilgrimage for many centuries. Some records suggest that Francisco Vásquez de Coronado interrupted a quadrennial pilgrimage in 1540. During the remainder of the Spanish and Mexican periods (1540–1846), however, the Zunis seem to have kept their pilgrimages secret in order to avoid religious persecution from Spanish authorities.

In 1848 with the signing of the Treaty of Guadalupe Hidalgo, the United States expressed sovereignty over Zuni's traditional territory. Zuni quickly signed a treaty with U.S. authorities. The United States agreed to respect Zuni boundaries and to give Zuni true freedom of religion. Zuni leaders especially welcomed the promise of religious freedom. Unfortunately, the treaty was never ratified, and the United States did not honor its promises of protecting Zuni's traditional territory and allowing it freedom of religion.

A little over thirty years later, in 1879, a young anthropologist named Frank Hamilton Cushing moved to Zuni and was eventually adopted into the tribe and initiated into the Bow Priesthood. Cushing took most of his Zuni religious duties very seriously and seems to have acted in good faith as a Bow Priest in most regards. But he also secretly gathered religious objects from Zuni shrines and sent them back to Washington, D.C., to be placed in the Smithsonian Institution museum. When he saw the quadrennial pilgrimage leave and return to the pueblo in 1880, Cushing determined to visit Kolhu/wala:wa. During the same year, a non-Indian who had made a homestead along the sacred trail to Kolhu/wala:wa attempted to stop the Zunis, but they militantly enforced their rights to the pilgrimage and the sacred trail along which they traveled. Later that year, Cushing quietly slipped out of the village and secretly traveled to Kolhu/wala:wa, where he looted the ancient shrines, stealing prayersticks and other religious offerings and then packing them, with the intention of then sending much of the material to Washington. Fortunately, the Zunis discovered Cushing's cache of religious offerings and tried him in a religious court for his offenses. He was fortunate to be released unharmed.

News of Cushing's discovery quickly spread, and other non-Indians looted the shrines at Kolhu/wala:wa. Other anthropologists, like Matilda Coxe Stevenson, also invaded the Zunis' sacred area and stole sacred religious offerings in order to put them in museums. At the same time, non-Indians began to collect and sell Zuni religious objects as though they were art, and traders engaged in an extensive business of selling things taken from Zuni shrines.

Ever since, Zuni religious and political leaders have used what means they have had to stop the desecration of their religious shrines and especially to protect their rights to Kolhu/wala:wa and the sacred trail there, which has been called *We:sak'yaya Onnane* (Barefoot Trail). Zuni leaders pressured the United States to make *Kolhu/wala:wa* and all the territory in between Zuni and *Kolhu/wala:wa* a part of the reservation. When that failed, in the early and mid-twentieth century Zuni leaders tried to have the government purchase the lands around *Kolhu/wala:wa* for the tribe's use. Special efforts were made in the 1930s and 1940s by Zuni leaders to obtain title to *Kolhu/wala:wa*. In the meantime, Zuni religious leaders never stopped making the quadrennial pilgrimages and always claimed their exclusive right to the sacred trail to and from *Kolhu/wala:wa* during those pilgrimages.

Zuni leaders continued to lobby for their rights to *Kolhu/wala:wa*, but little progress was made until the 1970s. In 1978 the American Indian Religious Freedom Act was passed. At Zuni, during hearings held to implement the legislation, leaders emphasized their rights to *Kolhu/wala:wa* and told of problems they had encountered with a rancher named Earl Platt, who owned a large portion of land through which the trail passed. The act was passed, but it did little or no good in helping the Zunis with their religious rights, perhaps partly because these problems occurred on private as well as public lands.

In the same year another act was passed that allowed the Zunis to sue the United States for lands taken without payment and for damages to their remaining trust lands that were caused by the United States. Zuni leaders had to tell the U.S. court what their "aboriginal" boundaries were and had to decide which lands they believed had been taken from them. Title to Zuni Salt Lake was returned to Zuni as a part of the passage of the 1978 act. The Tribal Council met and discussed the situation at many meetings and called in many religious leaders to provide their views. Eventually the Zuni Tribal Council determined the boundaries of the aboriginal territory and concluded that those lands had been taken from the tribe, with the exception of *Kolhu/wala:wa*. Of all of the aboriginal lands outside the reservation, there was only one parcel of land (along with access to and from that parcel) to which the Zunis claimed a right to title—*Kolhu/wala:wa*. The Zunis believed they should not take compensation for this land, so this area and its attendant access were withdrawn from the land claim. The tribe believed *Kolhu/wala:wa* had never been "legally" taken away.

While the land claim litigation continued, the tribe continued to lobby for a satisfactory solution to protect its rights to *Kolhu/wala:wa*. In 1983–1984 the Zunis obtained the support of prominent Republicans and Democrats in the Senate and House, and legislation was drafted that would arrange title to the area for the tribe. The Zunis and their attorney, Stephen G. Boyden, were successful in arranging a complex deal among the various, diverse entities: the two political parties, the Zunis and

Navajos, the non-Indian ranchers in the area, the Bureau of Land Management (BLM), and the state of Arizona. Many amendments were necessary before S. 2201 would become law. Senate 2201, a bill "To Convey Certain Lands to the Zuni Indian Tribe for Religious Purposes," was made law (Public Law 98-408) on August 28, 1984. The act established a method for Zuni to obtain the over 11,000 acres of land that make up the area around *Kolhu/wala:wa*. The tribe was given some of the lands outright and was allowed to purchase other of the lands and then place them all in trust status. Since the tribe was required to purchase some of the lands, Congress agreed to waive "offsets" in the claims cases. This compromise proved to be a very favorable one for the tribe because it meant that its monetary settlement in the claims cases would not be "offset," or reduced, by much of the money that the United States had spent on the tribe in the past. Later in the year a celebration honoring Senator Barry Goldwater (R-Ariz.) for his role in the passage of this legislation was held at Zuni. Today almost all of the land at *Kolhu/wala:wa* has been officially transferred to Zuni tribal trust status.

Zuni's problems in guaranteeing rights to *Kolhu/wala:wa* were not finished, however. The following year, in 1985, as the time for the quadrennial pilgrimage approached, Earl Platt, a wealthy attorney in his mid-seventies and owner of a large ranch along the route of the pilgrimage, notified the Apache County, Arizona, sheriff that he wanted the Zuni religious leaders arrested for trespassing when they passed along the trail through his property. Sheriff Art Lee notified the Zuni Tribe of Platt's intent, and the Zunis in turn contacted their attorney, Stephen G. Boyden. Since the pilgrimage was scheduled to begin in a few weeks, the tribe moved quickly. The Zunis, through their attorney, asked for support from the Justice Department. The department agreed to take the case. Hank Meshorer, chief of the Indian Section of the Division of Natural Resources in the Department of Justice, took the case for the United States and immediately went to federal district court in Phoenix and was granted a temporary restraining order against Platt on June 12, 1985.

Previously, the tribe had contacted the other landowners along the route. Arizona, through its Land Department, had already acquiesced in the tribe's claimed right of passage by granting the Zunis demand for a right-of-way. The Bureau of Land Management agreed to accept the Zunis' request for a permanent right-of-way across its lands. Other private owners of lands through which the pilgrimage trail passed also provided their acquiescence to the tribe's claimed right for the pilgrims to pass.

The 1985 pilgrimage was concluded without incident between June 12 and 15, although Earl Platt later was reported to have stated that he had intended to disrupt the pilgrimage in spite of the federal restraining order but was unable to locate the pilgrims as they crossed his land. Subsequent to the 1985 pilgrimage, the Department of Justice sued Platt for a permanent prescriptive easement.

Floyd A. O'Neil and I were hired as expert historians for the Department of Justice and asked to submit reports on the history of *Kolhu/wala:wa*. T. J. Ferguson submitted a report on the archaeology along the trail to *Kolhu/wala:wa*. In order to obtain an easement, it was necessary to map the trail. Many Zuni religious leaders assisted us in our work on these reports and this mapping process, including John Niiha, Solen Lalio, Ben Kallestewa, Curtis Lanyate, Philip Vicente, and Nelson Vicente. Ronald Stauber created the first map of the trail to *Kolhu/wala:wa*, with assistance in the field from Andrew Othole.

The legal proceedings involved in suing for the easement were extremely complex. Hank Meshorer, attorney for the United States, who represented Zuni, spent much of his time during the next five years learning all he could from the Zunis and the expert witnesses. Eventually it became necessary for the Bureau of Land Management to make another, formal survey of the route to *Kolhu/wala:wa*. This was completed in 1987, but because of the legal maneuverings, the trial still had not taken place by 1989, when the next quadrennial pilgrimage was set to take place. During preparations for the trial, head councilman Barton Martza acted as liaison with Zuni religious leaders and coordinated tribal efforts.

As the trial on the Zuni easement approached, Earl Platt again was reported to have threatened to disrupt the Zuni pilgrimage, which was scheduled for June 21–24, 1989. The United States asked for and received a second temporary restraining order, issued to ensure that Platt did not disrupt the pilgrimage. Unfortunately, this order was not enough to prevent Platt from doing so. Meshorer traveled to Zuni to be available during the pilgrimage should any problem occur, and although every possible precaution was taken, on the third day of the pilgrimage Platt drove his pickup through the line of pilgrims, reportedly hitting one of the horses and riders in the group. All of the Zunis on the pilgrimage had taken strict vows to avoid hostility or confrontation, and they quickly veered away from Platt and completed the remainder of the pilgrimage without further incident.

The Justice Department immediately vowed to prosecute Platt for contempt of court and on July 27, 1989, filed a petition to show cause why Earl Platt should not be held in contempt. The trial was set for August 31, 1989, in Phoenix federal district court and was presided over by Judge William P. Copple, who had signed the restraining order.

At the contempt trial the government called five Zunis as witnesses as well as the deputy who had observed the incident and several other non-Zunis. Earl Platt did not take the stand. Although his attorneys did not dispute the disruption of the pilgrimage, they claimed that he had not actually run into the horse and rider. Judge Copple rendered his decision on September 14, 1989, finding Earl Platt guilty of civil contempt. He said that to "penalize" Platt for violating the court order, he was ordering him to make a payment of $5,000 to the Zuni Tribe.

Prior to the trial on the prescriptive easement, the United States deposed Earl Platt. Platt, an attorney himself, claimed he had never known the Zunis made a regular pilgrimage over a defined trail across his ranch. He also said that on the occasions when he had been aware that the Zunis did cross his land, they caused damage to his fences and other property. He vehemently denied he had ever known of a four-year cycle or a regularly used trail.

Judge Earl H. Carroll presided over a second trial, held January 3–5, 1990, to obtain a prescriptive easement to *Kolhu/wala:wa*. Hank Meshorer represented the United States in behalf of the Zuni Tribe. He was joined at the plaintiff's table by Stephen G. Boyden and John Boyden for the Zuni Tribe and by Melvin A. McDonald, who acted as local counsel in behalf of the tribe in Phoenix.

The United States called five expert witnesses and eleven lay witnesses, three of them Zunis. My own testimony summarized the history of Zuni use of the trail. Questioning from both sides focused on the production of both the Stauber and BLM maps of the route. At the trial I produced a mylar overlay that proved the original map constructed under my direction by Stauber was virtually identical to the map produced using sophisticated instruments by the Bureau of Land Management cadastral survey crew. James P. Kelley, who headed the BLM crew, corroborated these statements and described the BLM's methods. T. J. Ferguson described the archaeological reconnaissance and the evidence of Zuni use of the trail that he had discovered. James I. Ebert discussed the aerial photographic and photogrammetric analysis that had led him to conclude that the trail preceded the construction of Platt's water tanks along the route. Finally, O'Neil summarized the entire body of evidence and conclusions based on documentary evidence and lay interviews.

The United States also called Jerry Cordova, who had been the superintendent of the Zuni Agency during the 1985 pilgrimage and was himself a Taos Pueblo Indian. He testified that the Zunis not only claimed a right to the pilgrimage route but had also frequently acted on that claim, such as in the construction of gates in fences along the route. Several non-Indian residents were called as witnesses and testified to the open and "notorious" nature of the pilgrimage over many, many years. Three other property owners along the route said they had long known of the pilgrimage and had no objection to the Zunis' use of the trail. One of them, Mabel Hinkson, owned land covering the portion of the pilgrimage from the reservation line nearly to Highway 666. She took pains through many years to protect the rights of the Zunis and the archaeological heritage on her ranch. Although appearance at the trial required a long trip and she was confined to a wheelchair, she gave strong testimony in the Zunis' behalf. A former Platt employee said he had been fully aware of the pilgrimage during the entire period that he worked for Platt, that he had seen the Zunis during the pilgrimages, and that as far as he was concerned, "I think everybody that's been around there knew about it." Both the sheriff and county attorney of Apache County testified about the county's efforts to protect the Zunis during their pilgrimage, including setting up roadblocks along Highway 666, under the Zuni religious leaders' direction, while the pilgrims passed over the road in order that non-Indians would not interfere with the pilgrimage. Former Secretary of the Interior Stewart Udall, who had grown up in the area and who has since written about the Zunis' use of the trail, also testified to the common knowledge of the Zuni pilgrimage in the community.

The first of the three Zunis who testified was Mecalita Wytsalucy, the High Priest of the North and *Kyakwemossi*. He emphasized the preeminent importance of *Kolhu/wala:wa* and the pilgrimage to all Zuni people. He was followed by John Niiha, who had been chosen by the Zunis and Meshorer to provide the direct testimony about the pilgrimage itself. Although many Zunis have been involved in past pilgrimages and many have significant and important knowledge about the pilgrimage, it was decided that Niiha, the *Kopekwin*, would best represent the tribe at this proceeding. He gave a detailed account of the pilgrimage, the route, the method that he used to remember the route as he helped lead the pilgrims down the trail, and the fact that the route had never changed during the decades that he had been going on the pilgrimages. Edmund J. Ladd, a Zuni and an anthropologist, acted as interpreter for Niiha and Wytsalucy. Ladd also worked with the experts throughout the preparation for trial in the long and difficult process of objectively translating the comments of Zuni witnesses to establish the facts of the case from the Zuni perspective. Governor Robert E. Lewis, the final Zuni witness, spoke eloquently in English of the Zunis' claimed rights to the *Kolhu/wala:wa* and the trail to that place, including where it crossed Platt's property.

The United States rested its case, and there was a short recess. But when the trial resumed, the Platts unexpectedly rested their case without calling a single witness. A long exchange among the attorneys ensued, during which Meshorer argued about the truthfulness of statements made in the past by Platt and asked to introduce some additional evidence relating to the veracity of Platt's statements. The judge did not allow the additional evidence, but he did make a biting comment. Judge Carroll reiterated his belief that the court's determination would be based on easement law and not religious rights and added at that point, looking out at the courtroom, "We used to have a saying in the courthouse years ago . . . that said, 'Truth will rise above lies as oil will rise above water.' " Meshorer agreed and concluded by saying, "Truth has risen."

Attorneys for both parties gave their final arguments, and then Judge Carroll immediately ruled from the bench in favor of the Zunis on most of the elements of an easement. On February 7, 1990, Judge Carroll issued his order, finding that all elements of easement law had been met and granting an easement to the Zunis over Platt's lands for their pilgrimage every four years, for up to sixty people on foot and horseback, at the time of the summer solstice. The order also stated that the easement should be fifty feet wide and that the Zunis should not interfere with Platt's water sources.

The decision was greeted with great joy and relief at Zuni and received newspaper headlines in both New Mexico and Arizona. Nevertheless, there were several aspects of the easement that both Zuni and the United States believed were unclear. The United States quickly notified the court that it would appeal the judgment to allow "off-year" pilgrimages, to allow the Zunis the use of water from tanks along the easement, and to expand the width of the easement at the second day lunch location. The United States also filed a motion to assess costs associated with the case against Platt. He objected and a hearing was held, but on June 19, 1990, the court assessed over $14,000 in costs to Platt. Platt appealed, but the court upheld the order.

Later in the year, with the Platts contemplating further appeals on the contempt fine and the costs award, and with the United States appealing for additional easement rights for the Zunis, discussions for a settlement of the case were initiated. On November 8, 1990, attorneys for Platt notified the Department of Justice that he was willing to allow the Zunis a larger easement area (200 yards by 200 yards) for the location where they stopped for lunch during the second day, rights to use water tanks for their horses along the route, and the right to "off-year" pilgrimages in times of drought in return for the United States asking the court to waive the $5,000 contempt fine and $14,000 court costs. This settlement was subsequently approved by the court.

Two additional complications relating to *Kolhu/wala:wa* developed during the ongoing litigation. First, it was discovered that Public Law 98-408, which conveyed title to *Kolhu/wala:wa*, had inadvertently left two of the most important sections out of the area being placed in trust status. In 1990 the Zunis and attorney Stephen G. Boyden, working with the New Mexico congressional delegation, managed to add language to a bill settling one of their land claims, which directed the Bureau of Land Management to exchange land with the private owner of the two sections desired by the Zunis. Negotiations to conclude the necessary exchange are still ongoing. Second, the Department of Justice notified the court that in the adjudication of the Little Colorado water basin, it was claiming rights to water at *Kolhu/wala:wa* in behalf of the Zunis. The Department of Justice commissioned me to complete a study of Zuni water use at *Kolhu/wala:wa*. A draft report, summarizing the history of Zuni use of water at *Kolhu/wala:wa* was submitted to the Department of Justice in August 1990. The final report was submitted in June 1991 and included the results of an archaeological reconnaissance of the area conducted by T. J. Ferguson. Evidence indicates Zuni religious use of water at *Kolhu/wala:wa* since time immemorial, and ancestral agricultural use of water on what are now the "Zuni Heaven" trust lands. In 1994, the Institute of the NorthAmerican West was commissioned to do supplementary ethnohistorical and archaeological work related to these Zuni trust lands to be used by the Department of Justice relative to Zuni's claim for water rights in the Little Colorado water rights adjudication. This work is being carried out by T. J. Ferguson and me at the time of this writing.

On September 5, 1990, the Zuni Tribe held a celebration for the court victory giving Zuni its easement to *Kolhu/wala:wa* and honoring those who had helped carry out the complex litigation. The tribe expressed particular gratitude to Meshorer for his tireless efforts in pursuing the litigation and relentless attention to the complex details in the case. After more than a century of work, the Zunis have now guaranteed their rights to go to and use *Kolhu/wala:wa*.

CHAPTER 20

The Sacred Trail to Zuni Heaven: A Study in the Law of Prescriptive Easements

Hank Meshorer

Someone once said that all cases are truly unique. I don't know if that is true, but I am certain that the litigation that led to the recognition of the right of the Zuni Tribe to conduct its quadrennial pilgrimage from its reservation in New Mexico to *Kolhu/wala:wa*, commonly known as "Zuni Heaven," in Arizona and return was, all things considered, a truly special case. In the spirit of John Nichols's 1974 novel *The Milagro Beanfield War*,[1] the controversy was fraught with long-standing grudges based partly on history and a clash of cultures but, if the truth is known, more on personality than anything else. Not that the controversy wasn't taken seriously because it was, and with deadly intensity. Quite simply, to the parties nothing less than a whole way of life was at stake. And with such high stakes no means of battle was considered inappropriate.

The United States Department of Justice initially heard of the matter in early June 1985, when the secretary of the interior first requested that the federal government, in its capacity as trustee for the Zuni Tribe, seek an immediate restraining order to prevent one Earl Platt, a large landowner in northeast Arizona, from interfering with a planned Zuni pilgrimage across his lands. Between 1876 and 1946 Zuni had lost control of that portion of their aboriginal territory on which Platt's ranch was located, and he had vowed to stop the Zunis from entering and "trespassing" on his property. The Zunis had expressed an equal intention of continuing their little-known but centuries-old quadrennial pilgrimage. To the Zunis, an interruption of their sacred trek was simply incomprehensible, a thought so foreign to their psyches that the possibility of it even occurring was beyond verbalization.

Nor were the Zunis particularly comfortable with asking the federal government for its assistance. Differences between the two had existed for several years. First, a long-standing suit brought by the Zunis against the United States, *Zuni Tribe of New Mexico* v. *United States*, alleging a taking of certain tribal ancestral lands was then currently under way. Although the Claims Court suit sought money damages for all of those lands allegedly taken from the Zunis, which claim geographically encompassed both Zuni Heaven as well as the sacred trail to and from the reservation, the tribe had fortuitously decided prior to the initiation of the Claims Court suit specifically to exclude from their claim the lands immediately surrounding Zuni Heaven as well as by inference the quadrennial access. To both the Zunis and the United States, then, a claim, consistent with both parties' positions in the Claims Court could now be made together for the sacred trail to Zuni Heaven. Nevertheless, at the outset both the tribe and the United States remained wary not only of Earl Platt but also of each other.

Second, the Zunis were also undergoing the last, delicate stages in the final acquisition of both the fee title to Zuni Heaven and a permanent quadrennial easement for the sacred trail. Pursuant to an act of August 28, 1984, to convey certain lands to the Zuni for religious purposes, the secretary of the interior had been directed "to immediately acquire by *voluntary* agreement the permanent right of ingress and egress to (Zuni Heaven) for the limited purpose of allowing the Zuni Indians to continue to use said lands for traditional religious pilgrimages and ceremonials."[2] Now both the Zunis and the United States were faced with one large and angry landowner who was absolutely refusing even to allow the Zunis on his lands, let alone entertain a "voluntary" acquisition of the sacred trail. Moreover, and perhaps most significantly, the landowner was hinting darkly of a possible violation of his constitutional rights under the First Amendment to the Constitution,[3] which charge might well have put in jeopardy the entire congressional scheme for the Zuni reacquisition of Zuni Heaven and the sacred trail.

Third, more or less contemporaneous with these events, the federal courts were also considering whether the First Amendment's Free Exercise Clause allowed certain tribes to halt the construction of a government road through an admittedly sacred former Indian area.[4] Very much on the minds of both the Zunis and the United States were the sentiments later articulated by the Supreme Court when it stated, "[Even though] the road-building projects at issue . . . could have devastating effects on traditional Indian religious practices . . . [and] . . . would virtually destroy the Indians ability to practice their religion, . . . the Constitution simply does not provide a principle that could justify upholding" the tribe's claims of a "religious servitude" over the subject lands.[5]

Simply stated, a claim based on the purely religious right to the use of the sacred trail seemed at best dubious and most certainly extremely problematic. Any claim based on a First Amendment basis was fraught with danger.[6] But to the Zunis, the whole idea of the pilgrimage was a fulfillment of a religious obligation. "Why," they asked, "could they not practice their religion free from interference on land they considered always to be their own?" "How," the landowner Earl Platt must have been asking at the same time, "can the government impose these Indian religious practices on me by forcing me to accommodate their pilgrimage across my lands? Isn't that a violation of *my* First Amendment rights?" Much on the minds of the government prosecutors was the fact that most, if not all, of the evidence to be offered by the Zunis would by definition reflect the very essence of the pilgrimage as very much a religious endeavor. On the eve of filing suit against Earl Platt, the shadow of *Lyng* indeed hung heavy on the parties. Perhaps mercifully, the Justice Department was not given much time to consider these imponderables because the case was thrust suddenly on it on the eve of the quadrennial pilgrimage of 1985. But let me first back up and set the legal landscape.

STATEMENT OF FACTS

For centuries approximately sixty Zuni religious priests had been making a religious pilgrimage from their central village in New Mexico along a sacred path learned by memory to an equally sacred area in northeast Arizona known as *Kolhu/wala:wa*, or "Zuni Heaven." The trek occurred once every four years at the time of the summer solstice and covered approximately 110 miles over a period of four days. The pilgrims, traveling by foot and horseback, were first witnessed by Spanish conquistador Francisco Vásquez de Coronado in 1540.

In 1985, the defendant, Earl Platt, one of the intervening landowners, challenged the right of the Zunis to cross his lands. To avoid the chance of violence (in 1882 the Zunis had burned out the last rancher to challenge their quadrennial right of passage), the United States secured a temporary restraining order on June 12, 1985, enjoining the defendant from interfering with that pilgrimage. The government also brought suit (*United States v. Earl Platt*) on that date seeking to establish a prescriptive easement under Arizona law that would afford the Zunis the right of ingress and egress on the subject lands once every four years for the limited purpose of traveling from their reservation to *Kolhu/wala:wa* and return.[7]

In what proved to be a most fortuitous strategic move, the government's pleadings were particularly drawn to avoid the obvious difficulties that would inure from any (favorable or otherwise) decision based on a First Amendment right either to support the Zunis in their claim or to support the defendant in his opposition.[8] Specifically, the government's suit purposely sought only to establish that the Zunis had satisfied the requisite elements, *infra*, necessary to establish a prescriptive easement under Arizona law solely to allow the tribe to cross Earl Platt's lands once every four years. No mention was made of any First Amendment–based privilege the Zunis may have retained to cross such lands. Rather, the only legally cognizable right sought was the distinctly nonreligious claim under state property law for an easement to enter on, cross over, and return through certain lands once every four years. The admittedly religious use of the claimed easement was thus forever rendered irrelevant to the court's limited inquiry.

For the next four years the defendant, a former state senator and county attorney and one of the largest landowners in Arizona (reportedly owning or controlling approximately 400,000 acres), tenaciously opposed the prosecution of this case. Virtually every motion, discovery request, or other matter was bitterly resisted by the defendant. Meanwhile, the next quadrennial pilgrimage was coming due, and a second temporary restraining order was granted on May 26, 1989, for the then-impending June quadrennial trek across Earl Platt's lands. During that pilgrimage, the defendant, in violation of the second restraining order, interfered with the pilgrimage by, inter alia, driving his truck through the pilgrimage and allegedly (but not proven at trial) hitting a horse and rider, cursing the pilgrims, and denying them access to water. After an August 31, 1989, hearing, the court held the defendant in civil contempt of court and fined him $5,000.

Over the centuries the Zuni pilgrimage had never been curtailed. Even with the sanctions of a civil contempt order, the entire Zuni nation was in a state of shock and anger because of the defendant's desecration of its ancient ceremonial pilgrimage. Members of the Bow Priests, who are charged with securing the safety of the religious beliefs of the tribe, along with a large contingent of the Zunis, attended the entire trial. For his part, Earl Platt was equally intent on blocking the Zunis from crossing his lands. Accompanying Platt were several of his ranch hands as well as his two sons, both of whom are hardened Arizona trial attorneys. The U.S. Marshal's Office was alerted to the possibility of open hostilities. It was in this charged atmosphere that the trial began in Phoenix on January 3, 1990.

The presentation of the government's evidence was made doubly difficult by virtue of the fact that the quadrennial pilgrimage had hitherto been a secretive activity unknown to most of the Anglo community. During the trial, the extensive preparation by the government's expert witnesses led to an avalanche of archaeological, ethnohistorical, and contemporaneous testimony to support the contention that the Zunis had in fact traveled to *Kolhu/wala:wa* under a claim of right once every four years over the same route, which route had been memorized by rote and passed on from one generation to another through song and prayer. Although the Zunis themselves were extremely reluctant to discuss the pilgrimage with any outsiders, the United States, through the services of its main expert witness, E. Richard Hart, was able to elicit invaluable testimony through the use of an interpreter of several elderly Zunis who could remember participating in numerous pilgrimages over the years. In addition, and again through the use of Hart, the government prosecutor was able to find several non-Indian local inhabitants, including Stewart Udall, the former secretary of the Interior, who stepped forward to testify on behalf of the Zunis.

STATEMENT OF LAW

Elements of Prescriptive Use

Under Arizona law, a prescriptive easement is granted when a claimant proves that he has retained "peaceable and adverse possession" of another's land for a ten-year period.[9] "Peaceable possession" means "possession which is continuous, and not interrupted by an adverse action to recover the estate."[10] "Adverse possession," in turn, is defined as "an actual and visible appropriation of land, commenced and continued under a claim of right inconsistent with and hostile to the claim of another."[11] Generally then, before title by adverse possession can be acquired it must be shown that the possession was (1) actual, (2) open and notorious, (3) hostile or under a claim of right, (4) exclusive, and (5) continuous for the statutory period.[12] On a showing of adverse use, the claimant becomes entitled to an easement in the adversely used property.[13]

To be sure, prescriptive easements are not favored because of the implied diminution or forfeiture of the rights of the record owner. Recognizing the vast, unfenced nature of the topography, Arizona law limits the scope of an easement to the actual use that gives rise to the prescription.[14] Moreover, unless notice of such use of unenclosed land, hostile to the record owner, is clearly brought home to the true owner, the use will be deemed permissive.[15] Once the requisite elements of prescription are demonstrated, however, the use will be presumed to be under a claim of right and not by license of the owner.[16] In order to overcome this presumption, the record owner must show that the use was permissive.[17] If the servient estate's owner fails to rebut this inference, the easement is established.[18]

Earl Platt argued that even under the alleged facts, several of the requisite statutory elements for adverse possession were not present. More specifically, the defendant contended that by merely crossing the subject lands once every four years, the Zunis had not treated the land as would an ordinary owner of the same land. Such minimal, sporadic use, the defendant argued, did not constitute "actual" possession.

The government countered by pointing out that the Zunis sought only an easement by prescription and not a full fee to conduct their quadrennial pilgrimage. To be sure, the tribe's claim of prescription required satisfaction of all the elements necessary to acquire full title by adverse possession, but a "satisfaction" that was measured by the fact that the Zunis sought only to establish a limited right to use the premises, not to own them.[19]

An easement, after all, is only a right to use the lands of another for a specific purpose. Therefore, it is only the use of the land that must be shown to be "open," "notorious," and "adverse" in order to establish an easement. For it is the actual use of the land that ultimately measures the easement. An easement does not involve possession or occupation of the land. It does not involve dominion over the premises except that which is necessary for the enjoyment of the use. It does not distort the legal title of the premises except as it was limited by the character of the easement.[20] Stated succinctly, the government argued that the scope of an easement is limited to the actual use that gave rise to the prescription.[21]

Thus, Arizona courts had had no difficulty finding two to three weeks' physical occupancy each year for approximately thirty years to be "continuous" and "peaceable," sufficient to establish adversity.[22] Actual occupancy similarly had been found not to be necessary to establish possession sufficient to support an adverse claim, the acts necessary being dependent on the circumstances of each case.[23] Moreover, "continuous" use of a right-of-way did not require its utilization every day for the statutory period, the scope of the right-of-way rather being defined only by the nature of its past usage.[24]

In the government's eyes, the unusual quadrennial nature of the pilgrimage did not in and of itself render that use any less prescriptive than would otherwise occur.[25] After all, the government pointed out, the Zunis did not seek fee title to the disputed lands. They were not asking for recognition to any property rights beyond that which they had exercised for centuries. What they sought, however, was an easement narrowly defined to allow them to cross defendant's lands on a date certain (summer solstice) on a quadrennial basis, on a fixed location, and only for the purpose of gaining access to Zuni Heaven.

As the courts in Arizona had stated, "The acts necessary to constitute peaceful possession (are) necessarily varied depending upon the circumstances of each case."[26] In determining matters of prescriptive rights, the Arizona courts had long concluded that there can be no one hard-and-fast formula on which a court can mechanistically lean in a summary fashion to determine the sufficiency of a claim of adversity. Rather, as the courts in *Kay* and *Fritts* recognized, each case must be judged on its own unique facts and circumstances, which by definition require a judicial examination of the individual facts at hand.

On consideration of the evidence compiled and presented by the experts, the government prosecutors concluded that the admittedly sparse use of the subject lands by the Zunis did, in fact and law, constitute a sufficient basis to claim a prescriptive easement. That the Zunis had made this quadrennial pilgrimage for centuries was obvious. There simply was too much direct evidence to dispute seriously this fact. Moreover, the evidence would show that the use of the right-of-way had been continuous and had never been interrupted by the acts of any of the owners of the land. Additional testimony would demonstrate that the Zunis' use of the trail had long been under a "claim of right," which was acknowledged by other property owners in the area. Indeed, the evidence indicated that it was common knowledge throughout the area that the Zunis claimed the right to use the trail on a quadrennial basis at the time of the summer solstice.[27]

The fact that the defendant claimed not to have personally known of the quadrennial trek across his lands did not discourage the government prosecutors. Under Arizona law, the claim of right does not have to be verbally communicated to the property owner. Rather, overt, nonverbal acts may well constitute notice of the users' intention to claim rights inconsistent with the owner's rights.[28] Nor must the prescriptive user express an "ill-will" or "evil intent" toward the record owner in order to establish a "hostile" interest. A mere showing that the one in possession of the land claims exclusive rights thereto and denies by words or acts the owner's title is all that is necessary.[29] Significantly, acts inimical to the owner's claim of exclusive possession and dominion over several years in excess of the statutory period can give rise in the Arizona courts to a presumption that the use is under a claim of right and not by license of the owner.[30] To overcome such presumption the owner then has the burden of showing the use was permissive.[31] Thus, the defendant here was faced with overcoming this heavy burden of an established adversity placed on him by virtue of the uniquely minimal, yet long use of his lands by the Zunis and the need for him to satisfy the burden of proving permissiveness.

Decision of the Court

After a full hearing on the merits, the court issued its opinion on February 8, 1990, "grant(ing) an easement over the land owned by Earl Platt . . . for the purposes of ingress to and egress from Kolhu/wala:wa." Based on the evidence presented, the court found that, as a matter of fact, all of the requisite elements for a showing of an easement by prescription had been established by the government. Moreover, the court concluded that, as a matter of law, such facts were sufficient to constitute an easement by prescription under Arizona law. "It is clear from the record that the plaintiffs have established that the Zuni Indians meet the standards of adverse possession, set forth in A.R.S. sec. 12-521 and the applicable case law for purposes of the limited use sought."

More specifically, the court found the Zuni use to have been (1) actual: "The tribe has had actual possession of the route used for the religious pilgrimage"; (2) open and notorious: "The use of the property, by the Zuni Indians, along the pilgrimage route has been open, visible and known to the community. The Court draws the reasonable inference, from all the facts and circumstances, that Earl Platt, the defendant, was aware that a pilgrimage occurred, that it occurred approximately every four years and that the pilgrimage went across his property"; (3) claim of right: "The evidence clearly illustrated that the Zuni Indians never sought permission to cross lands on their pilgrimage but rather it was believed said crossing was a matter of right"; (4) exclusive: "The Zunis participating in the quadrennial pilgrimage have (had) exclusive possession of the land upon which they cross enroute to Kolhu/wala:wa when they are crossing that land"; and (5) continuous: "The Zuni . . . use and possession of the . . . land has been actual, open and notorious, continuous and uninterrupted for at least 65 years and under a claim of right."

At bottom, the government had prevailed. The crucial issue of whether a mere quadrennial use of a vast and unpopulated area of rural Arizona could give rise to ownership by prescription had been decided in the Zunis' favor. As noted, the trial court found, as a matter of fact and law, that each and every element of adverse possession had been established. Most significantly, the court specifically concluded that "Earl Platt was aware that a pilgrimage . . . went across his property."

Absent a finding of such "actual knowledge" on the part of the owner, the government's case would have been much more susceptible to later modification on appeal. Without "actual knowledge," many of the other elements of prescription, such as "claim of right," "hostile," and "open and notorious," would have been easier to challenge as matters of law on appeal, despite the specific factual findings to the contrary, because of the vast and unenclosed nature of the subject property together with the minimal quadrennial use of the land. Although Arizona law requires mere implied knowledge of the adverse nature of the use, the near-clandestine quadrennial use found here would strain that doctrine quite possibly to the breaking point.[32] From a determination of "actual knowledge," however, there follows a much more facile legal conclusion that the other elements of prescription are legally sufficient as well. In other words, since the defendant knew of the quadrennial pilgrimage and never objected, the elements of actual, hostile, claim of right, and open and notorious attach much more easily to the prescriptive use, despite its admittedly rare and unusual nature.

LESSONS LEARNED

What have we learned? The first lesson is obvious: An aboriginal property right can be successfully established under state laws of prescription even when that usage is deemed at first blush rather minimal or even scarcely visible. Care should be taken, however, before expanding this rather particularized event into a generalized trend in Indian law. Three major factors unique to this case helped lead to its successful result.

The first distinguishing factor was the Zuni Tribe. An incredible sagacity of purpose, which remained crystallized throughout these proceedings despite a myriad of political, legal, and economic distractions, kept the tribe focused on maintaining its consistency of approach to the one true task at hand: to have recognized its unfettered title to Zuni Heaven and the sacred trail. Throughout the decade of proceedings at the Claims Court, during a similarly long period of congressional machinations, and throughout the five-year tumultuous litigation with Earl Platt, the Zunis were never distracted. I believe that a steadfast clarity of purpose derived from their cultural maturity uniquely guided the Zunis in their quest. How else can one explain the Zunis' near-clairvoyant approach in what for them was the easy decision to exclude, nearly ten years *before* the *Platt* litigation, both Zuni Heaven and the sacred trail from their Claims Court litigation? That is, to refuse consciously to accept monies for these lands being taken from them simply because in their psyche these lands had never left their possession. Or their courage and faith in our system of jurisprudence to reveal through statement and testimony certain aspects of their hitherto near-secret quadrennial pilgrimage in what to them was a foreign court of law? Or their resolve to stay the course despite Earl Platt's provocations in attempting to disrupt their quadrennial trek in both 1985 and 1989? A strong tribe indeed.

Second, throughout these proceedings the Zunis had been supported extremely well by their experts. Unique to this case, I can safely say that in my twenty-five-odd years of litigation I have never seen a cadre of more knowledgeable and dedicated consultants as I had the pleasure of associating with in the *Platt* litigation. Their preparation, intensity, and integrity well served the Zunis and their cause. With the secretive nature of the pilgrimage itself, let alone the natural reticence of the Zunis to testify in mind, the totality and clarity of evidence presented to me by these experts made my job infinitely easier. Without their help, this case may well have been decided otherwise. Indeed, the court as much agreed when it ruled in favor of virtually every major factual inference asserted by the tribe during the trial.

Third, let's face it: Earl Platt never got the point. Aside from other missed opportunities, Platt never fully realized the inherent weakness of the government's claim to a prescriptive easement based on such a minimal use of his vast and unenclosed land. Rather than focusing on a pointed demand that the Zunis first and foremost prove his "actual knowledge" of their quadrennial trek, he chose, for whatever reason, to avail himself of other less forceful legal arguments, including an attempt to stop single-handedly the pilgrimages of both 1985 and 1989, which led ultimately to the court finding him in contempt. Such tactics may appear to work in the movies, but they are not the most effective means to prevail in federal court. As noted earlier, if the defendant had steadfastly argued, despite the evidence offered by the government to the contrary, for a showing of "actual knowledge" on the part of the landowner, perhaps the court might have been more sympathetic to his cause.

Finally, a second lesson that can be taken from this case is the possibility that in other, similar situations where a long-standing native religious practice requires the crossing of non-Indian lands, a successful claim for a prescriptive easement narrowly drawn to conform to the actual Indian religious needs may be possible without regard to First Amendment problems. As in the Zuni situation, even though most, if not all, of the evidence would be of religious orientation, the specific activity, that is the actual physical *use* of the land (walking across, stopping and praying at certain shrines, camping overnight, lighting ceremonial fires, ritually bathing at designated locations, etc.) would not be presented to the court as a legally cognizable religious right but as mere indicia of the fulfillment of the requirements for a prescriptive easement.

PURPOSE VERSUS USE

Viewed in this context, then, the religious purpose for the Zunis' pilgrimage is irrelevant. The issue before the court is not whether the purpose of the activity is "religious" but whether that activity can satisfy the state law requirement for the finding of a prescriptive easement. For it is the alleged prescriptive *use* of the land, not the *purpose* for such use, that is determinant. For example, if I cross your lands every day to go from my house to a gambling establishment to participate in a prohibited activity (gambling) and I later decide to seek a prescriptive easement to cross your lands thusly, it would be no defense for you to point to the illegal *purpose* (or any other purpose for that matter) of my crossing your lands. The only issue would be whether my *use* of your lands (the actual physical crossing once per day) is sufficient to support the finding of a prescriptive easement. So, too, for the Zunis and perhaps for other tribes as well. It worked once. It might again. As in cases of this nature, only time will tell.

NOTES

1. John Nichols, *The Milagro Beanfield War* (New York: Random House, 1974).
2. 98 Stat. 1533 (1984), sec. 4; emphasis added.
3. The first clause of the First Amendment to the Constitution states that "Congress shall make no law respecting an establishment of religion." In essence, the landowner was arguing that by enactment of Public Law 98-408, which would provide the Zunis with a property right across his lands for a religious purpose, Congress had violated this portion of the First Amendment by, in effect, establishing a religion.
4. The Free Exercise Clause of the First Amendment to the Constitution provides that "Congress shall make no law . . . prohibiting the free exercise (of religion)." See *Northwest Indian Cemetery Ass'n* v. *Peterson*, 565 F. Supp. 586 (1883), *aff'd* in part 795 F.2d 688 (9th Cir. 1986) reversed *sub nom. Lyng* v. *Northwest Indian Cemetery Protective Ass'n*, 485 U.S. 439 (1988).
5. *Lyng*, 485 U.S. at p. 439.
6. See ibid.
7. Civ. No. 85-1478 USDC, Ariz. (1985). As noted earlier, in a previous suit, *Zuni Tribe* v. *United States*, the tribe itself had sued the United States for money damages based, in part, on the extinguishment of its aboriginal title to an area that included the lands on which the easement was located. During the Claims Court litigation, however, the tribe specifically excluded from its claim the present-day Zuni Reservation in New Mexico as well as the lands immediately surrounding Zuni Heaven. Access once every four years between the two parcels was also impliedly excluded, and the Zunis so acknowledged throughout both the Claims Court and the instant litigation. The Zunis simply had never asserted that their quadrennial right of access was ever taken from them. The position advanced by the United States on behalf of the Zunis in the *Platt* suit was based on the particular elements of a prescriptive easement under state law and was therefore not in conflict with the government's stance vis-à-vis the tribe in the claims suit.
8. See, e.g., *Lyng*.
9. A.R.S. sec. 12-526A. The section reads as follows: "A person who has a cause of action for recovery of any lands, tenements or hereditaments from a person having peaceable and adverse possession cultivating, using and enjoying such property, shall commence an action therefor within ten years after the cause of action accrues, and not afterward."
10. Ibid., sec. 12-521A2.
11. Ibid., sec. 12-521A1. *Kay* v. *Briggs*, 475 P.1 (1970); *LaRue* v. *Kosich*, 187 P.2d 642, 645 (1947); *England* v. *Ally Ong Hing*, 459 P.2d 498, 505 (1969).
12. *Ellington* v. *Fuller*, 563 P.2d 1339 (1973).
13. *Overly* v. *Crowley*, 664 P.2d 210 (1982).
14. Cf. *Krencicki* v. *Peterson*, 522 P.2d 762, 764 (1974).
15. *England* v. *Ally Ong Hing*, 459 P.2d at p. 505; *Combs* v. *DuBois*, 662 P.2d 140 (1982).
16. *Brown* v. *Ware*, 630 P.2d 545, 547 (1981); *Terry* v. *Luplow*, 442 P.2d 107, 111–12 (1968).
17. Cf. *LaRue* v. *Kosich*, 187 P.2d at 647.
18. *Brown* v. *Ware*, 630 P.2d at pp. 547–48.
19. *Etz* v. *Mamerow*, 233 P.2d 442 (1951).
20. Ibid., 233 P.2d at p. 445.
21. Cf. *Krencicki* v. *Peterson*.

22. *Kay* v. *Briggs,* 475 P.2d at pp. 4–5.

23. See *Wise* v. *Knapp,* 422 P.2d 96, 101–2 (1966), where the court found intermittent and confusing use of certain lands based on mutual mistake of facts to be sufficient grounds for adversity; and *Walker* v. *Northern Arizona Title Co.,* 433 P.2d 988, 1002 (1967), where the court noted that "the fact that the possessor of the lands does not realize that he is holding the property adversely or hostile to the interests of another person does not affect the application of the rule."

24. See *Gosheroski* v. *Lewis,* 167 P.2d 390, 393 (1946); *Brown* v. *Ware,* at p. 547.

25. See *Spillsbury* v. *School District 19 of Maricopa County,* 288 P. 1027, 1029 (1930), wherein the court, noting approvingly of a rather phlegmatic claim of occupancy by an adverse claimant, nevertheless stated: "It is suggested that to establish title by adverse possession there must be an actual occupancy of the land, as such use of it as is ordinarily adopted to. This court has held that neither actual occupancy nor cultivation nor residence is necessary to constitute actual possession and that what acts may or may not constitute a possession are necessarily varied, and depend upon the circumstances."

26. *Kay* v. *Briggs,* 475 P.2d at pp. 4–5; *Fritts* v. *Ericson,* 436 P.2d 582, 585 (1968).

27. Indeed, the Zuni leaders were in the habit of contacting the county sheriff to let him know the pilgrimage was under way and to request his assistance in blocking traffic on one of the state highways the Zuni procession had to cross.

28. *Sparks* v. *Scottsdale Mortgage Corp.,* 398 P.2d 916, 918 (1965), wherein the only overt notification of the claim of the right was the bare use of the easement.

29. *Leon* v. *Byus,* 565 P.2d 1312 (1977); *Tenny* v. *Luplow,* 442 P.2d at p. 110.

30. *Gosheroski* v. *Lewis,* 167 P.2d at pp. 393–94.

31. Ibid.

32. *Tenny* v. *Luplow,* 442 P.2d at pp. 107, 111–12. See *Establishment of Prescriptive Easements in Arizona,* 23 Ariz. L. Rev. 1487 (1983).

Postscripts

CHAPTER 21

The Zuni Claims Cases

Stephen G. Boyden

Nearly twenty years ago, my law firm was approached by the governor and the Zuni Tribal Council to represent the Zuni Indian Tribe as legal counsel. Governor Robert E. Lewis explained that Zuni tribal members had recently heard accounts of the aboriginal land claims of the neighboring tribes then pending before the Indian Claims Commission, which the Zunis felt were contrary to Zuni history and tradition. He also stressed that many tribal members were concerned that some of their sacred shrines were being endangered by third parties that might desecrate them or otherwise try to interfere with traditional Zuni worship. In short, Governor Lewis was fearful that Zuni customs, traditions, and religion were in jeopardy.

After holding several meetings with the governor and the Tribal Council and signing a general counsel contract and a claims attorney contract, we jointly established two primary goals. The first was to obtain the ownership of sacred lands for the Zuni Tribe, and the second was to institute a claims case against the United States for Zuni lands taken many years ago without compensation to the tribe. The goals were ambitious and very difficult to attain in light of intense opposition from the U.S. government and the limited resources of the Zuni Indian Tribe. We knew at the outset that both we and the Zuni Tribe would have to make a long-term commitment of time and resources to be successful, but everyone felt the cause would justify the extraordinary effort that would be required.

We began our work by personally interviewing a number of Zuni elders in the pueblo about Zuni traditional land use. The leaders spoke of the place of creation and the eventual migration of the Zuni ancestors to the Middle Place at the present site of the pueblo of Zuni. They spoke of many places of significance along the migration route, of the division of the people, of holy shrines, of places of worship, and of sacred paths and sites remembered and named in oral tradition. The Zuni people provided the information that we needed to formulate our original concepts of aboriginal Zuni land use and occupation.

The American West Center of the University of Utah under the direction of Floyd A. O'Neil had completed a number of oral interviews with the Zuni people and published a portion of them. E. Richard Hart, who was working with the center, assembled a number of interviews and historical documents pertinent to the issue of Zuni land use during the nineteenth century. He also drafted a preliminary narrative describing Zuni farming, livestock raising, hunting and gathering practices, and as contacts with Spanish, Mexican, and U.S. explorers, soldiers, missionaries, and settlers. The documentary record combined with the information received from the Zunis rounded out our preliminary assessment of Zuni claims.

Although it appeared that the Zuni claims had merit, the Indian Claims Commission statute of limitations had run out in 1951, and the United States was immune from further suit. Since the Zuni Tribe had not filed a lawsuit with the Indian Claims Commission, the tribe was precluded by law from bringing an action against the United States notwithstanding the validity of the claims. The only way open to Zuni was to present its case to Congress and ask that a special law be passed to allow the tribe to sue the United States for the taking of Zuni lands. We had to ask Congress to change its policy and make an exception for the Zuni Tribe, knowing full-well that Congress had repeatedly said after 1946 that it would never change its policy.

The major breakthrough came on May 15, 1978, when Public Law No. 95-280 was signed into law after six years of intensive lobbying in Washington, D.C., in the face of intense opposition by the Department of Justice and the Department of the Interior. This law conferred jurisdiction on the United States Court of Claims to hear, determine, and render judgment on any claims of the Zuni Indian Tribe of New Mexico against the United States with respect to any lands or interest therein held by aboriginal title or otherwise. The legislation not only opened the door to the lawsuits known as Zuni 1 and Zuni 2 but also returned Zuni Salt Lake, located south of the present Zuni Indian Reservation.

Using the guidance received in depositions and oral interviews with Zuni elders, we employed outstanding experts in the fields of anthropology, archaeology, ethnology, and history to document for the court the Zuni land use patterns predating the first Spanish *entradas* up to the present time. There was great harmony between the Zuni oral traditions and the historical and scientific records. We spent an immense amount of time in meticulously preparing for trial and correlating all of the evidence.

The trial was held in Salt Lake City in March 1982 before the Honorable Judith Ann Yannello. We presented evidence from numerous sources to establish that the Zuni Tribe had from time immemorial owned, used, occupied, and held by aboriginal title a large tract of land located in the present-day states of New Mexico and Arizona. The tribe presented archaeological-anthropological evidence, together with oral history, to demonstrate how Zuni land use involved a core area of permanent and seasonal settlements, where agriculture was intensively practiced, surrounded by a larger sustaining area, where floodwater farming was pursued, with extensive grazing, hunting, and gathering of numerous plants and minerals.

The tribe also presented evidence of a deeply rooted religious faith that was expressed by making use of a vast area both inside and outside the claim area for the specialized gathering of many objects used in connection with prayer offerings and other religious ceremonies. Numerous "markers," or shrines, were built and maintained throughout the area and served notice on travelers of Zuni ownership and protected the Zuni people from intruders. The boundaries of Zuni aboriginal lands were dictated in large part by the geography of the region.

Judge Yannello handed down her decision on May 27, 1987, holding the United States liable for the taking of all of the lands claimed by the Zuni Tribe. The decision was total victory for the Zuni people, carefully documenting the Zunis' rightful claims to their aboriginal lands. The question of value was left to the second phase of the lawsuit. We attempted to obtain interest, but the court found, as it did in all other aboriginal cases, that the Zuni Tribe was not entitled to interest on any judgment. The $25-million settlement, which we have recently concluded, represents a fair value for the lands at the time they were taken.

The major significance of Zuni 1 is that it provides the Zuni people with a true and correct history of their origins, land use, and relationship with other tribes and the governments of Spain, Mexico, and the United States. The money judgment, if protected, will provide the tribe with a source of income that will enable it to purchase more land or fund worthy programs. In our view, the preservation of the Zuni history, culture, tradition, and religion is the priceless legacy of the effort made by the tribe in Zuni 1.

In keeping with the original goal of obtaining ownership to Zuni sacred lands, we worked with Congress, especially Senator Barry Goldwater (R-Ariz.) in obtaining the lands of Zuni Heaven, located in the state of Arizona. The act of August 28, 1984, provided the tribe with an area of nearly 12,000 acres, which was part of a new Zuni reservation in the state of Arizona. This act protected the Zunis' right to make their traditional pilgrimage to the area without disturbance or desecration to the sacred site.

Difficulties arose regarding the pathway to Zuni Heaven, and we were able to convince the United States to protect the rights of the tribe against a landowner who wanted to interfere with the traditional pilgrimage. This litigation was concluded with a judgment in favor of the tribe not only to use the new reservation land in Arizona but also to travel along the pathway without interference.

Zuni 2 was a lawsuit designed to seek reparations from the United States for damages to the Zuni Reservation lands caused by acts or omissions of the United States. This lawsuit was extremely complicated because it dealt with erosion of tribal lands over a long period of time. From a legal standpoint, it was extremely difficult to prove what had caused the erosion to take place since much of it had happened before any living person was born. We were required to hire many technical experts who dealt with the issues of causation and damage.

Governor Lewis, being aware of the great length of time it would take to finally resolve the issues in litigation, suggested that we go forward with a legislative settlement. We were required to continue litigating the case while we attempted to settle the matter with Congress. This effort put a terrific strain on the time and resources of the attorneys and the tribe. We completed our preparations for trial while we spent three years lobbying in Washington, D.C.

Senator Pete Domenici (R-N.Mex.) championed the Zuni cause, which resulted in the act of October 21, 1990, the Zuni Land Conservation Act. We were able to accomplish two basic purposes: (1) draw attention to the need for a comprehensive sustainable development program for Zuni human, cultural, and natural resources; and (2) have the United States be responsible to appropriate money for the restoration of Zuni Reservation lands on a permanent basis. These purposes were accomplished by the creation of a $25-million trust fund that would provide income to the tribe on an annual basis for the land restoration work and sustainable development plant.

The twenty-year relationship that we have had with the tribe has been blessed with great success. We have had to work very hard at lobbying Congress, negotiating with the administration, and litigating in the courts all at the same time. The effort of the Zuni people likewise has been tireless and unfailing, and the experts employed by the tribe equally dedicated themselves to the Zuni cause. The Zuni people, their attorneys, and the experts could see the vision of regaining the sacred lands, restoring reservation lands to their original condition, and, above all, preserving the culture of the Zuni people. Gratefully, we have reached the time of fulfillment, but much lies ahead for future generations to continue the Zuni cause.

CHAPTER 22

The Zuni Land Case:
A Personal Reminiscence

Floyd A. O'Neil

In 1967 the University of Utah's American West Center, then called the Western History Center, became associated with the Zuni Tribe in a project to translate many of the oral histories the tribe had recorded. In connection with that project, I was sent to Zuni by the historian Gregory Crampton to handle some administrative details. In a characteristic act of generosity, Governor Robert E. Lewis showed me around the pueblo, discussed the history of his family, and even drove to Gallup that evening with his wife, Virginia, to join me for dinner. Our discussion led to some research into Zuni history and work with the Zuni schools in producing some printed items to be used by the local students.

As the research progressed on the history of the pueblo, Governor Lewis indicated that the research could be very useful in a legal problem the council was addressing. It was then he discussed the fact that the tribe had been advised by the Bureau of Indian Affairs not to file a land claim case, as most tribes in the country had done. Governor Lewis and his lieutenant governor, Theodore Edaakie, had already begun the process of getting the Zuni land issue into the courts.

At the time a student at the University of Utah, E. Richard Hart had begun his work with the American West Center. Hart took such an avid interest in Zuni history that he became the major researcher in that field. He developed friendships and relations of trust with the tribe that have endured and matured for the past quarter century. He took on a central role for the American West Center.

Part of the research work performed by Richard Hart and myself was funded by a small grant to investigate the land claim. During that investigative period, the tribe was in the process of changing attorneys. In a meeting with the Tribal Council, the question of an attorney came up. I was asked my opinion about an attorney who could handle the issue. I suggested Stephen G. Boyden and gave the tribe two reasons for my choice. The first was a tenacity I had seldom seen before, and the second was that I thought that congressional permission would be needed to succeed and that Boyden was very talented at working with Congress.

While I was still in the council chamber, Governor Lewis telephoned the U.S. solicitor for the Department of the Interior. The solicitor agreed in the choice but indicated that Boyden could not be hired because his firm represented the neighboring Hopi tribe. The governor suggested that there were no outstanding issues between Zuni and Hopi and that there had never been, so Boyden was approved and hired. In a three-way communication, the tribe, the American West Center, and the attorneys were in a constant exchange of materials and opinions about the facts. Hart took up the compilation of a very usable collection of materials on Zuni history. His role was far more intense than was my own in pursuing the issues in the case.

The case was finally allowed by a congressional act passed May 15, 1978, Public Law 95-280, which conferred jurisdiction on the U.S. Court of Claims for Zuni land claims. The early assumption that the approval of Congress would be necessary proved to be true. Boyden and Hart were both extremely important in the process. After the act was signed, the intense process of gathering even more detailed material began. The central gathering and processing place for correspondence, maps, notes, printed sources, archival material, and oral testimonies was the center.

Once the permission of Congress had been obtained to litigate the claims, a new role was described for me by Boyden. He asked my help in choosing expert witnesses. I named several whom I thought would be excellent: S. Lyman Tyler, director of the American West Center (Boyden had worked with Tyler before and thought the choice a good one); Myra Ellen Jenkins, state historian for New Mexico (her long service, deep knowledge, and pro–Indian interests attitude were welcome); and Ward Alan Minge of New Mexico, who had had long experience as a historian and had acted as an expert witness, especially at the pueblo of Acoma. All three agreed to serve. I also suggested Albert Schroeder of Santa Fe, but he decided not to serve. Boyden asked Triloki Nath Pandey of the University of California at Santa Cruz to assist. Pandey's study at Zuni made him a highly qualified participant. Boyden also invited the renowned professor of anthropology Fred Eggan of the University of Chicago to join the team. His work at Hopi had convinced the attorneys that he would prove valuable. At Zuni archaeologist T. J. Ferguson had begun to put together the Zuni Archaeology Program, which would become so wonderfully successful. He was retained to provide expert testimony on the archaeology of the claim area.

Governor Lewis and Lt. Governor Edaakie are the two people at Zuni, who more than any others, worked directly with us in making decisions. Never, at any point, was the dignity of the scholars questioned. When the question came up, "Can the scholars write whatever they please from the materials they find," the governor and the council decided in the affirmative: "Let us be open and honest." There was less partisan spirit in the proceedings than I have ever seen, and I have worked with thirty-four tribes in eleven states. So I have great admiration for Zuni's handling of this case.

Later in the process, Jenkins suggested that John Baxter of Santa Fe be added to the team because of his special research abilities. He was. But of all the experts who served, E. Richard Hart spent the most time and was more nearly a full-time participant than the rest of the experts. He also displayed a passion for the case and the interests of the Zunis. By that time Hart had left the American West Center and was employed at the Sun Valley Center for Arts and Humanities. The close liaison between the American West Center and Hart remained. The central gathering point for archiving of materials was the center. As the need arose, the maps for the case were drawn in the center under the careful instructions of Boyden and Hart. Zuni should know that the work was done diligently and well by all the those who gave expert testimony. It was indeed a work of scholarly love. The maps were tremendously effective, the first ever struck in that mode to produce a graphic evidence in regard to the Zuni areas, and American West Center cartographic work was carried out by Cathrine Patillo.

Under a request from Stephen Boyden, each of the expert witnesses wrote a major paper on their subject or period of history. The American West Center at the University of Utah had considerable responsibilities in regard to the Zunis' land claim case (Docket 161-79L). Governor Lewis and his council gave me research tasks, and in my office we coordinated the organization and submission to the court of all of the exhibits, the papers, and background documents. The center staff took the responsibility for reviewing all facts and every footnote. All sources in each of the papers were compared for overall continuity. Because the writings were extensive, the work was extremely detailed. Two graduate students, Kathryn L. MacKay and David R. Lewis, both of whom have since received Ph.D.s and professorships, did the lion's share of that work. Lyman Tyler, Gregory C. Thompson, and I each took turns at checking, verifying, and informing experts where opinions diverged. All of those preparing papers were cooperative in resolving what appeared to be conflicts. After all the papers were in final form, the attorneys borrowed staff (Kathryn L. MacKay) to help in computerizing the data derived from the papers and from other sources used.

When all of the exhibits for the case were complete, they filled eleven banker's boxes, each holding two cubic feet. I wondered at the time about the ability of the attorneys to find enough time to digest that much volume. I sincerely believe that no one on the government's side was ever given the time or resources to respond to that avalanche of scholarship.

When the issue of the trial was addressed, a decision was made not to hold the trial in New Mexico. Boyden obtained the Utah State Supreme Court chambers in Salt Lake City for the trial. The United States Court of Claims appointed Judge Judith Ann Yannello to sit without a jury. The tribe brought twelve Zunis to Utah. Stephen and Pat Boyden housed several of the Zunis, and my wife and I hosted two. The trial lasted two weeks, and the scene was very hectic.

The witnesses were on the stand for long periods. The expert witnesses were seven on the tribe's side and two on the government's. Watching the trial, I was amazed at the poor preparation by the Department of Justice. But it was suffering. The Reagan cuts had decimated the department's ranks, and overassignment was everywhere. I was buoyant as the trial ended. That was premature. The decision we expected within six months took four years! Even after every major point in the case was given to the plaintiff, the Department of Justice was reluctant to see an award. There were radical differences of opinion between the evaluators for the tribe and those for the government. Finally, the tribe and its attorney concluded that a congressional settlement was the only solution. I assisted with that process by testifying before Senator Daniel Inoye's (D-Hawaii) Senate Select Committee on Indian Affairs. The solution was provided by Congress, and another case was joined to it. With the passage of the act, the process was at an end for me.

Three months before the president's signature made the settlement law, I met Governor Lewis in Washington, D.C. I wondered if either of us would live to see an end. We laughed, but ruefully. The case was an active interest for me for twenty-four years, an a participant for twenty-three. Justice for an Indian tribe can be elusive, expensive, and time consuming.

It would be pleasant to end on an upbeat note, but I must end by saying that fair treatment is sometimes bought at too great a price. The case would never have seen a favorable end without the tenacity of three men: Governor Robert E. Lewis, E. Richard Hart, and Stephen G. Boyden.

CHAPTER 23

Achieving True Interpretation*

Edmund J. Ladd

I was appointed interpreter by the Zuni Tribal Council, who consulted closely with Zuni's claims attorneys: Stephen G. Boyden, assisted by John Boyden and Richard Hill. They were having a problem getting an interpreter who was fluent both in English and the Zuni language, and the Boydens recommended that the council select me, subject to tribal law and tribal authentication by Governor Lewis. Then I had to be accepted by the Justice Department as well—I had to be acceptable to both sides. When the case finally went to court, I went through a process of qualification, and both sides and the judge had to agree that they thought I would do an objective and fair job.

I had already done some work for the tribe working to recover the Zuni war gods (*Ahayu:da*) from the Smithsonian and from other organizations. So it wasn't anything that was brand new as far as integrity was concerned, except that it was more strenuous because of the exactness of the terminology that had to be used to translate. I had to take all possible care in my interpreting and translating so that the court heard both sides of the story—objective and straight. With the war gods, the work was strictly interpreting and strictly translating what the tribal elders had to say to the Board of Trustees of the Denver Art Museum and the Board of Trustees of the Smithsonian Institution. So the land claim work wasn't anything that was brand new as far as the process was concerned, but it was a project that was more frightening and more strenuous simply because of the accuracy of terminology that was required. I had to be very careful not to inadvertently put words into the mouths of the elders.

The depositions were probably harder to translate and interpret, because the attorneys had to rephrase and reread questions that were difficult to understand. In translation I had to put the questions into the proper context and make sure that the elders were given enough time to answer the questions that were being asked. Interpretation of the phrasing was necessary so that the elders could understand the

*From an interview by E. Richard Hart, Washington, D.C., June 29, 1993.

questions being put them. Those depositions are some of the most re-markable ethnological documents about Zuni that have ever been created for any purpose.

There are a whole host of words in Zuni that really have no equiva-lency in English. So in those cases you have to dig for the answers, dig for the interpreting and translating with the proper phrasing. It was probably the most difficult thing that I've ever had to do. I have basic knowledge of the Zuni religion system, but I don't have much of the proprietary knowledge as far as the esoteric religious ceremonies are concerned. For instance, I wouldn't have access to special knowledge of the *Koyemshis* ("Mudheads"). The priests are concerned with the origin and archaic place-names and esoteric knowledge that's only privileged to them. There I was with my basic knowledge trying to interpret to the Anglo world and the lawyers the difference between the Zuni language and the pressures of knowing and not knowing what the esoteric knowl-edge really meant. It was a very difficult process.

So there were areas of, not complete secrecy, but guarded statements that were made for the sake of the lawyers and the sake of the law, but the religious leaders' statements were very carefully composed. They would tell me, in essence, "This is not really for their [the outside world's] knowledge, but we still want to make it clear that they understand what our position is going to be." So I was put in a very tenuous and very difficult position of trying to know what to say at that point to keep it from being my words instead of theirs. It was very difficult. It was no simple thing that I had to do there.

There is a difference between interpretation and translation. Straight translation can be very inaccurate. Interpretation involves understanding vernacular in two languages. Take the simple phrase, "Do you work?" or "Are you employed?" You have to be careful to interpret it correctly. By saying in the Zuni language, "Do you work?" the answer would more than likely be, "No," because Zunis consider that phrase to refer to a "regular job," like an eight-to-five job. So that would be a mistranslation in terms of the interpretive aspect of the culture itself. So you have to say, "Are you employed?" or "How do you feed yourself and your children?" That's interpretive. So that's why the simple phrase of "Do you work?" becomes a problem of how you say it to the person so that he realizes the answer that is being requested, that is, "How do you make a living?" It's just like trying to juggle four balls instead of three balls. The three balls is relatively easy, but to get a fourth ball in it gets more complicated because there is more movement. The way the lawyer asks the question and the way you want to phrase it so that you get the response for the lawyer that he wants, you're looking for, and the way you feel he should be responding to in terms of the English that you know is right. When the lawyer said, "Do you work? Are you employed?" the response will be, "Well, no, I am not employed, but I have an income from my jewelry business."

We completed two depositions a day and did thirty of them with Zuni elders as a part of Docket 161-79L, a total of about two or three weeks. Some were easy to do, and some were most difficult because of the way the questions were phrased by the lawyers. The phrasing of the question was as important as eliciting the right response in terms of interpreting the request for information. I knew all of the deponents from past years, and they knew who I was, so I had talked to them before, and I knew what their positions were in the community and what kind of religious background they had. So it wasn't like we were strangers. Knowing who I was, they always greeted me as "younger brother." So it was a rather easy task in that regard, in that I knew most of them intimately and some of them distantly, but still I could speak with them on their terms.

The trial took more than two weeks, and it was pressurized. We had time to be with each other during the evenings and during the trial period, which was kind of difficult because I had to keep myself as much detached from them as I was detached from the opposing parties. Consequently, it was a strain, but knowing the situation, they were very helpful; they would try not to talk about the case, try and not talk about things they were going to discuss at the trial in front of the lawyers, in front of the judge. So it was a strain for the two weeks we were there, but once it was over it was a great relief and very relaxing.

As a Zuni I naturally wanted to see the Zunis win this case, but on the other hand I had to be a strictly impartial translator. It was probably one of the more difficult transitions that one could make. When the opposing lawyers were asking questions, I had to remember that they were asking their questions in just the same way as our lawyers were asking our opponents. I tried to completely neutralize myself to the point where I was just like a sieve, with information coming in one side and going out the other side and coming back from the tribe. The phrasing of the questions and the interpretation and the translation were most difficult because just through simple voice inflection I could get a different answer, different response. So it was one of the more strenuous exercises of self-control, not to overinterpret, not to overtranslate.

There were many instances that provided special difficulties in translation. For example, I remember one episode when I couldn't get the point across of what the lawyer was trying to say. The question was something to the effect that, "When did the Zunis become less hostile?" There is no word for "hostile" and there is no word for "less." So I was trying to interpret around that concept of "When did the Zunis become less hostile?" It became very difficult, and the response was coming back in the wrong context because I would say something like, "When did the time of goodness or nonwarfare begin?" And the concept of time would become so important because Zunis don't recognize time in terms of years. They say in Zuni, "a long time ago." I would say in Zuni, "What year were you born?" It was difficult to say, "What year?" It was difficult to achieve phrasing that would elicit the right concepts in terms of the time—but the time elements were so critical. It was very difficult to get through because in Zuni there is "now," "today," "tomorrow," and past tense, "very far in the past," and "extremely far" in the past tense. All are recognized as time markers, but they're not years. They don't say, "In 1984, 1968, 1970 . . . ," so I had to interpolate around those figures. I would ask in Zuni, using a direct translation, "What year were you born?" And they would say, "Well, I don't know because it was springtime."

There were also moments with some humor. Governor Lewis gave his answers in English. He was asked what Kiva group he belonged to. He belongs to the *Muhekwe*, the "Manure Clan," but when asked for an English equivalent his response was (with a straight face, too) that he was a member of the "Soil Restoration Clan." At first I was perplexed, and then all of a sudden, just like a light bulb, it dawned on me what he was saying.

It has really been a great victory for Zuni to finally win the land claim case. I feel very satisfied. It's been one of the highlights of my career as an anthropologist and archaeologist. My work with the tribe to successfully obtain the *Kolhu/wala:wa* easement was also a highlight of my career as interpreter. It was the hardest thing to try to be neutral and not phrase anything in a favorable way or a nonfavorable way for either us or the opponents. For this reason, especially, I had a feeling of accomplishment that I was responsible for something very important.

When we finally got to the Zuni 1 trial and the Zuni witnesses were ready to enter the Utah Supreme Court Chambers where the trial was held, three of the religious leaders went ahead of the rest, leading the way into the chambers for the first time. They were performing a War Ceremony of the Galaxy Society. No one was allowed to get ahead of them or cross their paths. The Zunis all stayed behind them, and it was done so tactfully that no non-Indians got in front of them either. And each of them was reciting all the appropriate prayers as they went along. There's a phrase that is used that hits the heart of the people that you are fighting against, and they used this phrase. It was used by the Zuni religious leaders to put themselves in an advantageous frame of mind, a frame of reference for what they were about to undergo. The prayers and ceremony provide stamina, perseverance, proficiency at what you're supposed to be doing, and bravery. So we all got behind him, and we walked very slowly up there, and nobody said anything. Nobody said a word until we got inside and then for a few more moments. That was one of the most awesome things because I'd only heard of these things before, and then I was actually a part of them.

CHAPTER 24

Afterword

E. Richard Hart

More than twenty-five years ago in the Zuni Tribal Council chambers, Governor Robert E. Lewis asked me if I would be willing to spend some time working on the Zunis' land claim. Even though almost everyone with whom the Tribal Council had consulted up to that time had said there was virtually no hope in getting the necessary legislation to file a claim, the Zunis remained resolute in their belief that they would eventually get their day in court. From the first, Governor Lewis and the council emphasized that their interest was not only in obtaining some kind of compensation for their lost lands but also in setting the historical record straight. They were deeply offended by the Indian Claims Commission's Navajo decision and frequently stated that it was more important to correct the official history than to get any money. They also stressed ethical considerations. They asked me to look at the history and to honestly tell them if I thought they had a claim or not, and if so, why the tribe hadn't filed before the Indian Claims Commission. They said to find out the facts and "let the chips fall where they may." I remember quite clearly, when first asked by the governor to work on the claims project, thinking that if I said "yes," this would probably not be a short-term commitment.

Indeed, it was not a short commitment, but it was an extraordinarily rewarding effort not only for me, I think, but also for all of those involved. It was a wonderful opportunity for me to work closely with Zuni religious leaders and tribal elders over a period of twenty-five years. The morning before the Zuni 1 trial began, the Zunis who were in Salt Lake City to testify rose early, and we all drove up City Creek Canyon. The Zunis had asked to be taken to the closest location to the court where a spring-fed stream could be found. We parked and the Zunis went to the stream, while the non-Zunis waited in the car. At the stream the Zunis prayed and made offerings of prayer meal. At almost the same moment that they returned to the cars, raindrops began to hit the cars' windshields. Rain kept up throughout most of the trial. While many of the non-Zunis complained about the continuing rain, the Zunis smiled and took it as a good omen.

I have great respect for the integrity of the religious leaders. They pondered, with excruciating patience and focus, over even the smallest considerations brought before them. Throughout the period, the successive Tribal Councils of Zuni took great care to maintain a commitment to established objectives and to deal fairly with all involved. I will remember no Zuni individual with more respect and admiration than Governor Lewis. He was remarkable in his tenacity, sometimes in the face of seemingly insurmountable odds. It was a special privilege to accompany him on Capitol Hill. At all times patient and exceedingly gracious, he is a person who simply will not accept a "no" when he knows he deserves a "yes." His determination in dealing with his congressional delegation earned him a substantial reputation.

It has been a rare opportunity to work in such detail over so many years to answer so many difficult and complex questions involving history, ethnology, and the sciences. The teams of experts truly worked in an interdisciplinary manner, stimulating each other and often finding more new questions than answers. Much of the intellectual fulfillment that came from these cases was really due to the persistent and curious nature of the two lead attorneys in the cases. Steve Boyden, the lead attorney in the Zuni 1 and 2 cases, demonstrated his intellect time and again. He mastered the reports of all of the disciplines and witnesses and displayed his grasp of that knowledge throughout the litigation process. Similarly, Hank Meshorer took such great care to absorb the details in my reports that at times I became convinced he knew my report better than I did. It was extremely gratifying to work with both men, who acted as strong advocates for their client, the tribe, while at the same time understanding the need for objectivity in the expert reports and pressing for that objectivity at all times.

Zuni is a dynamic, vital, and vibrant culture. It continues to be a great pleasure to me to visit Zuni, although I must admit that considerable stress has now been eliminated. As a result of the various settlements, in 1993 we saw a new, modern school at Zuni, construction finished partly with judgment funds. Congress delayed the full appropriation authorized under the Land Conservation Act by some three years, seriously undermining the budget and planning schedule put together by the Conservation Program. But under director James Enote, the Zuni sustainable development plan has been successfully completed, and I find it to be a very impressive document and commitment to the future by this tribe and a model that states, and even nations, should examine carefully. The quadrennial pilgrimage to *Kolhu/wala:wa* was carried out in the summer of 1993 without incident. All these things are heartening to see, especially in a community known for centuries for its hospitable and industrious nature.

At the same time, the intangible results of the cases are making themselves felt. The results of the historical, archaeological, and scientific inquiries carried out by the tribe and in its behalf are being integrated into many facets of tribal operations—education, economic enterprises, and political planning. It was not that long ago that Zuni was a nonliterate, theocratic society. Under today's constitutional Zuni government, the tribe has its own school district and has taken the lead in establishing and maintaining model educational programs for its people. The transition may have been painful at times, but from today's perspective it has been successful. Certainly, archaeological investigation neither proves nor disproves Zuni traditional religious beliefs regarding the first people's emergence and migration. But the integration of these new studies into Zuni society does help religious leaders in making recommendations to planning agencies on management of natural and cultural resources on the reservation and within the aboriginal homeland.

Even though Zuni leaders would be quick to point out that the judgment funds that Zuni has received can never pay the tribe for the extensive damages it has suffered, they have always spoken to me positively about their place within the United States. The Zunis are frequently patriotic and very proud of their many men and women who are veterans. They are confident that they can deal successfully with and under the judicial, executive, and legislative branches of the U.S. government, and they have a positive view of that government and their relationship to it. There is certainly something for all of us to learn from Zuni's experience with the federal courts.

Appendices

Findings of the United States Claims Commission Docket 161-79L, Aboriginal Area

IN THE UNITED STATES CLAIMS COURT

No. 161-79L
Filed: May 27, 1987

THE ZUNI TRIBE OF NEW MEXICO V. THE UNITED STATES

Indian Claims; Extent of Aboriginal Land and Title; Exclusive Use and Occupancy.

    For Plaintiff: Stephen G. Boyden, of Salt Lake City, Utah; John S. Boyden, Jr., G. Richard Hill, and Boyden, Kennedy and Romney, of counsel.
    For Defendant: D. Lee Stewart, with whom was F. Henry Habicht II, Assistant Attorney General; John C. Hitzelberg of counsel.

OPINION

YANNELLO, J. This case involved a claim by the plaintiff for just compensation in the alleged taking of its lands. The claim is of the type formerly addressed by the Indian Claims Commission under 25 U.S.C. §§ 70 et seq. (repealed with the termination of the Commission in 1978 when their jurisdiction was transferred to the Court of Claims and later to that court's successor, the Claims Court, under the Federal Courts Improvement Act of 1982, Pub. L. 97-164). Jurisdiction of this specific action, however, was conferred, by virtue of a special jurisdictional enactment, in section 2 of the Act of May 15, 1978, Pub. L. 95-280, 92 Stat. 244.
    Two of the issues presented in this case have been the subject of trial before this court: (1) the extent of the plaintiff's aboriginal land area which would allegedly be the subject of the taking; and (2) the events which allegedly constituted the taking. The parties have proposed findings of fact and briefed issues of law on both of these issues.
    Due to the volume of the evidentiary record and the complexity of the facts surrounding these issues, the court has addressed them separately. *This opinion, and the Findings of Fact accompanying it, address only the issue of the extent of the land in the claim area.* A separate opinion (with accompanying Findings) will address the events allegedly constituting the taking.

The Findings of Fact accompanying this opinion encompass the proposals of the parties to the following extent: plaintiff's proposed Findings Nos. 1 to 87 and defendant's proposed Findings Nos. 1 to 30 and No. 42. The remainder of the parties' proposed Findings relate to events after 1846, and thus are relevant to the issue of the alleged taking and will accompany the separate opinion addressing that issue.

Aboriginal title to an area claimed by Indians in cases of this type has been defined by the courts as actual, exclusive, and continuous use and occupancy for a long time (or from time immemorial).

Defendant contends that, in 1846, the Zuni area of exclusive use and occupancy was within what is presently the Zuni Reservation. Plaintiff contends that its use and occupancy at that time extended to the entire area claimed. As a factual matter, this court has resolved this issue in agreement with plaintiff, finding that the plaintiff had exclusive use and occupancy from time immemorial.[1]

The Zuni tribe unquestionably used the entire claim area for permanent living accommodations as well as for life-sustaining activities including farming, hunting, grazing, gathering, worshipping, and a host of other activities. While not all of the area was used for all of these purposes, the court finds as plaintiff contends, that the claim area encompasses those lands most thoroughly used for most purposes. (The claim area, for example, does not include the outer reaches used perhaps solely for religious worship and which the Zuni may have shared with other tribes. See e.g., defendant's brief, pp. 299–300.[2]

Considering the entire pattern of use by the Zunis of all territory within the claim area, in determining use and occupancy, is consistent with precedent. See e.g., Confederated Salish and Kootenai Tribes v. United States, 8 Ind. Cl. Comm. 40 (1959); San Carlos Apache Tribe v. United States, 21 Ind. Cl. Comm. 189 (1969); Pawnee Indian Tribe v. United States, 5 Ind. Cl. Comm. 268 (1957); Thompson v. United States, 8 Ind. Cl. Comm. 1 (1959); Snoqualmie Tribe v. United States, 9 Ind. Cl. Comm. 25 (1960); Gila River Pima-Maricopa Indian Community v. United States, 24 Ind. Cl. Comm. 301 (1970).

Defendant also contends that the claim area, particularly that area not permanently inhabited but merely used for life-sustaining activities (sometimes referred to as the "sustaining area") was used by other tribes as well, thus precluding a finding of exclusivity by the Zuni. This court has determined to the contrary.[3]

The use by other tribes, as described in the accompanying Findings, was either temporary and under agreement with the Zuni or was of specific short duration and the result of raid or other hostile intrusion. This court concludes that the use by other tribes, to such a limited extent, does not vitiate or detract from the court's finding of plaintiff's actual exclusivity of use and occupancy. See also: Snake of Piute Indians v. United States, 4 Ind. Cl. Comm. 608, 624 (1956); Omaha Tribe v. United States, 4 Ind. Cl. Comm. 627, 650 (1957); Red Lake, Pembina and White Earth Bands v. United States, 6 Ind. Cl. Comm. 247 (1958); Confederated Salish and Kootenai Tribes v. United States, 8 Ind. Cl. Comm. 40, 56–57 (1959); Quechan Tribe v. United States, 8 Ind. Cl. Comm. 111, 127 (1959); Nez Perce Tribe v. United States, 18 Ind. Cl. Comm. 119, 129 (1967).

Having resolved that plaintiff has established actual exclusive use and occupancy of, and aboriginal title to, the claim area, it is not necessary to examine the parties' contentions as to whether the special jurisdictional act in this case exempted plaintiff from the requirement of making such a showing.[4]

Having determined that the plaintiff has established aboriginal title (see, e.g., Pltf. brief, pp. 35–61; Deft. brief, pp. 295–301), it is unnecessary to treat the alternate contentions that plaintiff had "recognized title" (Pltf. brief, pp. 24–34; Deft. brief, pp. 310–312).

Conclusion of Law

Based on the foregoing, and the accompanying Findings, it is concluded that the plaintiff has established aboriginal title, and exclusive use and occupancy, of the area as claimed in its amended petition.

Judith Ann Yannello, Judge

FINDINGS OF FACT

These Findings are based on a review of the Findings proposed by both parties— including their objections to the proposals of the opposing party, and their replies to objections of the opposing party—together with the evidence cited by both parties in support thereof. By and large, the court's findings are patterned after those proposed by plaintiff, rather than those of defendant.

Much of the evidence introduced by the parties consisted of Expert Testimony and Reports, including the experts' opinions, and the records reviewed and analyzed by experts. While the experts of both parties were credible and impressive, the court found the scope of evidence given by plaintiff's experts to be the more persuasive.

To be sure, as defendant contends in its objections to plaintiff's requested Findings, for example, many of the opinions of the parties' experts differed and some contrary testimony was introduced. However, the evidence introduced by defendant—patterned after its contentions—tended to take a limited view; defendant tended to focus on limited scientific disciplines, on inferences in the absence of evidence (such as those relating to the presence of other Indians) and on limited land area use (such as that actually used for permanent homes).

The court concludes that plaintiff's proposals cite the most persuasive evidence and that the preponderance of the evidence (including the archaeological, anthropological, ethnological, as well as historical and cultural evidence) supports plaintiff's view and proposed Findings. The court's adoption of most of plaintiff's proposals thus in no way implies a lack of consideration of defendant's contentions.

(See also the discussion of the parties' legal contentions in the accompanying Opinion.)

A. JURISDICTION

Finding No. 1: Jurisdictional Status of Plaintiff

The Zuni Indian Tribe is a sovereign American Indian tribe organized pursuant to the provisions of the Indian Reorganization Act of June 18, 1934 (48 Stat. 984) as amended by the Act of June 15, 1935 (49 Stat. 378). The majority of its members now reside on the Zuni Indian Reservation in New Mexico. The constitution and by-laws of the Zuni Indian Tribe were adopted by the Tribal Council, ratified by a vote of the tribal members, and approved by the Secretary of the Interior, thus empowering the tribal government to represent the interests of the Tribe. The Zuni Indian Tribe thus described is the entity entitled to sue under the provisions of the Act of May 15, 1978 (92 Stat. 244).

Finding No. 2: Jurisdiction of the Court, Timely Filing

By the Act of May 15, 1978 (92 Stat. 244), jurisdiction was conferred upon the United States Court of Claims (and, now, its successor the Claims Court) to hear, determine, and render judgement on any claims of the Zuni Indian Tribe against the United States with respect to any lands or interests therein, in the states of New Mexico and Arizona, held by aboriginal title or otherwise which were acquired from the Tribe without payment of adequate compensation by the United States. The Zuni Indian Tribe timely filed its claim herein within three years of May 15, 1978, as required by the aforementioned jurisdictional act.

Finding No. 3: Description of the Claim Area

The Zuni Indian Tribe asserts a claim herein that a large tract of land in the States of Arizona and New Mexico was exclusively owned, used, and occupied by the Zuni Tribe from time immemorial (hereinafter the "claim area"), and that the lands so held by "aboriginal title or otherwise" were taken from the Tribe by the United States without payment of adequate compensation at various designated times between 1846 and 1939. The exterior boundary of the aboriginal land claimed by the plaintiff is outlined on the map appearing as Plaintiff's Exhibit No. 240 and is described as follows:

> Beginning at the point located on the summit of Humphrey's Peak of the San Francisco Peaks located in the present State of Arizona; thence south to Mormon Mountain; thence south to the lookout tower on Baker Butte; thence in a southeastery direction along the Mogollon Rim to McNary, Arizona; thence southeast to Baldy Peak in the Mt. Baldy Wilderness; thence south to Willow Mountain, in the State of Arizona; thence east to Willow Mountain in the State of New Mexico; thence northeast to Granite Mountain near the town of Magdalena, New Mexico; thence northwest to Cebollita Peak; thence in a northerly direction around the western fringe of the Maplais (lava flow) to Grants, New Mexico; thence northeast to Mt. Taylor; thence northwest to Hosta Buttes; thence northwesterly to Mexican Springs; thence westerly to Ganado, Arizona; thence west to Steamboat Canyon; thence west to Steamboat Wash; thence south along the Steamboat Wash to its junction with the Pueblo Colorado Wash; thence in a southwesterly direction along the Pueblo Colorado Wash to its junction with Cottonwood Wash; thence southwest along Cottonwood Wash to Winslow, Arizona; thence in a northwesterly [sic] direction along the Little Colorado River to Leupp, Arizona; thence west to the place of beginning.

Finding No. 4: Exceptions to Lands Claimed

The following three tracts of land are excluded by the Zuni Indian Tribe from the claim asserted herein:

(A) The present Zuni Indian Reservation, New Mexico, held in trust by the United States.

(B) The Zuni Salt Lake which was made part of the Zuni Indian Reservation by the Act of May 15, 1978 (92 Stat. 244), and is described as follows:

> Lots 3 and 4, east half southwest quarter, west half southeast quarter, section 30, township 3 north, range 18 west, lots 1 and 2, east half northwest quarter, west half northeast quarter, section 31, township 3 north, range 18 west,

southeast quarter, section 25, and east half northeast quarter, section 36, township 3 north, range 19 west, all of New Mexico principal meridian, New Mexico, containing approximately 618.41 acres, more or less.

(C) The lands immediately surrounding Zuni Heaven or *Kolhu/wala:wa* which are described as follows:

Beginning at the Northeast corner of Section 26, Township 15 North, Range 26 East, Gila and Salt River Base and Meridian; thence west to the Northwest corner of Section 28, Township 15 North, Range 26 East; thence South to the Southwest corner of Section 16, Township 14 North, Range 26 East; thence East to the Southeast corner of Section 14, Township 14 North, Range 26 East; thence North to the point of beginning.

ALSO all of Section 27, Township 14 North, Range 26 East, Gila and Salt River Base Meridian.

B. PHYSICAL FEATURES OF CLAIM AREA

Finding No. 5: Importance of Land Forms

The Zuni claim area contains a wide variety of land forms. In the north is the Colorado Plateau, a high table land containing mesas or valleys and broad plains broken by occasional mountain ranges. South and west of the claim area is the Basin and Range Province consisting of wide river valleys separated by long mountain ranges. Between the Colorado Plateau and the Basin and Range Province are the rugged and steeply pitched mountains of the Transition Zone. The steep escarpment of the Mogollon Rim separates the Colorado Plateau from the mountains of the Transition Zone. The eastern end of the Mogollon Rim is buried under the high volcanic mountain ranges of the Mogollon Slope, which enclose a large basin in the Plains of San Augustine. The highest mountains in the Zuni claim area are the San Francisco Peaks to the west at 12,633 feet, Mt. Taylor to the east at 11,389 feet, and Baldy Peak in the White Mountains to the south at 11,403 feet. Between the bottom of the Grand Canyon in the northwest corner of the claim area and the highest mountain peaks is found a vertical relief of over 10,000 feet. The claim area consists of diverse physical landscapes and varied environments and resources.

Finding No. 6: Zuni Use of the Land and Its Resources

The Zunis made use of resources from every part of their environment within the claim area.[5] The landscape of the Zuni claim area encompasses a highly varied physical environment offering many valuable resources needed to sustain human life. Geology, land forms, drainage, precipitation, temperature, and biotic communities all vary from place to place within the claim area, and the availability of many critical resources varies from year to year as well. This environmental variability requires an extensive and flexible land use system, so that if a particular resource is not available at one place when it is needed it can be obtained elsewhere.

Finding No. 7: Effect of Drainages and Hydrology upon Zuni Land Use

The drainages and availability of water were critical elements determining the location of cultivated crops and collectable plant materials traditionally used by the

Zunis. The drainages of the Zuni claim area are separated by the Continental Divide into east and west following streams. To the east, the streams flow to the Rio Grande. To the West, the streams, including the tributaries of the Little Colorado River, flow to the Colorado River. Water flows into but not out of the closed basins of the north plains and the Plains of San Augustine. To the north, the San Juan River drainage carries water east of the Chuska Mountains in a northerly direction to the San Juan River and thence to the Colorado River. Important areas of water resources include all of the high mountain peaks where winter snows provide surface runoff during the spring melt as well as a recharge subterranean water tables. In general, water resources in the claim area become increasingly scarce at lower elevations.

Traditional Zuni agricultural land use was concentrated in the drainage of the Upper Little Colorado River including the Zuni River Valley.

The Zuni also used the drainage of the Upper Little Colorado River for agricultural purposes. (This area is depicted on Plaintiff Ex. Nos. 240 and 245 including the area of the Upper Little Colorado River between Springerville and Winslow.) The heavily faulted geological structure of the Zuni Mountains has resulted in many springs in the Zuni drainage. Although instream flow of the Zuni River is not great, the presence in the Zuni River Valley of numerous springs and a water table high enough to allow wells to be dug by hand have provided water for domestic and agricultural use by the Zuni Indians through the centuries.

Finding No. 8: Effect of Precipitation and Climate upon Zuni Land Use

Precipitation in the form of rain and snow is one of the most important aspects of climate in the Zuni claim area. In general, the climate of the Zuni area is semiarid and temperate. Much of the climatic variability of the Zuni area is related to the region's diverse land forms. Higher elevations and mountain ranges tend to have greater precipitation, while lower elevations are generally drier. About one-half of the precipitation falls in the summer, often in the form of localized torrential rain storms which cause rapid runoff and soil erosion. Winter precipitation in the form of snowfall melts off gradually in the spring, recharging the water system of the region. Between the 6,000 and 7,000 foot elevations on the Colorado Plateau, the most favorable zone of human occupation, annual precipitation averages 11–16 inches per year. One of the most important aspects of climate in the Zuni claim is the variation in precipitation from year to year. In any given year, a particular area can receive either much more or much less rain and snow than the average. Localized droughts are common in the claim area, and they greatly affect the availability of plant and animal resources. This situation requires mobility and flexibility in the land use system, so that if resources are not available in one area, they may be obtained in another area. Thus, a relatively large "sustaining area" was required.

Finding No. 9: Effect of Temperature and Frost Free Season upon Zuni Land Use

Temperature is an important factor in the climate of the Zuni claim area because it controls the growth of vegetation and amount of evaporation. Like precipitation, temperature varies with elevation. Every 1,000 foot increment of elevation results in a decrease of 3.3 degrees Fahrenheit of the average annual temperature. Frost occurs when the temperature drops below 32 degrees, a condition which kills annual plants and crops. The annual growing season is thus determined by the length of the frost-free season between the last freeze in the spring and the first freeze in the fall. Zuni Pueblo, at 6,282 feet elevation, has an average frost-free season of 156 days. A few days difference in the length of the frost-free season can be vital to crops like corn which have a long maturation period. In the semi-arid climate of the Southwest, temperature also affects evaporation of moisture from soil and plants. High temperatures and winds in the spring and summer dry up available moisture, with a resulting adverse effect upon plant growth.

With the evidence of variations in elevation, temperature, and precipitation within parts of the Zuni claim area (and over time), it is established that agriculture (and the raising of livestock) would likewise vary. In anticipation of possible crop (and stock) losses, the Zuni were required to continue with traditional hunting and gathering practices as well.

Finding No. 10: Zuni Use of Biotic Communities

The rich diversity of wild plants and animals found within the claim area provided the Zunis with adequate food and materials to sustain life. Plants and animals live and function together in natural biotic communities. In the Southwest, these biotic communities are primarily structured by temperature and available moisture, which, in turn, are related to elevation. Each biotic community contains numerous species of plant and animals, but is named after the dominant form of vegetation. Many biotic communities are found in the Zuni claim area, offering a rich diversity of resources. In general, grasslands and scrublands are found at the lower elevations and woodlands and forests at the higher elevations. The Zuni Indian land use system made use of resources from every biotic community within the Zuni claim area.[6]

C. PREHISTORIC PERIOD (5000 B.C.–A.D. 1539)

Finding No. 11: Early Aboriginal Use of Claim Area from 5000 B.C. to A.D. 1,000

At least as early as 5000 B.C. the land now known as the American Southwest, including the portion now designated as the Zuni claim area, was inhabited. (From 5000 B.C. to approximately 1000 A.D. may be simply described for our purposes as the Archaic Period.) Among the inhabitants of the Southwest were the ethnological groups of, Hohokam, Mogollon and the Anasazai, the last of which, at least, may be said to be tied to Zuni ancestry. (See also Finding 14 infra.)[7] The Archaic period in the Southwest generally, including the Zuni claim area, began largely as a hunting and gathering life style and closed, with the introduction of agriculture from Mexico and the ability to grow crops in arid climates, with the introduction, at least, of a more sedentary lifestyle.

Finding No. 12: Wide Distribution of Early Zuni Habitation Sites

By the end of the Archaic Period (between 500 A.D. and 1000 A.D.) an early and extensive trade network was in operation, as shown by the presence of various trade goods in parts of the Zuni claim area. The trade system, together with the introduction of early agriculture, led to the development of more centralized communities; pithouses and underground habitations appeared within the claim area.

Between A.D. 900 and 1000, a large number of surface pueblos were inhabited in the Zuni claim area. By the year A.D. 1000, the culture within the Zuni claim area had become a part of the Chacoan complex, characterized by an expansive network of trade relations and very large communities with hundreds of rooms housing thousands of people near very large Kivas. In the Zuni claim area, ancestral pueblos of the Zuni such as the Kiatuthlanna, Villages of the Great Kivas, and White Water serve as examples of these early, large communities and ancestral Zuni homesites were located throughout the claim area. (See also Finding No. 14 infra.)

Finding No. 13: Areas of Ancestral Zuni Occupation

Both archaeological and anthropological research demonstrates a continuity of occupation of the claim area by ancestral Zunis, who developed knowledge of and economic dependence upon the entire claim area. Pottery shards and other archaeological findings indicate the substantially homogenous nature of the Zuni culture within the claim area. Dr. Leslie Spier's surveys show ancestral Zuni occupation of the region south of the San Francisco Peaks to the Mogollon Rim and southeast along the rim to the region of Baldy Peak in the Mt. Baldy wilderness area. Dr. Edward B. Danson has also confirmed Zuni occupation of the Little Colorado River country, the Zuni River and the Puerco River of the West and their tributaries, and the country as far as the Continental Divide south of Highway 66. Dr. John Renaldo noted that the Zuni culture area at its inception was broadly Chacoan and more closely related to the Anasazi culture than to the Mogollon. However, Mogollon influence in the Zuni culture can be seen as early as the 8th Century and became significant in the 14th Century, when Mogollon populations joined the ancestors of the Zuni people in the Zuni River Valley. The ancestral Zunis developed upon the lands within the claim area.[8] (See also Finding No. 14 infra.)

Finding No. 14: Merger of Mogollon and Anasazi into Zuni Culture

The Zunis trace their origins to the Mogollon and Anasazi cultures which merged in the Zuni claim area during prehistoric times. Between as early as A.D. 600 and continuing to A.D. 1350, the Zuni Indians' ancestors were members of both the Anasazi and Mogollon culture traditions. In the Zuni area there was a broad trend to about A.D. 1200 toward consolidation of villages and the building of larger and more sophisticated villages which were Anasazi in their cultural orientation and were so-called "Chaco Outliers," part of the Chaco Canyon network. As the importance of the Anasazi Chacoan area faded, the relative importance of the Zuni cultural area increased. The southern and western portion of the Chacoan interaction system appears to have reorganized to interface with new areas, principally the Little Colorado River Valley and the Mogollon Mountains.

The large pueblos constructed in the Zuni drainage between A.D. 1250 and 1540 reflected an interaction with Anasazi populations to the west and Mogollon populations to the south. The Mogollon culture was centered in the Mogollon Mountains, the mountainous zone on the southern edge of the Basin and Range province. In its later development, A.D. 1000–1400, Mogollon culture was influenced and became similar to Anasazi culture in terms of large pueblo Kiva architecture and increased religious paraphernalia. During this later period the Mogollon groups consolidated. Habitation in the Upper Gila area was abandoned about A.D. 1300, and the Mogollon people likely joined the Pima-Opata tribes and the Zunis to the northeast. The large pueblos in the White Mountains at the headwaters of the Little Colorado River were occupied to A.D. 1300, with the people moving thereafter to Zuni or Hopi or the Silver Creek area along the Mogollon Rim. Prominent Mogollones built large pueblos in the Winslow-Holbrook region such as Homolovi and Chevelon and when these villages were deserted some of the clans went to Zuni and others went to Hopi.

By A.D. 1450 the Zuni claim area was the center of cultural and economic activity for the region. Anasazi and Mogollon populations moved to the large pueblos in the upper Zuni valley by choice, not because of Athapaskan intrusion. There is no evidence of Athapaskan groups such as Apache or Navajo in the Zuni claim area during this period. Only those people ancestral to the present Zuni Indians used the area.

Finding No. 15: Zuni Absorption of Marginal Populations

Throughout the later prehistoric period (A.D. 1250 to A.D. 1350) period, a process of periodic absorption of marginal populations into the Zuni Tribe took place, coupled with gradual centralization of all people from the countryside of the far corners of the claim area into towns in the Zuni River Valley.

Finding No. 16: Zuni Language Serves as Unifying Force

The Zuni language unified the diverse elements of Zuni ancestry. The Zuni are considered by anthropologists to represent one of the early groups to develop pueblo culture in the southwest. The Zuni language is unique and is not shared by any tribe in New Mexico or Arizona. The Zunis nearest linguistic relatives are the Penutian-speaking tribes in the central valley of California. Marginal populations absorbed by the Zunis adopted the Zuni language as their own.

Finding No. 17: Zunis Did Not Abandon Outlying Portions of Claim
Area when Habitation Sites Were Consolidated

The Zuni culture grew stronger and more powerful as the Zuni people consolidated their homesites into the Zuni River Valley. By A.D. 1450, all of the habitation sites within the Zuni claim area had been consolidated into a series of villages within the Zuni Valley. Only Zuni Indians resided within the claim area, bordered on the northwest by the Hopis and on the east by the Acomas. The movement into the Zuni Valley from outlying areas may have been prompted by choice to live a communal lifestyle, to participate in social and religious functions, and to have access to a permanent and reliable water supply. The Zunis did not abandon[9] the outlying portions of their sustaining area or claim area when they consolidated their homesites, but continued to make traditional use of the entire area for farming, hunting, and other life-sustaining activities.

Finding No. 18: Continuous Zuni Knowledge and Use of Entire Claim
Area

Notwithstanding the homesite consolidation, the Zuni people retained their economic dependence upon the extensive lands of the claim area.[10] As the Zuni Valley consolidation took place, the inhabitants from the fringe areas brought with them an extensive and detailed knowledge of critical and useful resources from throughout the claim area. Exploitation of these resources continued unabated. Plants, animals, birds, clays, pigments, and/or minerals from within the entire area were utilized. The Zunis exploited water ways and watered lands, mountainous areas, and arid lands. Zuni resource use and procurement throughout the historical period demonstrates extensive knowledge and use of various resources from all parts of the claim area. Even today Zunis possess detailed knowledge of areas on the Little Colorado drainage, the Mogollon Rim, the Reserve Area, the San Francisco Peaks, and other sites distant from the claim area to west, north, east and south.

Finding No. 19: Zuni Sustaining Area

The extensive lands which surround the core area of Zuni habitation are referred to as the Zuni "sustaining area" because within such lands are produced the wild plants and/or animals and/or minerals upon which the Zunis sustained themselves. The severe limitations placed upon agriculture by the climate of the claim area meant that a large land base was necessary to support the native economy of the Zuni Indians. A large sustaining area was an ecological necessity to insure the long-term stability of a large concentrated population in the arid Southwest. Sufficient water was needed to support agricultural production, and to support the wildlife and wild plants that provided important economic and medicinal resources. The Zuni villages achieved a size and stability not usual in the Southwest. While modern communities have surpassed the Zuni Pueblo in size, they do not have the long-term self-sufficiency afforded by the traditional Zuni land use system. The most notable aspect of the physical environment of the Zuni region was its great diversity of altitude, land forms, geological resources, and biological communities. The Zuni sustaining area was larger than the claim area since the sustaining area included some areas of joint use with other Indian tribes outside of the claim area.

Finding No. 20: Zuni Subsistence Strategy

The Zunis used the sustaining area extensively as an integral part of their subsistence strategy. The subsistence strategy of the Zuni traditionally involved a mixture of agriculture, hunting, and plant gathering that could be adjusted to the varying climatic conditions through the use of various geographical regions within the claim area. Drought was a recurrent condition; thus, the large Zuni population had to have emergency resources to draw upon. When crops failed, the Zunis relied on surrounding grasslands and mountain forests to supply wild game and foodstuffs.

Finding No. 21: Zuni Pottery and Architectural Ruins

Pottery shards and architectural ruins found throughout the claim area attest to the fact that ancestral Zunis made extensive use of the sustaining area. Tremendous quantities of pottery shards of various designs found in strata underlying the entire claim area verify that the Zuni people and their ancestors occupied the claim area without interruption from A.D. 650 until the present time. The architectural/ archaeological sequence began with small pithouse villages, underwent a change to surface masonry structures, and culminated in large pueblos around A.D. 1300. The Zuni communities were the manufacturing centers of several pottery types that had wide distribution throughout the claim area as well as outside the claim area, indicating that pottery was often imported by other Indian Tribes as a tradeware in exchange for other goods.

Finding No. 22: Ancient Zuni Ties to the Land

The Zuni Indians have ancient cultural and historical ties to their land. The Zunis and their ancestors have lived along the Zuni River and used the surrounding country to sustain themselves for over a thousand years. During that time the Zunis have acquired an intimate knowledge of the resources and landscape of their homeland throughout the claim area. The ancient ties of Zuni people to their land is presently manifest in the tribal oral tradition about Zuni origin and migration and in the physical artifacts representing the archaeological history of Zuni culture.

The land of the claim area is marked by numerous religious shrines (and is today considered by the members of the Zuni tribe to be sacred).

Finding No. 23: Zuni Migration Tradition (as Recounted)

Zuni oral tradition and religion recount ancient migrations and sacred landmarks or shires which had continuing importance in the Zuni lifestyle.[11] According to Zuni tradition, the people at Zuni migrated from other places, particularly "The Place of Beginning" located at Ribbon Falls in the Grand Canyon. In their migration eastward from the Grand Canyon to their present location, the Zunis stopped at a number of places which are still remembered in their prayers and visited periodically to make offerings. After their emergence from the Grand Canyon, the first major stop was near the San Francisco Peaks where the medicine plants had "settled" so that the Zunis would have a source nearby. The next stop was Canyon Diablo near Two Guns, Arizona, where the ruins of their settlements are still visited and offerings are made to their ancestors. The Zuni people continued on to the Woodruff Butte southeast of Holbrook, Arizona, which is the course of a special medicinal plant used by their rain priests for divination and other purposes. The Zunis next stopped at a site located near the confluence of the Zuni River and the Little Colorado River where they resided for "four years" (a period of at least forty years).

Nearby this confluence of the Zuni and Little Colorado Rivers, is the sacred lake of Zuni, the site of "Zuni Heaven," the place where spirits of the deceased go to join their ancestors after death, and where the Council of the Gods resides. Pilgrimages from Zuni are made to this area regularly. Shrines are located in the Zuni Heaven complex in the Stinking Springs Mountains west of the Zion Reservoir and are closely related to the Kachina dance groups and the *Koyemshi* (sacred clowns). Additional Zuni shrines are also located in the mountains surrounding the headwaters of the Little Colorado River south of Springfield, Arizona. From the Sacred Lake near the Little Colorado River to the center of Zuni there are many springs where the Zunis stopped for varying periods. All the places mentioned in the oral tradition are of religious significance to the Zuni.

Thus, starting at "The Place of Beginning" in the Grand Canyon, the Zunis migrated to San Francisco Peaks and on across the State of Arizona to Zuni Heaven, then searched in several directions before finding the "center" or "middle place" in the upper valley of the Zuni River.

Zuni tradition states that during the migration to the Little Colorado River Valley the tribe split. Part of the people went into the Zuni heartland, part of the people went south, never to return, and part of the people first went north, then east to the Rio Grande Valley, finally returning to join the rest of the Zuni Tribe in the Zuni River Valley. The migration of the Zuni people into their heartland established sacred areas and shrines in all directions throughout the Zuni claim area and beyond. These areas and shrines were and are remembered in prayers and songs and were and are visited and cared for on a continuing basis to the present.

Finding No. 24: Absence of Other Indians in the Claim Area

During the prehistoric period, the sole occupants of the claim area were the Zuni people who used the area on a regular and continuing basis.[12] There is no evidence of Apache or Navajo use of the Zuni claim area during the prehistoric period. At the close of the prehistoric period the only neighbors of the Zuni were the Acoma Indians and Rio Grande Pueblos to the east, the Hopi Indians to the northwest, the Havasupi to the west, the Opata Indians to the south in Mexico.

D. ZUNI DURING THE SIXTEENTH CENTURY

Finding No. 25: First European Contact with the Zuni People

When Spanish explorers first entered the claim area, they searched for the Zuni people who had been the subject of earlier second-hand reports. First reports of the Zuni were received by the Spaniards from Nuño de Guzman in 1529 as he searched northward for wealth in New Spain. The Cabeza de Vaca group, which passed many miles south of Zuni in the early 16th Century, also heard tales of a highly civilized people to the north who lived in houses and wore cotton clothes. The reports from Nuño de Guzman and Cabeza de Vaca prompted the expedition of Fray Marcos de Niza in 1539. He was accompanied by one of the members of the Cabeza de Vaca party, the Moor Estevan. Estevan, in a vanguard group, reached Zuni in 1539 after crossing the *Despoblado*. The accounts of the expedition note that no other Indians were seen in the areas between the Gila River and the central Zuni villages.[13] Estevan was killed by the Zunis for inappropriate behavior, and Fray Marcos, after allegedly viewing the village of Hawikuh from afar, retreated quickly to Mexico.

Finding No. 26: Kingdom of Cibola Recognized by Spain

When the Spaniards first received vague reports of Zuni in the late 1530's, the Zuni people and their ancestors had been living in the claim area for over a thousand years. The "Kingdom of Cibola" was a term used by the Zuni to designate their sustaining area or claim area over which the Zunis exercised dominion. The Spaniards referred to the Kingdom of Cibola as a province occupied by the Zuni, within which were seven villages and wherein they expected to find the legendary "Seven Cities of Gold." Spaniards treated The Kingdom of Cibola as a foreign nation and not as an area occupied by a savage tribe. The Spanish king's dominion was formally extended over this area, in the Act of Obedience and Vassalage for Zuni of 1598.

Finding No. 27: Exclusive Zuni Occupation of the Kingdom of Cibola

The boundaries of exclusive Zuni use and occupancy are coextensive with the Kingdom of Cibola. The Zunis used and controlled the claim area, but also made more limited use of areas outside of the claim area to the northwest of the San Francisco Peaks up to the Grand Canyon; the area north to Chaco Canyon; Horse Lake in the Jucarilla Mountains; the Blue Mountains in Utah; and east to the Jemez Mountains and in the Sandia Mountains; and to the south of the Mogollon Rim in the Gila River Valley.

Finding No. 28: Zunis Battle Coronado

The Zuni warriors protected their boundaries and engaged in battle with the Coronado expedition. Prompted by the reports of Fray Marcos, Coronado organized and led a large expedition towards the province of Cibola in 1540. The Zunis met Coronado a number of miles away from the central villages, evidently warning the expedition not to continue into their territory. The Spaniards noted signal fires used by the Zunis to warn of their approach. At night the Zunis ran off the Spaniards' horses, but after a short battle at Hawikuh in which Coronado himself was wounded, the Zunis rendered obedience to the King of Spain on July 11, 1540. Following this episode, peace was maintained between Coronado's forces and the Zunis.

Finding No. 29: Coronado's Written Descriptions Confirm Extensive Zuni Use of Cibola

The written descriptions by the chroniclers of the Coronado Expedition confirmed extensive Zuni use of the claim area. The chroniclers of the Coronado Expedition described the conditions in the Zuni villages after they returned to Mexico City. They described the gathering, hunting, trading, and agricultural practices of the Zunis. Gathering practices included the collection of various plants which were used in the manufacture of native textiles. The Zunis were observed gathering pine nuts, one chronicler reporting that "the natives gather and stored pinon nuts for the next year." Others gathered items which the chroniclers observed were reeds used for mats and roofing and timbers used for building construction. The reports described Zuni domestication of turkeys and the use of turkey feathers for religious purposes. Trade of turquoise, salt, and other items were also observed. Hunting was of particular importance to the Zunis, as evidenced by chroniclers' reports that the Zunis possessed well-tanned skins from deer, rabbits and other animals, which were used for clothing and knee-boots. They also noted that heads of wild goats, paws of bears, and skins of wild boars were seen at the pueblo and described other game which included deer, leopards, and large elk. The Zuni lifestyle as described by Coronado's chroniclers indicated the storage of many food stuffs and other items to be used later in the year.

Finding No. 30: Rodriquez-Chamuscado Missionary Expedition of 1581

The Spaniards made an effort to convert the Zunis to the Christian faith with the Rodriquez-Chamuscado Expedition of 1581. Since general disappointment prevailed following Coronado's failure to find gold in Cibola, further expeditions were delayed to the Zuni claim area for forty years. Inspired by potential missionary work among the Pueblo Indians, Fray Augustin Rodriquez and Francisco Sanchez Chamuscado traveled up the Rio Grande as far north as Santa Fe and then westward to Acoma and finally to Zuni. The expedition recorded the cultivation of corn and the presence of large stone houses which were whitewashed and painted, each having passageways, windows, doorways, and wooden ladders.

Finding No. 31: Espejo Expedition of 1583 Protected by Zunis

In addition to the Espejo Expedition of 1583 noting Zuni irrigation of crops and hunting, they recorded how they were protected by Zuni warriors on the trip to Hopi. The expedition led by Merchant Antonio de Espejo reached Zuni in 1583 after traveling from the Rio Grande Valley. The Spaniards spent time at Zuni between excursions looking for mines, which they never found. They found crosses built by previous expeditions and three Mexican Indians left at Zuni by Coronado. Expedition members found evidence of irrigation and noted that the Zunis spun fiber and wove blankets. After spending some time at Zuni, Espejo traveled more than a dozen leagues towards Hopi stopping at the pueblo Matsaki and later camping at a water hole where the Zuni Indians caught many rabbits which they gave to the expedition. At least several dozen Zuni warriors accompanied the Spaniards over the trail to Hopi. On the way there the party met a group of Zunis returning from Hopi. The Zuni travelers warned the Spaniards that the Hopis planned to fight, but since the expedition was protected by Zunis, the visit to Hopi proved peaceful. The Zuni warriors gave the Spaniards protection from potentially hostile Hopis, since there were no other Indians in the area.

Finding No. 32: Spain Recognizes Zuni Nation with Acts of Obedience in 1598

Spain officially recognized the Zuni Nation and pledged Spain's support to protect the Zuni Nation against its enemies. Juan de Oñate was the first successful colonizer of the northern frontier of New Spain. He officially took possession of the area on April 30, 1598, and established a settlement near the San Juan Pueblo on the Rio Grande. He later moved his settlement to Santa Fe in the year 1608. His relationship to Zuni was important in that he placed the Zuni Province officially under the sovereignty of Spain with formal Acts of Obedience and Vassalage. In the official Act of Obedience and Vassalage by the Indians of Zuni, Oñate's men made the following representation:

> He told them that they had come to their lands to bring them to the knowledge of God and the King our Lord, on which depended the salvation of their souls and their living securely and undisturbed in their nations, maintained in justice and order, secure in their homes, and protected against their enemies, and that he had not come to do them any harm.

Finding No. 33: Exclusive Zuni Use of Claim Area[14]

The early Spaniards never saw other Indian groups within the claim area thus substantiating the Zunis claim to exclusivity. The Spaniards Fray Marcos de Niza and Coronado referred to the area between the Gila River and the Zuni Pueblo as the *Despoblado*. The *Despoblado* began in the country between the Gila River and the headwaters of the Little Colorado River in eastern Arizona and ended at the periphery of modern Zuni country; thus, Cibola was the first populated area encountered by the Spaniards as they proceeded northeastward from the Gila River Valley. None of the aforementioned expeditions (Coronado, Rodriquez and Chamuscado, Espejo) reported Apaches or Navajos within the Zuni area. The *Despoblado* gave the Zunis in Cibola a position of relative isolation, although the area was marked with trails used for conducting trade with tribes to the south and west.

E. ZUNI DURING THE SEVENTEENTH CENTURY

Finding No. 34: Zunis Land Rights Protected Under Spanish Law

Under Spanish law, the Indian tribes were required to live in pueblos or villages, but movement into a village did not result in the loss of their outlying lands. This

Reduccion Policy, as it is known, was interpreted by local Spanish authorities as allowing Indian people to continue to use land they had used prior to the imposition of Spanish government, while at the same time restricting habitation to villages wherein Indians could be taught the arts of civilization. Zuni people were not required to move since they were already living in villages.

Finding No. 35: Alcalde System Provided Political and Military Support for Zuni Land Use

The creation of the office of an *Alcalde Mayor* at the *Alcaldia* of Zuni in 1659 or 1660 was recognition of a political province or *Alcaldia* under Spanish law. The establishment of the *Alcaldia* had no adverse impact upon traditional Zuni land use. The Spaniards did not attempt to occupy the area but occasionally quartered soldiers there to protect the *Alcalde Mayor*. The only area which was occupied by the Spanish at Zuni was the church and cemetery and a small amount of space that a few soldiers used from time to time on a temporary basis.

Finding No. 36: Zuni Land Ownership Under Spanish Law[15]

The Zunis were secure in the use and ownership of their lands under the laws of Spain. The Zunis were considered vassals and subjects of the Spanish Crown. They voluntarily accepted Spanish jurisdiction by Acts of Obedience and Vassalage. According to Spanish law as set out in the *Recopilacion* the ownership of lands remained with the Spanish subjects upon their voluntary acceptance of Spanish sovereignty, and in turn the crown obligated itself to protect its vassals in their homes and lands. The Zunis were considered to be Pueblo Indians or civilized Indians under the law as distinguished from "wild or uncivilized tribes," and as such were given full protection of the law. The extent of the lands belonging to the Zuni Tribe, while never mapped or documented by Spanish chroniclers, were nonetheless determined by the Zuni people themselves according to their own tradition and included as part of the Spanish realm. The lands protected by the crown during Spanish rule were those lands of the traditional Zuni claim area. In 1812 the Spanish King issued a proclamation which was later interpreted to mean that all Pueblo Indians were citizens regardless of origin. As citizens they were still entitled to the use of their traditional lands.

Finding No. 37: Zuni Autonomy Under Spanish Law

The Zuni Tribe as an entity retained autonomy or the right of self-government under the law of Spain. The second *Audiencia* in Mexico, from 1530 to 1535, passed a series of ordinances which essentially revised administration of Indian pueblos and established traditions which exist today. Indian communities were granted the right of self government and the administration of justice under their own elected officials and the Tribe was considered to be the land owning entity. This practice was prevalent in New Spain by the time Oñate settled in New Mexico. Further policy changes occurred in 1620 when the Viceroy issued decrees by authority of the Spanish King to the Governor of the area designed to secure utmost autonomy for Pueblo Indians. Tributes were to be paid only on condition of the conversion of the Pueblo people to the Christian faith. Since the Spaniards considered the Zunis' conversion incomplete, they were exempted from paying tribute to the crown. Being exempted from tributes probably tended to lessen motives for official visits to Zuni.

*Finding No. 38: Zunis Resist Spanish Efforts to Stop Shrine
Visitation*

The Zuni people reacted violently when Franciscans attempted to stop the Zunis from practicing certain traditional religious ceremonies. The only recorded incident where Spain attempted to interfere with the Zuni custom and tradition was the episode of the Franciscan Fray Francisco Letrado. He apparently was interested in preventing the Zunis from practicing what he considered to be pagan religious ceremonies. He and Fray Martin de Arvide were killed by the Zunis in 1632. On October 7, 1672, La Purisima Concepcion de Hawikuh Mission was burned and destroyed and the missionary Fray Pedro de Avila y Ayala was killed. Evidence indicates that the Zunis blamed the attack on the Apaches, but it seems certain that the Zunis assisted since the raid was directed at the missionary because he did not tolerate their religious practices. Following that occasion the Zunis continued undisturbed at Hawikuh. During the Pueblo Revolt of 1680, Fray Juan de Bal, assigned to Halona, was killed by rebelling Zunis.

Finding No. 39: Zunis Revolt Against Spain

The resistance of the Zuni people to proposed change in their customs and religion culminated in the Zuni Tribe joining the Pueblo Revolt. The Pueblo Revolt of 1680 resulted in all of the Spaniards being driven out of New Mexico. The Zunis and the Hopis willingly participated in the hostilities and gave support to the neighboring pueblos on the Rio Grande. However, in expectation of retaliation from the Spaniards, the Zunis commenced fortification of Corn Mountain.

*Finding No. 40: Zuni Enhanced Defensive Capability with
Construction of Corn Mountain Fortress*

In anticipation of Spanish reprisals for the Pueblo Revolt, the Zunis enhanced their defensive capability by constructing the Corn Mountain Fortress. Corn Mountain is a large mesa with sheer walls which rise several hundred feet from the floor of the Zuni River Valley to the flat mesa top. Corn Mountain was a natural sanctuary or fortress where the Zuni people could go when under heavy attack. There is no indication of its use as a defensive site prior to the arrival of Coronado. The Zunis, after assessing the power of Spanish horses, guns, and armor, however, began making fortifications on top of Corn Mountain and used the Mountain as a refuge or defensive position during succeeding times of crisis. The mountain was so used during the decade following the Pueblo Revolt of 1680, the Zunis made extensive fortifications, built homes, stored quantities of food and water, erected archer booths, collected heaps of flingstones, and stacked ammunition of heavy rocks on the mountain. The Zunis did not live there permanently, but prepared the site for their own protection in the event of an anticipated retaliation by the Spaniards.

*Finding No. 41: Zunis Unite Villages and Strengthen Political and
Social Organization*

The Zuni people united themselves in a single village to strengthen and combine their political, religious and social organizations. The concern over Spanish reprisals in the years following the Pueblo Revolt of 1680 brought about tremendous internal and external changes in Zuni society. The Zuni leaders, recognizing the need for unity against the common Spanish enemy, rebuilt the Zuni villages after 1692 into one consolidated village. Smaller villages in the outlying area continued to be used seasonally. The supreme council Bow Priests, the arm of the Priestly Council, was also centralized. Communication was thus enhanced and central leadership provided Zunis with the ability to mobilize people for military purposes.

Finding No. 42: Voluntary Reinstatement of Spanish Sovereignty

The Zunis and Spaniards were able to reconcile without bloodshed, when the Zuni Tribe voluntarily accepted the reinstatement of Spanish sovereignty. On October 16, 1692, Diego de Vargas left Santa Fe to subdue the Western provinces of Acoma and Zuni as part of the Spanish reconquest of New Mexico. De Vargas had been forewarned by two Indians who had returned from Zuni that a great council had been held near Acoma to plan for the ambush of the expedition. Apparently the Zuni, Hopi, Jemez, and other Indians had been involved in the council. However, after traveling through Acoma, de Vargas met Zunis at El Morro on November 8, 1692. Ten or twelve Zunis had come from the Pueblo on horseback to welcome Governor de Vargas and his group to the Province of Zuni. When de Vargas arrived at Zuni he found that the inhabitants were located on top of Corn Mountain in anticipation of his arrival, although the Zunis were also using the other pueblos and their surrounding territory. Vargas' approach to the Zunis was friendly, and, therefore, he was received on top of Corn Mountain in a friendly manner.[16] De Vargas proclaimed that the Zunis were once again vassals to the king of Spain. Then he traveled to Hopi and returned to Zuni. He was led by Zuni guides back to the Rio Grande above Socorro, taking a short-cut known to the Zunis.

Finding No. 43: Apaches Located Outside of Claim Area During the 17th Century

Apache Indian bands traded and may have raided at the Pueblo of Zuni, but they did not live in, or otherwise claim Zuni lands as their own, as discussed further below. One of the earliest documented records of Apaches in the Zuni claim area concerns events of 1672 when the Apaches were ostensibly blamed for the killing of a priest at Hawikuh. There is speculation that the Zunis were in league with the Apaches to rid themselves of Spanish influence. There is no evidence of any injury to Zunis during the "Apache" raid on Hawikuh in 1672. On November 14, 1692, Diego de Vargas was at Zuni when he was approached on his camp's parade grounds by a chieftain of the *Salinero Apaches* and eight or ten braves who assured the Spaniards, "they had always entered this land and the province of the Zuni on terms of peace, that they were friends of the natives, and that it was their earnest desire that the Spaniards be their friends." The *Salinero Apaches* followed de Vargas and his men at a distance on their trip to Hopi and the return to Zuni. De Vargas then traveled to the Rio Grande area above Socorro. De Vargas made note of the Apache surveillance as they traveled from Zuni remarking that the Apaches had been inspecting his camp sites and following his trail.

De Vargas was led by a Zuni guide, Agustin de Cabezon, who had agreed to show him a shortcut. From El Morro the guide led de Vargas on a road which led southward. After traveling a league, the company stopped at a hill from which the Zuni pointed out a mountain he called *Sierra Prieta*. He also informed de Vargas that at a great distance beyond it was another mountain called *Pena Larga*, near which he said the *Apaches Colorados* had a rancheria. *Pena Larga* had been identified as being outside the Zuni claim area near the headwaters of the Gila River. The Zuni guides delivered de Vargas to the Rio Grande, above Socorro, and returned by way of Acoma to avoid confrontation with the Apaches trailing de Vargas.

No evidence is found of any Apache habitation, farming sites, or hunting activities within the Zuni claim area during the 17th Century. The only recorded evidence at the close of the 17th Century demonstrated a friendly relationship between the Apaches and Zunis, most likely founded upon trade. In fact, in 1696 Governor de Vargas was informed by Spanish allies that the Acomas, Zunis, and Hopis had been joined by Apaches in support of rebellious pueblos who had resolved to kill all Spaniards and again drive them from New Mexico. In July of 1696, the Acomas and Zunis lost men in the battle with the Spaniards near the Pueblo of Jemez. The Jemez, Acoma, and Zuni confederation was thus broken up.

Finding No. 44: The Fraudulent Cruzate Grant Has No Bearing on Zuni Land Use

The fraudulent Cruzate Grant, purportedly dated 1689, has no bearing whatsoever in determining Zuni use and occupation of the claim area. Historians generally agree that the "grant" purportedly issued to the Pueblo of Zuni in 1689 was forged by unknown persons, possibly during the late Mexican period. The fraudulent grant recites a spurious story in which the Governor and Captain General Don Domingo Jironza y Petros de Cruzate found a Zia Indian who assured the Governor that the Zunis would accept obedience; whereupon, the Governor granted the Zunis a one league grant, measured from the four corners of the Pueblo.

When the "grant" was finally measured in 1880 it excluded the Pueblo of Zuni itself. There is no evidence of any bona fide or non-spurious grants having been made to pueblos in New Mexico, except for Sandia in 1748. Instead, Spanish and later Mexican authorities applied Spanish decrees and ordinances which provided for protection of Pueblo Indian rights to the lands they used and occupied.

F. ZUNI IN THE EIGHTEENTH CENTURY TO THE MEXICAN PERIOD (1700–1821)

Finding No. 45: Zunis Kept Integrity of Culture

The Zunis maintained the integrity of their cultural values by killing Spanish soldiers who lived openly with Zuni women contrary to Zuni custom and tradition. During the first decade of the 17th Century, there were new reports of a Zuni-Apache alliance against the Spanish. Around 1700, Joseph Naranho began serving as *Alcalde Mayor* at Halona with a detachment of twelve soldiers. He doubtless notified Santa Fe of the troubles threatening to erupt there in 1702 involving a threatened uprising of Acomas, Lagunas, Zunis, and Apaches. A small force of soldiers came to Zuni to protect the mission priest Fray Garaicochea, and three of the group were left after the Spaniards determined that there was no immediate danger. The three soldiers behaved scandalously, living in public with Zuni women, and, in 1703, they were killed by the Zunis. Following the incident another force of soldiers was sent to Zuni. Some of the Zunis once again moved to maintain the mesa stronghold on Corn Mountain. In 1705, however, the Zuni-Spanish relations were normalized and the defensive position of Corn Mountain was deemphasized as in the past times of peace.

Finding No. 46: Apache Raids Directed at Spanish Interests

During the 17th Century Apache raids were directed at Spanish towns and ranches in Northern Mexico and the Rio Grande Valley rather than the Pueblo of Zuni where many Apache bands had friendly trade relations. Apaches began raiding Spanish Colonies on the Rio Grande and further south into Mexico. The Spaniards often suspected the Zunis and other Pueblos of being in alliance with the Apaches against the Spaniards. Spanish campaigns against Apaches brought them through Zuni on their way to the Gila River where Apache rancherias were located outside of the claim area. There does not appear to be any firsthand account of Apache conflict with the Zunis during the first half of the 18th Century.[17] While Apaches traditionally had friendly relations with the Zuni people, they were considered hostile by the Spaniards. Many of the reported hostilities at Zuni were aimed at the Spaniards residing there rather than the Zunis themselves. Fray Manual de San Juan Nepomuceno y Trigo visited Zuni in 1754 and reported that the Zunis were neighbors of the numerous Moqui (Hopi) apostates and were certainly very independent, for they never sowed any crops for their minister. Instead they had their own flocks of sheep and went about their own farming, and, from the produce, shared with the mission. They also furnished wood for the mission. In 1760 Bishop Pedro Tamaron y Romeral, Bishop of Durango, Mexico did not visit Zuni while he was making a visit to Acoma.[18] "One of the difficulties alleged against my going there was that I should not find even half of the inhabitants because they are so dispersed in their ranchos. They breed livestock, and large flocks of sheep come from there."[19] Since the Zunis did not share with the Spaniards the same fear of the Apaches, they traveled freely and dispersed to their ranchos.

Finding No. 47: Dominguez, Escalante, and Don Miera y Pacheco Visits Confirm Zuni Exclusivity

The visits of Fray Dominguez and Fray Escalante and Don Miera y Pacheco confirmed extensive Zuni use of the claim area and located Apache farmsites near the Gila River outside of the claim area.

A. In 1776, Fray Francisco Atanasio Dominguez passed through the Pueblo of Halona or Zuni, on his inspection of the New Mexican missions, and gave a thoughtful and detailed report on the mission at Zuni. He reported that the Zunis provided the fathers there one sheep per week, eggs, lard, salt, milk, and tallow candles, in addition to many other agricultural products.[20] He noted that timbers used in the building of the church and convent were collected from a far distance. He also described some Zuni farming. He made no mention of any settlements or farms in the claim area belonging to Navajos or Apaches.[21] The closest Apaches reported by Dominguez' companion Fray Francisco Velez de Escalante were said to be cultivating a valley about 18 miles north of the Gila River, thus outside the Zuni claim area. Those particular Apaches evidently had been subject to attack by Zuni (accompanied by a few Spanish).

B. In 1779, Don Miera y Pacheco, who had accompanied the Dominguez-Escalante Expedition of 1776, prepared a map of New Mexico showing its various political subdivisions. It is clearly a map of areas governed by the *Acalde Mayors* and not the areas controlled by various Indian groups. The area controlled by the Zunis is not indicated, particularly the extensive area needed to graze the over 15,000 sheep counted as Zuni-owned. The so-called "Miera map" is in reality a *Plano* and is not a topographical map. Miera's *Plano* was not detailed enough to render it susceptible to precise locations and cannot now be used to identify the specific locations of Navajo and Apaches in the area. The *Plano* indicated the eastern boundary of the Alcaldia of Zuni to be the lava flow between Acoma and Zuni. The other two lines indicate northern and southern borders of the Alcaldia, the distance between them about thirty miles. The western boundary is completely open as far as the coast of California.

Finding No. 48: Zunis Join Spaniards to Fight Apaches

Zuni Indians served as auxiliaries with Spanish troops to fight hostile Apaches bands when needed, however; Apache hostilities were infrequent and did not affect the traditional Zuni use of land within the claim area.[22]

Conditions in the Pueblo of Zuni by the middle of the 18th Century were not bad by standards of the times. The Zunis had domesticated a number of horses. In fact, they had more horses than any Spanish settlement. Increased mobility enabled Zunis to travel distances with greater ease and strengthen protection of their territory. Greater protection was needed as various Indian groups were dislocated and disrupted by Spanish intrusion. Comanche raids against the Spanish Pueblo settlements along the Rio Grande stimulated counter offenses by the Spaniards against the Comanches; in the period from 1767 to 1788, Governor Mindinueta launched an all out war against the Comanches, which in turn stimulated raids against the Spaniards by Utes, Navajos, and Apaches.[23]

An "open door" between Socorro and the Pueblos of Acoma and Laguna existed wherein Navajos and Apaches passed freely to make raids on the Rio Grande. In 1772, Apaches raided at Zuni and the skirmish resulted in the death of six Indians. In 1788, Zunis serving as auxiliaries to Governor Concha fought against the Apaches between the Pueblo of Laguna and the Rio Grande.

In 1795, Captain Zuniga traveled from Tucson through the Gila area to the Zuni Pueblo and back, searching for a trade route between Sonora and Santa Fe. Zuniga was also ordered to punish the Apaches along the way. Apaches were encountered only in the Gila River Valley well outside the Zuni claim area. In 1797, the Spaniards launched another offensive against the Apaches going as far as the Sierra de los Mimbres.

In 1807, Apaches robbed and killed a Spaniard near San Rafael. Spanish troops chased the Apaches into the Malpais or lava flow, but were unable to drive them out. Thereafter, three hundred Apaches attacked the Zunis, fighting from seven in the morning until three in the afternoon, killing one Zuni and wounding twelve others, then taking 600 sheep with them.

On October 25, 1809, twenty Gila Apaches attacked Zuni horse herds and killed five men and two women. Both the Zunis and the Spaniards retaliated after these attacks, but the records are incomplete as to the details.

The Apaches did not seize any Zuni territory by conquest or any other means during the entire Spanish period. It appears that while the Apache attacks on the Rio Grande were serious during the early part of the 19th Century, Apache attacks were generally focused to the south on towns in Mexico rather than to the north on Zuni. Despite isolated raids against Zuni by some hostile Apache bands, relations with other Apache bands were good, as evidenced by trade between them and Zunis.

Finding No. 49: Apache Farms and Homesites Located Outside of the Claim Area

Apache farms and homesites were located outside of the Zuni claim area during the entire Spanish Period. In 1747, Don Bernardo de Miera y Pacheco traveled as engineer and captain of the militia on a general campaign initiated by Spanish authorities to establish a road from Zuni, through the Gila country, to the presidios in Sonora. He later used the information gained on this trip to draw his 1779 *Plano*. Don Bernardo explored the area from Zuni towards the Gila and found no Apaches, but he did discover some Apache farms located in the valley north of the Gila River, located well to the south and outside of the claim area. He traveled the entire area from Los Mimbres, Rio de San Francisco, and to the area south of Acoma and noted no other Apache settlements.

Finding No. 50: Zuni Homesites Away from Pueblo

The Zuni people traditionally lived in farming villages or livestock camps away from the central Pueblos of Zuni during much of the year. The 1790 Census of Zuni, compiled by the *Alcalde Mayor* Juan Pedro Sisneros, showed that the Zunis not only lived at the Pueblo of Zuni, but also at Rancho Colorado, Rancho de Piedras Negras, Rancho de Galisteo, Rancho del Canoon and Rancho de Senora Santa Ana.

These outlying ranches were undoubtedly some of those noted in 1779 by da Anza as places where Zunis, who had not gone to stay at other pueblos during the drought, lived and from where they pastured large flocks of sheep.

These ranches were not described by Dominguez in 1776; however, his purpose was a visit to the mission to assess its condition, not to survey Zuni land. Don Bernardo Miera y Pacheco did not note these ranches on his 1779 *Plano*; his purpose was to indicate Acaldia administrative boundaries, not Zuni occupation.

Finding No. 51: Absence of Navajos Within Claim Area

Throughout the Spanish period, Navajo bands lived and used lands outside of and not within the claim area. Zunis were harassed by occasional Navajo thefts during the end of the Spanish period. In 1804–05 Zunis were recruited to join Spanish campaigns against the Navajos. In 1818–1821 reports were sent by Spanish officials at Zuni warning of Navajos preparing to attack the pueblo. The Navajo had been driven from their homeland in the upper San Juan region by the Utes and the Spaniards into the area north and east of Mt. Taylor. From there they began to raid Spanish settlements and the Pueblos. However, there is no evidence of Navajo settlements or land use in the Zuni claims area throughout the period 1700–1821.

Finding No. 52: Exclusive Nature of Zuni Use of Claim Area to 1821

To the close of the Spanish Period in 1821, there are continuing reports of Zuni uses of their land. Particularly notable are the reports indicating increase in sheep husbandry. There are also reports of the Zunis keeping large herds of horses, of farming at a number of locations, and of gathering timbers from far distances. These historical reports, coupled with archaeological and anthropological information, demonstrate that the Zunis' continued use of the claim area was exclusive.

Finding No. 53: Zuni Aboriginal Lands Remain Intact Under Spain

Since Spain had recognized the Zunis' right to aboriginal territory and had done nothing to disrupt or interfere with Zuni use and occupation, the Zunis became subject to the sovereignty of Mexico with their aboriginal lands intact.

[G. ZUNI IN THE MEXICAN PERIOD (1821-1846)]

Finding No. 54: Zunis Declared Mexican Citizens

In 1820, the Pueblo Indians of New Mexico became Spanish citizens. With the independence of Mexico and her acceptance of sovereignty over the area in 1821, the citizenship of the Pueblo Indians was affirmed. Citizenship was given to the Zunis under the *Plan de Iguala*, which declared all of the inhabitants of New Spain, "without distinction, whether Europeans, Africans or Indians," to be citizens, and that their "person and property would be protected by the government." These principals were reaffirmed by the Treaty of Cordova of August 24, 1821, in the Declaration of Independence of October 6, 1821, and by Act of the Mexican Congress. The Zuni people remained Mexican citizens during the entire Mexican period up to and including 1846. Relations between the Zunis and Mexico were at all times friendly, if distant. The Mexican government eventually provided a school teacher at Zuni and military support from time to time.

Finding No. 55: Navajo Homeland Outside of Claim Area

The Navajo area of occupancy was to the north and east of the Zuni claim area during the Mexican Period.[24] The traditional homeland or Dinetah of the Navajos was in the El Gobernador Canyon area north of Santa Fe; the Navajos having settled there about 1500. Pressures from Utes and other Indians pushed the Navajos to the west, deserting Gobernador and Big Bead Mesa by 1800.

Prior to 1821, some Navajos had settled in the area east of Mt. Taylor near Cebolleta. Mt. Taylor was considered to be the Navajos' sacred mountain of the south. Continuing pressures from the east resulted in the Navajos concentrating, by the close of the Mexican period, in the areas north of the Zuni claim area in Canyon de Chelly and the Chuska Mountains.

The Navajos were generally nomads and raiders and did not establish large, permanent settlements. The Mexican authorities made a number of campaigns against the Navajos. For example, in 1816, some Navajo temporarily gathered at Bear Springs, where a water source was available; in 1821 and 1836 they were attacked by Mexican authorities and removed (either through death or capture). (*See* also Findings 56 and 57 below.)[25]

Some Navajos were friendly and entered into peace treaties, which frustrated the Mexican officials in Santa Fe who learned that friendly Navajo chieftains only spoke for their own band. The first treaty signed by Governor Jose Antonio Vizcarro in February 1823 was unsuccessful, since it was followed by more raids and retaliatory campaigns by Mexican soldiers. The second treaty was signed in 1829. Still the raids and thefts continued. As authorities got better acquainted with Navajos, they learned that their strongholds were the La Plata and Chuska-Tunicha Mountains as the Canyon de Chelly, which are all north of the Zuni claim area.

Finding No. 56: Mexican Troops Protect Northern Border of Zuni

Mexican troops chased fleeing Navajos from the northern border of the claim area. In 1836, Governor Armijo ordered Jose Francisco Vigil to march against the Navajos. En route Vigil received word that the Zunis were possibly in league with the Navajos against the Mexicans. He arrived on Christmas morning at the Pueblo of Zuni in hopes of surprising the Zunis, but he found that the Zunis were not united with the Navajos. In fact, the Zunis turned over two Navajo captives to the Mexican soldiers. Vigil then sent a detachment of soldiers to Ojo del Gallo and thence to the Chuska Mountains and Ojo del Oso to battle any Navajos which might be found there. The Mexicans destroyed the rancheries, killed 20 Navajo men and took Indian women and 14 children captive along with 5,300 sheep. Vigil declared the Sierra De Tunicha to be the center of Navajo country, but noted that the Navajo had dispersed in many directions. Mexican forces traveled all the way to Canyon de Chelly (outside the claim area) and fought numerous skirmished with the Navajos. Navajo raiding appeared to increase in 1837 in retaliation for Zuni assistance to Mexican troops; however, rumors of Zuni-Navajo collusion continued.

Finding No. 57: Exclusive Nature of Zuni Use of Claim Area During Mexican Period

The Zunis continued to have exclusive use and occupation of the claim area during the Mexican Period. While there is some evidence that some Navajo families or bands made temporary use of Ojo del Oso, they were driven from the area by Mexican soldiers because Navajo Indians were at war with Mexico and their presence at Ojo del Oso was opposed by the Zunis and Mexican officials. During the period 1843 to 1844, although there were increased Navajo attacks throughout the rest of the province of New Mexico, none were reported at Zuni. Most of the Mexican military campaigns were directed at Navajos living north and west of Jemez, well outside of the Zuni claim area.

Finding No. 58: Mexico Recognized Zuni Ownership of Claim Area

During the brief period of Mexican sovereignty over the claim area, the new Mexican government continued to apply existing Spanish law respecting Indian tribes. Ordinances governing land and water were taken from the Laws of the Indies and adopted by the new regime. Thus from a legal standpoint, the period of Mexican rule was characterized by a continuity of Zuni property rights. The Mexican government recognized the Zuni right to permanently use and occupy the lands the Zuni had traditionally used and occupied, just as the Spanish before it had done.

Finding No. 59: Zuni Aboriginal Lands Remain Intact Under Mexico

Since Mexico had recognized the Zunis' right to aboriginal territory and had done nothing to disrupt or interfere with Zuni use and occupation, the Zuni became subject to the sovereignty of the United States with their aboriginal lands intact.

H. NATURE AND EXTENT OF ZUNI LAND USE AND OCCUPANCY AS OF 1846

Finding No. 60: Reference Points Defining Zuni Boundaries[26]

On Plaintiff's Exhibit 240, the numbered locations 1–20 described hereafter indicate the reference points of the boundary of Zuni territory as of 1846. A short description of each reference point together with a brief discussion of its significance follows:

1. San Francisco Peaks: These high peaks, which can be seen from the Zuni River Valley, are the Zuni sacred mountains to the west. In Zuni tradition, this area was one of the first stopping places on the migration of the Zunis

from "The Place of Beginning" in the Grand Canyon to their present location at the Pueblo of Zuni. The peaks were used for hunting, gathering, and as shrines. These mountains marked the western edge of exclusive Zuni use and occupation as of 1846 and the common boundary point between Zuni and Hopi and Havasupi lands.

2. Mormon Mountain: While Zunis claimed to use the area immediately south of the San Francisco Peaks as of 1846, the claim line was drawn in a southeasterly direction to Mormon Mountain so as to avoid possible overlap with the northern Tonto Apaches, who were also know to have used the area due south of the San Francisco Peaks prior to 1846. The Zuni claim area thus does not include any lands utilized by the Tonto Apaches in 1846.

3. Baker Butte: This butte is a large prominent landmark on the Mogollon Rim which separates the Strawberry and Verde Valleys to the west of the claim area from the Little Colorado River Valley to the east and within the claim area. The Strawberry River Valley was used for Apache farm sites and is thus not included within the Zuni claim area. There were no Apache farm sites within the Zuni claim area in 1846.

4. The Mogollon Rim: The Mogollon Rim is a prominent escarpment or cliff which forms a natural division between the Little Colorado River drainage area to the north, within the claim area to the north, and the Gila River Valley outside the claim area to the south. The rim separates two ecological communities. The various lookout points along the precipitous edge of the rim are used for Zuni ceremonial purposes, and Zuni war god shrines were placed along the rim as of 1846 to protect the Zuni area. Much Zuni hunting and gathering was carried on north of the rim itself. The Apaches lived to the south of the Mogollon Rim in small bands using semipermanent homes which can be identified by Mescal roasting pits. A Zuni watchtower on the rim was located in the late 1800's near the town of Springerville.

5. Mt. Baldy: Mt. Baldy is a high mountain of religious significance to the Zunis. In addition, the area was used extensively for hunting and gathering by the Zunis to 1846. This mountain marks the boundary between the Zunis and the Apaches to the southwest.

6. Willow Mountain, Arizona: This prominent mountain is the extreme southern boundary of the Zuni claim area in the State of Arizona as of 1846, serving as a religious area, and for the gathering and hunting of turkeys, and other birds and small game.

7. Willow Mountain, New Mexico: This prominent mountain is the extreme southern boundary of the Zuni claim area in the State of New Mexico as of 1846, serving as a traditional hunting and gathering area, as well as serving as a religious shrine.

8. Granite Peak: This peak is located near the present town of Magdalena and is clearly visible from Willow Peak and Cebolleta Peak. A line drawn from Point 7 to Point 8 on Map 240, included the Plains of San Augustin and the Datil Mountains used extensively for hunting purposes by the Zunis in 1846.

9. Cebolleta Peak: This prominent land mark stands by itself at the foot of the lava flow originating at Mt. Taylor. Its predominant place and landscape marked the division between Acoma and Zuni in 1846.

10. The Ice Caves: This geological phenomenon is located near the western fringe of the Malpais and was and is a focal point of the activities of many Zuni religious societies. It is also located near "The Place of the Deer," where Zunis believe that deer are created to replenish those hunted and used throughout Zuni

country. The Malpais itself is uninhabited and its barren nature served as a natural boundary between Zuni and Acoma.

11. Ojo del Gallo: This sacred spring was used by the Zuni people extensively in 1846 and times previous thereto. It is the last watering place upon leaving Zuni country for the Rio Grande Pueblos.

12. Mt. Taylor: This prominent landmark serves as the common boundary point between Acoma, Laguna, Navajo, and Zuni. As of 1846, the Zunis controlled their approach to the mountain from the west. Mt. Taylor was used by the Zunis in 1846 for hunting and gathering purposes and as a sacred religious shrine.

13. Hosta Butte: At the summit are separated drainage systems. Waters north flow to the San Juan River. Waters south in the Zuni claim area flow into the Rio Puerco. Ruins in the Upper Puerco River Valley just to the south of this butte were inhabited by ancestors of clans now domiciled in Zuni. The summit of Hosta Butte was the natural dividing point between the Zunis and the Navajo after the Navajos moved into the San Juan River basin area in the 1800's.

14. Mexican Springs: These springs are located at a place where the San Juan River drainage flows to the north and the Little Colorado River drainage and the Rio Puerco flow to the South. In 1846 this was the "Zuni side" of the southern tip of the Chuska Mountains which divided them from the Navajos.

15. Ganado: Ganado is located near the traditional Zuni site of Kintiel. This was a place where water could be found on the Zuni/Hopi trail and was often used by Zuni traders. In 1851, the United States constructed Ft. Defiance on the edge of the Zuni territory as a defense against raiding Navajos. Ft. Defiance is located on a line drawn between Points 14 and 15 on Map 240.

16. Steamboat Canyon: This canyon was, in 1846, and is the traditional and agreed upon boundary between Hopi and Zuni. Steamboat Canyon contains a Zuni shrine and a Hopi shrine indicating that the site served as their common boundary. Steamboat Canyon is located on the Zuni/Hopi trail.

17. Twin Buttes: Twin Buttes is located at the confluence of Steamboat Wash and the Pueblo Colorado Wash and was an ancestral site of Zuni habitation. The Pueblo Colorado Wash was an identifiable boundary between Hopi and Zuni in 1846.

18. The Confluence of the Pueblo Colorado Wash and the Cottonwood Wash: This area marks another place on the traditional boundary between Hopi and Zuni.

19. Confluence of the Little Colorado Wash and the Cottonwood Wash: In prehistoric times, the common ancestors of the Hopis and Zunis lived here, but later separated themselves during the migration period, some going to Hopi and some going to Zuni. The Little Colorado River from Winslow to Leupp completed the traditional and easily identified boundary between Hopi and Zuni, as recognized in 1846.

20. Leupp, Arizona: Based upon the archaeological discovery of numerous pottery shards of ancestral Zunis, this area is traditionally Zuni. It was used by the Zunis in 1846 for hunting, gathering, and for religious pilgrimages both to the San Francisco Peaks and to the Grand Canyon.

The foregoing points of reference were connected by a single line to form a boundary or perimeter of Zuni exclusive use and occupancy as of 1846. Since it is clear that actual Zuni use and occupancy for the purposes of farming, hunting, gathering, trade and shrine visitation exceeded this line, the boundary, as drawn accurately, reflects the area of exclusive Zuni use and does not include those lands which may have been used infrequently or jointly with surrounding tribes.

Finding No. 61: Physical Environment Determined Zuni Boundaries

Geography was an important factor in determining land use boundaries in the pueblo region. Such boundaries included mountain areas, lava flows, river basins and drainage systems, and biotic communities. The mountains on the margins of the Zuni aboriginal territory played an important role by serving as boundary markers. The mountains used by the Zunis as their boundary markers are easily discernible as one views the horizon from the Zuni River Valley, and anyone who stands on the summit of any of the peaks named in Finding 57 can see the length and breath of the Zuni claim area. Mountain areas also provided the Zunis with wild foodstuffs, and were sites for gathering medicinal plants, for hunting various animals, and for making prayer offerings to their deities and other perceived supernatural beings. The mountains are so sacred to the Zunis that they locate various shrines on the summit of each peak, which, by religious tradition and custom, must be visited periodically. The Mogollon Rim and the mountain ranges in that area were an important boundary marker between Zuni and Indians to the south, such as Apaches.

The great lava flows south of Mt. Taylor and the modern city of Grants on the eastern edge of the Zuni region were a forbidding boundary between Zuni and Acoma. This Zuni-Acoma boundary is still relevant since the Acoma farming villages stop at the eastern edges of the lava fields, and the areas of Zuni utilization, including ancient shrines and familiar places, begin on the western edge, in the vicinity of San Rafael and the Blue Lake Region.

Springs used for watering livestock, and by people, marked trails into Zuni. Sacred springs fed by mountain snows were visited periodically and offerings were made by Zuni priests. Available water determined agricultural boundaries and grazing boundaries. Drainage systems served as boundaries. An example is the area of Hosta Butte and the crest of mountains of which it is a part which form a portion of the northern boundary of the claim area. Water flows from this area south into the Rio Puerco of the claim area. North from Hosta Butte waters flow into the San Juan River Basin of the Navajo Area of occupancy.

Biotic communities served as boundaries, since materials used by the Zunis were found in certain of those communities. For instance, the area between the Little Colorado River and the Mogollon Rim as far west as the San Francisco Peaks was a large Zuni hunting and gathering area. The Mogollon Rim marked separate biotic communities; the one to the north used by Zunis, the one to the south used by Apaches.

Finding No. 62: Zuni Use of Boundary Markers

The Zunis used their own unique "flags" or boundary markers to designate their territorial limits. Practical restraints imposed by natural barriers determined to a great extent the area of exclusive use and occupancy of the Zuni people. Prominent landmarks, such as mountain peaks, mesa tops, cliff escarpments, lava flows, and rivers were easily recognized by any traveler in the claim area. A preliterate society, such as the Zuni Tribe, having no aid of maps or surveying equipment, relied on these landmarks to define their boundaries. These natural landmarks in turn were set apart or prominently marked by the Zunis placing clearly visible War God Shrines, masks, Zuni fetishes, prayer sticks, turquoise, shells, pottery or other materials readily identified as being Zuni. The Zunis were careful to mark many other places of significance within the claim area itself, giving rise to a large number of Zuni place names, which serve as very sacred symbols of identity or boundary markers.

Zuni tradition and religion preserved the knowledge of these exact locations by the use of oral tradition memorized by rote or in song and prayer, and passed from one generation to another without deviation. The retention of memory of these places is one way Zunis maintain their identity as a people.

In addition, Zuni people preserved and maintained these "markers" or locations by making regular visits or pilgrimages to deposit offerings and ask blessings upon the land. In depositions, priests and leaders of secret Zuni societies documented for the first time the general location of these "marked" or sacred places. In recent times, many of the Zuni markers or shrines have been lost, stolen, or destroyed.

Finding No. 63: Zuni Bow Priests Patrolled Zuni Borders

Invoking what were believed to be supernatural powers of the War Gods by the placement of war god masks on the Zuni borders, Zuni Bow Priests or warriors patrolled Zuni lands for the purpose of removing unwanted intruders. Zuni war gods, or *Ahayuda*, are believed to protect the Zuni people and their lands. Bow Priests from the village of Zuni placed imposing war god masks or figures representing the *Ahayuda* at various points on the periphery of the Zuni area as boundary markers. These War God shrines were visited regularly and maintained by the Zuni people with the intention of protecting their boundaries from intruders. Zuni warriors or Bow Priests had the authority to patrol the boundaries and to escort visitors from the Zuni territory. Zuni Bow Priests placed their unique signs or symbols of the War Gods on every trail crossing the Zuni boundaries to warn or give notice to travelers that they were entering Zuni territory. Since the Bow Priests were empowered to protect against alien invasion of their sacred lands, intruders who came into the Zuni area without permission were hunted down and scalped.

Finding No. 64: Zunis Continued Traditional Land Use as of 1846

The traditional Zuni area of land use as of 1846, for all purposes including farming, grazing, hunting, gathering and worship (*i.e.*, shrines) is depicted in Plaintiff's Exhibit 241.[27]

Traditional Zuni land use involved a core area of permanent settlements where agriculture was intensively practiced, a larger surrounding area containing seasonal settlements where dry farming and flood water farming were practiced and livestock was grazed, and a more expansive surrounding area where animals were hunted, and plants, minerals, and other items were gathered. All of these activities were conducted upon "chosen" lands to which the Zunis believed they were guided by the gods. The introduction of new agricultural crops and domesticated animals from both the Spaniards and the Mexicans supplemented the aboriginal economy, but Zuni land use as of 1846 was not significantly affected by Europeans; thus the traditional Zuni land use system continued unabated. It is this traditional Zuni land use system that enabled the Zuni people to be self-sufficient and to produce surplus agricultural goods and other commodities obtained by hunting and gathering for trade with other Indians and with the governments of Spain, Mexico, and the United States.

Finding No. 65: Zuni Religious Use as of 1846

Zuni maintenance of the land under aboriginal land tenure practices as of 1846 required that specific offerings, prayers, and rituals be prepared throughout the calendar year. In addition, they felt intense religious devotion to the land and consequent responsibility for its maintenance and its protection. The Zuni calendar, determined and maintained by the Sun Priest and his associates, determined when agricultural and ceremonial activities were performed, year after year, in unchanging sequence. Zuni loyalty to and responsibility for the Zuni claim area is, and traditionally was, so great that they believe the rain will not fall if their prayers are not made, and the land will be ruined without their religious activities. As of 1846, the Zunis protected their orders, including all of the lands in the Zuni claim area, with religious zeal described by Cushing as "fanatical." The Zunis practiced intense conservation and revered the entire Zuni claim area as though it were a single living organism. Religious use of the land naturally coupled with other types of usage.

Finding No. 66: Religious Boundaries of Zuni Land as of 1846

The Zuni sacred lands of 1846 are depicted in Plaintiff's Exhibit 242. The religious boundaries of Zuni land extended well beyond the Zuni claim area as of 1846: to the east the Sandia Mountains east of Albuquerque; to the north the Blue Mountains in Utah and Colorado; to the west the Grand Canyon and Mohave Desert; to the south the San Francisco River drainage south of the Willow Peaks. Notwithstanding the many visits and religious pilgrimages made to specific shrines or areas outside of the claim area, the Zunis respected the rights of other Indians to those areas as well. The frontier of Zuni exclusive use to the east is Mt. Taylor, and to the west, the San Francisco Peaks. Within the boundaries of the claim area itself are innumerable springs, ruins, cliffs, waterways, pilgrimage routes, mesas, buttes, mountains, and other places of special religious significance. Zuni religious leaders are obligated to visit these sacred places for a variety of purposes, including making prayer offerings, gathering medicinal herbs, collecting materials for prayer sticks, and capturing birds for feathers. The Zunis have a reciprocal relationship with nature and believe that payment should be made when water, plants, or animals are used to maintain human life. Therefore, the deities must be "paid" with prayer offerings taken to shrines and sacred places.

All water is sacred in the semi-arid climate. All streams and springs within the claim area are, therefore, sacred, and the entire length of the Zuni River has religious significance. Mountain tops are sacred because they attract necessary water and are the source of springs. They are the homes of kachinas and other deities and serve as special markers of territorial claim. Thus, mountains along the Mogollon Rim and in the Reserve area, the San Francisco Peaks, and Mt. Taylor are primarily religious shrines of the Zunis which the latter considered to guard their area of exclusive use and dominion. Although shrines are sometimes located on mountain peaks, the entire mountain will have religious significance as a site for gathering medicinal herbs and other ceremonial materials. Entire regions, as well, may take on important and unique religious values. Thus, each stopping place in the origin and migration narrative of the Zunis is a shrine area held in special esteem. Important shrines also exist at all ancestral villages of the Zuni, where offerings are made to the Zunis' ancestors.

Finding No. 67: Zuni Plant Gathering Area as of 1846

The traditional Zuni plant gathering area as of 1846 is depicted in Plaintiff's Exhibit 243. The Zuni people collected various plants from every biotic community in the Zuni area, from the Alpine tundra at the top of the San Francisco Peaks, to the

Mohave Desert scrub in the bottom of the Grand Canyon. In the same way that the Zunis had reverence for the landscape, they revered the plants of the Zuni claim area. Zunis were therefore highly protective of that resource. By gathering plants from every corner of the region they occupied, the Zuni people were able to fill their larders and storage bins with an abundant array of foods, medicines, ceremonial materials, basketry materials, and toiletries. The Zuni also collected wood for building purposes, utensils, and fuel.

In the hundreds of years during which the Zunis occupied their traditional territory prior to 1846, there is no evidence that their gathering practices in any way depleted any of the plant resources about them. The Zunis had arrived at a way of life, and had developed land use systems, which would sustain them indefinitely in their territory using the resources therein in a way that promoted conservation and sustained yield.[28] Much of the traditional knowledge which made possible this great Zuni achievement, the harmonious interaction with the land and environment, has continued to be passed down at Zuni to the present day.

Finding No. 68: Traditional Zuni Mineral Gathering Area as of 1846

The traditional Zuni mineral gathering area as of 1846 is depicted in Plaintiff's Exhibit 243. As of 1846, the Zuni people did not differentiate between organic and inorganic materials, but considered all things to be living: the earth, the stones, and minerals, as well as plants and animals. All types of inorganic materials were gathered within the Zuni area: minerals for pigments, clays for pottery, soils and water for religious and other use, and particular types of rocks for tools, jewelry, fetish making. Zunis gathered minerals from the petrified forest, the Malpais, the Grand Canyon, the Gallo and Mogollon Mountains, and every other corner of their country. Turquoise was obtained from copper mines in the Zuni Mountains, and the Cerrillos. Peridot was gathered in the White Mountains of Arizona. Salt from Zuni Salt Lake provided an essential nutrient as well as an important trade item. The Zunis made systematic use of minerals occurring over a wide territory.

Finding No. 69: Traditional Zuni Hunting Area as of 1846

The traditional Zuni hunting area as of 1846 is depicted in plaintiff's Exhibit 246. From the highest mountains to the driest deserts within the claim area, the Zunis hunted, trapped, and snared many different species of animals and birds. Zuni hunting parties ranged for hundreds of miles in both the mountains and plains. Some of the most important hunting was carried out communally such as ritual rabbit drives near the Pueblo of Zuni. In outer areas of their territory, the Zunis constructed and used long brush fences or "drive lanes" in communal hunts for deer and antelope. Hunting was also done individually for family or clan use, and as initiation into adulthood. Hunting activities had associated religious practices, with ceremonial rites and prayers for slain animals. Prayers and offerings were made at hunting shrines along the trails that led to hunting grounds. Hunting provided the Zunis with a crucial supply of meat, with hides for clothing, and with bone and sinew for tools and other manufactured articles. A great number of birds were snared to obtain feathers for religious use.

Finding No. 70: Zuni Grazing Area as of 1846

The traditional Zuni grazing area as of 1846 is depicted in Plaintiff's Exhibit 244. As of 1846, Zunis tended extensive flocks of domestic animals which were herded over a large portion of the claim area. Before contact with Europeans, the Zunis tended extensive flocks of turkeys which were herded over a large area. Turkey feathers were used for clothes, and the birds themselves were used for food during times of need. The Zunis later obtained livestock from the Spaniards including sheep, cattle, horses, burros, and other domestic animals. With the incorporation of livestock into their economic system, the Zunis began using extensive lands within their territory for grazing. The sheep industry was particularly well established by 1846, providing wool for weaving, as well as meat for food. During the summer the Zunis grazed their sheep in the grasslands as far as 70 miles from Zuni Pueblo. In the winter and during the spring lambing, the Zunis herded their sheep closer to Zuni Pueblo and the farming villages. Traditionally, flocks were rotated from one grassland to another to conserve range land and were often allowed to graze in agricultural fields after the harvest.

Finding No. 71: Zuni Farming Area as of 1846

The traditional Zuni farming area as of 1846 is depicted in Plaintiff's Exhibit 245. The economic base of traditional Zuni society was agriculture, stabilized by gathering and hunting. Since prehistoric times, through and including 1846, the Zuni people farmed in all of the well-watered drainages throughout the Zuni area. Crops included a variety of plants developed in the Southwest before European contact as well as a variety of plants acquired from the Europeans. While much of the farming was concentrated in the valley of the Zuni River, many small farms as far away as St. Johns, Arizona, were still being planted as of 1846. In addition, many sheepherders planted small plots of corn and squash in the outlying areas used for grazing. These small plots were tended by the sheepherders during the summer months while they were watching their flocks. In the Zuni River Valley, corn was planted wherever there was sufficient runoff to provide growth. Wheat and other irrigated crops were grown in large farms nearer to the villages. Small, hand-watered waffle gardens for chili, coriander, and onions were planted on the banks of the Zuni River at the Zuni Pueblo, and tended by women. The traditional agriculture of the Zunis employed dry farming and flood water farming methods, conserving the soil and making maximum use of available water. Irrigated agriculture was an indigenous technique at Zuni which included the use of viaducts made from large hollow logs.

Finding No. 72: Zuni Trade Relations as of 1846

Trade has been an important part of the Zuni economy for about a thousand years allowing the Zunis to exchange resources from their area for the products of other areas. (See also Finding 12.) As of 1846, the Zuni Pueblo was a hub in a large regional trade system connecting the Southwest with Meso-America, the west coast, the northern mountains, and the Great Plains. Active trade regularly took place along the north/south and the east/west trade routes. Zunis traveled far distances to trade, and other Indian people traveled far distances to Zuni. The Zunis also allowed, under certain conditions, other Indian people to collect salt within Zuni territory. Macaw feathers were traded for turquoise and blue paint; shells for corn; coral for pigment; and cotton thread and cloth for buffalo hides. Zunis also traded pinon nuts, wicker baskets, and ceramics. After the arrival of Europeans in the Southwest, trade continued to be conducted within Zuni territory, and beyond, with both Indian peoples and the Europeans. Disruptions in the trade caused by European efforts to regulate it, and by dislocations of Indian tribes, may have restricted some trade. Nonetheless, trade was augmented by new trade goods and new markets. Zuni trade established important social as well as commercial relationships with many different tribes and many Europeans.

Finding No. 73: Zuni Trails as of 1846

As of 1846, there were many trails throughout the Zuni area used for religious pilgrimages, used for hunting and gathering expeditions, and used to facilitate trade. The former uses have been discussed in Findings 65–68. Well-marked and well-worn trading trails went out from the main Zuni Pueblo as if it were the hub of a wheel. Two trails on either end of the Zuni Mountains led to Acoma, from there a trail went east to the Rio Grande Pueblos, with branches to Pecos, and Taos, and beyond to the buffalo plains. Two branching trails went northwest to the San Juan country and to the Hopi villages, and then on to the Grand Canyon. Another trail went to the Grand Canyon from Kothlualawa, following the ancient migration route. From Hopi and from Zuni, trails went west to the Colorado River and the tribes living along it. The Colorado River Trail went south to the Gulf of California. Another southern trail connected Zuni Pueblo with the Gila Country and Sonora, which was used by Coronodo. Several trails also went out from the Zuni Salt Lake.

The Zunis placed high priority on keeping their trails open and safe in order to promote their widespread trade. Zuni war chiefs acted against parties that restricted or endangered Zuni trails, but were willing to provide guides to peaceable strangers. As of 1846, Zuni country was spoken of as a very safe place in which to travel. Spaniards and Americans first entered the Zuni area traveling the Zunis' well-developed trails. Use of the Zuni trails within the Zuni claim area was by permission of the Zuni Tribe, either expressed or implied.

Finding No. 74: Zuni Government Remained Strong as of 1846

The Zunis used an advanced, civilized, and sophisticated political structure as of 1846. The religious leaders or Council of Priests formed a kind of theocracy which carefully watched over Zuni affairs. The Council tried to remain apart from secular affairs, however, which were left to the Bow Priests. Civic officials appointed by the priestly council were given titles from the Spanish system of government such as the Governor, and Teniente. The governor became the spokesman, selected by the priestly council, to cope with outside matters. Under the legal systems of both Spain and Mexico, the rights of the Zunis to govern themselves, in the lands they occupied, were respected. As outside pressures intensified, so did Zuni concern for maintenance of their territory. The Zunis were aware of their political boundaries and resisted any attempt at unauthorized intrusion within those boundaries. The governors, as the spokesman most generally knowledgeable concerning Zuni boundaries and Zuni obligations, became increasingly involved in diplomacy and negotiation.

Finding No. 75: Absence of Apache Occupation Sites Within Claim Area as of 1846

There is no physical or historical evidence of any Apache settlement within the Zuni claim area as of 1846. The only Apache archaeological sites are found well outside the claim area south of the Mogollon Rim. Likewise, Apache farming areas are found to the south of the Zuni claim area. As a general rule, the Apaches did not graze livestock; but what little livestock they had, was kept outside of the claim area. The only evidence of Apache presence in the Zuni claim area, as of 1846, indicates it was for raiding or trading purposes. Whatever little unpermitted use was made of the Zuni claim area by Apache Indians prior to 1846 was met with strong Zuni resistance.

Finding No. 76: Absence of Navajo Occupation Within Claim Area as of 1846

There is no archaeological evidence of any temporary or permanent homesite of the Navajos which predates 1846 in the Zuni claim area. The temporary rancheria of Navajos located at Ojo del Oso was destroyed in 1836 and the people were either killed or taken captive. The Navajos complained that when Navajo women were attempting to gather pine nuts in the Zuni mountains a few years prior to 1846, the Zunis had killed a number of them. The only evidence of Navajo presence in the Zuni claim area, indicated they were there for raiding or trading purposes. Whatever little unpermitted use was made of the Zuni claim area by Navajo Indians prior to 1846 was met with strong Zuni resistance.

Finding No. 77: Apaches and Navajos Without Central Government

Apaches and Navajos were without central government as of 1846. They operated in small, independent bands or as individual families, and as such were no threat to traditional Zuni land use. They did not develop into organized tribes until well into the United States period. The Zunis knew and traded with some Navajos and Apaches and also knew that other Navajos and Apaches were not to be trusted. The representatives of Spain, Mexico, and the United States also learned that making treaties to end raids on Indian pueblos and European settlement with certain representative bands of the Navajos and Apaches would not result in cessation of hostilities with other bands of Navajos and Apaches. Thus, it was possible that the Zunis might be trading and enjoying good relationships with certain Navajos and Apaches, and shortly thereafter might experience raids from others. There is no evidence that hostilities experienced between Zunis and their Navajo and Apache neighbors kept the Zunis from continuing their farming activities, their grazing activities, their gathering activities, and the uses of customary places connected with their religious life.

Finding No. 78: Written Account Concerning Northern Boundary of Zuni Territory as of 1846

The Robinson diary contains a first-hand written account of the northern boundary of Zuni territory as it touched Navajo lands as of 1846. In the Fall of 1846, military personnel carrying out orders given by General Kearny to Colonel A. W. Doniphan to protect New Mexicans from continuing Navajo attacks on the Rio Grande, found themselves at Cebolleta, northeast of the Zuni claim area in order to guard one of two main "war trails." A task force was dispatched to go to the Navajos in the Chuska Mountains and secure a peace treaty with them. A Navajo Chieftain Sandoval, whose band lived periodically in the Cebolleta area northeast of the Zuni claim area, volunteered to accompany the peace mission. Sandoval reported that the principal habitation or haunts of the Navajos as of that time were 200 miles west from Cebolleta in the neighborhood of the Tunicha Mountains, the dividing range between the Atlantic and Pacific on the borders of Red Lake. Private Jacob Robinson, a member of Captain John W. Reid's task force, kept a diary of the reconnaissance. Robinson's diary gives the earliest first-hand description of Navajo country by an Anglo, and gives definite indications concerning the extent of Zunis northern and northeastern boundaries at the time of United States occupation. The task force marched northwest from Cebolleta. In October 1846, while encamped at Red Lake, Private Robinson recorded:

> That night a Zuni Chief came to us and informed us that he was sent by his tribe to invite us to come and to see their women and children; he told us that on his side of the mountain they were very honest; that three of his children have been taken prisoners by the Mexicans and much stock stolen, but if he could obtain his children he would be satisfied; and they never had yet made war against the Mexicans, and never should. Captain Reid advised him to go to Santa Fe and see the governor.

Since the party was still in the Chuskas, the Zuni side of the mountain referred to that range. Captain Reid's party left Red Lake on October 20, rounding the southern end of the Chuskas to the "Zuni side of the mountain," near point 14 on Plaintiff's Exhibit 240. The next several days the party crossed the Continental Divide at Hosta Butte, at point 13 of the Plaintiff's Exhibit 240, then went on to Mt. Taylor region before finally reaching Cubero.

Finding No. 79: Absence of Navajo Hunting, Livestock Grazing, Farming, and Gathering in the Zuni Claim Area as of 1846

There is no evidence of Navajo hunting within the Zuni claim area for some time after 1846. The Navajos were nomadic and pastoral people, having large flocks of sheep which they grazed in areas north and northeast of Zuni. There are no hogan sites as of 1846 in the Zuni claim area. Navajo hogan sites in the extreme northern part of the Zuni claim area have been archaeologically dated in the post-1868 or Navajo Reservation Period. Navajos occasionally stole Zuni livestock, but they did not graze the livestock in the Zuni area at their leisure after stealing it. Rather, they moved the livestock north as quickly as possible to avoid recapture by the Zunis. While there is some evidence of early Navajo farming outside of the Zuni claim area, there is no evidence of any Navajo farm sites within the Zuni claim area until well after 1846. An attempt by the Navajos to use the Zuni Mountains for gathering purposes was staunchly opposed by the Zunis shortly before United States sovereignty. Many military campaigns of the United States against the Navajos forced individual groups to cross the Zuni territory to avoid capture by United States troops and some may have found refuge with Zunis. However, Navajo settlement within the Zuni claim area did not occur until after the Navajos had been released from Bosque Redondo (1868).

Finding No. 80: Absence of Apache Hunting and Gathering in the Zuni Claim Area as of 1846

Apaches lived outside of the Zuni claim area. Despite the occasional reports of Apaches in the country between the Zuni Pueblo and the mountains to the south, the homeland of the Apaches was in the mountains, surrounding valleys, and desert country south of the Mogollon Rim. Few Apaches farmed; those who did farmed south of the Mogollon Rim, outside the Zuni claim area. As of 1846, the Apaches subsisted on raiding; they did not have livestock of their own that they grazed. Apache raiding was directed primarily to the south at the Mexican cattle ranches and settlements where Apache plunder trials became well known. The Apaches did gather mescal which they roasted in pits before eating. The mescal plant is located to the south of the Zuni claim area. Grenville Goodwin reported from oral interviews taken in the 1930's that the Apaches hunted and gathered to the north of the Mogollon Rim about 1850. However, it appears that the second-hand account by aged Apaches were of hunting and gathering activities more likely conducted after 1860, when the Apaches came into closer contact with the Navajos. There is no historical or archaeological evidence of any Apache settlement in the Zuni claim area prior to 1846.

Finding No. 81: Absence of Acoma Hunting, Gathering, Farming, and Grazing in the Zuni Claim Area as of 1846

The barren Malpais region extending southward from Mt. Taylor and modern Grants forms a natural boundary between the Acoma and Zuni cultures. All of the archaeologists who have recently conducted intensive field investigations in the Zuni Mountains have concluded that the late prehistoric pueblo sites there, including the five villages of El Morro, are all ancestral Zuni sites. The archaeological evidence thus indicates that Zuni settlements were concentrated west of The Malpais and that prehistoric Acoma settlements were located on Cebolleta Mesa east of The Malpais. Earlier archaeological work which assumed Acoma usage in the Zuni claim area during the late prehistorical period had been discredited by more recent and more reliable work. The report of Dr. Robert Rands, involving Acoma use west of The Malpais, is exclusively based upon materials which are outdated and unreliable, or upon oral interviews dealing with a time period subsequent to 1876. During the Spanish and Mexican periods, the various activities of the Acoma had been confined to the east of The Malpais, as observed by both Spaniards and Mexicans. While Acomas carried on friendly and active trade relations with the Zuni, Acoma farming and stock grazing did not extend west of The Malpais until after the coming of the railroad in the 1880's. The only isolated instance of temporary or permitted Acoma hunting was recorded by Lieutenant A. W. Whipple in late November of 1853 when he met several Acomas near Agua Fria at the eastern edge of the Zuni claim area, who claimed to have been hunting in the nearby Zuni Mountains. As of 1846 the aboriginal lands of the Acoma and Zuni abutted one another commencing at Mt. Taylor in a southerly direction along the lava flow to Cebolleta Peak.

Finding No. 82: Absence of All Other Indians from the Claim Area

As of 1846 other Indians such as the Hualapai, Havasupai, Hopi, Pima and Yavapai all used and occupied lands outside of the Zuni claim area. These tribes, however, maintained friendly trade relationships with the Zuni. The Hopis, in particular, had a common agreed boundary with the Zunis as shown by points 16 through 20 on Plaintiff's Exhibit 240.

Finding No. 83: Zunis Watch Their Lands Carefully as of 1846

Zunis made frequent religious pilgrimages to their shrines. Bow Priests frequently reconnoitered the area to check the boundaries. Zunis traveled far distances to trade. In so doing, Zunis reported back to the pueblo on the conditions of the lands, animals, birds, and plants in the area they traversed. The constant criss-crossing of the Zuni claim area by the Zuni people gave Zuni leaders up-to-the-minute information on all changing conditions of their area and most certainly on the intrusion of any unwanted people. As reported by Coronado, after crossing the *Despoblado* below the Mogollon Rim, he came under the constant surveillance of the Zunis, his progress being carefully relayed back to Zuni by means of smoke signals. Information of importance to other pueblos was relayed by Zuni runners. In turn, any important information from Mexico or the Rio Grande was similarly passed on to the Zunis. The extensive trade carried on at Zuni brought them news from throughout the entire Southwest, from the Gulf of California to Mexico, and from the north and the plains.

Finding No. 84: Description of Zuni Aboriginal Lands as of 1846

The Zuni aboriginal tract of land is depicted in Plaintiff's exhibit 240 as circumscribed by the black line connecting points 1 through 20. From 1846 up to and including July 4, 1848, the Zuni Indians held by actual exclusive, and continuous use and occupancy, since time immemorial, a large track of land described generally as follows, to wit:

> Beginning at the point located on the summit of Humphrey's Peak in the San Francisco Peaks located in the present State of Arizona; thence south to Mormon Mountain; thence south to Lookout Tower on Baker Butts; thence southeast along the Mogollon Rim to Baldy Peak in the Mt. Baldy wilderness; thence to Willow Mountain, in the State of Arizona; thence east to Willow Mountain in the State of New Mexico; thence northeast to Granite Mountain near the town Magdalena, New Mexico; thence northwest to Cebolleta Peak; thence north around the western fringe of The Malpais (Lava Flow) to Grants, New Mexico; thence northwest to Hosta Butte; thence west to Mexican Springs; thence west to Ganado, Arizona; thence west to Steamboat Canyon; thence west to Steamboat Wash; thence south along Steamboat Wash to its junction with the Pueblo Colorado Wash; thence southwest along the Pueblo Colorado Wash to its junction with Cottonwood Wash; thence southwest along Cottonwood Wash to Winslow, Arizona; thence northwest along the Little Colorado River to Leupp, Arizona; thence west to the place of beginning.

I. INTRODUCING THE UNITED STATES PERIOD[29]

Finding No. 85: Introduction in 1846

The Zuni in 1846 were living as described in the previous findings.[30] Also in 1846, a war began between Mexico and the United States. An American General, Stephen Watts Kearny, occupied Santa Fe on August 22, 1846, and issued a formal proclamation of annexation, stating that New Mexico was a territory of the United States.

Thereafter, in mid-1848, a formal treaty, the Treaty of Guadalupe Hidalgo, was signed between the United States and Mexico. This formalized American jurisdiction over the Zuni Indians. Under this treaty, former citizens of Mexico now under American jurisdiction (including the Zunis) were permitted to elect either Mexican or American citizenship. The Zuni, like all inhabitants of the area, were guaranteed protection of liberty and property and security in the free exercise of their religion. (The Zuni did not elect Mexican citizenship and thus were considered to have elected American citizenship, to be conferred at the proper time. By the

Indian Citizenship Act of 1924, Indians, including the Zuni, who were not yet citizens were given citizenship.)

Finding No. 86: Zunis, Navajos, and the United States

Major Gilpin of the United States Army described Ojo del Oso (Bear Springs) as being within the Territory of the Zuni. Major Gilpin met with American Colonel Doniphan at Bear Springs, then marched south to the Zuni pueblo, where they were hospitably received (as was Captain Monroe Parsons who arrived in the pueblo after pursuing Navajo raiders).

The Zunis, and other Indians in and around New Mexico, continued to be harassed by raiding or pillaging Navajo bands. On November 26, 1846, the Zunis and Navajos signed a treaty of peace and amity, under the guidance and arbitration of Colonel Doniphan.

Also in November 1846, Colonel Doniphan (on instructions of General Kearny) signed a treaty of peace with certain Navajo. (Additional disagreements and treaties with the Navajo were to be seen later.)

Finding No. 87: Other Indians after 1846[31]

Pursuing Navajos reportedly raiding Zuni territory, American military, in 1847, did not sight any Navajo in the Zuni claim area, particularly inasmuch as the Navajo continued to retreat from the military pursuit.

Military officers of the United States (*i.e.*, Americans) joined by an American Indian Agent and a topographical engineer reported that the Navajo raids were for the purpose of plundering.

In the mid-1800's, American military reported that the Zunis had large herds of sheep and horses and extensively cultivated the soil, and noted evidence of agriculture in outlying areas. (Some expeditions also noted the commandeering of livestock and supplies, property of the Zunis, by a band of California emigrants.)

In a meeting in October 1849 with Americans, the Zunis requested military material to enable them to repulse Navajo raids. (Instead, the Americans promised to provide military protection. Various treaties and agreements were discussed.)[32]

The Navajo raids continued throughout the mid-1800's. During this period, American expeditions described the Zuni presence throughout the claim area, denoting the "Navajo Country" in the Chuska Mountain (north of the Zuni claim area) and the Apaches below the Mogollon Rim (south of the Zuni claim area).

Such expeditions also described the northern Zuni-Navajo border to be north of Fort Defiance at the south end of Canon Bonito (between points 14 and 15 on Plaintiff's Exhibit 240).

Throughout the mid-1800's, American (United States) military and other expeditions (including some trailblazers) received a considerable amount of various supplies from the hospitable Zunis. Descriptions by Americans, during this period, note the Zunis' raising of sheep, horses and mules, and their practice of agriculture, on an extensive basis.

In 1854, Hispanic stockmen attempted to intrude upon Zuni (as well as Navajo) territory to graze their flocks. Apache bands increased their raids (including south of the Zuni claim area) in 1856. American military expeditions (sometimes joined by Zuni warriors and/or scouts) followed the trail of marauding Apaches. The Zunis and Apaches reached an apparent peace in 1858.

Navajo presence in Zuni territory, for the purpose of raiding, was again recorded by an American Indian Agent in 1857.

In August 1857, an American military officer again noted the abundant and extensive Zuni resources; he also sighted some Navajo grazing animals just northwest of the main Zuni pueblo and a few Yavapai who had been trading at Zuni.

In 1858–59, American military reconnaissance expeditions patrolled the Zuni claim area and reported that there was no evidence of any Navajo or Apache habitation within the area.

In the 1860's, some Navajo were found in the Zuni claim area (particularly in the area of the Zuni Mountains) and were repulsed, or killed, by the Zuni.

In 1868, after four years of captivity under the Americans at Bosque Rendondo, the Navajos signed a treaty with the United States which allowed the Navajo to return to a reservation north of the Zuni territory (although the Zunis may have consented to a small group of Navajo families settling in the Ramah area).

In the mid to late 1860's, some Navajo and Apache (seeking refuge from the United States military) and some Hispanic and "Anglo" settlers began to push into Zuni territory. The Zunis continually complained of this Navajo and Apache encroachment.

A major battle between the Zunis and the Navajos, on the banks of the Rio Puerco of the West, was reported in 1873. In 1875, the Zuni complained to the American Indian agent in Santa Fe that Mexicans (or Hispanics) were bringing large flocks of sheep into what they, the Zuni, considered their territory.

Between 1846 until 1900's (approximately) the Zunis were subject to the territorial laws of the United States.

In 1850, the Zuni signed an agreement with the United States which bound the latter to protect the former from Navajo raids (refusing to the Zunis the ability and capability of doing so themselves).

Finding No. 88: Ultimate Finding[33]

A. The Zuni Tribe, plaintiff herein, had aboriginal title to the land contained in the area claimed by plaintiff (as described in Plaintiff's Exhibit 240 and Finding 60).

B. This aboriginal title existed from time immemorial beginning as early as 5000 B.C. (at the latest) and continuing through and including at least 1846.

C. The Zuni, exclusively, used and occupied this claim area.

This entire claim area was used by the Zuni for one purpose or another including: habitation (chiefly in pueblos as well as in some of the outlying areas) and life-sustaining activities including farming, hunting, grazing, gathering, and religious worship. (This use continued even during periods of attack from others.)

The Zunis' use was exclusive. The presence of any other Indians or individuals was under particular specific circumstances, not detracting from the exclusivity of the Zuni use and ownership. Some other Indians were present in the claim area with Zuni permission for such purposes as trade or travel; some were also given permission to use certain limited areas during particular designated seasons for limited purposes (such as agriculture). (Other individuals, namely the Mexicans and Spanish, were also present, with Zuni permission, for brief periods for the various purposes of, for example, travel including peaceful and military expeditions, trade, and activities related to government administration.) Other Indians, particularly the Apache and Navajo, were also present in the claim area for brief, and various, periods of time and for the sole purpose of raiding; their presence was objected to, and was resisted and/or repulsed, by the Zuni.

Judith Ann Yannello, Judge

NOTES

1. Defendant suggests that evidence in the form of testimony by tribal elders requires corroboration to be entitled to probative weight. Whatever the merits of that contention, this court would note that it has considered all the evidence including testimony by several expert witnesses, source material relied upon by witnesses and accompanying their written reports, and the documentary evidence, and considered the lay testimony in that context.

2. Defendant also contends that the small Zuni population (1,500 to 2,500 by 1846) could not possibly have exclusively used and occupied the entire claim area (of some 15,000,000 acres). Defendant offers no factual support for this contention, however; in any event, the matter could not be resolved solely by noting that Zuni population and acreage but rather would require examination of the patterns of all populations of all similar areas at that time. *See* also Finding Nos. 8, 9, and 10.

3. Defendant contends that the claim area was used or occupied by the following: Acoma, Hopi, Havasupai, Apache, and Navajo. With respect to the Acoma, the evidence primarily relied upon was prepared for another action and related to periods after 1870 (not before 1846) or is, for other reasons, not considered probative. With respect to the Hopi, the persuasive evidence addressed only those areas wherein the Hopi and Zuni shared traditional borders and such boundaries are the limit of the Zuni claim area, with Zuni use and occupancy within its boundaries. With respect to Havasupai habitation, the evidence shows that, if such habitation did occur, it ceased around 1400. With respect to the Apache and Navajo, the evidence established that their presence within the claim area was sporadic, for purposes of raiding, and was repulsed by the Zuni.

With respect to all these allegations and most of the Findings made by the court, there is again disagreement between the expert witnesses. As noted in the footnote to the Findings, the court had resolved these differences based on the preponderant and most persuasive evidence. (With respect to evidentiary citations, *see also*, plaintiff's proposed findings; plaintiff's response to defendant's objections to plaintiff's proposed findings; and plaintiff's objections to defendant's proposed findings.)

4. It is however, important to note that that special jurisdictional act did provide as follows:

Any award made to any Indian tribe other than the Zuni Indian Tribe of New Mexico before, on, or after the date of . . . this Act, . . . with respect to any lands that are the subject of a claim submitted by the [Zuni] shall not be considered as a defense, estoppel, or setoff to such claim, and shall not otherwise affect the entitlement to, or amount of, any relief with respect to such claim.

Accordingly, contrary to the suggestion of defendant, this court concluded that any other findings by the Indian Claims Commission or any other court (and any evidence introduced in the course of proceedings before those tribunals but not before this court in the instant case) as to the use of the claim-area lands by any other tribes (including the Navajo) is not relevant here and cannot be used in the government's defense against plaintiff's claim.

5. Additional findings, infra, address a matter which may be summarized here. During a brief 12 year period after the Pueblo Revolt (1680 to 1692), the Zuni retreated to the environs of Corn Mountain, which served as a defensive stronghold when Spanish soldiers threatened Zuni security. The evidentiary record nonetheless supports a finding that, even during this time, the Zuni ventured into other regions of the claim area (or otherwise collected or made use of the resources of the claim area) to sustain and augment life when restricted to Corn Mountain. (See also Finding 40 infra.)

6. This Finding addresses Zunis use of the biotic communities in the claim area. (Additional descriptions of Zuni use are set forth below for various periods of time. *See* Nos. 60 at seq. for the periods of alleged takings, beginning in 1846.)

The Finding is not refuted or rendered inaccurate even if, as defendant contends in its objection, other tribes, for limited times, used some of the resources of some of the claim area for various purposes. (*See* also accompanying opinion.)

Moreover, the court finds persuasive the arguments and evidence set forth in plaintiff's response to defendant's objection. (See also Findings Nos. 43, 46, 48, 49, 75, and 80 re: Apache; 81 re: Acoma; 14 re: Hopi; 51, 55, 76 and 79 re: Navajo; and 24, 33, 52, 57–79 and 82 generally.)

7. These ethnological cultures were described by Gordon R. Wiley (Defendant Ex. 19, pp. 180–81) as follows:

The Anasazai subarea has been linked with the present Pueblo Indians among whom are the Hopi and Zuni in the west and the Rio Grande towns of the east.

The historic Patayan subarea is linked to the historic and modern Yuma and the Havasupai, Yavapai, and Walapai.

There may be a link between the Hohokam and the modern Pima and Papago.

Less certain is the link between the Mogollon and their modern relatives.

See also Finding No. 14 infra.

8. In addition to the experts noted in the Finding, defendant points to the 1930 report of Frank H.H. Roberts, Jr. who at that time excavated Kiatuthlanna and examined its pottery. Plaintiff's expert T. J. Ferguson relied upon several studies conducted after 1930, in addition to his own extensive research. The court finds plaintiff's evidence persuasive.

9. In the testimony, scientific experts such as archaeologists used the term "abandonment" to refer to physical presence; thus tribes might "abandon" sustaining areas to consolidate their housing. These witnesses did not address "abandonment" as that term is used in the law relating to use and occupancy. This finding employs the term in its legal sense.

10. Some additional comment on the limitations of language may address some of defendant's objection to this (and similar) Findings. Defendant states:

Defendant denies this [evidence] represents claim areawide use of plants and animals by the Zuni. The above [evidence] only proves the likelihood of the use of specific plants and animals in a particular section of the Zuni Claim Area.

The court would note that individual citation to specific evidence addresses particular resources in certain parts of the claim area. An amalgam of the collective evidence does establish that the Zuni derived resources of one sort or another from within, or otherwise used, the entire claim area.

11. The court recognizes that this particular Finding incorporates in part the modern Zuni tribe-members' description of present religious observation and their belief and understanding of their history. Nonetheless, such beliefs have been established and are a part of the record. Moreover, this Finding is intended to be read in context with the other Findings based, unless otherwise noted, on objective evidence (e.g., expert testimony).

Beyond a present recounting of belief and understanding, and in addition to the citations cited in plaintiff's proposed Finding, plaintiff also points (in its response) to the observations of Mr. Roberts (Pltf. Ex. 1115 at pp. 6, 8–9) corroborating, at Kiatuthlanna in 1930 (prior to the enactment of the Indian Claims Act), similar Zuni beliefs particularly in their religious observations. (Mr. Roberts concluded his Report of this 1930 study with a caution against "too much" reliance being placed on modern recounting of primitive history.)

The court acknowledges that, like any religious history, oral recounting throughout generations can become less than accurate. Again, however, this Finding is to be taken in context with all other Findings. Moreover, the court is persuaded by the testimony of plaintiff's experts that, to the Zunis as to members of other tribes, the transmission of historical data and tradition was always of great import with little, if any, reliance placed on any written documentation. Defendant conjectures, but offers no evidence to contradict or impeach the Zuni recounting of their history. And, given the import attached to the oral transmission of history and religious observation by the Zuni, there is no reason to suspect gross or deliberate distortion. Accordingly, the court is persuaded that, notwithstanding some insufficiency, this recounted history is of evidentiary probity.

12. There is ample evidence of the Zuni presence. Defendant, however, contends that the Zuni may not have been the sole occupants of the claim area but that others (Athapaskans or Apache or the Navajo) may have lived there. Defendant notes that no evidence of such other occupation exists because such groups customarily do not leave archaeological evidence. Even if this contention is archaeologically or scientifically correct, this court must conclude – in the absence of any evidence of occupation by any other group – that the Zunis were the only occupants.

13. Defendant, again, contends that "non-sighting" of other Indians does not confirm their absence. The court, however, must weigh existing evidence – namely that no other Indians were seen and the presence of other Indians has not been in any way shown – and cannot speculate further. (See also the footnote to Finding 24.)

14. See also the footnotes to Findings Nos. 24 and 25.

15. Defendant objects that this Finding is supported solely by testimony of plaintiff's expert and is not corroborated by any documentation. However, expert opinion and testimony before the court, it matters such as these, is sufficiently probative.

16. De Vargas described the entrance into "the pueblo which the natives of the pueblos of the Zuni tribe have on [the mountain's] mesa top." (Pltf. Ex. 4039, pp. 198–200) The court disagrees with defendant's conclusion that "the facilities on top of Corn Mountain were considered *the* pueblo of Zuni." Rather the evidence established that the tribe consisted of multiple pueblos (plural), one of which was on the mountain. The court is also persuaded that not only the mountain but portions of the claim area were used to contribute to the tribe's subsistence.

17. Mission burial records, showing cause of death, show only approximately 20 Zuni killed by Apache in the 50 year period, 1700–1750.

18. What prevented the bishop's visit was information given him expressing concern for the lives of the mules, there was extreme heat, the mules were swollen, and there was only one watering hole and no pasturage.

19. Defendant, in objecting to this finding, contends that the descriptions (such as fn 2 above) of Zuni life warrant a conclusion that very little of the claim area was being used. The court does not agree but finds, as plaintiff argues, that the historical, archaeological, and other expert testimony and evidence established wide-area use, as described here and elsewhere throughout these Findings.

20. To some extent Dominguez apparently described directly the activities of Laguna and then, by reference, the Zuni, saying that what applied to Laguna also applied to the Zuni. Nonetheless, the description applies.

21. Although not mentioned, there was, in 1779, apparently a group of Navajo north of Zuni (about twice as close as El Morro) and in the claim area; this settlement was a permissive farmsite granted to a few individuals temporarily to grow corps for a season.

The hostile Apache referred to by Dominguez were located particularly on the road from El Gallo to Laguna and within the Spanish Kingdom (including New Mexico in general) but not within the Zuni claim area or Kingdom of Cibola. (See also Finding 26.)

22. One exceptionally extensive engagement occurred in 1807 when 300 Apaches attacked the Zunis in an all-day battle (with only 1 Zuni fatality). See also discussion in the text infra. The Apache raids were not intended to homestead members (and families) of that tribe in the Zuni claim area, or to permanently use or occupy that land.

Again, the reports of Dominguez of hostile forces addressed not the claim area but the Spanish Kingdom, particularly areas at the borders of the Zuni area (see also Finding No. 47, fn 2).

23. It is apparently the Comanche threat, between Mexico and New Mexico (in areas outside the Zuni claim area), which attracted the Spanish attention in fortification of the Spanish Kingdom generally.

24. The Mexican period being 1821–1846, Navajo presence (or absence) in 1754, 1779, and 1816 is not particularly relevant here. (See also Finding 47, fn 2, re: 1779.)

The defendant's general contentions about 1816 rely on a report speculating that it was possible that some Navajo movement occurred; movement to Canyon de Chelly—the only location described by defendant and supported by primary source material—is outside the claim area. (See also the following text of the Finding.)

25. The court rejects defendant's contention that any Navajo occupation was permanent or that it vitiated in any way the exclusive use and occupancy of the Zuni. Rather, the court finds the evidence (and contentions) advanced by plaintiff to be preponderant and more persuasive.

26. Both parties introduced expert testimony concerning the boundaries of Zuni aboriginal territory (and proper claim area). Again, the court finds the evidence introduced and relied upon by plaintiff (including the related archaeological, ethnological, historical, religious, and other evidence) to be the more persuasive. The court adopts plaintiff's exhibit 240 and its 20 reference points as described in the text.

27. Defendant objects generally to depiction of areas of use outside the claim area. Actually this applies almost entirely to areas designated as shrines or areas of worship. (These areas are shown separately on Plaintiff's Exhibit 242.)

The areas shown in the exhibit (241) depict use only (and is not intended to show use necessarily exclusive of other tribes). The area of exclusive use is designated by plaintiff as the claim area. (The claim area found to have been Zunis' exclusive use and aboriginal title area has been determined by the court considering all the evidence surrounding all aspects of Zuni activity.)

28. The text describes the Zuni efforts and achievement. It should also be noted, as defendant points out, that part of the achievement was complemented by the abundancy of the resources available and by the degree of demand upon them.

29. This section incorporates some of the proposed findings of Plaintiff in its Nos. 85–87 and of Defendant in its Nos. 25–30.

30. The court does not dispute defendant's proposed Findings Nos. 25 and 29, to the extent that, in 1846, undoubtedly one large pueblo did exist within the area now designated as the Zuni Reservation, and that many Zuni lived there. The court also finds, however, that the Zunis also occupied the entire area of their claim; this occupation included some living accommodations—either seasonal (or temporary for the use of those hunting, gathering, worshipping, or for any of a variety of activities) or permanent—and, to a larger extent, the occupation included continuous and extensive use of the area for the many agricultural, gathering, hunting, religious, and other purposes described in the above Findings.

31. This Finding addresses some matters (and the parties' proposed findings) beyond those enumerated in the Opinion above. They are not intended to deal comprehensively with such proposals (or their subject matter) or to address the allegations concerning the events of the purported taking. Rather, they are included here only insofar as they may be relevant to the issue addressed herein: the extent of plaintiff's aboriginal lands—that area over which plaintiff had exclusive use and occupancy. Here too this court finds the preponderant, substantial, and persuasive evidence to be cited in support of plaintiff's requested findings (and plaintiff's response to defendant's objections thereto).

32. Throughout this period, the United States was to continually, and without any long-lasting success, attempt to negotiate peace treaties with the Navajo (addressing issues of peace not only with the United States but with its citizens including the Zunis). Among the many difficulties was the disparate nature of the many separate Navajo bands.

33. This ultimate finding is based on the facts found in all previous findings. To the extent that the conclusions herein involve concepts of law, they are also discussed in the opinion accompanying these Findings.

Findings of the United States Claims Commission Docket 161-79L, Taking Dates

IN THE UNITED STATES CLAIMS COURT

No. 161-79L
Filed: May 27, 1987

THE ZUNI TRIBE OF NEW MEXICO V. THE UNITED STATES

Indian Claims; Events and Dates of Taking of Aboriginal Land.

　　For Plaintiff: Stephen C. Boyden, of Salt Lake City, Utah; John S. Boyden, Jr., G. Richard Hill, and Boyden, Kennedy & Romney, of counsel.
　　For Defendant: D. Lee Stewart, with whom was F. Henry Habicht II, Assistant Attorney General; John C. Hitzelberg of counsel.

OPINION

YANNELLO, J. Two of the issues presented to this court have been the subject of trial: (1) the extent of the plaintiff's aboriginal land area which would allegedly be the subject of a taking; and (2) the events which allegedly constituted the taking. The parties have proposed findings of fact and briefed issues of law on both of these issues in a single submission.

　　For convenience, in view of the extensive nature of the evidentiary record and the parties' proposals, the court had prepared two opinions. A separate opinion addresses the first issue, the extent of plaintiff's aboriginal land area, and concludes that, as of 1846, the plaintiff had aboriginal title to the land area claimed. (This area may be seen on plaintiff's exhibit 240, circumscribed within the locations 1 to 20.)

　　The instant opinion now turns to the second issue: the events and dates which purported to constitute a taking of the aboriginal land.

　　Again here, as in the opinion describing the extent of the aboriginal land, the court has reviewed the record and the parties' proposed findings and adopts the contentions advanced by plaintiff as being the most persuasive and finds the evidence cited in support thereof to be the preponderant and most persuasive evidence.

Indeed, in connection with the issues addressed in the instant opinion, the events and dates of any alleged taking, defendant has proposed but a few limited findings. Rather, the thrust of defendant's position has been that the Zuni aboriginal land was limited to the area of its central pueblo (rather than to the area used and occupied exclusively by Zunis for life-sustaining activities). *See, e.g.,* defendant's proposed findings Nos. 13, 22, 25, and 29. From this premise, defendant argues that, since this area of the pueblo is within the Zuni reservation, there has been no taking, *See e.g.,* defendant's proposed findings Nos. 39 and 42. Defendant has proffered no alternative findings addressing the dates and events which, if plaintiff's aboriginal land was found to exceed the pueblo area as plaintiff claims, may (or may not) have constituted an alleged taking.[1]

This court, in a separate opinion, has rejected defendant's premise concerning the extent of plaintiff's aboriginal land. This, however, does not lead to an automatic adoption of plaintiff's proposed findings concerning the dates and events of the alleged taking. Defendant, although not proposing any alternative findings, has opposed plaintiff's proposals, offering citations to evidence and refutations to argument.

The court, in the instant opinion, has thoroughly reviewed all the proposals, objections, and responses, and the evidence with reference thereto. It is as a result of that review that the court has concluded that the accompanying Findings, patterned largely upon plaintiff's proposals, are warranted by the record.

The accompanying Findings speak for themselves, and no legal arguments, other than those grounded on resolution of factual disputes, are presented in the briefs.[2]

Suffice it to say here that, as plaintiff contends, any loss of Indian lands can be compensable only if caused by or the result of acts or omissions of the United States. The accompanying Findings illustrate a number of acts and omissions of the United States.

Plaintiff cites a number of cases in which such acts or omissions have been held sufficient to constitute a compensable taking by the United States. *See* for example *Pillager Band* v. *United States,* 192 Ct. Cl. 698 (1970) (re: United States exercise of dominion inconsistent with Indian use and occupancy, such as ceding land to another); *Tlingit and Haida Indians* v. *United States,* 147 Ct. Cl. 315 (1959); *Pueblo of Laguna* v.*United States,* 17 Ind. Cl. Comm. 615, 697 (1967) (re: failure to protect Indians from encroachment and creating reservations for other Indians on aboriginal land); and a host of other cases cited by plaintiff with respect to the United States' use of aboriginal land for non-Indian grazing, townsites, homesteading, railroad construction (*Cabazon* v.*United States,* 21 Ind. Cl. Comm. 119, 128–32 (1969)), for schools in newly recognized states (*Three Affiliated Tribes of Fort Berthold Reservation* v.*United States,* 182 Ct. Cl. 543, 558–61 (1968)), and treating aboriginal land as public land (*Cowlitz* v.*United States,* 25 Ind. Cl. Comm. 442, 448, 450 (1971)).

It is concluded that the acts and omissions found by the court here are sufficient to constitute a taking requiring just compensation.

Conclusion of Law

Based on the foregoing, and the accompanying Findings of Fact, it is concluded that plaintiff's aboriginal title was extinguished by acts or omissions of the United States by virtue of the events, and on the dates, described herein.

The matter will not proceed to a determination of the amount of just compensation to which plaintiff is entitled. The parties shall within 120 days of the date of this opinion, file a Joint Status Report suggesting a schedule of further appropriate proceedings.

Judith Ann Yannello, Judge

FINDINGS OF FACT re: TAKING OF ZUNI LANDS[3]

1. TAKING OF ZUNI LANDS (1846 TO 1876)

Finding No. 1: United States Assumes Sovereignty over Zuni Claim Area

Following a war with Mexico, Brigadier General Stephen Watts Kearny, on August 18, 1846, took possession of Santa Fe, the capital of New Mexico, in the name of the United States. On August 22, he issued a formal proclamation of annexation and stated that New Mexico was a territory of the United States. With the imposition of the Kearny Code of 1846, the United States began its exercise of sovereignty over the Southwest area, and the Zunis. The Treaty of Guadalupe Hidalgo was signed February 2, 1848, ratification exchanged with Mexico on May 30, 1848, and proclaimed July 4, 1848. This Territory formalized United States jurisdiction over the area, and the Zuni.

Prior to the statehood of Arizona and New Mexico, in 1912, inhabitants of the area, including the Zuni, were subject to the Territorial Laws of the United States.

Finding No. 2: Zuni Property Rights Recognized Under Treaty of Guadalupe Hidalgo

The Zuni Indians were recognized as vassals and subjects under the Spanish crown and later as citizens of Spain. Spanish citizenship was affirmed by Mexico on February 24, 1821, in the *Plan de Iguala* which declared that all inhabitants of New Spain, whether Indians or not, were citizens and their persons and property protected under the new Mexican government. These rights were reaffirmed in the Treaty of Cordova of August 24, 1821, in the Declaration of Independence of Mexico on October 6, 1821, and by Act of the Mexican Congress.

Under the Treaty of Guadalupe Hidalgo of 1848, citizens of Mexico, which included the Zunis, were entitled to the guarantees of protection of "liberty and property" and security "in the free exercise of their religion" without restriction. Since Spain and Mexico had recognized the Zunis' right to permanently use and occupy their aboriginal territory, the Zunis became subject to the sovereignty of the United States with the same right to aboriginal lands intact.

Finding No. 3: Ojo del Oso Described as Zuni Territory

Ojo del Oso (which is marked by an "X" on Plaintiff's Exhibit 240) was described by Major Gilpin of the United States Army as being in the Territory of the Zunis. A detachment led by Major William Gilpin, later to become the first governor of Colorado, reconnoitered Navajo country by following the San Juan and then traveling south into the Tunicha Mountains and descending into Canyon del Chelly. He talked with nine Navajo chiefs and then met Colonel Doniphan at Ojo del Oso or Bear Springs, in what he described as "the territory of the Zunis," thus definitely locating Ojo del Oso within the Zuni claim area as of 1846. Colonel Doniphan and

Major Gilpin's parties, after meeting at Bear Springs, marched south to the Pueblo of Zuni where they were hospitably received. Shortly before Colonel Doniphan and Major Gilpin's visit to Zuni, Captain Parsons had also visited Zuni. After pursuing Navajo raiders west of the Chuska Mountains, sixty men under Captain Monroe M. Parsons came to Zuni destitute of supplies, after an exhausting three days march. As recorded by Private Marcellus Ball Edwards, the soldiers had nothing but praise for the warm hospitality and generosity of the Zuni people.

Finding No. 4: Major Walker Finds No Navajos in Zuni Territory

Because of many Navajo raids upon the New Mexico settlements in the summer of 1847, Major W.H.R. Walker was sent on a punitive expedition against the Navajos in early September. Leaving the Rio Grande below Albuquerque the troops marched westward through Zuni then north to Red Lake outside of the claim area as far as Canyon de Chelly. The troops had used most of their supplies before reaching Zuni, and when they turned to the north to look for hostile Indians the Navajos kept moving farther north as they were pursued by the troops. No Navajos were encountered by United States troops in the Zuni Claim area in 1847. No crops were found in Canyon de Chelly. The troops were forced to turn back to Zuni. When the Zunis found United States troops in distress, they gave them provisions and treated them kindly and hospitably.

Finding No. 5: Zunis Protected Themselves Against a Navajo Raid

In the late summer of 1849 Colonel John M. Washington launched an expedition northwest from Jemez into Navajo country. He was accompanied by the newly appointed Indian Agent James S. Calhoun and Topographical Engineer James H. Simpson. After completing a peace treaty with Navajo leaders in Canyon de Chelly in September of 1849, a report was received that Apaches had attacked Zuni. The expedition returned by way of the Pueblo of Zuni to find that Navajos, and not Apaches, had made an attempt to run off livestock, but had been repulsed. The unburied body of one of the Navajo raiders was found only one-half mile from the Pueblo of Zuni. The expedition received a hearty reception from the Zuni upon its entry into the Pueblo, and the party was fed bread in many varieties, watermelons, muskmelons, and peaches.

Agent Calhoun had lengthy discussions with Governor Pedro Pino of the Zunis. Calhoun later wrote to Commissioner Medill that (based on his own knowledge obtained during Washington's expedition against the Navajos) the Navajo raids were for plunder rather than out of necessity since the Navajos possessed in their own country extensive fields of corn, wheat, melons, squash, beans, peas, and peach orchards in addition to their immense flocks of sheep, mules, and horses.

Finding No. 6: Military Officers Observe Extensive Zuni Land Use

Lieutenant James H. Simpson reported that the Zunis had large herds of sheep and horses and extensively cultivated the soil. As he moved up the Pescado Valley from the Pueblo of Zuni, he noted further evidence of Zuni agriculture in outlying areas: "We have met today, as we did yesterday, a number of Zuni Indians carrying bags of wheat upon horses and burros to their Pueblo. These people seem to have discovered the principle of industrial accumulation, and therefore of social progress, more than of any Indians I have seen." The expedition was also informed of a band of California emigrants that had commandeered livestock and supplies from the Zuni's accumulations. Calhoun wrote that the emigrants committed "outrages" against the Zunis and, with the same frequency and as flagrant, against the Laguna. Such outrages, as described by Calhoun, included "taking in the name of the United States such horses, mules and sheep and grain as they desired. . . ."

Finding No. 7: United States Prohibits Zunis from Protecting Themselves

On October 15, 1849, Governor Pedro Pino and the Grand Captain of War from Zuni, together with a Zuni delegation met with Calhoun in Santa Fe. Calhoun reported that the Zunis asked for arms and ammunition and for permission to make a war of extermination against the Navajos. The Zunis spoke confidently of their ability to protect and defend themselves against the aggressions of the Navajos and Apaches and stated that if permitted to form a combination of Pueblos, they could and would exterminate those tribes. The Zunis' request for fire arms and ammunition was denied by Agent Calhoun. Colonel Washington would not give his consent to the Zuni taking any direct action against either the Apache or the Navajo. (The general United States policy was not to arm any Indian tribes.) Promised military protection by the United States was ineffective and in January of 1850 the Zunis reported that Navajos had again raided the Pueblo, stealing livestock and carrying off two women. A United States officer then sought out the Navajo raiders, but without success.

Finding No. 8: Calhoun Requests Treaty Authority to Protect Pueblos

On November 15, 1849, Calhoun recommended to the Commissioner that he be authorized to make treaties with the Pueblos to bring them under the protection of federal law. In reviewing the Pueblo Indians' former relationship with the government of Spain and New Mexico, he made the following observation:

> The former government of this territory, having never interfered with their peculiar form of governments, each Pueblo has had, for time immemorial, a separate and distinct political existence—Instances are now occurring of Prefects and Alcaldes extending the operation of some of the laws of this territory over these people—a matter they can not comprehend, and of which, they daily complain, and beg for relief. Add to this, the fact, they are no longer authorized to make reprisals upon the wild Indians who annoy them so much, and you have the causes of the uneasiness, and the distrust, which they sometimes manifest.

Finding No. 9: Pueblo Treaty of 1850 Never Ratified

Agent Calhoun was granted authorization by Commissioner Brown on April 24, 1850, to negotiate Pueblo treaties. Zuni Governor Pedro Pino arrived at Santa Fe on August 7 and signed, on behalf of the Zunis, a treaty which provided the boundaries of each Pueblo Tribe would be settled and never diminished, as set out in paragraphs 4 and 5 of the Treaty:

> 4. The Government of the United States will, at its earliest convenience, afford to the contracting Pueblos its protecting power and influence; will adjust and

settle, in the most practicable manner, the boundaries of each Pueblo, which shall never be diminished, but may be enlarged whenever the Government of the United States shall deem it advisable.

5. It is expressly understood and agreed by the contracting parties that the respective Pueblos are to be governed by their own laws and customs, and such authorities as they may prescribe, subject to the controlling Power of the Government of the United States.

On the occasion of the treaty signing, the Zunis bluntly criticized the government's lack of good faith illustrated by four years of empty promises of protection.[4]

The United States, through its Senate, failed to ratify the treaty drafted on August 7, 1850.

Finding No. 10: Breach of Treaties Protecting Zuni

Military and other government officials negotiated several agreements with Navajo and Pueblo leaders in efforts to stop the Navajos from molesting or stealing and to bring peace to the New Mexico area.

Among these negotiations were the following.

The first treaty, was signed on November 21, 1846, but was not ratified by the U.S. Senate. This document was directed to the Navajo, but specifically included the Pueblo Indians in its provisions. Article One of that treaty provided for the firm and lasting peace and amity between the American people and the Navajo Tribe. Article Two provided that the Pueblo Tribe of Indians were included in the term "American people."

In July 1848, Lt. Colonel Henderson P. Boyakin, Zuni Governor Pedro Pino and War Commander Antonio Chapeton signed Articles of Convention. The articles provided that the Zuni Tribe would be: "Protected in the full management of its right of private property and religion, by the authorities, civil and military, both in New Mexico and the United States." (No formal treaty was drafted based on these articles.)

The treaty of 1850 was signed by Governor Pino in the presence of a Zuni delegation that traveled to Santa Fe to sign the treaty with James S. Calhoun. The draft treaty was not ratified by the U.S. Senate. In that draft treaty, the United States bound itself to protect the Zunis from raiding Navajos, while the Zunis themselves were prohibited from pursuing military campaigns against the Navajos without the consent of the territorial authorities of Santa Fe.

On October 26, 1851, Major Electus Backus, without authorization from Commander Colonel Edwin V. Sumner, entered into a verbal agreement jointly with the Navajo headmen and representatives of the Zuni and Hopi tribes. The agreement was made at the newly constructed Ft. Defiance. The first condition was that, "the Navajo Indians shall be at peace with, and shall cease to molest or steal from, the people of the United States, the Mexican people and our friends the Zuni and Moca [Hopi] Indians."

Governor Calhoun and Colonel Sumner met with a large group of Navajos at the Pueblo of Jemez on December 25, 1851, and informally agreed to ratify Backus' agreement. (See also preceding paragraph.) Major Backus, who (although the agreement was not ratified by the U.S. Senate) insisted on calling the verbal agreement "The Treaty of October 26, 1851," informed Colonel Sumner on January 4, 1852, that Zarcillos Largos, Navajo headman, had assured him that all Navajos considered the agreement binding and were anxious to abide by it.

Notwithstanding the foregoing agreements made, or treaties proposed or drafted with, the United States, the Navajos continued raiding and harassing the Indian Pueblos and the settlements along the Rio Grande. The Zunis were prohibited by the United States government officials from taking any action to defend themselves. Orders of the United States provided that arms were not to be furnished to the Zunis and withheld any consent to the Zunis to take any direct action against either the Apache or the Navajo.

Finding No. 11: Expedition of Captain Lorenzo Sitgreaves Observes Zuni Agriculture

In 1851, an expedition of Army topographical engineers under the direction of Captain Lorenzo Sitgreaves, which included cartographer Lieutenant J. G. Parke and civilian draftsman Richard H. Kern, accompanied a military expedition led by Colonel Edwin V. Sumner. The engineers were dispatched to explore and map the area westward from Zuni to California following the Zuni River to its junction with the Colorado and the latter river to its mouth. When the expedition reached Zuni, they received complaints of Navajo harassment and Colonel Sumner directed the campaign towards Canyon de Chelly. The campaign against the Navajos was unfruitful because of the Navajos' refusal to stay and fight and Sumner returned to Santa Fe. However, he had directed Major Backus to construct Ft. Defiance.[5] Meanwhile, the Sitgreaves party remained at Zuni until Major H. L. Kendrick was available to serve as military escort.

The group traveled from Zuni to the Colorado River and west to San Diego. Sitgreaves noted the extensive Zuni cultivation along his route, observing that: "The cornfields of the Zuni Indians extended at intervals for several miles down the stream, their crops and orchards being planted on the edge of the valley or in the fertile gorges of the mountains." Traveling down the right bank of the Zuni River, the expedition crossed the steam bed just before reaching the Little Colorado River. The next day, just prior to reaching the Little Colorado River, they met a party of *Coyotero Apaches* driving mules to trade at Zuni. The official map of the expedition drawn by Kern, depicts the Chuska Mountain north of the Zuni claim area as "Navajo Country" and places the Apaches south of the Zuni claim area below the Mogollon Rim.

Finding No. 12: Domenech Describes Northern Boundary of Zuni Country

Abbe. Em. Domenech claimed to be in the Zuni region for seven years in the 1850's. During his travels, he came from the San Juan River area of the north into the Canyon de Chelly area describing that as Navajo country. Then he described the border between the Zuni and Navajo country: "On emerging from Canon Bonito you penetrate into the Zunis country. . . ." This description identified the northern boundary of the Zuni claim area in the 1850's to be north of Ft. Defiance at the south end of Canon Bonito between points 14 and 15 on Plaintiff's Exhibit 240.

Finding No. 13: Ft. Defiance Established on Zuni Boundary

The construction of Ft. Defiance at the direction of Colonel Sumner, with the accompanying permanent location of United States troops at the Zuni border, brought a measure of protection to the Zuni Pueblo from Navajo depredations. The

Fort was commanded by Major Backus in approximately 1851–52 and, beginning on September 8, 1852, by Major H. L. Kendrick.[6] Major Kendrick made a determined effort to treat the Navajo fairly and to encourage and assist them in peaceful pursuits, but at the same time to confine them to their own area of habitation. His task was complicated by continuing pressure on the Navajo by the Utes to the north. The Zuni Tribe provided most, if not all, of the corn supply for horses at Ft. Defiance.

In 1853, Kendrick opened a new road from Fort Defiance to the Ojo del Oso and through the Wingate Valley on the east side of the Zuni Mountains to intercept the old trail which led from the Ojo del Gallo. Supply trains then began purchasing corn at Laguna Pueblo. As a result of the Kendrick road, Ojo del Oso became a regular stopping place for military wagon trains.

Navajos began to reside in the immediate area of the United States forts, at Defiance and Ojo del Oso. Later those Navajos were forcibly removed to Bosque Redondo.

Finding No. 14: Zuni Economy Robust in 1853

Francois X. Aubry, a Southwestern trailblazer, returning from California in September of 1853, noted in his journal that when his party reached the Pueblo Zuni from the west they were" . . . met with a hospitable and civilized population from whom we obtained an abundance of good provisions, over which we greatly rejoiced. We have subsisted for a month on mule and horse flesh, and for most of that time on half or quarter rations."

In late November of 1853 the Whipple expedition traveled through Zuni country. The Expedition was part of the War Department's Congressionally-mandated project to survey the Trans-Mississippi in order to locate the best route for the railroad to the Pacific coast, and was under the direction of the Army Corps of Topographical Engineers. After leaving the Laguna Pueblo, one group followed the Kendrick or Ojo del Oso road through the Wingate Valley. Whipple, with the main survey and supply trail, used the Ojo del Gallo route and came south through the Zuni Mountains using the Camino del Obisbo, passed by Inscription Rock, and through the Zuni farming lands of the Pescado Valley.

The Whipple group camped at Black Rock and waited for the arrival of the other group. Several Zunis came to the camp. According to Baldwin Mollhausen, the expedition's naturalist and draftsman:

> The project of establishing a direct communication with the coast of the Pacific seemed to strike them [Zunis] wonderfully, and it was not long after they were informed of it, before Pedro Pino, the *Gobernador* of Zuni, made his appearance in state costume with two of his chiefs, to introduce himself to us, and obtain further information concerning the direction of our journey. . . .

Mollhausen also made the following statement about the Zuni economy:[7]

> The Zuni Indians are more favorably disposed to civilization than those of the other Pueblos. They breed sheep, keep horses and asses, and practice agriculture of an extensive scale. The harvest was over when our Expedition passed, but in all directions fields of wheat and maize stubble, as well as gourds and melons, bore testimony to their industry, and they also raise in their gardens beans, onions, and capsicums [peppers]; the latter especially, immense quantities of which were hanging to dry in garlands over the

houses. Besides agriculture and cattle breeding, they, or rather their women, are skillful in the art of weaving, and like the Navajos manufacture durable blankets.

Finding No. 15: Zuni Guides Used in Zuni Hunting Grounds

Lt. Whipple was particularly anxious to secure Zuni guides to lead the expedition through the area to the west of Zuni. His requests were made known to the Zunis, and they deliberated on the matter for some time before assigning him three guides. Mollhausen commented that the securing of guides in their own lands was crucial. As Mollhausen described the situation as follows: ". . . The services of natives who possessed an intimate acquaintance with their own hunting-grounds would be of more avail to us now, than the general knowledge of the most experienced trappers." [See plaintiff's response to defendant's objections to its proposed findings, at pages 181–82; see also quote from plaintiff's exhibit 6108 at page 99.]

On November 28, 1853, the Zuni guides described to the expedition the area over which they would be traveling. Mollhausen noted: "They described the country to the Colorado Chiquito as being a nearly level plain, with springs or permanent water at convenient distances. This is their hunting grounds." Supplied with several hundred bushels of Zuni corn, the expedition moved down the Zuni River some nine miles then turned west to Jacobs Well. The guide Hacha then led the expedition to the Little Colorado; the other two guides went to Hopi to secure other guides. Hacha led the Whipple expedition through the Petrified Forest, and crossed the Leroux Wash on December 5, 1853. Anxious to return to the village as soon as possible, since it was the Zuni ceremonial season, Hacha, nevertheless, returned to the Pueblo only after having led them to the vicinity of the present day Holbrook, Arizona.

Finding No. 16: Surveyor General Fails to Determine True Nature and Extent of Zuni Tribe

In July of 1854, Congress established the office of Surveyor-General in the territory of New Mexico to investigate land titles in the region. His duties included a charge to investigate and report on all land claims originating under Spain and Mexico which were recognized and protected under the Treaty of Guadalupe Hidalgo. Lands in the area were prohibited from sale or other disposal by the government until Congress had acted on his recommendations.

Pursuant to the above legislation, a Surveyor-General was appointed to investigate Pueblo titles. However, he failed to fulfill the congressional mandate with respect to Zuni by failing to include Zuni Pueblo in his initial evaluation of Pueblo titles and by failing to determine the true nature and extent of Zuni title within the framework of Spanish and Mexican law as the legislation required. As a result, Zuni title to lands within the claim area was not protected by Congress as it should have been had the government fulfilled its obligations to the Zunis.[8]

Finding No. 17: Zunis Protest Hispanic Trespass in Zuni Mountains

In 1854, several Hispanic stockmen from the Rio Grande Valley attempted to graze their flocks on the slopes of the Zuni Mountains and in the general area of Mt. Taylor. Both Navajo and Zuni people complained about the encroachment in their respective territories and were accused of maltreating the herders. The

Navajos made off with large numbers of livestock, and it was theorized that the sheepmen may have deliberately encouraged such theft so that the government would pay them for their losses. No action was taken to apprehend the trespassers. After negotiating another peace treaty with the Navajos in July 1855, things remained relatively calm to the extent that an entire company of soldiers was withdrawn from Ft. Defiance. However, in the early spring of 1856, raiding in the eastern area again became widespread. Matters became so serious that Major Kendrick urged Commander Garland to plan a general campaign against the Navajo. Troops were ordered back to Ft. Defiance and the situation again quieted. Kendrick urged the Zunis to increase their planting, and the Zunis provided large amounts of corn, not only to the United States military, but to individual Navajos or bands of Navajos.[9]

Finding No. 18: United States Military Action and Apache Attack at Zuni

Apache bands located in the San Francisco River drainage north of the Gila River and south of the Zuni claim area had been increasing their raids throughout the settlements west of the Rio Grande during the summer of 1856. Gileno and Mogollon Apaches had been particularly aggressive, striking the villages north from Socorro as far as Tome. Lieutenant Colonel Daniel J. Chandler led a scouting expedition following the trail of marauding Apaches to the Gila River and inflicted losses on the bands of the Mimbres Apaches. The United States military action was followed by increased and more widespread Apache raiding and reprisal. In October, a band of Coyotero Apaches seized a flock of Zuni sheep. The Zunis pursued the raiding Apaches, recaptured the flock, and killed one Apache. Prior to that time, the Coyotero Apaches had frequently come from their area south of the Mogollon Rim between the White Mountains and the Pinals to trade at Zuni. Due to widespread Apache hostility, Major Kendrick led a detachment out of Ft. Defiance in November to patrol the region south of Zuni. He was joined by Salvador, the Zuni war captain and several Zuni warriors. Also accompanying the expedition was Navajo Agent Henry L. Dodge. Leaving camp to hunt for deer, Dodge was killed some thirty miles south of Zuni by a group of Coyotero and Mogollon Apaches. The soldiers tried, but could not find the fleeing Apaches. Shortly thereafter, the Apaches attacked Cubero, east of the Zuni claim area, killing nine Anglos, they seized sheep from Laguna, and raided into the Puerco. The Apaches then attacked Zuni, on December 22, killing ten people and stealing 1,200 sheep and other stock. The United States military tried to enlist Zunis as spies and guides in the Apache Campaigns, but the Zunis refused.[10] The army defeated bands of Coyotero, Mogollon and Warm Springs Apaches and by September, 1858, the Apaches were on peaceful terms with the United States, and with the Zunis as well.

Finding No. 19: Zuni's Northern Boundary and Navajo Attacks

During October of 1857, a new agent was assigned to the Navajo Agency, William R. Harley. He was soon made aware of deteriorating relations between the Zunis and the Navajos due to Navajo thefts from Zuni fields. He planned to go to Zuni in person, but before he left the Navajo Agency, the Zuni Governor, with a war captain and nine others, arrived at his office in an attempt to settle the difficulties. Harley reported:

I immediately caused a council of the Navajos to be assembled. It appeared during the investigation that the Navajos had been committing depredations on the cornfields of the Zunias [sic] and that a Navajo women had been killed by the Zunias [sic] whilst taking corn. The Zunias [sic] had taken a number of horses belonging to the Navajos. . . .

Harley settled the matter by requiring the Navajos to pay for the corn and the Zunis to return the horses and pay for the death of the Navajo women according to "the Indian usage." In the following year, Zunis willingly volunteered to serve as guides and scouts for the United States military forces in a campaign against the Navajos. Approximately 160 warriors with four head war chiefs served with Colonel Dixon S. Miles. The Zunis saved the Fort Defiance cattle and horse herd in Canon Bonito by driving off 300 mounted Navajos. Unfortunately, the Zunis viewed Colonel Miles' ability as an Indian fighter as inept and this caused the Zunis to return home in disgust.

Finding No. 20: Zuni Agriculture Continues to Prosper in 1857

Lieutenant Edward F. Beale received the assignment to construct a wagon route along the 35th parallel from Ft. Defiance to the Colorado River. The experimental use of 76 camels as draft animals was unique and his group became know as the "Camel Corp Expedition." Arriving at Zuni on August 29, 1857, Beale noted the extensive cornfields along the way and the excellence of the wheat. As described by Lt. Beale, the amount of corn traded the next day was so great that it took his crew all day and half the night to shell it; at the Jacob's Well camp two days later, in commenting on the efficiency of his camels, he noted that each carried some 750 pounds of corn. On the trip west, Beale had sighted no Indians until well past the San Francisco Peaks outside of the Zuni claim area.

On his return trip, in January and February of 1858, Beale met some rather aloof Navajos with horses and sheep in the vicinity of Navajo Springs. This is the first evidence of any Navajo grazing northwest of the Zuni Pueblo.[11] Just before reaching Zuni he met two Yavapai Indians who had been trading at Zuni. While passing through the Pescado Valley after leaving the Pueblo, Beale commented on Zuni agriculture: "Here the fine wheat of the Zunians is principally raised, and the stubble remaining on the imperfectly cultivated patches, show clearly the natural resources of this beautiful valley."

Finding No. 21: Military Reconnaissance Discloses No Apache or
Navajo Habitation Within the Claim Area as of 1859

In 1858–1859, reconnaissance expeditions were conducted. One such expedition, in 1859, was led by Major O. L. Shepherd and included two companies led by Lieutenants Bell and Walker.

Major Shepherd, in his daily account for September 9, recorded sighting some Navajo Indians who were encamped in an area outside the Zuni claim area. Describing events on September 13 in the Cebolla Chequito, east of the Zuni claim area, Major Shepherd noted that Navajo appeared to have wintered there. In the account for September 15, Major Shepherd reported that he marched in the old trail from Acoma to the Rita Quemado and "found no Indians had been living here, contrary to what was supposed, probably being too near the Apaches. It is, perhaps, a neutral ground."

The expedition moved to the Zuni Salt Lake, along the Zuni trail, and to the Zuni Pueblo. In the account of September 20, 21, and 22, marching from the Zuni Pueblo and returning to his post, the major noted: "Judging from the absence of signs on the route from Acoma Mountains to the Pueblo of Zuni, the Navajos do not frequent the region south of the Zuni Mountains, although the climate is warm and the pasturage abundant during the winter months."

Finding No. 22: United States Military Pressure in 1861 Temporarily Forces Some Navajos into Zuni Claim Area[12]

In 1860–61, the United States engaged in actual war with the Navajo. The pressures of troop movements and burned crops forced some Navajos to seek refuge in Zuni territory in the region along the north bank of the Puerco of the west and into the Zuni Mountains. Reports of troop movements indicated that these were areas of refuge rather than of previous occupation.

Finding No. 23: Zunis Drive Navajos from Zuni Mountains

Captain Lafayette McLaws was in charge of a large force which covered the area north of the Puerco as far as the Little Colorado. He found very few Navajos in that area. He found a few Navajos near Jacob's Well and upon questioning the Navajos concerning the country, noted that they represented to him that they had never heard of that Little Colorado River and had not know of its existence. McLaws met Governor Pino and a party of Zunis who were returning from a Navajo "hunt" or expedition of their own. Governor Pino told them that another Zuni group was still out and that his people intended still further expeditions against the Navajo. Colonel Edward R.S. Canby dispatched troops from Ft. Fauntleroy (the Fort established in 1860 at Ojo del Oso) to pursue raiders who had stolen mules from Blue Water east of the fort and then fled to a hideout in the Zuni Mountains. The camp was finally located deep in the Zuni Mountains as were the bodies of three dead Navajos. Col. Canby reported that the camp had probably been attacked by Zunis.

Finding 24: Navajos Taken by Force to Bosque Redondo

General John H. Carleton laid plans for a systematic campaign, first against the Apaches, then against the Navajos, placing Christopher (Kit) Carson in command in September of 1862. In October, Fort Wingate was established at the Ojo del Gallo in preparation for the Navajos campaign. Ft. Sumner, established on the Pecos River in a region known as the Bosque Redondo, was designated as a reservation for the Mescalero Apaches and the Navajos when they surrendered or were captured. By the spring of 1863, Carson assembled his forces at Ft. Defiance, which was temporarily renamed Ft. Canby. For the next five months, Carson carried out a devastating campaign throughout the heartland of the Navajos, scattering them in all directions as they tried to elude the United States troops. Some Navajos evaded capture by hiding within the mountain areas on the periphery of the Zuni claim area. However, reconnaissances made throughout the 1860's offered no evidence of occupation of any Navajos other than those hiding and moving frequently to avoid United States troops.

The Zunis participated in the campaign by direct action of their own as well as in furnishing supplies and guides for the troops. Carson obtained corn and secured the services of guides to take him through the Little Colorado River area. The Zunis joined Carson in his slash and burn rampage, but soon it became evident that the Army was not completely discriminating in its practices; there are indications that Zuni fields were burned and Zuni people victimized.[13]

Nonetheless, Carson had high praise for the services of the Zunis, whom he described as "employed as spies; I am greatly indebted for the zeal and ability displayed by them. . . ." During the Carson campaign, Roman Catholic Bishop John B. Lamy and Father J. M. Coudert witnessed a scalp dance in the Pueblo of Zuni celebrating a victory over the Navajos.

Navajo resistance weakened, and, by the end of 1864, Navajos numbering some 8,000 were incarcerated at Bosque Redondo. It is estimated that this number accounted for three-fourths of the Navajo people. Many Navajos remained at large but moved deeper into their own country, while a few friendly Navajos may have been hidden or harbored by the Zunis.

Finding 25: Navajos Released from Bosque Redondo to Reservation on North Side of Claim Area

In 1868, after four years of captivity at Bosque Redondo, the Navajos signed a peace treaty with the United States allowing them to return to a reservation north of Zuni territory. Sometime after 1868, a small group (of perhaps several families) of Navajos settled in the Ramah area, contrary to the stipulations of the treaty. A Navajo presence, however, was not noted by military reconnaissance of this area in the late 1860's and early 1870's. There are indications that these Navajo families settled in the area with the consent of the Zunis.

Relatively large numbers of Navajos, who had found refuge in the mountainous areas along with southwestern, southern and southeastern periphery of the claim area, stayed on and settled in these areas, as did Apaches fleeing from United States troops in the south. The establishment of the Navajo reservation did not confine the Navajo to their heartland.

With the final subjugation of the Navajos completed, both Hispanic and Anglo settlers began to push into Zuni territory. In 1869, the area around San Rafael was settled by Hispanic homesteaders. At least one Hispanic settlement was established at St. Johns some time prior to 1873.

Finding 26: Zunis Fight Further Encroachment Until Ordered by United States to Stop

Throughout the 1870's, the Zunis defended their borders against encroachments of Navajos and non-Indians. The press reported that a major battle was rumored to have taken place in 1873 between the Zunis and the Navajos on the banks of the Rio Puerco of the West was reported. The fight reportedly claimed the lives of thirty Navajos and fifteen Zunis. In that same year, Timothy O'Sullivan, the early western photographer, happened to document a war dance at Zuni. (It cannot be said with certainty whether this dance related to victory in the rumored confrontation with the Navajos or commemorated some other event.) According to Zuni customs, such a dance is held spontaneously to celebrate a sudden or unexpected victory. The O'Sullivan photograph shows spears, muskets, and rifles in the hands of Zuni men, who were dancing.

In 1875, when the Zunis complained to the agent in Santa Fe that the Mexicans were bringing large flocks of sheep into what they considered to be their country, they were told by the Indian Agent that they could not drive the tres-passers away, but that they should share the range. The Agent advised that, beyond the area of the Zuni central pueblo, the Zuni and anyone else had equal rights. (Such equal rights applied, for example, to "adjacent grazing country" claimed the Agent.)[14]

The Zunis followed the counsel of their Agent in Santa Fe and the legal authorities of the United States and, instead of using force to drive the Mexican-Americans out of their country, they abided by the orders given to them by the United States government.

Finding No. 27: Acts or Omissions of the United States Resulting in Taking of Zuni Land

During the period 1846 to 1876, the following acts or omissions of the United States resulted in the loss of land by the plaintiff Zuni Indian Tribe:

A. The United States, from the time it assumed jurisdiction over the Southwest in 1846 and as commemorated in the Treaty of Guadalupe Hidalgo (and as echoed in U.S. officials' agreements directly with the Zuni), guaranteed to protect the Zunis' rights to their property. Notwithstanding this obligation, the United States, by Acts of Congress and actions of U.S. officials implementing government policy, failed to respect and protect the Zuni rights to its aboriginal lands (particularly the "sustaining area"). Rather, the U.S. acknowledged the Zuni rights only in their central pueblo area. (See, e.g., Findings 16 and 26, and footnote 1 therein.)[15]

B. United States military efforts to maintain peace throughout the area, and related efforts to quell the Navajo and Apache raids, caused Navajo and Apache to intrude into Zuni lands. (See, e.g., Finding 18, 22, 25, and 26.)[16]

For example, when U.S. Col. Kit Carson sought to capture Navajo for containment in Bosque Redondo, individual Navajos, in an attempt to evade Carson, began to occupy portions of the Zuni claim area where they previously had never been (specifically in the western portion of the claim area in the State of Arizona, south of the Little Colorado River, in the high mountains in the southern periphery of the claim areas in the States of Arizona and New Mexico, and in the southeastern portion of the claim area in the Datil Mountains).

Moreover, as part of its policy of peace and against arming Indians, the United States forbade any Zuni defensive or retaliatory military action, promising instead to provide U.S. protection. The U.S. protection was ineffective. For example, in October 1849, a Zuni delegation asked Superintendent Calhoun for arms and ammunition and permission to make war against the Navajo, since the U.S. had failed to provide adequate protection. The request was refused. The Zunis also complained about the allocation and deployment of the U.S. military. (See, e.g., Findings 7 and 9, including footnote 1.)[17]

C. The United States appropriated land and water for its own use around Ojo del Oso in the Wingate Valley with the building of the Kendrick Road in 1853 and the establishment of Ft. Fauntleroy in 1860. The United States established Ft. Wingate at Ojo del Gallo in 1862. In 1868, both forts were combined at the original site of Ft. Fauntleroy, and the size of the fort called Fort Wingate was increased substantially. Army officers shortly thereafter began to appropriate grazing lands for their own animals in the vicinity of Ft. Wingate, as well as allowed individual Navajo families to settle in close proximity to the fort.

D. In 1868, the United States, by treaty of 1868 with the Navajo Indians, took the northern fringe of the Zuni claim area including the southern fringe of Chuskas and Mexican Springs. [See Plaintiff's proposed Finding 111(G) and Defendant's proposed Finding 38.]

E. In 1876, Mormon settlers established the towns of St. Joseph, Holbrook, and Woodruff along the Little Colorado River in the western Zuni claim area in the State of Arizona. The United States permitted the establishment of said settlements in derogation of the Zunis' rights to the area.

F. The United States exercised dominion over Zuni lands and resources and over the ways of life of the Zuni people, inconsistent with, and without consideration for, Zuni interests, treating Zuni land as though it were in the domain of the United States.[18]

G. The United States allowed trespass on Zuni lands for the purpose of mining, homesteading, timber cutting, and other uses totally inconsistent with Zuni ownership.

Finding 28: Description of Land Taken (1846–1876)

The descriptions of the Mormon settler Ammon Tenney in 1876, of ethnologist Frank H. Cushing in 1885, and as found in other evidence submitted at trial, outline the lands held by Zuni as of 1877. The balance of the claim area (*i.e.*, the lands which have been found to have constituted the aboriginal area in 1846 but were not within the description of lands held by Zuni in 1877) can be described as follows:

> Beginning at a point located on the Little Colorado River at Leupp, Arizona; thence west to Humphrey's Peak of the San Francisco Peaks located in the State of Arizona; thence south to Mormon Mountain; thence south to the lookout towner on Baker Butte; thence in a southeasterly direction along the Mogollon Rim to Baldy Peak in the Mt. Baldy wilderness; thence south to Willow Mountain, in the State of Arizona; thence east to Willow Mountain in the state of New Mexico; thence northeast to Granite Mountain near the town of Magdalena, New Mexico; thence northwest to Cebollita Peak; thence in a northerly direction around the western fringe of the Malpais (lava flow) to Grants, New Mexico; thence northeast to Mt. Taylor; thence northwest to Hosta Buttes; thence northwest to Mexican Springs; thence west to Ganado, Arizona; thence west to Steamboat Canyon; thence west to Steamboat Wash; thence south along the Steamboat Wash to Twin Buttes, Arizona; thence east to Houck, Arizona; thence in a northeasterly direction up the Rio Puerco of the West to a point where the Atchison, Topeka and Santa Fe Railroad crossed the Continental Divide, thence southeast along the Continental Divide to the Ice Caves; thence in a southerly direction around the western fringe of the Malpais (lava flow) to the southernmost tip of the lava flow; thence south to Allegros Mountain; thence southwest to Mangas Mountain; thence southwest to Eagle Peak; thence west to the town of Reserve, New Mexico; thence due west to the Arizona/New Mexico state line; thence northwest to Springerville, Arizona; thence north along the Little Colorado River to the point of beginning at Leupp, Arizona.

This tract of land (the land taken) is depicted by cross-lines on Plaintiff's Exhibit 248. (Plaintiff's exhibit used colored tape to mark the cross-lining, which color did not photocopy adequately. Hence, the court also includes, as an unofficial exhibit, an enhanced map.)

2. TAKING OF ZUNI LANDS (1877 TO 1900)

Finding No. 29: History of Taking of Zuni Lands

During the period 1877 to 1900, the United States took a large portion of the remaining Zuni land; this land was particularly valuable because of its water resources.

Early in the period, military officers at Ft. Wingate, engaging in cattle business, appropriated land and water from the Zunis. In 1876, the Mormons settled in a place called San Lorenzo (in western New Mexico) and early in 1877 commenced a settlement in Savoia as well. Shortly thereafter, decimated by smallpox, San Lorenzo appears to have been entirely abandoned and Savoia nearly so. Resettled in 1882, the latter was called Navajo for a time and finally given the name Ramah, New Mexico.

On March 16, 1877, the Zuni reservation was established by Executive Order. The Zuni people in the area had no survey description whatever of the actual boundaries of the reservation. The reservation was enlarged by Executive Order of May 1, 1883 (to include, inter alia, Nutria Springs and the Ojo Pescado).[19]

In the early 1880's, additional Anglo settlements, including St. Johns, were established on the little Colorado River drainage; the United States conveyed title to those lands to the settlers allowing mining claims, desert entries, and homesteading. The Atchison, Topeka and Santa Fe Railroad arrived in Gallup in 1882; this resulted in even further intrusions into Zuni aboriginal land area.

Navajos encroached southward between the Pueblo Colorado Wash and the Rio Puerco in violation of their treaty of 1868. The United States did nothing to restrain the Navajos; in fact, the United States appeared to condone such trespassing by issuing individual settlement allotments of land to trespassing Navajos.

Anglos encroached to the south of Zuni; an Anglo obtained title to the Zuni Salt Lake and attempted to prohibit Zuni use of the lake. Some ranchers used the water from the Rio Puerco and the Little Colorado to the west of Zuni.

In the early 1890's, due to a large portion of the Zunis' outlying resources (*e.g.*, portions of the sustaining area), there were reports of starvation at the Pueblo of Zuni. Problems were exacerbated by the United States' attacks on the political authorities of Zuni through a series of arrests and imprisonments of Bow Priests.

In 1893, serious clear cutting of timber on a large area in the Zuni Mountains began. Many people employed by the logging companies moved into settlements in the Zuni mountains, such as San Rafael, Grants, and Blue Water.

Finding No. 30: Acts and Omissions of the United States Resulting in Taking of Zuni Lands (1877 to 1900)

The following acts and omissions of the United States resulted in the loss of land by the Zuni Indian Tribe during the period 1877 to 1900:

A. The United States, under mining, homestead, and desert entry laws, encouraged numerous settlements in the Arizona portion of the Zuni claim area (specifically in the towns of Snowflake, Taylor, Shumway, Pinedale, Showlow, Lakeside and Pinetop) during the period 1877 to 1878 and the settlements of St. Johns, Springerville, Eager, Greer, Nutrioso and Alpine in the period 1879 to 1880. All of these settlements were on lands claimed by the Zuni Tribe; nonetheless, the

United States conveyed said lands to third parties, in derogation of the rights of the Zunis.

B. The actual surveying and construction of the Atchison, Topeka, and Santa Fe Railroad authorized by the Act of July 27, 1866, did not begin until approximately 1880 on any lands within the Zuni claim area. The major part of the construction of the railroad took place during the period of 1880 through 1884. The actual surveying of the checkerboard areas authorized by the 1866 Railroad Legislation was not commenced until the late 1880's and early 1900's. The taking of lands for railroad purposes by the United States directly affected the Zuni claim area, allowing third parties to occupy lands previously used by the Zunis. The influx of many people into the area as a result of the railroad culminated in the taking of a substantial portion of the Zuni claim area.

C. The United States authorized the granting of alternate sections along the railroad running through the claim area from Grants, New Mexico, through Gallup, New Mexico, and from Winslow, Arizona, to Flagstaff, Arizona. Following the authorizing legislation, the railroad surveyed lands, occupied the route, received patents from the United States, cut timber, *mined coal*, and sold lands to third parties. These actions were in disregard of the Zunis' interest in the land.

D. In connection with the building of the railroad, merchantable saw timber was clear cut from the Zuni Mountains within the Zuni claim area. The Zuni Tribe received no compensation for the timber. The bulk of the timber was harvested between 1880 and 1910.

E. Commencing in 1877 and continuing through 1882, copper miners appropriated all of the Zuni aboriginal copper mines located in the Zuni Mountains near the present towns of Coppertown and Tinaja, New Mexico. The United States allowed such mining activity by treating the area involved as though it were public lands in derogation of the Zuni rights to the lands. [See also Finding 26, supra, and footnote 1 therein.]

F. The United States, as trustee, failed to seek recourse under existing laws to obtain legal title to lands belonging to the Zunis.

G. The United States allowed the appropriation of Zuni Indian water rights in violation of the reserved water rights doctrine.

Finding 31: Description of Lands Taken Between 1877 and 1900

As a result of the aforementioned acts and omissions by the United States, the following lands were taken from the Zuni Indian Tribe by the United States:

Beginning at a point located on the Pueblo Colorado Wash at Twin Buttes, Arizona, thence southwesterly along said Wash to its junction with Cottonwood Wash; thence southwesterly along said Wash to its junction with Cottonwood Wash; thence southeasterly up the Little Colorado River to Springerville, Arizona; thence southeasterly on a straight line to the Arizona/New Mexico state line located due west of Reserve, New Mexico; thence due east to Reserve, New Mexico; thence east to Eagle Peak; thence northeast to Mangas Mountain; thence northeast to Allegros Mountain; thence north toward the southernmost point of the lava flow, but ending at a point due east of the Zuni Salt Lake; thence west to North Mountain located in the State of Arizona; thence northwest to the Flattops located in the Petrified National Forest; thence north to the Haystacks located in the Petrified National Forest; thence northeast to a point located seven miles south of Gallup, New Mexico on State Highway 32; thence due east to McGaffey, New Mexico; thence southeast to Tinaja; thence southeast to Ice Cave; thence along the Continental Divide in a northerly direction through the Zuni Mountains, where it crossed the railroad in Wingate Valley; thence to Ojo del Oso; thence along the Rio Puerco of the West to Houck; thence to the point of beginning in Twin Buttes, Arizona.

This tract of land is depicted in Plaintiff's Exhibit 249 by cross-lines.

3. TAKING OF ZUNI LANDS (1901 TO 1912)

Finding 32: History of Taking of Zuni Lands (1901–1912)

During the period 1901 to 1912, the Zuni population increased. Zuni livestock grazed their herds many miles outside of reservation boundaries and farmers continued to work their fields in outlying areas. Government officials planned and built, between 1904 and 1907, the Black Rock Dam located above the Pueblo of Zuni on the Zuni River in an effort to supply irrigation water to tribal lands. Zuni farmers were encouraged to leave traditional farm sites and use new lands located below the dam which would rely upon impounded water for irrigation. Prior to the completion of the dam in 1907, the Zunis had cultivated over 5,000 acres by traditional methods.

After the dam was built, the Zunis cultivated the smallest acreage of farm land in their history. Shortly after its completion, the Black Rock Dam broke and destroyed much of the newly developed farm lands. After its repair, the dam could not hold as much water as originally projected, and farming was further curtailed.

The sheep industry continued to be of great importance to the Zuni people. By 1907, their herds numbered 60,000 and grazed over a wide area. Zunis complained to United States government officials when others started to use traditional Zuni grazing lands.

By 1907, the Zunis still believed that their reservation was much larger than it actually was, and they continued to request surveys to enable them to prevent trespass by other people on what they considered to be "their lands." A survey team arrived in April of 1908, and by July had finished a survey of the reservation boundaries. The new survey, instead of enabling the Zunis to pursue grazing, farming and gathering on their traditional lands, staked out a very limited area for their use. The Zunis requested that the United States enlarge the reservation to include additional lands in all directions, including the Zuni Salt Lake. The Zunis presented many petitions to the government requesting return of their aboriginal territory or the enlargement of the reservation to encompass large tracts of their former territory. Friction arose between Zunis and non-Zunis settlers, over the Zuni use of the southern mountains area (a traditional area of Zuni use) for hunting purposes.

The United States attempted to reduce the area of Zuni use by allotting to individual Zunis small acreage of land for personal rather than tribal use, but the Zuni people resisted.

*Finding 33: Acts and Omissions of the United States Resulting in
Taking of Zuni Lands (1901 to 1912)*

The following acts and omissions of the defendant United States resulted in the loss of land by the plaintiff Zuni Indian Tribe during the period of 1901 to 1912:

A. The United States continued to encourage the settlement of third parties upon Zuni lands under authority of the Homestead and Desert Entry laws in derogation of the rights of the Zunis to those lands.

B. In violation of its duty as a trustee to protect and defend Zuni land, the United States continued to treat Zuni land as though it were public domain, conveying specific parcels to third parties, with no compensation to the Zuni Tribe.

C. The United States provided services to Navajo Indians in the Ramah area and failed to prevent Anglo, Hispanic, and Navajo trespass onto Zuni lands.

D. The United States allowed third parties to drive the Zunis from their lands and actively prevented the Zunis from controlling their land.

E. The United States controlled the size of Zuni herds and restricted the size of their grazing area, thus depriving the Zuni people of their right to use their own lands.

F. The United States, first by authorizing legislation and then by administrative action, created national forests, national parks, and national monuments on aboriginal lands, owned and occupied by the Zunis.

Finding 34: Description of Lands Taken Between 1901 and 1912

As a result of the aforementioned acts and omissions of the United States, the following lands were taken from the Zuni Indian Tribe by the United States:

> Beginning at a point located at North Mountain in the State of Arizona; thence northwest to The Flattops located in the Petrified Forest National Park in the State of Arizona; thence north to The Haystacks located in the Petrified Forest National Park,; thence northeast to a point located seven miles south of Gallup, New Mexico on State Highway 32; thence east to McGaffey, New Mexico; then southeast to the Ice Cave; thence in a southerly direction around the western fringe of the Malpais (lava flow) to the southernmost tip of said lava flow; then south of a line toward Allegros Mountain to a point due east of the Zuni Salt Lake; thence northwest to Veteado Mountain; thence west to the Zuni Salt Lake; thence northeast to Chimney Hill thence north to El Morro; thence northeast to Brennan Spring; thence due west to a point approximately ten miles south of Gallup, New Mexico on State Highway 32, thence southwest to Bluebird Well located in the State of Arizona; thence south to Witch Wells; thence south along Highway 666 to a point on the highway where it intersects a line between the Zuni Salt Lake in the state of New Mexico and North Mountain in the State of Arizona; thence west along said line to North Mountain, being the point of beginning.

This tract of land is depicted by cross-lines on Plaintiff's Exhibit 250.

4. TAKING OF ZUNI LANDS (1912–1924)

Finding 35: History of Taking of Zuni Land (1912–1924)

The admission of both the States of Arizona and New Mexico into the union in 1912, under their respective enabling acts, entitled each state to four sections of land in each township. Although much of the Zuni claim area (aboriginal lands) was unsurveyed, the school sections were thus owned and administered by the states. With the western boundary of the reservation clearly marked, at this time, by the Arizona/New Mexico state line, surrounding ranchers began to press in on what had formerly been used exclusively by Zuni stockmen for the grazing of their cattle and sheep. In answer to the February 1912 petition of Zuni leaders for more lands, the Commissioner of Indians Affairs suggested that individual Zuni members located outside of the reservation boundaries apply for individual allotments. Zuni Superintendent Robert J. Bauman persisted in requesting more lands for the Zunis, noting that "the Zunis have [traditionally] grazed their flocks very extensively outside of the reservation." Reservation land provided on a per capita basis only about one-sixth as much grazing land as any other Indian Reservation in New Mexico or Arizona.

Government officials who investigated conditions at Zuni during these years supported Zuni requests for additions to their reservation. In 1917, a small addition was finally made to both the north and south ends of the reservation. Despite these additions, the Zunis still did not have nearly adequate grazing lands within the reservation confines and were increasingly beset with competitors for use of the off-reservation lands.

In 1917, there was increased allotment activity by the Navajos who submitted applications for some tracts of land north of the reservation and to the east near Ramah. Rural and isolated regions within the overall Zuni claim area remained largely unpopulated to 1917; however non-Zunis exercised control over much of the land. Zunis were discouraged from using their traditional hunting grounds to the south of the reservation in the Reserve area and some Zunis were arrested for hunting out of season by state officers. The period 1918 to 1924 was the busiest period in terms of land entries filed and entries far exceeded anything in the past. By 1924, Zuni stockmen were forced from their lands and consequently reduced their herds to 35,000 sheep, 6,000 goats and 500 cattle. Some Zunis resorted to leasing lands outside of the reservation; others continued to graze stock on their traditional lands and resisted paying for leases.

Finding 36: Acts and Omissions of the United States Resulting in Taking Zuni Lands (1912–1924)

The following acts or omissions of the United States resulted in the loss of aboriginal land by plaintiff during the period 1912–1924:

A. The United States granted state school lands to Arizona and New Mexico in violation of the Zunis' rights to said lands.

B. The United States granted individual Indian allotments in an area to the north and to the east near Ramah, New Mexico to individual Navajos in violation of the Zunis' rights in that area.

C. The United States permitted third parties to trespass upon Zuni lands and utilize said lands for their own purposes, forcing the Zuni people and their livestock off their lands.

Finding 37: Description of Lands Taken (1912–1924)

As a result of the aforementioned acts and omissions of the United States, the following lands were taken from the Zuni Indian Tribe by the United States:

Beginning at a point on Highway 666 in the State of Arizona where it intersects a line from the Zuni Salt Lake in the State of New Mexico and North Mountain in the State of Arizona; thence north along said Highway 666 to Witch Wells, Arizona; thence southwest on a line between Witch Wells, Arizona and the Zuni Salt Lake in the State of New Mexico to a point where it intersects the Arizona/New Mexico state line; thence east to Carpenter Lake; thence north to Brennan Spring; thence southeast to El Morro; thence south the Chimney Hill; thence southwest to the Zuni Salt Lake; thence west on a line from Zuni Salt Lake to North Mountain in the state of Arizona to a point where it intersects Highway 666 in the State of Arizona, being the point of beginning.

This tract of land is depicted by cross-lining on Plaintiff's Exhibit 251.

5. TAKING OF ZUNI LAND (1925–1935)

Finding 38: History of Taking of Zuni Land (1925–35)

Although the Zuni Reservation had been surveyed in 1908, the Zunis continued to graze wherever they could, paying no attention to the reservation boundaries. Superintendent Trotter complained in 1927 of the absence of a map of the reservation, and in 1929 said that lines had never been definitely located and that there was much doubt as to the location of the reservation boundaries. Original stone corner markers had been removed.

In 1934, the Zunis continued to press for expansion of their reservation. The passage of the Taylor Grazing Act tended to limit the Zunis' ability to use what the United States considered to be "public lands." Fencing of the reservation was completed in 1935, finally confining Zuni grazing activity to the reservation. Although the Zuni people continually asked for additional land, by 1935 they had effectively been fenced out of surrounding public lands except in a small area to the north described in Finding No. 32. With that exception, all lands which are the subject of the instant suit were finally taken by the United States in 1935 by the fencing of the Zuni Indian Reservation. Water from the Zuni River was impounded and diverted by the United States for the benefit for third parties as part of the Ramah Dam Project.

Finding 39: Acts and Omissions of the United States Resulting in Taking Zuni Land (1925–35)

The following acts and omissions by the United States resulted in the loss of land by plaintiff from 1925 to 1935:

A. The United States administered Zuni lands as public lands, allowing homesteads to be taken up by third parties.

B. The United States implemented grazing reduction programs, thereby curtailing Zuni use of their own lands.

C. The United States fenced the Zuni Reservation lands held in trust and attempted to confine the Zuni Indians to reservation trust lands only.

D. The United States appropriated Zuni water for use by third parties, particularly for the Ramah Dam project, in violation of the Zunis' reserved water rights.

Finding 40: Description of Land Taken (1925–35)

As a result of the aforementioned acts and omissions by the United States, the following lands were taken from the Zuni Indian Tribe by the United States:

Beginning at a point at Witch Wells, Arizona; thence north to Bluebird Well; thence northeast to a point approximately ten miles south of Gallup, New Mexico on State Highway 32; thence due east to Brennan Spring; thence south to Carpenter Lake; thence west to a point on a line between the Zuni Salt Lake in the State of New Mexico and Witch Wells in the State of Arizona where said line intersects the Arizona/New Mexico state line; thence northeast to Witch Wells, Arizona, the point of beginning—excepting therefrom, however, the present Zuni Indian Reservation and the following described tract of land know as Area No. 6, to wit: All of the West; Township 10 North, Range 19 West; Township 11 North, Range 19 West; and Township 11 North, Range 18 West; except those portions of said Townships which are included in the present Zuni Indian Reservation.

This tract of land is depicted by cross-lining on Plaintiff's exhibit 252.

6. TAKING OF ZUNI LANDS (1936–1946)

Finding 41: History of Taking of Zuni Land (1936–46)

Under the authority of the Indian Reorganization Act of 1934, the Bureau of Indian Affairs conducted a Sub-marginal Lands Acquisition Program in the Southwestern United States. The program as carried out at Zuni was designed to purchase or administratively transfer lands to be used for grazing by the Zuni Indian Tribe. By 1938, approximately, 100,000 acres surrounding the Zuni Reservation had been acquired by the project. That acreage outside of the then existing reservation boundaries was still being used exclusively and continually by the Zunis. The Zuni people fully expected the entire 100,000 acres to be added to the reservation, but Commissioner Collier, in 1939, administratively drew a "compromise line" excluding approximately 40,000 acres of the original 100,000 acres acquired by the sub-marginal land programs. A fence was constructed along the line and the Zunis excluded from the northern area. This tract of 40,000 acres taken from the Zunis by the administrative action of Commissioner Collier represents the last parcel of Zuni lands taken by the United States.

Finding 42: Acts and Omissions by the United States Resulting in Taking Zuni Land (1936–46)

The following acts and omissions by the United States resulted in the loss of land by the plaintiff during 1939:

The United States, through the administrative action of Commissioner John Collier, drew a line and fence the Zuni people out of a 40,000 acre tract of land in the North Purchase area in 1939 and thereafter allowed individual Navajos to settle thereon and appropriate it for their own use in violation of the rights of the Zunis to said tract.

Finding 43: Description of Land Taken (1936–46)

As a result of the aforementioned acts and omissions by the United States, the following lands were taken from the Zuni Tribe in 1939 by the United States:

All of Township of 11 North, Range 21 West; Township 11 North, Range 20 West; Township 11 North, Range 19 West; and Township 11 North, Range 18 West; except those portions of said Townships which are included in the present Zuni Reservation.

This tract is depicted by cross-lining on Plaintiff's Exhibit 253.

NOTES

1. Likewise, the defendant's brief argues only that, since the Zuni exclusively used and occupied only the area of their central pueblo, the creation of the reservation (as described in the court's Finding) terminated any Indian title and constituted a taking, if any, as of 1883 (when the reservation created in 1877 was enlarged). Similarly, defendant contends that, at that date (1883), the Zuni tribe had abandoned all lands beyond the reservation (if indeed any such lands had been considered aboriginal land).

2. The parties do raise an issue concerning whether plaintiff is entitled to interest on any judgement awarding just compensation. This argument seems grounded in a discussion of "recognized" title, whereas the court, in its separate opinion, has found Zuni aboriginal title. In any event, based on the Findings in that separate opinion as well as the instant opinion, such legal issue can be addressed at a later time (when the amount of just compensation is under advisement).

3. The court issued a separate opinion concerning the extent and location of the plaintiff's aboriginal land area. (The Findings of that opinion are incorporated herein to the extent they may be relevant.) In that separate opinion, the court set forth its findings with a footnote. That footnote is incorporated herein as well. The Findings herein, relation to the events and dates of taking, like the findings on aboriginal land, follow closely the findings proposed by plaintiff. The court found plaintiff's contentions, and the evidence cited in support there of including the extensive testimony of its expert witnesses and their reports and supporting material, to constitute the preponderant, and the more persuasive, evidence.

4. Some of the Zuni discontent centered on the removal of American troops from Cebolleta (there affording protection to the Zuni) to Albuquerque (there affording protection to the Rio Grande area)—at a time when the Zuni were being subjected to Navajo attack.

5. The location of Fort Defiance is shown on the map in Plaintiff's Exhibit 240, and related sequential exhibits. The court had found, in a separate opinion, that the area of the Zunis aboriginal land area is depicted on that exhibit as the area circumscribed within locations 1 to 20. Throughout the parties' proposed findings there appears to be some semantic disagreement concerning the location of Fort Defiance. Based on the court's Findings in its separate opinion concerning Zuni aboriginal land it is concluded that the Fort is located between points 14 and 15 on Exhibit 240, and that at that location it lies on the edge of or just beyond northern boundary of the Zuni claim area. (The aboriginal land area was determined in the separate opinion based on considerable evidence wholly apart from the location of the Fort itself.) For sake of convenience, in this opinion, the court is comfortable in adopting plaintiff's phraseology in locating the Fort "at Zunis' northern boundary."

6. For a brief period between Majors Backus and Kendrick, the Fort was commanded by Colonel J. H. Eaton. Eaton's descriptions at the time have been challenged as to accuracy and impartiality by expert witnesses. This court concurs and concludes that little probity should be attached to these descriptions.

7. The quote appears in Plaintiff's Exhibit 6109, a portion (pages 97–98) of an article. The right hand margin of the photocopy is slightly marred, and plaintiff's proposed finding contains in the quote, after reference to capsicums (i.e., peppers or berries) the word "later." The court, upon examining this exhibit (as it has examined all cited exhibits generally) believes the word should be "latter." (The

original is not available to the court, but the different reading is without substantive significance in any event.)

8. See also the court's separate opinion on the extent of plaintiff's aboriginal land area, and Finding 44 regarding spurious land grants.

9. Plaintiff notes that, as this court has found, the Navajo did not act in a united or concerted tribal way but rather by disparate bands—some friendly, some hostile—both in their treatment of the Zunis and in negotiating with the United States.

10. The parties have cited evidence suggesting a variety of reasons for this refusal, including the fact that the request was made at a time of Zuni religious observance and the Zuni appraisal that the weather was not auspicious (with deep snow and their horses too thin). The court does not conclude that a resolution of the reasons for the refusal is substantively significant.

11. Beale's first-hand sighting was confirmed as to point in time by testimony of plaintiff's expert witnesses.

12. Defendant here, in Finding 22, as in some of the findings addressed in the separate opinion concerning aboriginal title, objects to plaintiff's proposed finding as being based solely on the unsupported statement of plaintiff's expert witness. In cases of the type here, expert testimony is quite appropriate and the expert's opinion (including re-creation of facts through expert deduction and hypothesis), if based on adequate premises and background or underlying supporting evidence, is entitled to form the basis of a fact finding.

13. See also note to Finding No. 22.

14. Accordingly to the letter written to the Zuni by the Indian Agent, his appraisal was based on the following:

I went to the Surveyor General's office to see your original grant from the Mexican Government—the papers you left there last year for safe keeping—and find that the Pueblo of Zuni was granted by this document a tract of land described as follows: . . .

You see by this that you are actually entitled to one league [in] each direction from the Pueblo.

(Pltf. Ex. 7360. The court also provides this citation only because it does not appear in the citations furnished by the parties in connection with the proposed finding or objections thereto.)

It is not entirely clear to the court to what grant the Agent was referring, but only one grant has been called to the court's attention—and it contains the same description of land as in the grant noted by the Indian Agent. That grant is the subject of the court's Finding No. 44 in its separate opinion on aboriginal title. There the court found that the alleged grant referred to here was spurious.

Notwithstanding the grant in issue, the Mexicans, as the Spanish before them, recognized the Zunis' right to, and permitted the Zunis to, continue such use and occupancy of lands as they had been accustomed prior to the assumption of Mexican, or Spanish, jurisdiction (i.e., to the lands the Zuni had used since time immemorial).

The American Indian Agent was apparently acting in accord with United States policy. The Act of July 1854 established the office of Surveyor-General (S-G) and provided that the S-G was to determine, inter alia, the scope of Indian lands areas and titles and further provided that, until Congress acted on the S-G's recommendations, no lands in the area were to be disposed of. (See also Finding 16.)

The United States government apparently determined Indian land based solely on recorded grants. Whatever the merit of this approach in general, in the case of the instant Tribe this treatment deprived the Zunis of their land. Even if the United States government had reason to accredit the grant in issue (without further verifying its authenticity), the fact remains that, through 1846, the Zunis had aboriginal title to (and exclusively used and occupied) an area much larger than the area of its pueblo (which pueblo area is described in the alleged grant). Indeed, the Zuni aboriginal area has been found by the court to include a much larger area sometimes referred to as the "sustaining area." The United States neither recognized nor respected the Zunis aboriginal title but indeed, apparently relying solely upon the grant in issue, treated the larger area of "sustaining area" as public or in the public domain. (This continues to be defendant's express view. See, e.g., objections to plaintiff's proposed finding 111 (G), (H), (I) and (J).)

15. Certain findings are specifically cited merely for convenience. This by no means implies that the cited findings and/or event is the only, or even the primary, support for the conclusions stated herein.

16. The defendant contends that its efforts and proscriptions were laudable peace-keeping activities. However this might be, it nevertheless caused intrusion on Zuni land and rights.

17. Defendant argues that the allocation, or reallocation, of its resources was appropriate to the needs of the entire Southwest region. Again, the reasonableness of the United States' action is not the issue. However appropriate its action may be, the United States nonetheless failed to protect the Zunis (while the Zunis were, at the same time, prohibited from taking their own action as they had for hundreds of years previously).

18. See also the discussion in the last paragraph of footnote 1 in Finding 26. Again note that defendant acknowledges that it treated areas outside the central pueblo location (which location it contends is the only Zuni aboriginal land) as in the public domain. (See defendant's objections to plaintiff's proposed findings III (I), and similar objections.)

19. Under the Preemption Act of 1841, 5 Stat. 453, as amended by the Act of July 22, 1854, the President had authority to establish and enlarge Indian reservations in order to prevent encroachment on tribal lands.

With respect to the 1883 enlargement, Congress appropriated funds for the maintenance of the enlarged reservation.

The reservation was also enlarged by Executive Order of November 20, 1917, and by Acts of Congress on June 20, 1935, and May 15, 1978 – the latter of which included Zuni Salt Lake.

The Zuni Land Conservation Act of 1990

PUBLIC LAW 101-486 – OCT. 31, 1990

104 Stat. 1174

An Act

To authorize appropriation of funds to the Zuni Indian Tribe for reservation land conservation, and for other purposes.

Be it enacted by the Senate and House of Representatives of the United States of America in Congress assembled,

SHORT TITLE

Section 1. This Act may be cited as the "Zuni Land Conservation Act of 1900."

ZUNI RESOURCE DEVELOPMENT PLAN

Sec. 2. (a) Before the first day of the third fiscal year beginning after the date of enactment of this Act, the Secretary of the Interior and the Zuni Indian Tribe shall jointly formulate a Zuni resource development plan for the Zuni Indian Reservation, which shall include (but not be limited to) –

(1) a methodology for sustained development of renewable resources;

(2) a program of watershed rehabilitation;

(3) a computerized system of resource management and monitoring;

(4) programs for funding and training of Zuni Indians to fill professional positions that implement the overall plan;

(5) proposals for cooperative programs with the Bureau of Indian Affairs and other private or public agencies to provide technical assistance in carrying out the plan; and

(6) identification and acquisition of lands necessary to sustain Zuni resource development.

(b) The Resource Development Plan shall be implemented in a manner that protects resources owned and controlled by the Zuni Tribe and promotes sustained yield development.

TRUST FUND

Sec. 3. (a) There is hereby established within the Treasury of the United States the Zuni Indian Resource Development Trust Fund (hereafter in this Act referred to as the "Trust Fund"). The Trust Fund shall consist of amounts appropriated to the Trust Fund and all interest and investment income that accrues on such amounts.

(b)(1) The Secretary of the Interior shall be the trustee of the Trust Fund and shall invest the funds in the Trust Fund with a financial institution.

(2) The Secretary of the Interior shall not deduct any amount from the Trust Fund for administrative expenses or charge the Zuni Indian Tribe for expenses incurred by the Secretary in acting as trustee.

(c)(1) The funds appropriated to the Trust Fund under the authorization of section 4 shall constitute the corpus of the Trust Fund and may be expended, subject to paragraph (2), only for the following purposes:

(A) payment of any loans, debts, or future expenses incurred by the Zuni Indian Tribe to any person for the purchase of land or obtaining or defending rights of access to the area described in Public Law 98-408;

(B) payment of up to $600,000 per year for two years for the formulation of the Zuni resource development plan described in section 2;

(C) payment of all costs, attorneys' fees, and expenses incurred prior to September 30, 1990 by the Zuni Indian Tribe in the prosecution of docket numbers 327-81L and 224-84L of the United States Claims Court; and

(D) payment of all invoices submitted by any person to the Zuni Indian Tribe for which proper vouchers have been received prior to September 30, 1990, and subsequently approved by the Secretary of the Interior.

(2) The total amount of the corpus of the Trust Fund that may be expended under paragraph (1) shall not exceed $8,000,000.

(3) The interest and investment income that accrues on the corpus of the Trust Fund may be expended by the Secretary of the Interior pursuant to the Zuni resource development plan described in section 2.

(4) No funds appropriated under the authority of this Act may be used to make per capita payments to members of the Zuni Indian Tribe.

(5) All sums paid pursuant to this Act shall be offset against any judgment entered in favor of the Zuni Indian Tribe in docket numbers 327-81L and 224-84L, but not against any judgment entered in docket number 161-79L, of the United States Claims Court.

(6) Nothing in this Act shall be construed to affect in any way the trust status of Zuni Indian Reservation land or resources.

AUTHORIZATION OF APPROPRIATIONS

Sec. 4. There are authorized to be appropriated to the Zuni Indian Resource Development Trust Fund $25,000,000. Such funds shall remain available without fiscal year limitation.

ADDITIONAL LANDS

Sec. 5. The first section of the Act entitled "An Act to convey certain lands to the Zuni Indian Tribe for religious purposes," approved August 28, 1984 (98 Stat. 1533), is amended by adding at the end thereof the following: "Also, all of the sections 13 and 23, township 14 north, range 26 east, Gila and Salt River Meridian, such lands to be acquired and held in accordance with sections 2 and 3 of this Act."

Approved October 31, 1990.

Plan for the Use of Judgment Funds Docket 161-79L

Plan for the Use of Judgment Funds
Awarded to the Zuni Indian Tribe
in Docket No. 161-79L
Before the United States Claims Court*

The funds appropriated January 31, 1991, in satisfaction of the award granted to the Zuni Indian Tribe in settlement of Docket 161-79L before the United States Claims Court, less attorney fees and litigation expenses, and including all interest and investment income accrued, shall be used as follows:

1. EXPENSES

A. Outstanding Loans

The sum of $175,000 plus accrued interest shall be paid to satisfy existing loans made to the Zuni Indian Tribe by the Jicarilla Indian Tribe and the United New Mexico Bank in the amounts of $50,000 and $125,000, respectively.

B. Education

The amount of $1,700,000 will be provided to the Zuni Public School District for completion of construction of A:SHIWI Elementary School for the purpose of enhancing educational opportunities for all Zuni community children. Any residual funds from paragraph 1A and 1B of this plan shall be transferred to the investment activity and utilized pursuant to Section 2 of this plan.

C. Land Purchase

The amount of $250,000 will be used to pay the Bureau of Indian Affairs for the down payment of the Ellsworth Ranch.

*This plan was presented to the Zuni people on May 26, 1992, by the Zuni Tribal Council. Numerous possible expenditures were discussed during the course of the meeting.

D. No Per Capita Payments

None of the funds shall be paid as per capita or dividend payments.

2. INVESTMENTS

A. Management

All the remainder of the funds not expended pursuant to the preceding paragraphs shall be invested by the Secretary of the Interior in an investment program. If in the future, the Zuni Indian Tribe should desire to undertake the investment of the funds instead of having the investment made by the Secretary, the Tribal Council may present an investment plan to the Secretary for approval. Upon the Secretary's approval of the investment plan, the investment funds, at a mutually agreed upon time, will be transferred to the Zuni Indian Tribe and thereafter the Secretary will have no responsibility for such funds.

B. Authorized Purchases

All funds, including accrued interest, shall be invested and managed pursuant to paragraph 2A hereof until such time as the Tribal Council authorizes their use for any tribal development program, including land purchases, or other tribal programs or other tribal loan repayments not included in paragraph 1A above. No authorized program shall provide per capita or dividend payments to tribal members.

The Zuni Resource Development Plan: Executive Summary and Foreword

The Zuni Resource Development Plan:
A Program of Action for Sustainable Resource Development

A:widen dehul'an kwayná, Yadok an dek'ohannakwin de'china
Zuni Conservation Project

Edited by
James Enote, Steven Albert, and Kevin Webb

EXECUTIVE SUMMARY

Overview

The Zuni Resource Development Plan was written to meet the requirements of the Zuni Land Conservation Act of 1990 (Public Law 101-486). The Act is a result of a lawsuit brought against the United States by the Zuni Tribe to compensate the Tribe for resources damaged as a result of federal improprieties related to trust responsibilities (Docket No. 327-81L). The planning and writing of the plan was directed by the Zuni Conservation Project and assisted by the U.S. Department of the Interior and several private foundations and international development institutions. Implementation of the plan will be accomplished using interest derived from the Act's $17 million Zuni Resource Development Trust Fund.

The Conservation Act mandates that six specific subjects be addressed in the plan. These subjects form the framework for a program that will rehabilitate damaged Zuni lands through an integrated approach.

1. a mechanism for sustained development of renewable resources;
2. a program of watershed rehabilitation;
3. a computerized system of resource management and monitoring;
4. programs for funding and training of Zuni Indians to fill professional positions that implement the plan;
5. proposals for cooperative programs with the Bureau of Indian Affairs and other private or public agencies to provide technical assistance in carrying out the plan; and

6. identification and acquisition of lands necessary to sustain Zuni resource development.

All six subjects are addressed and accomplished in the plan and can be reviewed in the plan introduction.

Purpose and Need

The Past. The approach of developing specific projects to justify general policy has not served to connect Zuni land users to those policies. In fact, it has alienated many Zunis from policies which directly affect them, but which they are very eager to criticize.

Difficulties have arisen from federal plans where compliance with federal planning standards in reality means meeting minimal requirements where community input is concerned. This situation is complicated because federal standards to not consider Zuni consultation protocol, customs or etiquette. Also, several other agencies and institutions can become involved which further confuses the situation. This condition reflects poorly on government programs, frustrates well-meaning staff, and fuels distrust towards all governments.

The guidance for the 1967 Pueblo of Zuni Comprehensive Plan was obtained through a house-to-house survey. This survey helped create the plan and showed that even in the 1960s, innovation was necessary to gather meaningful Zuni views on community issues. It is evident that the Zuni Comprehensive Plan introduced an important concept for Zuni participatory planning.

Today. Current opinions and perspectives are again being gathered by going out to the community, this time for the formulation of the Zuni Resource Development Plan. Because the size of the Zuni population has doubled since the house-to-house surveys of the sixties, a similar but new approach to participatory planning was needed.

The contemporary approach focuses on Zuni staff explaining to individual tribal members or small groups what the intent of the Conservation Act is. This was followed by explaining what the roles of the many Zuni institutions are, such as, tribal, BIA, IHS, Zuni schools, etc. The informed community members are then asked, what course is Zuni capable of taking in developing Zuni resources?

Examining reservation policy, or lack of, with the community, has given direction on how to adjust or reorient policy for Zuni needs. Zuni community members can now suggest changes with an informed view and give support to specific projects with a clearer understanding of their responsibility and the responsibility of supporting agencies. This general to specific approach is much better understood by the Zuni community than the specific (projects) to support general policy approach of the past. It should also be understood that there is a wide variety of Zuni opinions and attitudes towards developing resources and this is where the Zuni Conservation Project communication strengths are most positive.

Issue Identification. The Zuni land user community has highlighted several issues that they believe are obstacles to improving the land and their way of life. Understandably, Zuni land users have many opinions of what should be done to improve the land. Some want to develop specific projects like developing water for livestock or controlling erosion, others carefully scrutinize the planning work to be sure the community is involved in any action. But the consensus of Zuni land users is that something needs to be done to untangle the confusion regarding responsibility and decision-making. In short, land users want to know ahead of time what is going to be implemented on the reservation. They have developed a great distrust for government because they were not involved in project or program designs and decisions in the past and they want this process stopped. Also, the responsibility issue is an important one because many Zunis still believe that the federal government (BIA) is responsible for nearly everything wrong on the reservation.

"Why did they build that?"
 —Zuni land user

"We want to know what the Zuni public wants, but nobody shows up at our meetings."
 —BIA

"Why didn't they tell us what they're doing?"
 —Frequently heard throughout Zuni

"I thought that's what the BIA is for."
 —Zuni land user

Implementation

Key Elements and Tasks. The Zuni Resource Development Plan serves as a blueprint and plan of action for the Zuni community to *effectively* address rehabilitation of damaged Zuni lands through an integrated, community-motivated approach. By listening to individuals at home and in the field and by meeting with members of Zuni community groups, we believe environmental degradation, including erosion, can only be dealt with by directly addressing policy confusion, community distrust in government, and segregated agency objectives. This listening, learning, and integrating with the community essentially "empowers" or enables members to understand and affect processes which influence Zuni resources and their lives. Therefore, community "empowerment" facilitates action and change in a responsible and knowledgeable manner.

Consequently, before beginning reservation-wide programs or projects which will affect large areas and many people, we will assess and reorient or adjust natural resource policies to make them *understandable* and *supportable* for the Zuni community. With community support the restoration of lands and protection of the environment can be accomplished much more efficiently. Simultaneously, watershed conservation and erosion control demonstration projects like the one already begun at the Nutria Pilot Project will be implemented.

During the first year of implementation (1994), the Zuni Resource Development Trust Fund will not have generated sufficient funds to carry out large scale restoration. Therefore, work will focus on small labor-intensive demonstration projects selected by the community and Conservation Project. Work will continue to integrate grazing, forest use, farming, wildlife, watersheds, and other land use concerns to respond to the restoration of Zuni lands from all perspectives. Most important is the work to assess natural resource policies that will set the framework for Zuni governments and the Zuni community to address all the *program areas* described in the plan.

From 1995 to the end of the century we will accomplish the *program areas* through the *activities* described in the plan. Our success during the next two years and in the distant future will depend on the success in focusing on the key tasks that will be addressed in 1994 and 1995.

Responsible Agencies and Institutions. The implementation of the plan will involve a large collection of agencies and institutions within Zuni and from outside Zuni lands. Several Zuni community groups and associations along with individual tribal members will be a part of this organization. A large part of the implementation effort will involve organizing these groups into a cooperative team to ensure compatible assignments and sharing of responsibilities consistent with Zuni community direction. As previously mentioned, Zuni environmental and developmental decision-making has been a confusing process which has not been consistent over the years. Given the number of institutions which are involved in Zuni land use matters, a solid and consistent process for decision-making will be the decisive mechanism for successful project implementation. Within the next two years, a regulatory process for reviewing proposed development projects will be established to ensure that all parties affected by land management decisions are consulted with. This process will be the responsibility of the Tribe's Department of Natural Resources, the Zuni Conservation Project.

Funding. Currently, the Zuni Resource Development Trust Fund has generated approximately $350,000 for application to 1994. Compared to the current budget of approximately $800,000 in 1993, 1994 will be a difficult year for implementation. Several hundred thousand dollars have been contributed by large foundations and institutions in 1992 and 1993 and it is hoped that these contributions will continue.

Funds for implementing the plan will be divided into 2 basic categories: (1) resources needed to carry out demonstration and pilot projects to begin efforts towards restoration of the damaged watersheds; and (2) work required to support the cooperative mechanisms of community and government. This second category is essentially community participation and policy assessment work, which in turn is fundamental to the entire conservation and restoration effort. In each of these categories, maximum utilization of all available institutions and resource is needed to spread the costs and interweave responsibilities.

An estimate of costs for each category is:

1. *Restoration of damaged watersheds*
   personnel $300,000 Zuni Tribe (Trust Fund)
                             $300,000 U.S. Agencies (Federal appropriations)
   equip. and supplies $200,000 U.S. Agencies (Federal appropriations)

   Total $800,000

2. *Community participation and policy assessment*
   personnel $75,000 Zuni Tribe (Trust Fund and private foundations)
                             $25,000 U.S. Agencies (Federal appropriations)
   equip. and supplies $10,000 Zuni Tribe (Trust Fund and private foundations)

   Total $110,000

Grand Total 1994 $910,000

During the remaining part of this century and beyond, costs must be distributed to all participating institutions. The *Zuni Resource Development Trust Fund* should generate at least $1 million dollars per year depending on interest rates and investment instruments selected by the Zuni Tribe. Ideally, an annual budget of approximately $2 million per year would allow full development of a Zuni Conservation Program as estimated in the *Financing and Cost Evaluation* portion of each Conservation and Management chapter. Additional support may come from federal agencies through appropriations or contracts and from private institutions and development centers.

Ratio of Planning to Implementation. The Conservation Act required two years of planning before actual implementation. However, a pilot project area was selected in January of 1993 to establish a location where the Conservation Project can test its ability to work with the Zuni people. Also tested are technical attributes necessary to develop a comprehensive watershed restoration program. The Nutria area of the reservation was chosen because it represented the most complete combination of Zuni land use activities and incorporated very well into the companion Zuni River Watershed Act studies, which are anticipated to begin in 1994. Therefore, the ratio of planning to implementation in 1993 has been approximately 1 : 1 in terms of time and resources expended. In 1994, it is anticipated that the ratio will be approximately 1 : 3. As work continues into the next century, the ratio may change depending on Zuni needs, national change, or global economic influences.

Summary

The Zuni Resource Development Plan as a Zuni community plan of action, addresses needs specific to the Zuni people. Where separation of responsibilities exist, the plan will serve as a guide to develop coherence and cooperation. Where damaged Zuni lands are to be restored, the plan is a framework for community involvement in decision-making and support where integrated and comprehensive planning will be needed to assure individuals, groups, and government will work together. For the future, the plan sets the stage for fundamental rethinking of where the Zuni people are today and what securities are needed to ensure that resources available today are available for future generations.

FOREWORD

For thousands of years we Zunis have lived in a complex and delicate environment that has sustained our ancestors and that continues to bring great benefits to our people today. But with the continuing growth of our population and the increasing demand for limited natural resources, the time has come to decide what means we will use to ensure that the resources and benefits available to our ancestors will be available for future generations.

Today Zuni could probably be described as both a developing nation and a prosperous community. Our contemporary habits are approaching the patterns of the United States in general, but our culture and ways of life remain consistently and uniquely Zuni. We are faced with the enormous challenge of moving into the next century maintaining our traditions and values, yet needing the modern technical capability to deal with the environment and development issues that confront us.

The Zuni Resource Development Plan is designed to ensure that any actions that affect the Zuni environment follow an integrated approach that consults with and involves the Zuni people in planning and decision making. The plan is innovative and is the first major planning document produced by a sovereign group or tribe that follows the United Nations Agenda 21 format. Agenda 21 was developed as a blueprint for sustainable development by over 170 nations and was distributed to the world at the Earth Summit in Rio de Janeiro, Brazil, in 1992. Zuni has become recognized worldwide for its innovative approach in developing new paths of public awareness and involvement and by advancing the spirit of Agenda 21.

There is still an enormous amount of work to be done. While many members of the Zuni community are currently involved in the planning process for natural resources, there remains a large part of the population that needs to be informed and included in natural resource decision making. Our work must be inclusive and equitable. The measure of our success will be in how the elected tribal representatives, the Zuni people, and relevant governments accept responsibility for the future.

James Enote, Project Leader

A Partial Listing of Expert Reports and Depositions in the Zuni Claims Litigation

ZUNI LAND CLAIM, DOCKET 161-79L
EXPERT REPORTS AND DEPOSITIONS

Eggan, Fred. 1980. "Aboriginal Land Use of the Zuni Indian Tribe."
Eggan, Fred. 1981. "Rebuttal Report."
Elam, Earl H. 1980. "A History of Zuni Land Utilization in Arizona and New Mexico, 1539 to the Present."
Elam, Earl H. 1981. "Deposition of Earl H. Elam."
Elam, Earl H. 1981. "Rebuttal Report."
Ferguson, T. J. 1980. "Zuni Settlement and Land Use: An Archaeological Perspective."
Ferguson, T. J. 1981. "Rebuttal Report."
Hart, E. Richard. 1980. "Boundaries of Zuni Land: With Emphasis on Details Relating to Incidents Occurring 1846–1946." 2 vols.
Hart, E. Richard. 1981. "Rebuttal Report."
Hart, E. Richard. 1981. "Zuni Trade."
Jenkins, Myra Ellen. 1980. "The Pueblo of Zuni and United States Occupation."
Jenkins, Myra Ellen. 1981. "Rebuttal Report."
Jenkins, Myra Ellen. 1981. Deposition of Myra Ellen Jenkins.
Minge, Ward Alan. 1980. "Zuni in Spanish and Mexican History."
Minge, Ward Alan. 1981. "Deposition of Ward Alan Minge."
Minge, Ward Alan. 1981. "Rebuttal Report."
Pandey, Triloki Nath. 1980. "Some Reflections on Aboriginal Land Use of the Zuni Tribe."
Pandey, Triloki Nath. 1981. "Rebuttal Report."
Tyler, S. Lyman. 1980. "The Zuni Indians Under the Laws of Spain, Mexico, and the United States."
Tyler, S. Lyman. 1981. "Rebuttal Report."
Worcester, Donald E. 1981. "Rebuttal Report."

ZUNI LAND CLAIM, DOCKET 161-79L
CHRONOLOGICAL LIST OF DEPOSITIONS
OF ZUNI LAY WITNESSES

Hustito, Alonzo. 1980 Deposition of Alonzo Hustito. February 19, 1980.
Mahooty, Chester. 1980. Deposition of Chester Mahooty. February 20, 1980.

Edaakie, Theodore. 1980. Deposition of Theodore Edaakie. February 21, 1980.
Awelagte, Tom. 1980. Deposition of Tom Awelagte. February 21–22, 1980.
Eriacho, Sefferino Sr. 1980. Deposition of Sefferino Eriacho, Sr. February 22, 1980.
Vacit, Frank. 1980. Deposition of Frank Vacit. February 22, 1980.
Nastacio, Alvin Lynn. 1980. Deposition of Alvin Lynn Nastacio, February 23, 1980.
Quam, Ralph. 1980. Deposition of Ralph Quam. February 24, 1980.
Bowannie, Fred Sr. 1980. Deposition of Fred Bowannie, Sr. February 26, 1980.
Gaspar, Chester Hart. 1980. Deposition of Chester H. Gaspar. February 26, 1980.
Nastacio, Oscar. 1980. Deposition of Oscar Nastacio. February 27, 1980.
Wytsalucy, Mecalita. 1980. Deposition of Mecalita Wytsalucy. February 27, 1980.

ZUNI LAND CLAIMS, DOCKETS 327-81L AND 224-84L
CHRONOLOGICAL LIST OF
ZUNI EXPERT WITNESSES

Hart, E. Richard. 1985. Damage to Zuni Trust Lands (3 volumes). Plaintiff's Exhibit 1000.
Geoscience Consultants, Ltd. 1985. Changes in Geomorphology, Hydrology, and Land Use on the Zuni Indian Reservation, McKinley and Cibola Counties, New Mexico, 1846–1985. Plaintiff's Exhibit 2000. July 18, 1985.
Dean, Jeffrey S. 1985. Dendrochronological Dating of Floodplain Erosion on Zuni Indian Lands, Northwest New Mexico. Plaintiff's Exhibit 14,000. August 14, 1985.
Hall, Stephen G. 1985. Erosion of Zuni Indian Reservation Lands. Plaintiff's Exhibit 3000. July 31, 1985.
Ford, Richard I. 1985. Zuni Land Use and Damage to Trust Land. Plaintiff's Exhibit 7000. August 15, 1985.
Rose, Martin 1985. Present and Past Climate of the Zuni Region. Plaintiff's Exhibit 5000. September 13, 1985.
Ferguson, T. J. 1985. Patterns of Land Use and Environmental Change on the Zuni Indian Reservation, 1846–1985: Ethnohistorical and Archaeological Evidence. Plaintiff's Exhibit 6000. September 30, 1985.
Hart, E. Richard. 1986. Deposition of E. Richard Hart. Volume 1. December 4–5, 1986.
Hart, E. Richard. 1987. Deposition of E. Richard Hart. Volumes 2 and 3. March 30–31, 1987
Wiget, Andrew. 1987. Review and Discussion of Certain Statements Concerning Oral History Contained in the Testimony of Thomas R. Wessel. Plaintiff's Exhibit 12,000. December 1987.
Baxter, John O. 1988. Patterns of Land Use Within a Portion of the Pueblo of Zuni Land Claim. Plaintiff's Exhibit 9000. February 10, 1988.
Monson, Samuel C. 1988. The Changing Meanings of Arroyo. Plaintiff's Exhibit 11,000. June 23, 1988.
Ford, Richard I. 1988. Rebuttal Report: Zuni Land Use and Damage to Trust Land. Plaintiff's Exhibit 7000. August 15, 1988.
Ferguson, T. J. 1988. Rebuttal Report: Land Use and Land Damage on the Zuni Indian Reservation, 1846–1988. Plaintiff's Exhibit 6000. August 31, 1988.
Hart, E. Richard. 1988. The Zuni Mountains: Chronology of an Environmental Disaster. Plaintiff's Exhibit 13,000. September 11, 1988.
Limerick, Patricia. 1988. Evaluation of "Federal Government Activity on the Zuni Reservation," by Thomas R. Wessel. Plaintiff's Exhibit 16,000. November 7, 1988.

Hart, E. Richard. 1988. Rebuttal Report: Damage to Zuni Trust Lands. Plaintiff's Exhibit 15,000. November 23, 1988.

Ebert, James. 1988. Historic Photographs: Photointerpretation and Photogrammetry Using Terrestrial and Aerial Photographs in and around the Zuni Indian Reservation to Define the Nature and History of Watercourse Erosion and Forest Cutting. Plaintiff's Exhibit 10,000. September 12, 1988.

Hall, Stephen G. 1988. Rebuttal Report: Erosion of Zuni Indian Reservation Lands. Plaintiff's Exhibit 3000. September 27, 1988.

Geoscience Consultants, Ltd. 1988. Rebuttal Report: Geomorphology, Hydrology, and Land Use on the Zuni Indian Reservation, 1846–1988. Plaintiff's Exhibit 2000. October 26, 1988.

Ferguson, T. J., and E. Richard Hart. 1988. Rebuttal Report: Interpretation of Historical and Contemporary Photographs. Plaintiff's Exhibit 8000. December 7, 1988.

Dean, Jeffrey S. 1989. Rebuttal Report: Dendrochronological Dating of Floodplain Erosion on Zuni Lands. Plaintiff's Exhibit 14,000. January 30, 1989.

Rose, Martin. 1989. Rebuttal Report: Present and Past Climate of the Zuni Region. Plaintiff's Exhibit 5000. August 31, 1989.

ZUNI LAND CLAIMS, DOCKETS 327-81L AND 224-84L
CHRONOLOGICAL LIST OF DEPOSITIONS OF
ZUNI LAY WITNESSES

Idiaque, Tom. 1984. Deposition of Tom Idiaque. September 17, 1984.
Eriacho, Sefferino. 1984. Deposition of Sefferino Eriacho. September 17, 1984.
Kanteena, Dempsy. 1984. Deposition of Dempsy Kanteena. September 18, 1984.
Neumayah, Sidney. 1984. Deposition of Sidney Neumayah. September 18, 1984.
Telsee, Kathlutah. 1984. Deposition of Kathlutah Telsee. September 18, 1984.
Walewa, Bob. 1984. Deposition of Bob Walewa. September 18, 1984.
Ondulacy, Sol. 1984. Deposition of Sol Ondulacy. September 19, 1984.
Vacit, Frank. 1984. Deposition of Frank Vacit. September 19, 1984.
Bowannie, Belle. 1984. Deposition of Belle Bowannie. September 20, 1984.
Ondulacy, Pacque. 1984. Deposition of Pacque Ondulacy. September 20, 1984.
Pinto, Ella. 1984. Deposition of Ella Pinto. September 20, 1984.
Bowannie, Fred. 1984. Deposition of Fred Bowannie. September 21, 1984.
Calavaza, Clarence. 1984. Deposition of Clarence Calavaza. September 21, 1984.
Harker, Mazone. 1984. Deposition of Mazone Harker. September 21, 1984.
Lewis, Robert E. 1984. Deposition of Robert E. Lewis. September 22, 1984.
Eustace, Calvin. 1984. Deposition of Calvin Eustace. September 24, 1984.
Panteah, Lowell. 1984. Deposition of Lowell Panteah. September 24, 1984.
Tsabetsaye, Joe. 1984. Deposition of Joe Tsabetsaye. September 24, 1984.
Ghaccu, Frank. 1984. Deposition of Frank Ghaccu. September 25, 1984.
Mahooty, Chester. 1984. Deposition of Chester Mahooty. September 25, 1984.

ZUNI LAND CLAIMS, DOCKETS 327-81L AND 224-84L
CHRONOLOGICAL LIST OF REPORTS AND DEPOSITIONS
OF DEFENDANT'S WITNESSES

Wessel, Thomas R. n.d. Federal Government Activity on the Zuni Reservation. Defendant's Exhibit 11,000.

Potter, Loren. 1986. Ecological Interpretations of the Zuni Reservation, N.M. Defendant's Exhibit 17,000. Letter Reports of October 19 and October 31, 1986.

Wells, Stephen G. 1987. A Quantitative Analysis of Arroyo Development and Geomorphic Processes in the Zuni River Drainage Basin, West-Central New Mexico. Defendant's Exhibit 12,000 (two volumes). May 8, 1987.

Balling, Robert C. 1987. Analysis of Zuni Indian Reservation Precipitation Patterns during the Period of Instrumental Record. Defendant's Exhibit 15,000. May 1987.

Jacoby, Gordon. 1987. Dendrochronological Investigation of the Zuni Indian Reservation. Defendant's Exhibit 14,000. May 1987.

Box, Thadis W. 1987. Range Management on the Zuni Indian Reservation, 1846–1946. Defendant's Exhibit 16,000. June 1, 1987.

Resource Consultants, Inc. 1987. Analysis of Changes in Hydrology, Hydraulics, and Sediment Transport, Zuni Indian Reservation, New Mexico. Defendant's Exhibit 13,000. June 1, 1987.

Box, Thadis W. 1987. Deposition of Thadis W. Box. November 17, 1987.

Wells, Stephen G. 1987. Deposition of Stephen G. Wells, December 3–4, 1987.

Potter, Loren D. 1987. Deposition of Loren D. Potter. December 7, 1987.

Wessel, Thomas R. 1987. Deposition of Thomas R. Wessel. December 9, 1987.

UNITED STATES V. PLATT

Floyd A. O'Neil. 1986. "The Trail to *Kolhu/wala:wa*."

E. Richard Hart. 1986. "The Barefoot Trail: Access to Zuni Heaven," with appendices and maps.

OTHER RELATED DOCUMENTS

Hart, E. Richard. 1988. Statement of E. Richard Hart before the Committee on Interior and Insular Affairs, United States House of Representatives. July 2, 1988.

O'Neil, Floyd, and E. Richard Hart. 1990. Fraudulent Land Activities by United States Officials Affecting Title to Zuni Lands: Conclusions. Testimony submitted to the Select Committee on Indian Affairs. 101st Congress. May 7, 1990.

Hart, E. Richard. 1990. Statement of E. Richard Hart. Select Committee on Indian Affairs, United States Senate. May 7, 1990.

Statement from Experts Relative to S. 2203, 1990. Statements from: John O. Baxter, Jeffrey S. Dean, James I. Ebert, Environmental Systems Research Institute, T. J. Ferguson, Richard I. Ford, Geoscience Consultants, Stephen A. Hall, Martin Rose, Barry Sadler, Andrew Wiget. Select Committee on Indian Affairs, United States Senate. May 7, 1990.

About the Contributors

JOHN O. BAXTER, a resident of Santa Fe, New Mexico, holds degrees in history from Princeton University and the University of New Mexico. His dissertation at the latter institution is entitled "Water Administration in New Mexico Prior to Statehood." Baxter is also the author of *Las Carneradas: Sheep Trade in New Mexico, 1700–1860,* published in 1987 by the University of New Mexico Press. In recent years, his work has focused on the agricultural history of the Southwest, particularly titles to land and water rights. As an expert witness, he has prepared reports for the State Engineer Office concerning priorities of use in several New Mexico systems. He has also performed extensive research for the Pueblo of Zuni in support of its claims for compensation against the federal government. A former *alguacil* ("sheriff") of the Santa Fe Corral of Westerners, Baxter presently serves as a director of the Historical Society of New Mexico.

STEPHEN G. BOYDEN was lead counsel for the Zuni Tribe during the two land claims cases (Docket 161-79L and Docket 327-81L). He is a member of the bar of the U.S. Supreme Court and the U.S. Court of Claims and holds a J.D. from the University of Utah (1967). He is formerly a member of the firm Boyden, Kennedy and Romney and has served as counsel for the Ute Tribe, the Hopi Tribe, and the Zuni Tribe. His work for Zuni on the two land claims cases stretched from 1970 to 1992. In 1992 he began serving a mission in Mexico for the Church of Jesus Christ of Latter-Day Saints.

JEFFREY S. DEAN is professor of dendrochronology in the Laboratory of Tree-Ring Research at the University of Arizona, Tucson. Born in Lewiston, Idaho, in 1939 he attended the Universities of Idaho and Arizona, receiving B.A. (1961) and Ph.D. (1967) degrees in anthropology from the latter. His interests include archaeological dating theory, Southwestern prehistory, Navajo ethnoarchaeology, and paleoenvironmental reconstruction. He has done archaeological and tree-ring research at prehistoric sites, Navajo sites, and inhabited pueblos and has helped produce dendroclimatic reconstructions for several areas of the Southwest. He is author or coauthor of numerous publications, including "Chronological Analysis of Tsegi Phase Sites in Northeastern Arizona" (1969), "Dendroclimatic Variability in the American Southwest, A.D. 680 to 1970" (1977), "Independent Dating in Archaeological Analysis" (1978), "Dendrochronology and Paleoenvironmental Reconstruction on the Colorado Plateaus" (1988), "The Chronology of Cultural Interaction in the Gran Chichimeca" (1993), and "The Medieval Warm Period on the Southern Colorado Plateau" (1994).

FRED EGGAN was a cultural anthropologist who specialized in studies of Hopi Indians, western Pueblos, and natives of the Philippines. Eggan was a central figure in twentieth-century American anthropology, whose works included the acclaimed *Social Organization of the Western Pueblos* and *Social Anthropology of North American Tribes*, both classics in the field. He began his studies at the University of Chicago in the 1930s, where he received two doctoral degrees and began his work with natives of the Philippines. During World War II he served as chief of research for the Philippine government in exile. For many years he assisted the Hopi Tribe in its disputes with the U.S. government, and he served as an expert witness for the Zunis in the field of anthropology. At the time of his death in 1991, he was a senior fellow at the School of American Research in Santa Fe and was working with the University of New Mexico Press and the University of California to update their published anthropological works.

T. J. FERGUSON, an anthropologist who specializes in the archaeology and ethnohistory of the southwestern United States, currently serves as director of Southwest Programs for the Institute of the NorthAmerican West. Ferguson lived at Zuni pueblo for six years in the 1970s and 1980s while employed by the Zuni Tribe, serving as director of the Zuni Archaeology Program from 1977 to 1981 and from 1984 to 1985. His subsequent research at Zuni has been conducted as a research associate of the Pueblo of Zuni. Ferguson served as an expert witness in the Zuni 1 claims case, the Zuni 2 claims case, and the litigation to obtain an easement to *Kolhu/wala:wa*.

E. RICHARD HART is executive director of the Institute of the NorthAmerican West. In addition to *A Zuni Atlas* (co-authored with T. J. Ferguson), he has written or edited another five books and has numerous publications in the fields of folklore, history, ethnohistory, and contemporary critical issues. He has received national awards and federal appointments in the fields of history and folklore. Having worked for and with the Zuni Tribe for more than twenty-five years, he has acted as an expert witness in several lawsuits relating to Zuni natural resources, including both of their claims cases, their religious easement claim, and their water adjudications. In addition to the written and oral expert testimony he has provided in court cases, he has testified many times on behalf of the tribe at hearings held by Senate and House committees.

MYRA ELLEN JENKINS was one of the most distinguished scholars of New Mexico history. Born on a cattle ranch in Colorado, she received her B.A. and M.A. degrees from the University of Colorado and her Ph.D. from the University of New Mexico in 1953. She worked for six years as an expert witness for the United States Indian Claims Commission, using her skills as translator of Spanish and Mexican documents. From 1960 to 1980 she headed the State of New Mexico Records Center and Archives. She received many awards and distinctions for her contributions to New Mexico and Southwest studies and was inducted into the New Mexico Women's Hall of Fame. Her works include *A Brief History of New Mexico* (with Albert H. Shroeder). She also directed a project to microfilm and to prepare guides and calendars for the Spanish, Mexican, and Territorial Archives of New Mexico. She served as expert witness in land claims cases involving the pueblos of Laguna, Acoma, Taos, Namb, Ysleta del Sur, and Zuni. She testified for the Zuni Tribe on its history in the New Mexico territorial period and was continuing in her work for the tribe at the time of her death in 1993.

EDMUND J. LADD, a Shiwi (Zuni), was born in Fort Yuma, California, and grew up at the Pueblo of Zuni. He is of the Coyote Clan and child of the Deer Clan. He is a member of the *U/tsa na:que* (Small Group Kiva). He attended the Christian Reform Mission and the government Zuni day schools on the reservation. If not for World War II, he would have graduated from the Albuquerque Indian School in 1944. He served in the armed forces during the war in the Pacific and the Mediterranean and was honorably discharged on December 7, 1947. In 1941 he had entered the University of New Mexico, receiving his B.S. in 1944 and his M.A. in 1964. He served with the Department of the Interior as Pacific Archaeologist stationed at Honaunau, Kona, Hawaii, retiring in 1984. He now works with the Museum of New Mexico, Laboratory of Anthropology, Santa Fe, New Mexico.

ROBERT E. LEWIS has been one of the most influential political leaders at Zuni in the twentieth century. He has served as governor of Zuni from 1964 to 1974, 1978 to 1982, and 1986 to 1994. He has also served in several important national positions representing Native Americans, including a term as chairman of the National Tribal Council Association. Both land claim dockets and the easement claim case were begun and concluded under his tenure as governor of Zuni. Lewis also testified at the trial of Docket 161-79L.

HANK MESHORER has been chief, Indian Resources Section, Environment and Natural Resources Division, U.S. Department of Justice, since 1982. He received an A.B. degree from Clark University in 1963, the LL.B. from Southern Methodist University in 1966, and an LL.M. from George Washington University in 1972. He was a captain in the U.S. Marine Corps from 1967 to 1970, serving in Southeast Asia. From 1970 to 1980 Meshorer served as senior trial attorney for the Justice Department, litigating some of the most significant environmental cases of that decade. From 1980 to 1982 he was trial counsel for Mobil Oil Corporation. Meshorer returned to the Justice Department in 1982 where he has been actively engaged in virtually all of the natural resource litigation of the United States on behalf of Indian tribes. He lives in Annapolis, Maryland.

WARD ALAN MINGE received his M.A. degree from the University of the Americas, Cholula, Mexico, and his Ph.D. in history from the University of New Mexico. He has retired from his position as chief historian at the U.S.A.F. Special Weapons Center and Weapons Laboratory, Kirtland A.F.B. He served as chairman of the New Mexico Public Records Commission for many years. He has worked closely with and provided expert testimony for the Pueblo of Acoma and is the author of *Acoma: Pueblo in the Sky*. He served as expert witness for the Zuni Tribe in the history of the Spanish and Mexican periods. His awards include a 1994 award from the New Mexico Endowment for the Humanities for his outstanding contributions in that field.

SAMUEL C. MONSON, professor emeritus of English at Brigham Young University, was educated at Utah State Agricultural College and Columbia University. His graduate work was in the history of the English language. He taught English at the University of Western Ontario, Ricks College, California State College of Arcata, and, as a Fulbright Scholar, at Zagreb University in the former Yugoslavia, as well as twenty years at Brigham Young University. For twelve years he was executive editor of the Thorndike-Barnhart dictionary series at Scott, Foresman and Company.

FLOYD A. O'NEIL has worked for the American West Center at the University of Utah for the past twenty-seven years. During that time his work with American Indian tribes, including the Zuni, has involved working with Indian tribes in producing tribal histories, helping to gather large quantities of American Indian oral testimony, serving as an expert witness in cases concerning American Indians and American Indian rights, and working extensively with curriculum projects in the public schools where Indians are taught. O'Neil has served as the chairman of the board of the Institute of the NorthAmerican West and is currently director of the American West Center, University of Utah, where he has been honored for his teaching abilities.

TRILOKI NATH PANDEY, professor of anthropology and Fellow of Crown College at the University of California at Santa Cruz, has been working among the Zuni for three decades. He has published papers on the methodology of his fieldwork as well as on Zuni history, culture, and politics. His latest paper is on patterns of leadership in Zuni and Hopi pueblos, published in *North American Indian Anthropology: Essays on Society and Culture* (1994), edited by Raymond DeMallie and Alfonso Ortiz. Pandey served as an expert witness in the Zuni land claim (Docket 161-79L) and was a special consultant for *People of the Desert*, a 1993 Time-Life book.

RONALD L. STAUBER has been chief cartographer for the Office of Contract Archaeology at the University of New Mexico since 1987. Prior to that he worked for the Zuni Archaeological Program. He lived at Zuni for a number of years and worked for the tribe on both claims cases and on the *Kolhu/wala:wa* easement case, providing research in General Land Office archives on surveyors and their notes. He also mapped the trail from Zuni to *Kolhu/wala:wa* as a part of his work for that case. He has done considerable archaeological work in New Mexico and the Southwest. A number of publications include maps drawn by him, including *A Zuni Atlas*. He has also worked in museum exhibit production and helped to produce several major exhibits on Zuni culture, archaeology, and pottery.

S. LYMAN TYLER has written several works on federal Indian policy, including *A History of Indian Policy*, and has translated important Spanish documents relating to Indian history in the Americas. In the 1950s, working with the Pueblos' attorney, he studied the history of irrigation among the Pueblo Indians. He provided expert services to the Ute, the Gila Pima, and the Maricopa Tribes over a long span of years and testified on behalf of the Zunis during their land claim trial on the subject of Spanish and Mexican law. His publications on Spanish law include *Spanish Laws Concerning Discoveries, Pacifications, and Settlements Among the Indians*, and *The Indian Cause in the Spanish Law of the Indies*. He was professor of history at the University of Utah from 1966 to 1985 and served as director of the American West Center there from 1971 to 1985.

ANDREW WIGET received his B.A. and M.A. from John Carroll University and his Ph.D. from the University of Utah, where his dissertation was a two-volume study, *The Oral Literature of Native North America*. He has published four books on Native American subjects, including *Native American Literature*. The author of numerous other published essays and technical reports, he has worked with members of many North American tribes, including Zuni and the Ramah Chapter of the Navajo Nation. He is the past president of both the Association for the Study of American Indian Literatures and the New Mexico Folklore Society and has been director of the New Mexico Heritage Center at New Mexico State University since 1986. His work at Zuni included expert testimony on Docket 327-89L, as well as extensive field recording of contemporary Zuni storytelling.

Index